Competition Law Compliance Programmes

Johannes Paha
Editor

Competition Law Compliance Programmes

An Interdisciplinary Approach

Springer

Editor
Johannes Paha
Department of Economics and Business
Justus-Liebig-University
Gießen, Germany

ISBN 978-3-319-44632-5 ISBN 978-3-319-44633-2 (eBook)
DOI 10.1007/978-3-319-44633-2

Library of Congress Control Number: 2016955412

Printed on acid-free paper

This Springer imprint is published by Springer Nature
The registered company is Springer International Publishing AG Switzerland

Preface

This anthology reviews and presents multidisciplinary research on competition law compliance programmes. The chapters are based on presentations held during a workshop at the Center for Interdisciplinary Research (Zentrum für interdisziplinäre Forschung, ZiF) in Bielefeld, Germany, in November 2015. I am very grateful for the funds and assistance provided by ZiF and the opportunity to conduct this workshop as part of my 5-year fellowship there. In particular, I would like to thank Dr. Britta Padberg who so successfully manages this research centre and Trixi Valentin who took care of all the organisational details of the workshop. I would also like to thank all other employees of ZiF who, just to name a few examples, operated the equipment, prepared the rooms and the meals, did the accounting, and announced the workshop to the press. Your work is outstanding, and ZiF does a great service to the scientific community.

I would also like to thank the renowned researchers who reviewed the chapters of this book and gave the authors helpful recommendations: Prof. Florian Baumann (Bonn), Prof. Roger Blair (Florida), Dr. Peter Cserne (Hull), Prof. Georg Götz (Giessen), Prof. Theresia Theurl (Muenster), and Prof. Frank Walter (Giessen). It is your dedication and voluntary service that made this publication possible and further improved the quality of the final product.

I would like to thank the numerous Springer employees involved in the publishing process. Your efforts helped us as researchers to concentrate on research while you took care of the production and distribution of this book both online and in print. Further dedicated editing services were provided by my student assistant Daniel Lüke whose employment was made possible by a grant provided to me by Justus-Liebig-University Giessen.

Above all, I would like to thank the authors of the chapters of this volume and three further presenters at the workshop in Bielefeld (Prof. Anja Jacobi, Prof. Bernd Marcus, and Prof. D. Daniel Sokol). Some of you may have considered it an experiment when I invited you to this multidisciplinary workshop in late 2014/early 2015. Crossing the disciplinary boundaries is not always easy, but it is often fruitful. Hopefully, your task was made somewhat easier when I asked you to *only* present the state-of-the-art research and ideas on an inherently interdisciplinary topic (i.e. competition law compliance programmes) from the viewpoint of your discipline and *simply* make it accessible for a multidisciplinary audience. I found your presentations very insightful and enjoyed our discussions. Thank you so much for the great efforts you undertook when writing the chapters of this volume that convey our ideas to an interested audience both in academia and practice.

Giessen, Germany
10 June 2016

Johannes Paha

Contents

Part I
Introduction

Chapter 1
Introduction

Johannes Paha

Improved detection, rising fines, a greater relevance of private damages claims (especially in Europe), and longer prison sentences (for example in USA) have raised the necessity for firms to implement measures that prevent their managers and other employees from violating competition laws (e.g., by engaging in price fixing or the abuse of a dominant position).[1] Competition law compliance programmes have increasingly been implemented by European firms since about the year 2005 while having been in use by, e.g., US-American firms already for a somewhat longer period. Yet, research on this topic is often relatively new and sparse. Such work has mainly been done by legal scholars but increasingly also by researchers in business administration and economics. However, concepts relevant for competition law compliance have been examined by psychologists and political scientists, too. This poses two challenges. First, researchers sometimes work on this topic within the confines of their disciplines without necessarily knowing all the relevant concepts and results established in other fields. Second, practitioners had to implement and design competition law compliance programmes to the best of their knowledge without necessarily getting the scientific advice they may have wished for.

This volume addresses both challenges and may ideally be a step towards overcoming them. This is done by reviewing and presenting state of the art research from legal studies, economics, business administration, and psychology that addresses aspects relevant for competition law compliance programmes. Ideally, this will not only be interesting for researchers who learn how other disciplines approach the topic of antitrust law compliance. The chapters of this volume may

[1]The terms *competition law* and *antitrust law* are used synonymously in this volume.

J. Paha (✉)
Department of Economics and Business, Justus-Liebig-University, Licher Straße 62, 35394 Gießen, Germany
e-mail: johannes.paha@wirtschaft.uni-giessen.de

J. Paha (ed.), *Competition Law Compliance Programmes*,
DOI 10.1007/978-3-319-44633-2_1

also be insightful for practitioners who learn what scholars from different fields think how antitrust law compliance programmes can be designed and implemented best. Especially this interdisciplinary approach is new. The book aims at building a bridge not only from academia to practice but also between different sciences.

In this context, Stefan Frübing and Kai Hüschelrath provide an overview about competition law compliance programmes taking a law and economics perspective. They establish the key advantages of adherence to competition laws such as the avoidance of corporate fines, individual sanctions, repayments for damages, litigation costs, and counsel fees. They also suggest that compliant behaviour may affect stock prices positively and enhances firms' reputation before discussing the key challenges of competition law compliance programmes (e.g. setting the right incentives). Based on this discussion, they review relevant compliance measures such as appropriate remuneration schemes and effective organisational structures. Their chapter concludes with an analysis how competition law compliance programmes relate to competition authorities' law enforcement efforts, also touching upon the question whether the firms should be rewarded for the implementation of such programmes by granting them a reduction of the fine imposed on wrongdoing.

Georg Götz, Daniel Herold, and Johannes Paha provide an overview about the compliance efforts of European firms. They surveyed firms in Germany, Austria, and Switzerland and present what compliance measures these firms employed in early 2014. The participants were mainly compliance frontrunners (i.e. large firms and former cartel participants) who had a greater interest in ensuring compliance with competition laws than most firms. And still, the survey identifies some room for improvement when it comes to measures that go beyond training employees in matters of competition law. Such complementary measures are necessary because 71 % of the firms whose employees had violated competition laws in the past had already trained their employees before the misconduct occurred. Complementary measures to mitigate antitrust risks (e.g. codes of conduct and remuneration schemes) are, therefore, analysed in this book.

For example, Peter Kotzian, Thomas Stöber, and Barbara Weißenberger study the effectiveness of codes of conduct and challenge the assertion that these codes and compliance training cannot prevent illegal conduct if such behaviour generates net benefits for the firm and/or the misbehaving manager. They argue that besides pure economic reasoning one must not neglect the (informal) rules within a firm and its corporate culture, which also implies that antitrust compliance must not be treated in isolation but should be shaped in the context of a business ethics strategy. In doing so, they explore the boundaries between the rational choice theory of corporate crime and sociological as well as psychological explanations for misconduct. The firms should establish a culture that condemns all sorts of illegitimate behaviour where managers and other employees not only obey the laws but behave ethically. The authors infer conclusions about the effectiveness of codes of conduct from a factorial survey using a sample with 1800 managers who are employed by a large European corporation. Therefore, their chapter combines the results of original research with a review of the relevant literature. Kotzian et al. conclude that codes of conduct and compliance training help to reduce unlawful conduct but should be complemented by additional measures.

One such measure is studied by Daniel Herold who reviews principal-agent theory showing what needs to be considered when designing employment contracts in a way intended to reduce anticompetitive conduct. He argues that sometimes cartel conduct may be beneficial for the misbehaving employees even if—in the light of fines, repayments for damages, litigation costs, reputational damage etc.—it lowers the profit of the firm. Therefore, the owners of the firm may have an incentive to design managers' remuneration in a way that deters collusive conduct best. Well-designed employment contracts may even prevent cartel conduct that would, otherwise, raise the profit of the firm. On the contrary, badly designed remuneration schemes may not only fail in preventing collusive conduct, they may even be the cause of managers' misconduct if, for example, a bonus can only be attained by illegal means. However, one must also bear in mind a trade-off insofar as remuneration schemes that prevent collusive conduct effectively may come at a cost, i.e., they may lower managers' incentives to exert work effort. Even more badly, if managers are not appropriately incentivised to work hard they may even become more likely to collude as this allows them to generate higher profits without exerting much effort.

The chapter provided by Ulrich Schwalbe broadens the scope of antitrust compliance beyond the prevention or early detection of cartel conduct. Compliance officers may put an additional focus on the prevention of abuses of a dominant position. Ulrich Schwalbe reviews conduct that may classify as an abuse of a dominant position and makes suggestions how to screen for such behaviour. Basic versions of such screens are already available today. Yet, future research may help to refine them. This is particularly important when it comes to abuses of a dominant position in online markets. They are not only special by often being characterised as platform markets offering services to (and charging prices from) both the sellers and the buyers of a good. Online markets also allow for the collection of data from the customers and forms of price discrimination that are not present in the offline world.

While these chapters analyse what the firms themselves can do to promote compliance with competition laws, later chapters study the role of competition authorities. Andreas Ransiek answers the question whether criminal sanctions (as opposed to administrative sanctions) should and can be imposed on firms whose employees violated competition laws. This discussion is not only relevant when comparing European competition laws to US antitrust laws. The discussion must also be seen in the context of recent advances in Germany calling for a criminalisation of corporate lawbreaking. The chapter asks whether a corporation can be personally culpable for conduct of its employees and studies whether it makes truly a difference if a sanction is called administrative or criminal. Andreas Ransiek argues that, say, a 10m EUR criminal sanction has no stronger effect than a 10m EUR administrative sanction. Administrative sanctions may even comprise elements similar to criminal sanctions such as imprisonment. This is because imprisonment deprives individuals of their liberty to go where they would like.

Depriving firms of their liberty to, e.g., submit bids in public tenders has a very similar effect. Therefore, the author does not see an advantage in holding corporations *criminally* liable for infringements of competition laws over the current situation in Europe and many European member states that impose administrative sanctions.

Andreas Ransiek continues by arguing that one should, however, also "think twice before introducing criminal sanctions against board members or employees of a corporation in antitrust cases". Such an in-depth discussion of individual sanctions is provided by Florian Wagner-von Papp who advocates sanctions, and in particular criminal sanctions, being imposed on the managers of a firm. He fears that, otherwise, sanctioning the firm only may not create sufficient deterrence. First, if the expected fines imposed on the firms are lower than the expected benefits the firms may not have an incentive to prevent their managers from colluding. Second, even if the fines imposed on the firms would in principle be deterrent collusion might still generate private benefits to the managers (e.g. greater job security, bonuses, or better chances to get promoted). In the absence of individual sanctions these managers would not be deterred by the corporate sanctions especially if they expect to work in another department or even for a different firm once the cartel will be revealed.

By reviewing the current state of law, Florian Wagner-von Papp shows that criminal sanctions are already applied by European member states such as the United Kingdom. Other countries such as Germany, Austria, Hungary, and Poland impose criminal sanctions on individuals only for specific offences such as bid rigging. Based on a detailed analysis, the author does not consider it justified to treat bid rigging substantially different from other cartel offences. Florian Wagner-von Papp is well aware of and presents arguments in favour of and against criminal sanctions being imposed on individuals. He suggests that a criminal fine is truly a *sanction* while an administrative fine is rather a *price*, and that a criminal sanction exerts a stronger deterrence effect. For example, being considered a criminal may cause a manager to lose social prestige and/or the esteem of his/her peers. The author provides both empirical and anecdotal evidence that supports his claim. Weighing these arguments against their counterarguments the author concludes that criminal sanctions against individuals would be a desirable feature of competition enforcement.

Firms sometimes ask whether competition authorities could reward their compliance efforts by reducing the fines that are imposed on anticompetitive conduct. Florence Thépot summarises the advantages created by compliance programmes and studies how competition authorities can encourage compliance efforts in order to improve the prevention and detection of collusive practices. In particular, the author discusses the effects of fine reductions that many competition authorities are reluctant to give as they fear this might undermine the deterrence effects of the fines. This is although such reductions are not infrequently granted in the fight against bribery and corruption. Florence Thépot reviews some literature analysing why fine reductions may actually improve compliance efforts. In line with Kotzian et al., the author suggests that (non-)compliance should not only be researched in a mere rational choice framework that takes the firm as the object of analysis. Taking into account organisational and cultural aspects, while focusing on employees as the unit of analysis, can instead help to understand (non-)compliance better and to set the right incentives for the introduction of compliance programmes. This may include fine reductions that according to Florence Thépot should, however, only be granted if the firms are able to demonstrate the effectiveness of these measures along with a strong commitment to compliance.

Per Rummel is more sceptical about such fine reductions and presents the negative side effects and legal obstacles that may prevent fine reductions from being the best way of promoting compliance programmes. To arrive at this conclusion, he studies different designs of this *compliance defence* asking, e.g., whether a fine reduction should only be granted for the implementation of a new compliance programme or also for the existence of a programme that was implemented even before the infringement occurred. He also questions whether a reduction of the fine of only 10 %, which is typically presumed in this context, provides a sufficiently strong incentive for the firms to intensify their compliance efforts. Per Rummel also presents what legal norms may require German firms to implement compliance measures. These norms may serve as an alternative to fine reductions when it comes to making firms invest in compliance programmes.

Competition law compliance programmes are often discussed from the viewpoint of legal studies, business administration, and economics. Agnieszka Paruzel, Barbara Steinmann, Annika Nübold, Sonja Ötting, and Günter Maier add a new perspective to this discussion. They show what psychology may contribute to this topic because violations of antitrust laws share common elements with counterproductive work behaviour, workplace deviance, and especially unethical pro-organisational behaviour. Based on these established concepts Paruzel et al. develop the *onion model of competition law compliance* arguing that in order to understand (non-)compliance better one must take into account certain intra-organisational factors (i.e. the individual, the group, and the organisation) that interact with influences in the (market) environment. On the individual level it may be important to take into account the personality traits of the employees (i.e. emotional stability, extraversion, openness to experience, agreeableness and conscientiousness) along with their needs for achievement, affiliation, and power. However, individual behaviour can on the group-level also be shaped by, e.g., social norms and perceptions of justice. These can potentially be affected by elements like ethical leadership that in the compliance-context is related to the *tone at the top*. The concepts described by Paruzel et al. relate to aspects studied by Kotzian et al. who both emphasise the importance of organisational elements like firms' corporate social responsibility activities and the creation of an ethical work climate to foster compliance.

To summarise, the book shows that antitrust compliance is an inherently interdisciplinary topic and can only be understood fully when crossing disciplinary boundaries. The law sets the stage for compliance issues, with legal studies defining what specific types of conduct are legal or illegal especially when this is far from clear. Firms' compliance efforts themselves may have a legal dimension such as data protection when using, for example, e-discovery methods. Economists then analyse the risks in the market environment that facilitate or even trigger collusive conduct. Such knowledge is necessary to concentrate compliance resources at the departments and during times where they are needed most. It is however not sufficient to study the effect of the market environment on the profit of the firms only. Misconduct is being carried out by the employees of the firms. This requires both to understand their individual incentives and to implement organisational measures that make anticompetitive conduct undesirable at an individual level. Here, knowledge generated by economists on, e.g., incentive-compatible employment contracts and remuneration schemes goes hand in hand with the results obtained by business scholars. Business administration and behavioural economics also build a bridge to psychology. Researchers in the latter field help to understand the individual motivations of firms' employees better, which is necessary to design the organisational environment as well as the employment contracts optimally.

In this context, it may be important for future research to understand these individual incentives better. For example, learning in what ways employees behave rationally while pursuing objectives other than a maximization of lifetime income is relevant when setting the *right* incentives. Even an ideal incentive scheme may not prevent misconduct that is emotionally driven, individual-specific, unsystematic and, thus, unpredictable. Improved knowledge about these limits of organisational measures also has implications for antitrust compliance. For example, knowing about unsystematic causes of illegal conduct (be they rational or irrational from the viewpoint of the decision maker) is necessary when measuring the effectiveness of the implemented compliance measures and demonstrating it to, e.g., a competition authority.

These considerations underline how this book may be source of reference both for researchers and practitioners in the compliance-field. It presents the current state of antitrust compliance efforts (mainly but not exclusively) in Europe and summarises key concepts from multiple disciplines. Ideally, researchers will take up some of these ideas in their future studies, and practitioners will find the concepts helpful in further refining their compliance programmes.

Chapter 2
Competition Law Compliance Programmes: A Law and Economics Perspective

Stefan Frübing and Kai Hüschelrath

Abstract We provide a law and economics perspective on competition law compliance programmes (CLCPs). Building on a general discussion of various motivations to ensure compliance with competition law, we discuss both key challenges in the design of an effective CLCP as well as the main building blocks of such programmes. Subsequently, we provide an overview of recent discussions by both academics and practitioners on the role of CLCPs in fine setting procedures as part of competition law enforcement. We close the article by providing a brief review of its main insights.

2.1 Introduction

Firms that operate in today's markets are confronted with a multitude of laws and regulations – labour law, competition law or environmental regulations to name only a few. By imposing various laws and regulations, policy makers ideally aim to improve market outcomes through the correction of market imperfections or market failures created by natural monopolies, externalities or asymmetric information.

However, the design and implementation of socially desirable laws and regulation alone appears insufficient as long as firms do not comply with them. Assuming that moral commitment alone is insufficient to reach compliance, policy

---

Sections 2.2. and 2.3. are updated versions of the respective sections in Hüschelrath (2010a). We are grateful to Michael Hellwig for comments on an earlier version of the article.

S. Frübing (✉)
ZEW Centre for European Economic Research, Competition and Regulation Research Group and MaCCI Mannheim Centre for Competition and Innovation, Mannheim, Germany
e-mail: fruebing@zew.de

K. Hüschelrath
ZEW Centre for European Economic Research, Competition and Regulation Research Group and MaCCI Mannheim Centre for Competition and Innovation, Mannheim, Germany

University of Mannheim, Mannheim, Germany
e-mail: hueschelrath@zew.de

J. Paha (ed.), *Competition Law Compliance Programmes*,
DOI 10.1007/978-3-319-44633-2_2

makers are forced to design and implement enforcement mechanisms. A cornerstone of such mechanisms typically is the imposition of civil, administrative or criminal sanctions for violations of the respective laws and regulations. With the introduction of such sanctions, policy makers aim to alter the cost-benefit assessment on the firm's side sufficiently to make compliance a rational investment.

From a firm's perspective, the challenges of ensuring compliance with laws and regulations appear quite different. Although the policy maker's cost-benefit calculus with respect to the desired deterrence of violations appears self-evident, real firms are not single entities but rather a collection of individuals driven by their own personal objective functions. Therefore, the key challenge for a firm's management — willing to comply — lies in the design and implementation of strategies to, first, assure that the employees gain knowledge of the respective laws and regulations and, secondly, to provide incentives to comply with them.

In this context, we provide a law and economics perspective on competition law compliance programmes (CLCPs). The subsequent second section identifies the key motivations of firms to comply with competition law. In addition to the avoidance of negative consequences of competition law infringements — such as, e.g., corporate and individual sanctions or negative effects on stock prices and firm reputation — it is shown that the inclusion of competition law compliance into a broader code of conduct or code of ethics should also be a cornerstone in a firm's motivation to ensure compliance.

The third section develops and discusses the building blocks of the design of a best practice CLCP. Starting from the identification of two key challenges — providing information and providing incentives — the proposed framework differentiates between the development of a compliance strategy, the determination of structures and procedures, the implementation of incentives and sanctions and the organisation of efforts to control the success of the programme and to develop improvement potential.

The fourth section takes account of recent discussions among academics and practitioners on the role of CLCPs in fine setting procedures as part of competition law enforcement. In addition to a summary of the main general arguments raised in the debate, we also provide a review of current practical approaches followed by a selection of competition authorities. The final fifth concludes the article by summarising its main insights.

2.2 Motivation to Ensure Compliance with Competition Law

Neither the economics nor the management literature provides a standard definition of compliance. In general, regulatory compliance can be described as all efforts undertaken by a firm to ensure that its employees are aware of and take steps to comply with relevant laws and regulations. Given the fact that the policy makers' key strategy to reach compliance typically is through the imposition of sanctions for infringements of competition law, any discussion on the motivation behind the compliance activities of firms has to depart from an assessment of these negative consequences of detected competition law infringements. Although the characteristics of the respective consequences can differ between jurisdictions, the general categories analysed in the following paragraphs are similar and include corporate fines, individual sanctions, damages, litigation costs and counsel fees, effects on stock prices and effects on firm reputation.

2.2.1 *Corporate Fines*

In many jurisdictions, competition authorities together with the responsible courts are entitled to impose (pecuniary) fines on undertakings for proven infringements of competition law. Corporate fines typically are a major building block in the entire concept to create a deterrent effect. Although the exact methodologies to set fines differ between jurisdictions, the basic amount for each firm is typically related to a proportion of the value of sales, but often also depends on the degree of gravity and the number of years of infringement. Additionally, competition authorities and courts may take into account circumstances that result in an increase or decrease in the basic amount. Aggravating circumstances can, e.g., be repeat offenders, refusal to cooperate with the respective authority or a role of leader in an infringement. Mitigating circumstances can, e.g., be the provision of evidence that the undertaking terminated the infringement or that the infringement has been committed as a result of negligence. Additionally, many competition authorities apply leniency programmes which provide possibilities for firms to reduce their corporate fines under specific circumstances.

The exact quantification of the fine is dependent on the jurisdiction. In the European Union, a ceiling of fines that can be imposed on companies is fixed by Article 23(2) of Council Regulation No 1/2003 to 10 % of the undertaking's total turnover in the preceding business year.[1] The Commission's revised guidelines[2] provide that fines may be based on up to 30 % of the company's annual sales to which the infringement relates, multiplied by the number of years of participation in the infringement. Moreover, a part of the fine may be imposed irrespective of the duration of the infringement. Finally, repeat offenders are also be fined more than under the old guidelines.

[1] A detailed overview of the fine setting procedure is provided by the European Commission itself, e.g., in the form of a brochure on 'Fines for breaking EU Competition Law' available at http://ec.europa.eu/competition/cartels/overview/factsheet_fines_en.pdf (last accessed on 29 March 2016).

[2] European Commission, Competition: Commission revises Guidelines for setting fines in antitrust cases, Press release IP/06/857, 28 June 2006, Brussels.

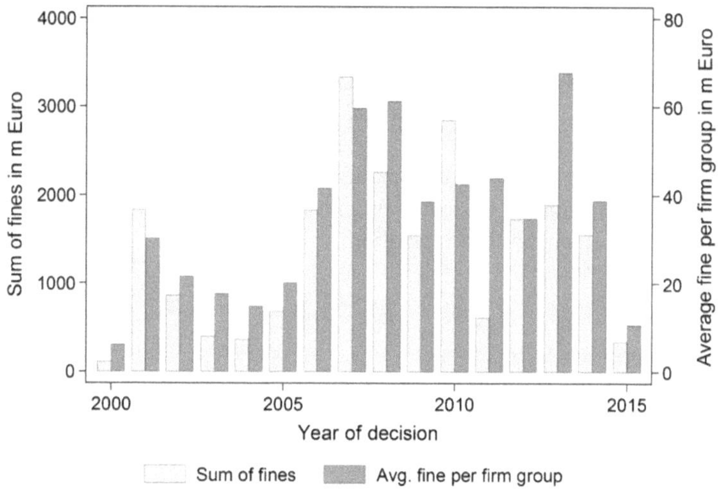

Fig. 2.1 Sum of fines and average fine per firm group for all EC cartel cases, 2000–2015. *Source*: own analysis based on data published in EC cartel decisions

Turning from the characterisation of the general fine calculation procedure to its actual implementation in practice, Fig. 2.1 below shows the sum of cartel-related fines as well as the average fine per convicted firm group[3] imposed by the European Commission (not adjusted for court judgments) on a yearly basis from 2000 to 2015.

As shown in Fig. 2.1, both the sum of fines as well as the average fine per firm group experienced a substantial increase in the years following 2005. While the sum of fines values still show large variation — at least partly being explained by the differences in the number (and size) of decided cases in a given year — the average fine per firm group values show a substantially smaller variation suggesting that firms convicted for cartelisation in recent years on average have to pay larger fines than they would have paid for the same infringement in more distant years.[4] Ceteris paribus, such an increase in the (expected) costs of cartelisation leads to increased incentives to invest in the avoidance of such infringements — with the design and implementation of best practice compliance programmes being one cornerstone in an overall firm's strategy to comply with existing laws and regulations.

[3]Firms within one group are linked through ownership and are jointly liable for cartel fines.

[4]Although five cartel cases were decided by the European Commission in 2015, the respective fines imposed were low resulting in the substantial reduction in both 'sum of fines' and 'average fine per firm group' shown in Fig. 2.1.

2.2.2 *Individual Sanctions*

In some jurisdictions, courts are not only entitled to impose (pecuniary) fines on undertakings for proven infringements of competition law but can also punish the responsible individuals for (specific) infringements of competition law with either pecuniary fines and/or prison sentences. Prison sentences are generally considered as the most effective way to deter and punish cartel activity as they directly affect the individual and not only the company. Individual punishment is normally not limited to the prison term as such but is often extended through a reduced employability of the manager afterwards. Furthermore, the loss of the respective manager can have an additional punitive effect on the firm, especially if the manager was important for the business success and cannot be replaced easily.

Although the legal system of the European Union currently does not allow for individual sanctions, the legal situation in several member states such as the UK or Germany allows individual sanctions for specific serious infringements such as cartelisation in general (UK) or specifically bid-rigging (Germany). In the United States, individual sanctions for price-fixing have a longer tradition and can result in a prison sentence of up to 3 years. Interestingly, referring to detailed information provided by the U.S. Department of Justice (DOJ)[5] as responsible authority in criminal antitrust cases, the possibility of imposing individual sanctions was increasingly used in the recent past. While the 1990–1999 enforcement period saw an average number of individuals sentenced to prison (in each year) of about 13 persons, the respective values experienced increases to 21 persons for the 2000–2009 enforcement period and to 29 persons for the (shorter but most recent) 2010–2014 enforcement period. Furthermore, the U.S. DOJ complements this information with additional facts in the form of the average prison sentence (in months) imposed for price-fixing. The respective values recently increased substantially as well from about 8 months in the 1990–1999 enforcement period via 20 months (2000–2009 enforcement period) to 25 months in the most recent (shorter) 2010–2014 enforcement period.

2.2.3 *Damages*

Competition law infringements typically cause harm to customers and final consumers. These third parties can be entitled to sue the infringing firms for damages. Although damages generally aim to cover the harm caused by competition law infringements such as, e.g., price-fixing conspiracies, they can also be interpreted as an additional punitive weapon. For example, in the United States, damages are an

[5]The respective information is available (and updated on a regular basis) on the website of the U.S. Department of Justice at https://www.justice.gov/atr/division-update/2015/criminal-program-update (last accessed on 29 March 2016).

important cornerstone of the entire enforcement strategy and damaged parties are entitled to sue for up to treble damages. Furthermore, class actions are allowed to bundle the interests against the cartelists. In the European Union and most of its member states, private damage claims have not played a huge role so far, however, (at the latest) since the Directive on Antitrust Damages Actions[6] was signed into law in late 2014, these cases are expected to gain in importance in the European Union's Member States in the coming years.

Technically, the damage is typically calculated by multiplying the difference between the price charged by the cartel and the price that would have existed in the absence of the cartel (the but-for price) with the respective sales volumes (see, e.g. Hüschelrath et al. 2016 for further discussions). Although the basic calculation is straightforward, its practical implementation is often challenging due to difficulties to derive the but-for price, the price actually paid by the customers (taking, e.g., different forms of rebates into account) or the degree of downstream pass-on of the overcharge. Comparable challenges also exist in dominance cases in which, e.g., a new entrant was harmed by a predation strategy of the incumbent and demands restitution.

2.2.4 Litigation Costs and Counsel Fees

Detected competition law infringements lead to investigations by the competition authority but can also lead to long trials in court. These procedures not only incur direct costs such as litigation costs and counsel fees but also cause substantial in-house costs, e.g., as employees need to invest part of their working time in the provision of information for the investigation or trials. These costs might be complemented by contract renegotiation costs if it turns out that contracts including anticompetitive practices are void and therefore need to be renegotiated.

The actual size of litigation costs and counsel fees depends to a large degree on the type, size and length of the respective case. For the United States, Baker (2003) assumes average costs of an antitrust case of $2.5 million (covering filing fees, lawyers and economic consultants). For the European Union, Neven (2006) reports that the costs and fees spent by Airtours in the EC merger investigation of *Airtours/First Choice*[7] add up to more than €2.2 million overall with about 80 % of these costs referring to the work of lawyers and the remaining 20 % to the work of economists.

---

[6]Directive of the European Parliament and the Council on Certain Rules Governing Actions for Damages under National Law for Infringements of the Competition Law Provisions of the Member States and of the European Union (PE-CONS 80/14). The Directive was signed into law on 26 November 2014 leaving the Member States 2 years to implement it in their national legal systems.

[7]Case No IV/M.1524 — Airtours/First Choice.

Although for EC cartel cases, such cost estimates are not available to the best of our knowledge, general EC cartel enforcement data can provide insights on one important driver of litigation costs and counsel fees: the duration of the investigation. In this respect, an empirical analysis by Hüschelrath and Laitenberger (2015) finds — for all EC cartel cases that were decided between 2000 and 2014 — an average duration of almost 50 months from the start of the investigation to the respective decision by the European Commission. Furthermore, additional evidence by Hüschelrath and Smuda (2016) suggest that roughly half of the convicted firm groups decide to file an appeal with either the General Court (formerly known as Court of First Instance) as first-stage appellate court or the European Court of Justice as second-stage and highest appellate court in the European Union. On average, the respective investigations increase the duration of the entire cartel case further by additional about 49 months creating substantial amounts of additional litigation costs and counsel fees. Furthermore, in case of international cartels, these costs may be boosted further by the respective public and private enforcement actions in multiple jurisdictions.

2.2.5 *Effects on Stock Prices*

The stock prices of a firm change as a result of market forces and are an indicator for the perceived value of the firm. An important factor that affects the value of a company is its profits and profit expectations. A detected cartel involvement reduces the profits and profit expectations and therefore expects a drop in the stock price. Ceteris paribus, such a development must be considered as an additional negative consequence of detected competition law infringements.

With respect to a quantification of such an effect, Aguzzoni et al. (2013) use an event-study approach to investigate the impact of various events of EU antitrust enforcement on the respective firm's stock market value. Their results show that dawn raids reduced the firm's stock market value by 2.89 % on average on the day of the raid. Furthermore, the formal decision of the European Commission led to another reduction of 3.57 % (on average) of the firm's stock market value. Interestingly, court judgments do not have a statistically significant further effect.

Motivated by the question whether the negative effects of antitrust enforcement on stock prices are only temporary or rather long lasting, Richards et al. (2015) investigate the equity price impact of announced cartel investigations. For a set of 160 firms who, first, were convicted for their involvement in international cartels between 1994 and 2010 and, second, whose securities are publicly traded in the American market, the authors estimate normal returns using the Fama-French three-factor model. They find that, first, cartel investigation announcements have a long lasting negative share-price effect of about 2 % (for firms that do not receive leniency only). Second, as this 2 % loss is notably less than the estimated present value of profits lost due to cartel termination, the authors conclude that that cartel participation is profitable.

2.2.6 Effects on Firm Reputation

Infringements of competition law detected by the competition authority usually cannot be kept in secret. Therefore, a further negative consequence of such infringements must be seen in adverse publicity causing negative effects on firm reputation. The knock-on effects of such a decrease in reputation can be multi-faceted. For example, in addition to a general reduction in future business opportunities, especially public sector customers might have to debar the firm from doing business with them. Furthermore, a damaged firm reputation might complicate the process of hiring high potential employees and therefore causes negative effects on future firm performance. Additionally, the payment of substantial fines and damages can cause a competitive disadvantage due to reduced possibilities to undertake investments in the firm's operations or research and development. Depending on the general financial situation of the firm and the competitive situation in the respective markets, the competitive disadvantages might become so severe that the firm's existence is at stake and therefore fortifies the negative effects on firm reputation (see, e.g., Hüschelrath et al. 2011, for further discussions in light of the 2003 revision of Swiss competition law).

Given the identification of negative consequences of competition law infringements, the question after the relevance of these factors is evident. Although empirical evidence is sparse, in 2007, the Office of Fair Trading (2007) published a Deloitte study which generally focused on the deterrent effect of competition enforcement. As part of a larger survey on the topic, business managers as well as competition lawyers were asked about the relative importance of various sanctioning options in deterring infringements of competition law. The results show that while both groups rank 'criminal penalties' highest, business managers rank 'disqualification of directors' before 'adverse publicity', '(corporate) fines' and 'private damages actions'. The interviewed lawyers, however, rank '(corporate) fines' before 'disqualification of directors', 'adverse publicity' and 'private damages actions'. However, following a later survey among larger UK companies conducted by the OFT (2010, p. 29), the adverse reputational impact of a competition law infringement has become the key driver of compliance efforts with an even greater relevance than corporate fines.

Although the negative consequences of competition law infringements are the natural starting point of a study of the motivations for CLCPs, a broader perspective suggests that excellence in compliance does not only lead to the avoidance of negative consequences of competition law infringements, but can also have positive effects on the efficiency and efficacy of internal processes. For example, managers well trained in competition law are not only more likely to make correct decisions but they can expect to make these decisions quicker and therefore free up resources for other activities. Additionally, a well implemented best practice CLCP helps managers to differentiate between strategies that hurt competitors but are nevertheless procompetitive (e.g., aggressive pricing strategies) and strategies that are anticompetitive and therefore likely to be punished (e.g., predatory pricing strategies). As a consequence, such firms can make sure that managers stay as defensive as necessary but as aggressive as possible to gain and defend competitive advantages.

Furthermore, an effective CLCP not only reduces the risk of competition law infringements due to ignorance but also helps with the internal detection of infringements leaving the top management more options to react and to minimise the negative impact on the firm. In case the firm decides to actively report the infringement to the competition authority, it can expect a significant reduction in the imposed fines (in addition to a possible reduction through the application of a leniency programme). Additionally, in some countries such as the UK or Italy, proof of the effective implementation of a best practice CLCP can lead to a further reduction in fines and therefore provides an additional incentive to invest in these programmes (see Sect. 2.4.2 below for a detailed assessment).

Still extending the perspective of the motivations for making compliance efforts, management approaches see competition law compliance as part of an integrated concept of 'Corporate Social Responsibility'. Following such an approach, firms — permanently monitored by share- and stakeholders — have to comply with, e.g., competition law not because it possibly avoids negative consequences such as fines but in order to meet their own moral and ethical standards set by a code of conduct or a code of ethics[8] (see generally Grüninger 2005). If such an approach works frictionless, even the complete abandonment of public fines would not change the firm's compliance efforts. It therefore challenges the neoclassical deterrence approach followed by most competition authorities in Europe and the rest of the world.

2.3 Design of an Effective Competition Law Compliance Programme

The following assessment of the design of an effective best practice competition law compliance programme (CLCP) is separated into two sub-sections. While Sect. 2.3.1 concentrates on the identification of key challenges, Sect. 2.3.2 discusses the building blocks of an effective CLCP.

---

[8]See generally Rodger (2005, p. 354f.) for an overview. Following such an approach, competition law infringements are not the consequence of deliberate wrongdoing by 'amoral calculators' but rather happen because of 'organisational incompetence' of different 'compliance school' approaches.

2.3.1 *Key Challenges in the Design of an Effective Competition Law Compliance Programme*

Although the policy makers' cost-benefit calculus with respect to the desired deterrence of violations appears self-evident, real firms are not single entities but rather a collection of individuals driven by their personal objective functions. As a consequence, a suitable starting point for a discussion of the challenges in the design of an effective CLCP is the development of an understanding of the drivers of non-compliance from the perspective of an individual. Extending an overview of Beckenstein and Gabel (1986, p. 674), answers to the question include a lack of information, a low probability of detection ('lack of supervision'), the structure of industrial markets, a dichotomy between management's and firm's objectives, ambiguity in the laws, the 'munificence' of a firm's environment, and individuals' risk preferences. Although it is beyond the scope of this article to provide a detailed discussion of all these factors, the majority of them will be addressed in the following by differentiating between 'providing information' and 'providing incentives' as the two major challenges in the design of an effective CLCP.

2.3.1.1 Providing Information

A necessary condition for an effective compliance programme is the efficient provision of the relevant information. At first sight, such an endeavour might look trivial; however, the fact alone that real firms consist of a large number of individuals with different backgrounds and tasks suggests that such an efficient provision of the relevant information is anything but straightforward. As discussed by Beckenstein and Gabel (1986, p. 676ff.), in large firms, problems such as the existence of imperfect information and uncertainty, costly communication, perverse incentives or bounded rationality make it difficult to achieve compliance even if it has a high priority as a management objective. As a consequence, competition law infringements by employees must not necessarily be motivated by the assumed individual cost-benefit assessment but can also be a consequence of the organisation's failure to provide the relevant information.

Attempting to disentangle the key drivers of an efficient provision of the relevant information a little further, it is important to realise that such a provision is costly for the firm. The activities necessary to keep employees informed cannot be reduced to the printing and distribution of a compliance brochure or the provision of check lists but needs to include, e.g., periodic trainings (face-to-face and/or with e-learning tools) to make the key messages memorable on the one hand and to allow for updates of the respective laws or the business environment on the other hand. Given the positive costs of the provision of information, it is on the one hand not optimal for the firm to aim to provide the full set of information to all employees.

On the other hand, the limited resources for the provision of information[9] confront the firm with the need to identify the areas within the firm where the likelihood and the impact of risks[10] are greatest.

With respect to competition law, an efficient provision of the relevant information basically demands the identification of the relevant competition law risks for the respective employee or group of employees (exposed to the respective competition law risk). The general risks are at least partly determined by competition law (and its enforcement) and include cartelisation, the abuse of a dominant position (e.g., by setting predatory prices) or the imposition of certain vertical restraints such as tying or resale price maintenance. By construction of the respective competition law, the different types of anticompetitive behaviour already allow a categorisation of the impact of possible infringements. For example, an involvement in a cartel may cause a higher risk than the implementation of an anticompetitive tying strategy, e.g., as the former might be classified as felony while the latter is only an infringement of competition law. In such an environment it would, ceteris paribus, be optimal to invest more in the avoidance of cartels than in the avoidance of tying.

An important insufficiency of such a general risk analysis is its implicit assumption that every form of anticompetitive behaviour is of equal relevance for the respective firm. However, depending on the industry specifics, the own market position and the organisational structure of the firm, the firm-specific risks for the various forms of competition law infringements might be distributed unevenly. For example, the risk of cartelisation might be elevated significantly in a firm that operates in a concentrated homogenous good industry and provides product managers with a high degree of autonomy in setting prices compared to a firm with inverted characteristics. Generally, a firm-specific risk analysis demands the identification and assessment of those forms of anticompetitive behaviour that are likely of the greatest importance for the specific firm. The result of such an assessment could be that it is, ceteris paribus, optimal to invest more in the avoidance of tying than in the avoidance of cartels (see, e.g., Paha and Götz (2015) for a more detailed discussion).

From a broader perspective, the identification of firm-specific risk areas should on the one hand include an assessment of past competition investigations in the respective industries complemented by a comparison of the industry and firm characteristics with the key drivers of the different forms of competition law infringements.[11] On the other hand, an assessment of organisational characteristics

[9]Another argument for a clear focus on the provision of the relevant knowledge is limitations in the absorptive capacity of individuals.

[10]In general, risk management can be defined as all policies, procedures, and practices involved in the identification, analysis, assessment and control of risks. An effective risk management aims to avoid, minimise, or eliminate unacceptable risks; its successful implementation depends on the correct adoption to the business specifics in the respective industry.

[11]Such a proposal is in line with, e.g., Kolasky (2002) who analyses the specificities of detected cartels and argues that an effective CLCP has to incorporate these factors.

within the firm such as the exposure of employees to direct contact to competitors, the ability to set prices or the responsibility for specific client accounts (see generally Bournonville and Brankin 2009) can be helpful for an assessment of the firm-specific risk areas.

Potential ambiguities in the law provide a final key difficulty in the efficient provision of the relevant information. The less specific the law provisions, the harder it is for a company to provide detailed information and advice to its employees. For example, while the definition of a hard-core cartel is relatively straightforward to communicate, other forms of anticompetitive behaviour such as the abuse of a dominant position are much harder to delineate and communicate. As a consequence, competition law infringements can not only be caused by insufficient deterrence or organisational failure to provide the relevant information but also by the policy makers themselves through the implementation of vague rules and regulations.[12]

2.3.1.2 Providing Incentives

Although providing the necessary information to the relevant employees is a necessary condition for the implementation of an effective compliance programme, such activities do not foreclose the possibility that employees decide to infringe competition law. Therefore, complementary to the provision of information, firms have to implement strategies for the efficient provision of incentives to comply with competition law. With respect to positive incentives to comply, the firm can, e.g., take compliance performance as a parameter in the derivation of the personal remuneration or promotion decisions. Furthermore, in setting personal task for departments or employees, the top management has to consider that unrealistic commercial objectives combined with group pressure may cause employees to break the law (see Economiesuisse 2010, p. 8). Such a situation might be further aggravated by connecting these objectives with the personal remuneration.

With respect to sanctions, their effectiveness is driven by especially two factors: types (and levels) of sanctions and the probability of detection. With respect to the former, firms generally can choose among several sanction options reaching from an official warning, promotion freezes or pecuniary fines up to immediate dismissal or the turn over to government authorities. In general, the sanction type and level should depend on factors such as the severity (i.e., the firm-specific risk classification) or the duration of the infringement.

[12]As a consequence, policy makers have to assure that competition rules are as clear as possible (e.g., by the provision of guidelines or possibilities for firms to consult the competition authority with specific competition problems). Furthermore, internal legal service departments might face a loss of trust if they are not able to give clear advice to the manager on the pro- or anti-competitiveness of certain behaviour. Such a 'loss of trust in legal advice' might raise the incentives for competition law infringements (see OFT 2010, p. 7).

With respect to the probability of detection, the firm can basically make use of comparable tools as a competition authority. Following a detailed assessment by Hüschelrath (2010b), these tools include both reactive and proactive methods. Reactive methods include the creation of incentives to self-report through the implementation of an internal leniency programme or the installation of an internal whistleblower programme that provides anonymous possibilities to report misbehaviour. Additionally, the firm can make use of proactive methods to detect competition law infringements. For example, as proposed by Abrantes-Metz et al. (2010) and Abrantes-Metz and Sokol (2013), an essential step to create robust compliance systems is to apply tools that screen market data for certain red flags[13] which are viewed as an indication for the presence of a competition law infringement. Due to the usually better data situation within the firm compared to the competition authority, such techniques can be valuable tools for the internal detection of competition law infringements.

Generally, all tools together have the important task to signal employees that it is likely that competition law infringements will be detected and it is hoped that they therefore decide to refrain from the implementation of such anticompetitive strategies. However, from an economic perspective, it would be inefficient to keep up the same high probability of detection in every area of the firm. An efficient provision demands the identification of the high risk areas and the implementation of strategies to mitigate these risks by a selective increase in sanctions and the probability of detection.

2.3.2 *Building Blocks of an Effective Competition Law Compliance Programme*

The discussion of the key challenges in the preceding section already suggests that the design of an effective best practice CLCP is a complicated exercise. In an early attempt to provide a structure to competition law compliance, Beckenstein et al. (1983) differentiate between three different (typically subsequent) strategies of compliance with competition law: basic decision-enhancing, advanced decision-enhancing and decision-restructuring strategies. The first 'basic decision-enhancing' strategy is guided by the belief that the provision of information about competition rules and the consequences of violations to the employees will be sufficient to prevent violations. The second 'advanced decision-enhancing' strategy assumes that competition law infringements are motivated by the expected personal benefits. As a consequence, the firm aims to strengthen external enforcement with complementary in-house policing such as the imposition of sanctions for violations

[13]Following Kolasky (2002), such red flags include trade association activity, sales transactions between the firm and competitors, stable market shares over a long period, or sudden unexplained price increases.

or competition law audits. The third 'decision-restructuring' strategy aims at reducing the probability of violation "... by constraining managers' decision autonomy or by restructuring the organization" (Beckenstein et al. 1983, p. 95). Examples of such measures are prohibitions for managers to set anything other than the list price, requirements that all prices cover fully allocated costs, a systematic rotation of key sales and marketing personnel or a prohibition of employee membership in trade associations. Although all measures are helpful in protecting the firm from competition law violations, there is a high risk that the respective firms overcomply with the law and are consequently deterred from the realisation of business strategies which might be harmful for competitors but are nevertheless procompetitive.

With respect to the design of a best practice CLCP, several alternative frameworks exist. For example, following the U.S. Sentencing Guidelines,[14] to have an effective compliance and ethics programme, an organisation shall "... (1) exercise due diligence to prevent and detect criminal conduct; and (2) otherwise promote an organizational culture that encourages ethical conduct and a commitment to compliance with the law. Such compliance and ethics program shall be reasonably designed, implemented, and enforced so that the program is generally effective in preventing and detecting criminal conduct." Furthermore, the Office of Fair Trading (2011) provides guidance on an effective competition law compliance culture and suggests a four step approach consisting of risk identification, risk assessment, risk mitigation and review. Most recently, the Competition Bureau Canada (2015) has published a detailed bulletin providing guidance regarding credible and effective corporate compliance programmes designed to ensure compliance with Canadian competition law. In particular, the bulletin, first, sets out measures that Canadian individuals and businesses should consider in order to minimise their risk of engaging in illegal anti-competitive activities and to detect any illegal activities. Second, it provides tools to help businesses develop compliance programmes and, third, the bulletin examines hypothetical case studies illustrating how the Bureau may consider the credibility and effectiveness of a compliance programme.

In addition to the definition of such official approaches, further proposals for the design and implementation of CLCPs exist, e.g. from an academic perspective (e.g., Rodger 2005; Sokol 2012; Abrantes-Metz and Sokol 2013, or Riley and Sokol 2015), a consultancy's perspective (e.g., Grüninger 2005), a lawyer's perspective (e.g., Desai 2005 or Banks and Jalabert-Doury 2012) or an industry association's perspective (e.g., Economiesuisse 2010). Based on a detailed assessment of the different framework proposals from the different perspectives and underlying motivations, the following Table 2.1 defines and characterises the building blocks of an effective CLCP.

[14]U.S. Sentencing Guidelines, Chapter 8, §8B2.1. Effective Compliance and Ethics Program (2009 Guidelines Manual, effective November 1, 2009). In the United States, the effective implementation of a compliance and ethics programme can lead to a reduction in fines for detected competition law infringements.

Table 2.1 Building blocks of an effective competition law compliance programme

Building block	Characterisation
Compliance strategy	• Clear, unambiguous and ongoing commitment to compliance from the top management • Definition of compliance goals (e.g., prevention and detection) • Risk identification and assessment (e.g., current practices, policies and agreements; past competition law problems in the firm/industry) • Development of the general (risk mitigating) strategies for the creation of an effective compliance culture (e.g., deterrence-based, prevention through moral standards, principles vs. rules) • Integration into a broader concept of corporate culture (e.g., 'code of conduct')
Structures	• The top management bears the ultimate organisational responsibility • Definition of the structural organisation of the compliance standards and processes (e.g., joined or separate functions, internal/external reporting bodies, coordination between various compliance-relevant departments of the firm) • Installation of an employee responsible for the overall implementation • Installation of individuals responsible for day-to-day operational aspects • Allocation of the necessary resources, powers and reporting lines to the responsible individuals • Inclusion of subsidiary firms in the compliance structure of the parent firm • Development of, e.g., competition law compliance handbooks and compliance checklists for employees containing all relevant competition law infringements • Specification sheets for compliance officials including the examination of new agreements, conducts, products and markets
Procedures	• Definition of procedures to communicate the basic compliance principles to all employees on a periodic (not one-time) basis • Definition of procedures to communicate specific knowledge tailored to each employee's respective role and responsibilities on a periodic (not one-time) basis (e.g., face-to-face training, eLearning tools, conducted internally or by external lawyers) • Definition of procedures to check new agreements or conducts for competition law compliance • Definition of procedures to check existing agreements or conducts for competition law compliance on a periodic (not one-time) basis (which is necessary due to changes in law, the markets and the market position or product portfolio of the firm) • Definition of procedures for dealing with compliance questions (e.g., helpline) • Definition of procedures in case of the (internal or external) detection of an infringement • Definition of procedures in case of dawn raids

(continued)

Table 2.1 (continued)

Building block	Characterisation
Incentives and sanctions	• Integration of a compliance performance parameter in the recruiting and remuneration of managers • Installation of a system to anonymously report misbehaviour; provision of protection and possibly rewards for internal whistleblowers • Installation of an internal leniency programme to encourage employees to report misbehaviour • Installation of a system to actively detect employees who fail to comply (e.g., red flags, screens) • Installation of a system of sanctions for employees who fail to comply (e.g., official warning, promotion freezes, pecuniary fines, immediate dismissal, turn over to government authorities)
Control and development	• Reoccurring internal monitoring and (re)evaluation of implementation and effectiveness of the compliance strategy (e.g. detected infringements, number of investigations by the competition authority, costs of compliance, compliance culture) • External evaluation by lawyers ('mock dawn raids') • Assessment of reasons for detected infringements and implementation of strategies to avoid them in the future • Monitoring and adoption of changes in (case) law, laws and regulations, the own market position and the industry • Oversight by the governing authority

Source: Hüschelrath (2010a)

In general, Table 2.1 only provides an overview and characterisation of the building blocks of an effective CLCP. The respective best practice design and implementation for a specific firm depends on a multitude of external and internal factors such as the respective industry, the market position and size of the firm as well as its organisational structure. In other words, Table 2.1 should be viewed as a menu selection device in the sense that it delineates the important steps and provides general guidance for the design of an effective CLCP.

2.4 Competition Law Compliance Programmes and Competition Law Enforcement

Subsequent to our discussions of the motivations to ensure compliance and the design of an effective competition law compliance programme (CLCP), in this section, we aim at relating CLCPs to competition law enforcement in general and the fine setting procedure in particular. While Sect. 2.4.1 provides a normative perspective on the issue whether the presence (or absence) of a CLCP should have a reducing (or elevating) effect on the final fine, Sect. 2.4.2 describes how selected competition authorities currently handle the issue in practice.

2.4.1 *Competition Law Compliance Programmes and the Fine Setting Procedure*

Over the last few years, a considerable discussion among both lawyers and economists emerged around the question whether and how the presence of a CLCP should affect fines for breaching competition law. While some commentators argue that CLCPs should be considered as a mitigating factor in the fine calculation process, others are of the opinion that they should either not be taken into account at all or even viewed as an aggravating factor if no (or an apparently imperfect) programme was implemented at the time of the infringement. In this context of a rather large spectrum of proposals on how to treat CLCPs in the fine setting procedure, we aim at providing an overview of the most important arguments from both ends of the spectrum. We will proceed by, first, describing the main arguments raised in an article by Wils (2013) and the reply to this article by Geradin (2013). Second, we add further important arguments brought forward in additional law and/or economics articles.

In his seminal article, Wils (2013) acknowledges the positive effects of CLCPs for competition law enforcement,[15] however, argues that CLCPs should neither be considered as aggravating nor as mitigating factor in the fine setting procedure. A classification as aggravating factor appears inappropriate as the implementation of a CLCP is not a necessary condition for being compliant (and thus there should not be an implicit obligation to have such a programme). However, according to Wils (2013), the presence of a CLCP should also not be considered as a mitigating factor in the fine setting procedure either as, first, such programmes might have been implemented just for the purpose of reducing the fine (in case of detection) rather than for actual compliance. In other words, treating CLCPs as mitigating factors would make them a rather cheap insurance against antitrust violations.

Second, as competition authorities would only observe instances where a CLCP did not prevent an infringement — but not the cases of successful prevention — the authorities are unable to distinguish between best practice and ineffectual CLCPs. Assuming that the costs of creating a CLCP are small compared to the potential gains from antitrust violations, immunity from fines or significant reductions could create an incentive for firms to actually encourage infringements.

Furthermore, granting immunity would also be unfair as firms would technically keep part of their benefits from their infringement. Wils (2013) also rejects the idea of using sanctions for responsible individuals as a substitute as this would give firms the incentive to trigger infringements by setting targets that could not be reached with compliance. He argues that a fine reduction would have the same effect as immunity, just to a lesser degree. Taking stock of all these arguments, Wils (2013)

[15]Wils (2013) sees substantial positive effects of CLCPs in situations when they prevent antitrust infringements that would otherwise have occurred, when they lead to an on-going infringement being terminated earlier and when they lead to an infringement being reported to the competition authority that would otherwise not have been reported.

concludes that — if there is a political willingness to subsidise CLCPs — this should be implemented for all firms and not only for those that violated competition law.

In a direct reply to Wils (2013), Geradin (2013) provides arguments why competition authorities should in fact reward the implementation of CLCPs under certain conditions. He particularly challenges Wils' view that it would not be possible to distinguish between best practice and ineffectual CLCPs, partly referring to a list of 20 criteria compiled by Murphy and Kolasky (2011). A competition authority that would reward only programmes which are deemed to be sufficiently robust would actively promote that those kinds of valuable CLCPs are actually adapted and thus result in a higher level of compliance with competition law.

Moreover, Geradin (2013) refers to experiences with compliance programmes in the fight against corruption where several authorities take compliance efforts into account when deciding on a sentence. He criticises the absolute refusal of allowing any fine reductions — even in cases where only low level employees were involved in the infringement and where it seems especially appropriate to distinguish between firms that attempted to prevent infringements and those that did not.

In addition, Geradin (2013) generally claims that, first, Wils underestimates the positive effects of compliance programmes by not taking into account that CLCPs are a very effective form of competition advocacy. Second, he believes that the potentially negative effects of CLCPs are in fact smaller than suggested by Wils (2013) — basically because effective CLCPs include an effective monitoring of employees which in fact reduce the possibilities that CLCPs make employees learn how to circumvent the respective rules. Furthermore, the danger that CLCPs could lead to internal detection and subsequent destruction of evidence is also considered as unlikely due to the existing strong incentives to apply for leniency.

Last but not least, Geradin (2013) also criticises Wils' (2013) sympathy with the idea of giving a fine reduction to a company that starts a CLCP after an infringement has been detected — basically because such a rule would reduce the incentives for companies to introduce such a programme before the first infringement occurred (and was detected by the competition authority).

In addition to the seminal contributions by Wils (2013) and Geradin (2013), recent additional research provides further interesting perspectives on the role of CLCPs. For example, Riley and Sokol (2015) suggest that there is a need for proactive encouragement regarding CLCPs as competition authorities will never have the resources to police the entire economy. By facilitating more effective CLCPs, competition authorities could manage to change the ethics in business. The authors view fine reductions as one feasible way to promote CLCPs, but also consider alternatives such as removing parent liability in case a subsidiary clearly violates the parent companies' CLCP.

Furthermore, in an earlier article summarizing the results of a compliance survey among practitioners in the U.S., Sokol (2012) finds that certain structural limitations inside firms often prevented them from having effective CLCPs. He suggests that appropriate incentives for individuals at all levels within the firm must be created in order to sufficiently promote the implementation of effective CLCPs. Therefore, guidelines provided by the competition authorities and support for

CLCPs — possibly in the form of fine reductions — are important cornerstones in promoting compliance with competition law.

Lachnit (2014) generally studies the question of how to improve the approach of competition authorities towards CLCPs and discusses fine reductions as one serious option. In particular, she argues that the granting of such fine reductions would promote the implementation of CLCPs thus creating positive external effects for both the competition authority and the general business culture. In fact, she argues that a fine reduction could actually be the necessary push for a firm to introduce a CLCP. However, she also takes account of a key additional argument against such a reduction, namely that the default situation should be one in which the law is obeyed (without providing any subsidies in the form of fine reductions). In sum, Lachnit (2014) concludes that fine reductions for well-functioning CLCPs appear reasonable; she expects that the detailed case investigations should allow competition authorities to assess to a sufficient degree whether a best practice CLCP was implemented at the time of the infringement or not.

Complementary to these contributions from a law and economics perspective, Miller (2014) and Paha (2014) both apply the tools of economic theory to the question of the most suitable role of CLCPs from a social welfare perspective. Miller (2014) particularly discusses the challenge of an evaluation of the effectiveness of a CLCP further and proposes to apply economic methods rather than a long list of criteria. From an economic point of view, an effective CLCP would consist of the set of policies and procedures that rational firms should establish when facing expected sanctions equal to the social costs of the violation. In such a world, Miller (2014) shows that fine reductions can be socially optimal as soon as the competition authority needs to invest less in detection (as CLCPs take over a part of that role).

Paha (2014) develops a rich model in which firms are subject to imperfect information about law enforcement and have to decide about both welfare-enhancing and welfare-reducing cooperation among them. In this model world, the introduction of a CLCP teaches firms which behaviour is legal. Since the introduction of a CLCP is costly and firms may freeride on their rivals, firms do not necessarily adopt a CLCP. However, if the antitrust authority reduces a fine, the adoption of a CLCP can in fact be promoted. The argument especially holds in situations where firms underestimate the detection probability. However, the fine reduction must not to be too high since otherwise firms would find cartelisation profitable.

2.4.2 *Treatment of Competition Law Compliance Programmes in the Fine Setting Procedure by Selected Competition Authorities*

In this sub-section, we complement our normative assessment of the role of CLCPs in the fine setting procedure by providing evidence on how the issue is actually treated by selected competition authorities. In the *European Union*, the Commission has never granted a fine reduction because of the existence of a CLCP at the time of the infringement (see Wils 2013). However, in some of its older decisions between 1982 and 2001, the Commission reduced the corporate fines in case of full cooperation of the respective firm and proof of undertaken measures to implement a CLCP to avoid future infringements. In its more recent decisions since 2001, however, the Commission (as well as the European courts) refrained from providing such fine reductions as they do not alter the reality of the infringement found in the respective case (see Wils 2013). According to Jalabert-Doury et al. (2015), this general position of the Commission remained unchanged in recent years — despite the (partly significant) recent changes in some EU Member States characterised below.

The *United States* also apply a 'strict liability approach' as discussed in detail in Riley and Sokol (2015). Although the US Sentencing Guidelines allow corporate fine reductions in case of the implementation of an 'effective compliance and ethics program' at the time of the infringement, such fine reductions are subject to very restrictive conditions. These include, for instance, that no managers or other personnel with substantial authority was involved in an infringement — a condition that will hardly ever be fulfilled in antitrust cases (see Wils 2013). As a consequence, the U.S. DOJ has typically ignored (the presence or absence of) CLCPs as part of its fining decisions. However, most recently, Gibson and Dunn (2015) report that the Department of Justice has started to rethink its tough policy by possibly considering fine reductions — as part of negotiated plea or settlement agreements — in cases where firms adopt a CLCP as part of their response to an U.S. antitrust investigation.

In *Germany*, the Federal Cartel Office sees compliance as a legal obligation and therefore considers neither the existence nor the quality of a CLCP as a mitigating (or aggravating) factor in the fine calculation procedure (see Jalabert-Doury et al. 2015). However, the authority clearly encourages firms to implement CLCPs as an important tool to prevent competition law infringements (and the substantial costs attached to them in case of detection). In this respect, effective CLCPs contain further benefits for the respective firms such as, e.g., an increased likelihood of an internal detection of infringements and therefore an increased likelihood to receive a fine waiver as first leniency applicant (see Jalabert-Doury et al. 2015).

For *France*, Jalabert-Doury and Sproul (2012) report that the French competition authority intensified its compliance-related initiatives in 2008 with the commissioning of a study on compliance programmes. Guided by the results of the study and subsequent discussions, in 2012, the authority published both a framework document and a brochure on the design of an effective best practice CLCP in general and the treatment of CLCPs in French competition law enforcement in particular (see Autorité de la Concurrence 2012a, b). According to those documents, fine reductions of up to 10 % are possible for firms committing to set up or to upgrade an existing compliance programme according to the best practices specified by the authority in the above mentioned two documents. However, as discussed in greater detail in Lachnit (2014), such fine reductions are typically only granted in the course of the settlement procedure. In the regular fining procedures, the authority sees CLCPs neither as mitigating nor as aggravating factor (as the existence of such a programme does not alter the reality of the infringement itself).

In the *United Kingdom*, the old Office of Fair Trading published a detailed guidance paper on achieving compliance with competition law already in 2011 (OFT 2011). Although the paper focuses on the development of a risk-based approach to compliance — with risk identification, risk assessment, risk mitigation and review as the four compulsory steps — it also provides a discussion on the possible impact of CLCPs on the amount of a penalty. In essence, the OFT can reduce the amount of a financial penalty by up to 10 % where adequate steps have been taken with a view to ensuring compliance with UK competition laws. While the 'adequate steps' are specified by the mentioned four-step approach — and are investigated by the authority on a case-by-case basis — it is important to add that fine reductions are in principle possible for both pre-date the infringement or where they were implemented quickly after the firm became aware of the infringement (see OFT 2011, for further information). According to Jalabert-Doury et al. (2015), the new Competition and Markets Authority (CMA) appears to continue the OFT's policy of imposing less stringent fines on companies with best practice compliance programmes. However, as its predecessor, the CMA emphasises that it is the substance — not the mere existence — that determines whether a CLCP is accepted as a mitigating factor in the fine calculation procedure.

In 2014, *Italy* introduced the possibility of a fine reduction of up to 15 % in case of "... the adoption and observance of a specific compliance program, which is in line with European and international best practices" (Pezzoli 2015, p. 4). Key elements of such a best practice CLCP — explicitly mentioned by the Italian competition authority — are an involvement of the top management, the precise identification of persons in charge, the identification and assessment of risks in the precise context, the organisation of training adapted to the size of the company, incentives to comply with the programme as well as sanctions, follow-up and audit mechanisms. According to Jalabert-Doury et al. (2015), so far, the Italian competition authority has not yet granted any fine reduction for the implementation of a CLCP.

Summing up the main insights of this sub-section, it becomes apparent that competition authorities have different opinions (or possibilities set by law, respectively) on whether to allow fine reductions for the (ex-ante and/or ex-post) implementation of a CLCP or not. For those jurisdictions who do offer a fine reduction, the degree of that reduction lies in a range of 10–15 %. Furthermore, proof of a best practice CLCP seems to be required by all jurisdictions who consider fine reductions in response to the implementation of such programmes. However, the fact that it is still unclear how a best practice CLCP should look like — together with the additional fact that many jurisdictions have only recently introduced the respective rules — makes a meaningful evaluation of the respective approaches a difficult endeavour for the time being.

2.5 Conclusion

The enforcement of competition laws has gained considerable momentum in recent years in many jurisdictions around the world. Taking cartel enforcement in the European Union as an example, the European Commission — acting in concert with national competition authorities — introduced (and reformed) a leniency programme, implemented a major revision of the fining guidelines, promoted the private enforcement of anti-cartel laws and intensified cooperation between competition authorities (particularly in the fight against international cartels).

These considerable efforts to promote competitiveness by detecting and punishing cartels are visible not only in the increased number of cartel cases handled by the Commission every year, but also in the substantial rise in the fines imposed on the cartel members. For example, while the Commission decided 10 cartel cases in the 1995 to 1999 period imposing fines of in sum about €0.3 billion, the most recent 5 year period from 2010 to 2014 experienced 30 decided cases with total fines of about €8.9 billion imposed by the Commission.[16] In other words, a tripling of the number of cases is accompanied by a roughly 30-fold increase in fines.

From a firm perspective, the recent trend of an improved competition law enforcement in combination with larger fines suggests that it has not only become more likely that infringements of competition law are detected but also that — in case of actual detection — the fines are expected to be substantially larger than for similar infringements in the past. Ceteris paribus, such a situation makes it rational to invest additional resources into the development and implementation of so-called competition law compliance programmes (CLCPs) that aim at providing both information and incentives to the employees to comply with competition law thereby reducing the likelihood of the occurrence of actual infringements.

Against this background, the article has provided a law and economics perspective on competition law compliance programmes (CLCPs) with a particular focus on the motivations to ensure compliance, the building blocks in the design of an effective CLCP and the implications of the presence (or absence) of a CLCP for competition law enforcement in general and the fine setting procedure in particular. With respect to the *motivation* for such programmes, it was shown that corporate sanctions are only one element of the negative consequences of competition law infringements — which may also include individual sanctions, damages, litigation costs and counsel fees, effects on stock prices and effects on firm reputation. Complementary to such an enumeration of the negative consequences, it was argued that ensuring compliance can also be interpreted as a competitive advantage as soon as it is understood as an integral part of a broader concept of corporate culture.

[16] The respective data (not adjusted for court judgements) is published (and frequently updated) by the European Commission's Competition Directorate-General on the following website: http://ec.europa.eu/competition/cartels/statistics/statistics.pdf (last accessed on 29 March 2016).

The *design* of an effective best practice CLCP faces two key challenges: providing information and providing incentives. With respect to the former, it was shown that an efficient provision of the relevant information to the relevant individuals in the firm should be based on an identification and assessment of the relevant competition law risks. With respect to the latter — providing incentives — the firm should implement a mix of (positive) incentives to comply and (negative) sanctions which apply in case of detected antitrust infringements. Based on these two challenges and incorporating existing research and practical experiences, the proposed building blocks for an effective best practice CLCP differentiated between the development of a compliance strategy, the determination of structures and procedures, the implementation of incentives and sanctions and the organisation of efforts to control the success of the programme and to develop improvement potential.

The general discussion of the *implications* of a CLCP for the fine setting procedure has brought up several arguments in favour or against fine reductions. For example, the opponents of the role of an implemented CLCP as mitigating factor in the calculation of the fine argue, for example, that, first, such programmes might have been implemented just for the purpose of reducing the fine (in case of detection) rather than for actual compliance. Second, as competition authorities would only observe instances where a CLCP did not prevent an infringement — but not the cases of successful prevention — the authorities are unable to distinguish between best practice and ineffectual CLCPs. The supporters of fine reductions acknowledge that it is not always easy to identify a best practice CLCP, however, they not only argue that it is generally possible but also expect that the respective costs are much lower than assumed by the opponents. Furthermore, and even more important, the promotion of best practice CLCPs though fine reductions is likely to create substantial additional benefits through reaching a higher level of compliance in the respective jurisdiction that are likely to surpass the respective additional costs created by such a policy reform.

In comparing and valuing these various arguments, a possible compromise would be to hold out the prospect of moderate fine reductions of about 10 % for serious (and proven) compliance efforts. Given that a number of competition authorities have already adopted such an approach, it will be interesting to observe in the years to come whether and how (and to what extent) the respective new possibilities are used in practice. In any case, the success of the new rules are closely tied to, first, the derivation of clear criteria of how a best practice CLCP looks like and, second, the possibilities of the respective competition authorities to find out whether these criteria are met in the case at hand.

References

Abrantes-Metz, R., Bajari, P., & Murphy, J. (2010). *Antitrust screening: Making compliance programs robust.* Working Paper, New York.

Abrantes-Metz, R., & Sokol, D. (2013). *Antitrust corporate governance and compliance.* Research Paper 13-18, University of Minnesota Law School, Minneapolis.

Aguzzoni, L., Langus, G., & Motta, M. (2013). The effect of EU antitrust investigations and fines on a firm's valuation. *Journal of Industrial Economics, 61*, 290–338.

Autorite de la Concurrence. (2012a). Framework-Document of 10 February 2012 on Antitrust Compliance Programmes, Paris.

Autorite de la Concurrence. (2012b). Antitrust Compliance and Compliance Programmes – Corporate Tools for Competing Safely in the Marketplace, Paris.

Baker, J. (2003). The case for antitrust enforcement. *Journal of Economic Perspectives, 17*, 27–50.

Banks, T., & Jalabert-Doury, N. (2012). Competition law compliance programs and government support or indifference. *Concurrences* N° 2-2012.

Beckenstein, A., & Gabel, L. (1986). The economics of antitrust compliance. *Southern Economic Journal, 52*, 673–692.

Beckenstein, A. R., Gabel, H. L., & Roberts, K. (1983). An executive's guide to antitrust compliance. *Harvard Business Review, 61*(5), 94–102.

Bournonville, D., & Brankin, S.-P. (2009). *Building an effective antitrust compliance program in Europe*. Washington, DC: European Briefings, Association of Corporate Counsel.

Competition Bureau Canada. (2015). Corporate compliance programs, Bulletin, Ottawa.

Desai, K. (2005). Antitrust compliance programmes. *The European Antitrust Review*, London, 15–20.

Economiesuisse. (2010). Fundamentals of Effective Compliance Management: Dossierpolitik, Number 7, Zurich.

Geradin, D. (2013). Antitrust compliance programmes and optimal antitrust enforcement: A reply to Wouter Wils. *Journal of Antitrust Enforcement, 1*, 325–346.

Gibson and Dunn. (2015). *2015 mid-year criminal antitrust and competition law update*. Available from www.gibsondunn.com/publications/Documents/2015-Mid-Year-Criminal-Antitrust-and-Competition-Law-Update.pdf. Accessed 28 March 2016.

Grüninger, S. (2005). Corporate governance & responsibility. Presentation, 2nd Constance Academy of Business Ethics, 21 September 2005, Constance.

Hüschelrath, K. (2010a). Competition law compliance programmes: Motivation, design and implementation. *Competition Law Journal, 9*, 481–506.

Hüschelrath, K. (2010b). How are cartels detected? The increasing use of proactive methods to establish antitrust infringements. *Journal of European Competition Law and Practice, 1*, 522–528.

Hüschelrath, K., & Laitenberger, U. (2015). *The settlement procedure in EC cartel cases: An empirical assessment*. ZEW Discussion Paper No. 15-064, Mannheim.

Hüschelrath, K., & Smuda, F. (2016). The appeals process in the European Commission's cartel cases: An empirical assessment. *Journal of Empirical Legal Studies, 13*(2), 330–357.

Hüschelrath, K., Leheyda, N., & Beschorner, P. (2011). The deterrent effect of antitrust sanctions: Evidence from Switzerland. *Antitrust Bulletin, 56*, 427–460.

Hüschelrath, K., Müller, K., & Veith, T. (2016). Estimating damages from price-fixing: The value of transaction data. *European Journal of Law and Economics, 41*(3), 509–535.

Jalabert-Doury, N., & Sproul, G. (2012). Enforcers' consideration of compliance programs in Europe: Are 2011 initiatives raising their profile or reducing it to the lowest common denominator. *CPI Antitrust Chronicle, 2*(1).

Jalabert-Doury, N., Harrison, D., & Schmidt, J. (2015). Enforcers' consideration of compliance programs in Europe: A long and winding — but increasingly interesting — road. *CPI Antitrust Chronicle, 6*(2).

Kolasky, W. (2002). Antitrust compliance programs: The government perspective. Address Before the Corporate Compliance 2002 Conference, 12 July 2002, San Francisco.

Lachnit, E. (2014). Compliance programmes in competition law: Improving the approach of competition authorities. *Utrecht Law Review, 10*, 31–50.

Miller, G. (2014). *An economic analysis of effective compliance programs*. NYU Law and Economics Research Paper, New York.

Murphy, J., & Kolasky, W. (2011). Role of anti-cartel compliance programs in preventing cartel behavior. *Antitrust, 26*, 61.

Neven, D. (2006). Competition economics and antitrust in Europe. *Economic Policy, 21*, 741–747.

OFT. (2007). *The deterrent effect of competition enforcement by the OFT*. OFT 962, London.

OFT. (2010). *Drivers of compliance and non-compliance with competition law*. OFT1227, Final Report, London.

OFT. (2011). *How your business can achieve compliance with competition law*. OFT1341, London.

Paha, J. (2014). *Lower sanctions, greater antitrust compliance? Cartel conduct with imperfect information about enforcement risk*. MAGKS Joint Discussion Paper Series in Economics, No. 60-2014, Marburg.

Paha, J., & Götz, G. (2015). Screening und das Compliance-Risikomodell: Konzepte zurunternehmensinternen Aufdeckung von Verstößen gegen das Kartellverbot. *WUW: Wirtschaft und wettbewerb=Concurrence et marché=Competition and Trade Regulation, 65* (12), 1198–1210.

Pezzoli, A. (2015). *Fines, discounts, compliance programs and competition culture*. Working Paper. Available from http://www.eui.eu/Projects/ENTRANCE/Documents/entrance2015/ComplianceWorkshop/AndreaPezzoliAgcm.pdf. Accessed 28 March 2016.

Richards, D., Yuan, H., & Bianconi, M. (2015). *Equity prices and cartel activity*. Working Paper, Tufts University, Medford.

Riley, A., & Sokol, D. D. (2015). Rethinking compliance. *Journal of Antitrust Enforcement, 3*(1), 31–57.

Rodger, B. (2005). Competition law compliance programmes: A study of motivations and practice. *World Competition, 28*, 349–376.

Sokol, D. (2012). Cartels, corporate compliance, and what practitioners really think about enforcement. *Antitrust Law Journal, 78*, 201–240.

Wils, W. (2013). Antitrust compliance programmes and optimal antitrust enforcement. *Journal of Antitrust Enforcement, 1*, 52–81.

Part II
Compliance in Business and Economics

Chapter 3
Results of a Survey in Germany, Austria, and Switzerland on How to Prevent Violations of Competition Laws

Georg Götz, Daniel Herold, and Johannes Paha

Abstract This report presents the results of a survey on competition law compliance in Germany, Austria, and Switzerland in which 86 large companies participated. The study shows that 80 % of the firms have implemented measures to identify and mitigate the risks of violating competition laws. The majority of firms and measures concentrate on legal risks (e.g. insufficient awareness of the content and scope of competition laws), whereas risks related to changes in the economic environment (e.g. entry into the market, competition by imports, and more intense competition) are rarely addressed. Risk mitigation heavily relies on competition law training, even though these measures hardly seem sufficient. This is obvious from the fact that 71 % of the firms whose employees had violated competition laws in the past had already trained these employees before the misconduct occurred. We conclude from our study that those measures should be improved that help to detect cartelisation risks at an early stage. Furthermore, sanctions imposed by the firms on the offenders of competition laws require a clearer design and more systematic communication.

3.1 Introduction

Non-compliance with competition laws is a substantial source of risk for the providers of equity, the managers, and more generally for the stakeholders not only of large but increasingly also of mid-sized firms. Since 1990, the European

---

G. Götz • D. Herold
Department of Economics, Justus Liebig University Giessen, VWL I - Industrial Organization, Regulation and Antitrust, Giessen, Germany
e-mail: georg.goetz@wirtschaft.uni-giessen.de; daniel.herold@wirtschaft.uni-giessen.de

J. Paha (✉)
Department of Economics and Business, Justus-Liebig-University, Licher Straße 62, 35394 Gießen, Germany
e-mail: johannes.paha@wirtschaft.uni-giessen.de

J. Paha (ed.), *Competition Law Compliance Programmes*,
DOI 10.1007/978-3-319-44633-2_3

commission has decided 122 cases where an infringement of Art. 101 TFEU was found. In these cases, 815 companies were involved and were sentenced to an overall fine of 25.9 billion Euros. The average fine imposed during the years 2012-2016 was 310 million Euros per case, with the highest fine (2.9 billion) being imposed on the producers of trucks in the year 2016 (European Commission 2016). Over the last few years, private claims for damages have also gained importance. There may be additional losses in the medium to long term since many of these cases go public and may cause a loss of customers or an increase in capital costs because of the greater volatility of returns. Moreover, the risk of detection has increased over the last 25 years due to the leniency policy implemented by the European commission in 1996 (See Miller 2009).

With these developments in mind, we conducted a survey among companies in Germany, Austria, and Switzerland in order to shed light on compliance measures implemented by these companies to prevent violations of competition laws (in particular, § 1 GWB in Germany, § 1 KartG in Austria, Art. 5 KG in Switzerland, and Article 101 TFEU in Europe).[1] Our questionnaire was mainly answered by executive employees in the legal or the compliance department or by members of the executive board of the participating companies. To ensure an adequate design of the study, we considered comments and suggestions made both by competition authorities and (future) participants when setting up the survey.

Early studies that address competition law compliance were conducted in the US in the 1980s (Beckenstein and Gabel 1982). They have gained additional attention only recently (Sokol 2012). While these surveys addressed competition lawyers, our survey reveals new insights into compliance programmes by using the assessments of executive employees within the legal or the compliance department or by members of the executive board. Additionally, our survey complements studies conducted by audit firms and universities during the last few years. For example, while addressing the same regions (i.e. Germany, Austria, and Switzerland) as a KPMG study on economic crimes (Van Heerden et al. 2013) we investigate more deeply the subject of *antitrust law* violations. Our study can also supplement the research conducted on compliance by the University of Applied Science in Konstanz (Grueninger et al. 2014). Whereas their study is concentrated on medium-sized firms, our survey analyses mainly large businesses. Many connections can also be drawn between our study and that of Bussmann et al. (2013). This study was commissioned by PricewaterhouseCoopers with the objective to examine anti-corruption and antitrust law compliance programmes.

We complement the study of Bussmann et al. (2013) by investigating the risk factors of anticompetitive conduct in greater detail. We asked the participants to comment on five groups of risks: (i) risk factors in the legal environment, (ii) changes of demand, (iii) risks in the competitive environment, (iv) changes of profits, and (v) adverse incentives of employees. Each of these risk groups consisted

[1]Gesetz gegen Wettbewerbsbeschränkungen (GWB, Act Against Restraints on Competition), Kartellgesetz (KartG in Austria or KG in Switzerland, Anti-Trust Law).

of up to eight questions as well as the opportunity to enter free text. Our survey shows that respondents are in general well-informed about the risk factors in the legal environment. A large portion (i.e. 85 %) of the companies participating in our survey stated that their employees might be poorly informed about competition laws and the consequences of violating them. In particular, 79 % fear that their employees underestimate the risk of detection (see also Murphy and Kolasky 2012). Therefore, more than 90 % attempt to prevent competition law infringements by offering competition law compliance training and providing additional information on these issues. At the same time companies seem less familiar with the risk factors in the economic environment. Only about one third of the firms consider economic risk factors such as demand shocks or an increasing intensity of competition as relevant. This opinion stands in contrast with both the knowledge generated by economic theory and the experience gained from case evidence. We discuss the responses in the light of that knowledge and show how competition economists might be prolific advisers when it comes to structuring, implementing, and evaluating competition law compliance programmes.

Our survey is based on the compliance guidance of the British Competition and Markets Authority (CMA) who recommends a set of five different competition law antitrust measures (OFT 2010): First, companies shall identify the risk factors of competition law violations; second, they shall assess the intensity of those risks; third, the firms shall mitigate the identified risks; fourth, they shall review their compliance programme regularly to ensure the effectiveness of the first three steps; fifth, the companies shall establish an appropriate *Tone at the Top*, i.e., the top-level management shall set an example for other employees by adhering to the laws and communicating this conduct. Our study focuses mainly on the first three of the above-mentioned measures of compliance (i.e. risk identification, assessment, and mitigation).

The remainder of this chapter is organised as follows. Section 3.2 discusses the data. Section 3.3 is concerned with risk identification and assessment. Risk mitigation is analysed in Sect. 3.4. Section 3.5 discusses the results of our survey and points out avenues for future work on antitrust law compliance programmes.

3.2 Data

This section presents the data collected by our online-survey between November 2013 and May 2014. When answering the questionnaire, the participants had the opportunity to withhold their answer (not specified, *ns*) or to quit the survey early (*qs*). To make sure that percentage shares are comparable throughout the chapter, we exclude these responses (i.e. *ns* and *qs*) from the calculation of the shares.

The dataset contains responses of 86 companies (Germany: 75, Switzerland: 4, Austria: 7) who mainly operate in manufacturing (20 %), services industries (14 %), chemistry (12 %), transport and logistics (9 %), banking and insurance (8 %), or pharmaceuticals (6 %). The majority of the participating companies

(89 %) are large according to § 267 of the German Commercial Code (Handelsgesetzbuch, HGB), i.e., at least two of the following criteria are met: Total assets at least 19.25 million EUR, total revenue at least 38.5 million EUR, number of employees at least 250. Most of the German (51 %), Austrian (60 %), and Swiss (67 %) firms do business globally. They were mainly active in industries where cartels had occurred in the past (62 %). Almost half of them (45 %) had participated in at least one cartel themselves.

50 participants provided information on their work experience and educational background. 44 % of the participants characterised themselves as an "employee of a company who works on issues related to competition law compliance (except for: legal counsel within the firm)". 28 % were employed in the legal department of the company and work on issues related to competition laws. In general, the respondents belonged to one of three groups: (i) (chief) executive or division manager, (ii) compliance officer, (iii) general counsel. The majority of the participants (56 %) who provided information on their experience worked on issues of antitrust law or antitrust law compliance for more than 3 years and were also employed at the current company for more than 3 years (61 %). Most respondents hold a degree in law (69 %) or business/economics (41 %). The numbers indicate that some hold a degree in both disciplines. Only a minority was trained in, for example, natural sciences (3 %) or engineering (5 %). Asked about their personal experience with violations of competition laws, 57 % said they had none. 27 % stated that their company had violated competition laws and they were involved in defending the company. Only 1 participant answered that his/her company was harmed by a violation of competition laws and that he/she was involved in claiming damages.

The dataset predominantly samples firms that either had previously violated competition laws or had been members of compliance associations. 45 % of the companies in our sample had been found guilty of violating competition laws and 83 % had implemented a Compliance Management System (CMS). Sampling mainly compliance frontrunners and firms being exposed to an above-average risk of anti-competitive conduct is a desirable feature of the dataset. If we find room for improvements within the antitrust law compliance programmes of these firms one may conclude that there is even more room for improvements for average firms.

Before we go into the details of antitrust law compliance we give an overview of the general evolution of the compliance activities of the firms in our sample and the determinants of this development. 71 of the participating companies stated that they had implemented a Compliance Management System. Within this group, 56 firms also provided the year of implementation. This data shows that there has been a steady and considerable increase in the number of CMS since 2005 (Fig. 3.1).

The reasons for implementing a CMS in their company can be summarised into five groups. These are the reputation of the company, legal requirements, the strategy of the parent company, risk avoidance, and a recent trend to install a CMS.

First, the firms believe that CMS enhance their reputation towards a variety of stakeholders such as investors, employees, customers, and politics. They would like to satisfy requirements or recommendations of the stakeholders

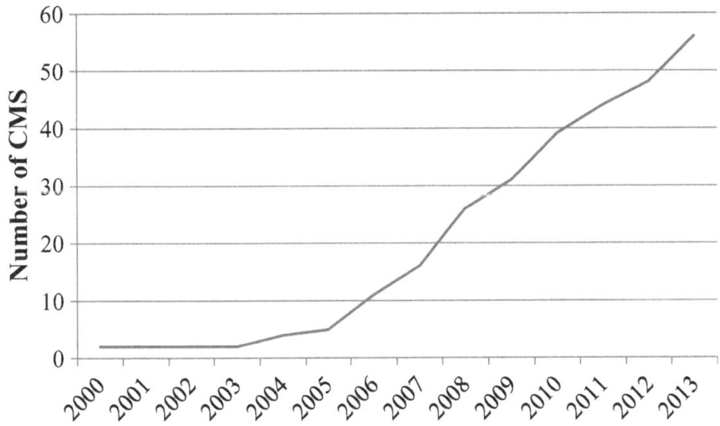

Fig. 3.1 Implementation of a CMS

(e.g. recommendation of the initiative Corporate Governance of the German housing industry). Concerning the customers of a firm, the reasons for implementing a CMS can be split into two groups. The first one is to construct a unique selling point, and the second is to meet the requirements of important customers. Thereby, a compliance programme was occasionally considered as a way to gain a competitive advantage that can enhance the value of a company.

Second, a necessity to implement a CMS can also be inferred from a variety of laws and regulations. Among them are corporate governance codices, requirements that must be met to be traded at certain stock markets, competition laws, anti-corruption and anti-bribery laws, accounting and governance laws (e.g. Sarbanes Oxley Act, German stock corporation act), or sector specific laws such as Solvency II or the German Minimum Requirements for Risk Management (MaRisk 2012).

Third, antitrust law compliance is frequently conducted as part of a broader compliance programme (e.g. Code of Conduct, anti-corruption). Within these compliance programmes, the development of a homogenous set of compliance measures is often desirable. Subsequently, many subsidiaries implement CMS in accordance with the strategy of their parent company.

Fourth, compliance programmes may also serve as a form of insurance that shall limit the liability of the members of the executive board in case their employees violate antitrust laws. Our survey suggests that avoidance of liability risks is another driver for implementing a CMS. For instance, the participants of our study perceived a "necessity of compliance" being caused by legal provisions. Other responses referred to the goal of securing the company's existence and the minimisation of liability risks.

Fifth, there is also a trend to implement a CMS which may be driven by recommendations of audit firms. The audit standard 980 of the Institute of Public Auditors in Germany (Institut der Wirtschaftsprüfer in Deutschland, IDW) may be attributed some importance. Moreover, the importance of compliance measures is generally considered rising.

3.3 Risk Identification

Risk identification measures are used by 56 out of the 86 companies that participated in our survey. 49 of these 56 companies specifically engage in the identification of antitrust risks. The following analysis concentrates on these 49 companies.[2] The participants of our survey were confronted with scenarios that might cause collusive conduct. These scenarios can be grouped into five categories: (i) Risk factors in the legal environment, (ii) changes in demand, (iii) risk factors in the competitive environment, (iv) changes in profits, and (v) objectives of the employees as a risk factor. The companies were asked: "Is this scenario considered a risk factor for cartel conduct in your company?" They could answer *yes*, *no*, refuse to answer (not specified, *ns*), or quit the survey (*qs*).[3] 27 of the 49 respondents said that their companies had participated in a cartel in the past. They were also asked: "Does this scenario apply to the cartel conduct that was observed in your firm in the past?"

3.3.1 Risk Factors in the Legal Environment

A majority of the participants believes that the employees of their company possess incomplete information about antitrust laws (85 %) and about the consequences of violating antitrust laws (82 %). These assessments seem to overestimate the true importance of these factors, as can be inferred from the answers given by the respondents whose firms had participated in cartels in the past.[4] Incomplete information about antitrust laws was only considered a trigger for past misconduct by 50 % of the respondents. 57 % attributed a role to incomplete information about the consequences of antitrust law violations. We interpret this discrepancy between the perceived and the actual relevance of risk factors as an overestimation, or, in the contrary case, as an underestimation of the risk of cartelisation.

This apparent misperception of the true risk factors for collusive conduct may be seen particularly well when considering that 80 % of the participants treat changes in competition laws, which make formerly legal actions illegal, as an important

[2]Note that five of them had quit the survey before answering the detailed questions on risk identification. Another 12 firms quit during the process of answering these questions.

[3]As before, we calculate the percentage shares of the answers *yes* and *no* while excluding *ns* and *qs*. This ensures the comparability of percentages even when the firms quit the survey. To provide an example, consider two situations A and B:

A: $yes = 40 \quad no = 40 \quad qs = 6$

B: $yes = 30 \quad no = 30 \quad qs = 26$

Our calculation ensures that *yes* and *no* are assigned a percentage share of 50 % in both cases.

[4]Paha (2014) provides a theoretical foundation of the decision behaviour in situations where agents possess imperfect information about competition law enforcement.

factor for past competition law offences. However, only 17 % hold changes in competition laws responsible for collusive conduct in the past.

The answers of the respondents are in line when it comes to the detection probability. 79 % believe that the employees of their firm underestimate the probability that cartel conduct is discovered and sanctioned. In comparison, 70 % of the participating companies deemed this factor important for antitrust law violations in the past. In the literature, the behaviour that underlies the concept of this risk factor is called hubris (Murphy and Kolasky 2012, p. 63). Hubris leads to the opinion that one's own misconduct will not be detected although others have already been punished for the same behaviour.

3.3.2 Changes in Demand as a Risk Factor

The participants were also confronted with a scenario where a change in demand for the products or services offered (such as a decrease in demand) affects the company or one of its business units. The respondents should indicate whether they consider (i) a sudden and persistent, (ii) a sudden and transitory, or (iii) a continuous (following a trend, non-transitory) demand shock a risk factor for cartel conduct.

Only some respondents considered a sudden and persistent (40 %), a sudden and transitory (30 %), or a continuous (38 %) demand shock a risk factor for cartel conduct. Hence, they attribute a lower importance to these factors than to the risk factors in the legal environment that were discussed above. More importantly, almost none of the participants considered a change in demand a relevant factor for violations of antitrust laws that had occurred in their companies in the past. This finding stands in stark contrast to the role that both the economic literature and case evidence attribute to these factors. Therefore, we argue that the effectiveness of compliance programmes can be improved by screening for risk factors in the economic environment of the firms.

The importance of demand trends on the emergence of cartels can be better understood when examining some European cartel cases (Herold and Paha 2016). For example, the French beef cartel had its roots in the repercussions of the BSE crisis (COMP/C.38.279/F3). In the year 2000, when an increasing appearance of bovine spongiform encephalopathy was observable, customers reacted by buying less beef, and thereby provoked economic troubles to beef producers. To handle this issue, beef producers came up with cartel-agreements. Another exemplary case of an infringement of competition laws caused by a change in demand can be seen in the price-fixing case of the fine art auction houses Christie's and Sotheby's (COMP/E-2/37.784). Both companies had been operating since the eighteenth century and ran into serious economic problems in the beginning of the 1990s when a recession hit the art market. As a consequence, they decided to utilise collusive pricing schemes that were evidently employed between the years 1993 and 2000.

Both cases suggest that the cause of collusive conduct can be found in a non-persistent change in demand. However, there are also well-known events where a persistent decrease in demand is followed by a violation of competition laws, as can be seen in the cartels of, e.g., carbonless paper (COMP/E-1/36.212), professional videotapes (COMP/38.432), thread (COMP/38.337), or TV and monitor tubes producers (COMP/39.437).

Even an increase in demand for a product can promote collusive conduct. This could be observed in the cartels among the producers of rubber chemicals (COMP/F/38.443), copper plumbing tubes (COMP/E-1/38.069), and flat glass (COMP/39.165). The latter conspiracy was preceded by a new regulation regarding energy efficiency, and a subsequent increase in demand for specific glass like E-glass or safety glass in the years 2005 and 2006. However, this increase in demand was accompanied by a steady decrease in prices. This highlights the fact that the interaction of opposing effects can lead to economic troubles, too. Either way, all of the above-mentioned cases make clear that changes in demand play a role in the emergence of collusive conduct.

The same conclusion may be drawn from the theoretic literature. For example, Rotemberg and Saloner (1986) analyse the impact of random demand shocks on the incentive to deviate from a cartel agreement. The authors find that cartel stability is higher during a recession. This is because there is little to gain from a deviation while demand is low. In such a situation, setting a lower than the agreed-upon price would not attract many new buyers. In their model, collusion is harder to sustain when demand is high which makes a deviation quite profitable for the firms. More generally, the economic literature of the last 25 years shows that cartel stability depends on the nature of the demand change (e.g. expected economic trend or unexpected demand shock), and, additionally, on the availability of production capacities. There may be complex interactions between these variables with the result that one cannot state a simple relationship between a change in demand and cartel stability. Rather, the impact of a change in demand on cartel formation has to be evaluated on a case-by-case basis.

To summarise, an investigation of changes in the economic environment is a valuable avenue for further improving the effectiveness of compliance programmes. One should screen for conspicuous changes in demand and possibly intervene with precautionary measures such as increased training and the communication of sanctions. This may be an important step to prevent cartels before their formation is actually attempted.

3.3.3 Risk Factors in the Competitive Environment

Our data suggests that a change in the competitive environment is being underestimated as a risk factor, too. A change in the competitive environment (e.g. increased competition by imports and changes in the costs of production) can facilitate collusive conduct as is known from case evidence and economic theory. However, the majority of the participants of our survey assume that these risk factors had no relevance for violations of antitrust laws in the past. These responses are quite surprising and they suggest a need for further communication between competition economists and compliance officers.

Only 42 % consider entry of new competitor(s) in the market a risk factor for cartel conduct. And none of the participants thinks that this scenario applies to the cartel conduct that was observed in their firm in the past. A similar pattern emerges when inquiring about increased competition from imports (considered a risk factor by 23 %/considered important for anti-competitive conduct in the past by 6 %), a perceptible increase in the firm's own production costs (27 %/11 %), competitors introducing new variants of their products (25 %/0 %), or a perceptible decrease in competitors' production costs (38 %/11 %).

In contrast to these answers, case evidence shows that entry into a market or intensified competition from imports may have caused cartels in the past. Both factors lead to a higher degree of competition in the market and therefore increase economic pressure on firms. An example of a cartel that has its roots in increased competition by imports is the sorbates cartel (COMP/E-1/37.370). The first connections between the cartel firms from Europe and Japan date back to the years between 1974 and 1975. The Japanese companies are said to have operated very aggressively in the European market during this time period to raise their exports. The description of events provided by the European Commission suggests that the Japanese producers of sorbates tried to increase their sales in the European market by lowering prices significantly. Hence, the European producers of sorbates were subject to more intense competition from imports.[5]

A further example for the impact of the competitive environment on the emergence of collusive conduct is the sodium gluconate cartel (COMP/E-1/36.756). The European Commission describes that in this case the first collusive arrangements were made in 1981. In this year prices for sodium gluconate were very low due to "tough competition between three European producers" (ibid. paras. 116, 119). It is also remarkable that prices fell around 50 % when the cartel fell apart in 1984. In the light of this price decrease the producers met once more to arrange a new cartel agreement (ibid. paras. 126, 127).

3.3.4 Changes in Profit as a Risk Factor

Only a relatively small share (24 %) of the participants considers a transitory reduction of profits a risk factor for future violations of competition laws in their own company. None of them thinks that a transitory reduction of profits caused the cartel conduct that was observed in their firm in the past. A greater volatility of profits is considered a risk factor for future violations by 24 % while being given no

[5]Similar developments can be seen among others in the following law proceedings: Zinc phosphate (COMP/E-1/37.027), monochloroacetic acid (COMP/E-1/C.37.773), fittings (COMP/F-1/38.121) organic peroxide (COMP/E-2/37.857).

credit for past violations. Only 11 % fear that an increase in profits may cause explicit collusion in the future and do not report any cases where it would have caused a cartel in the past. The respondents also attribute a greater role to realised (as opposed to expected) changes of profits. Only 33 % think that a future, expected change of profits may be a cause for cartel conduct, while 6 % attribute a role to such expected movements for the formation of cartels that were observed in the past. The respondents are more sceptical about adverse and fairly permanent profit shocks. 50 % of the respondents think that a permanent reduction of profits or a reduction of profits that threatens the existence of the company or one of its business units may be a cause of cartel formation. When it comes to cartels in the past, 13 % attribute a role to a permanent and 6 % to an existence-threatening reduction of profits.

Case evidence appears to contradict at least some of these assessments. For instance, the relevance of a change in profit on the emergence of cartels can be seen in the plasterboard cartel (COMP/E-1/37.152). A company that had participated in this cartel stated that all its participants had agreed on the subject that the ruinous price war had to stop, and the members should attempt to establish economically sustainable competition (ibid. para. 55). The company also mentioned that the firms incurred losses due to a price decrease of around 50–75 % between the years 1988 and 1992 (ibid. para. 71). Hence, in view of the establishment of the plasterboard cartel in the year 1992, we see a link between the development of profits and the emergence of collusive conduct.

Expectations about future developments of profits were relevant for infringements of antitrust laws, too. This was the case in the chloroprene rubber cartel (COMP/38.625). Six producers of chloroprene rubber started to engage in collusive activity due to a decrease in demand, excess capacity, and intensified competition from imports. In this case, the European Commission concluded that an expected decrease in prices had been the cause for the emergence of the cartel even though it was not fully able to reconstruct the chronology of the events preceding the infringement.

Note that changes in profits or more intense competition are consequences of fundamental changes in a market. These changes may be caused, for example, by the entry of competitors or increased imports that themselves may be triggered by other events such as technological change. Therefore, observing more intense competition is rather a further symptom of the causes that may also lead to cartel formation than being a cause itself. Both in view of preventive interventions that follow a compliance programme as well as from an economic standpoint, it would be important to learn the reasons responsible for the intensification of competition. Still, observing increased competition and a fall in profits can be used by compliance officers as a first indicator for impending violations of antitrust laws.

3.3.5 *Objectives of the Employees as a Risk Factor*

Our study also investigates risk factors that result from specific objectives of the employees. 36 % of the respondents think that employees of their firms might initiate cartel conduct to secure their jobs. 6 % report that this objective played a role for the formation of cartels, in which their firm participated. Employees' objective of promoting their career is considered a risk factor of cartel conduct by 36 % of the respondents and was also observed in former cartels by 24 % of the respondents. The objectives of employees being interested in raising their income (29 %), reducing the volatility of their income (21 %), preventing a reduction of income (36 %), reducing their workload (15 %) are considered somewhat important as risk factors but—according to the responses—hardly played a role in past cartel cases. The same is true for employees being attracted to illegal conduct (allure of the forbidden), which is considered a risk factor by 30 % while being given no credit for cartels in the past.

However, a majority (75 %) of the participants regard ambitious targets in working contracts and bonus schemes as risk factors. This is in line with the literature in economics since collusive agreements facilitate the attainment of, e.g., profit and sales targets (Murphy 1999, 2001). In some (extreme) cases, these targets can only be met by engaging in collusive conduct. 20 % of the respondents report that ambitious targets were a cause of cartels that their company had joined in the past.

In this context, the question arises who is generally involved in violations of antitrust laws. Empirical studies and case evidence suggest that violations of antitrust laws have been initiated by employees both lower or higher in a firm's hierarchy. Harrington (2006) attributes the responsibility for collusive conduct to the top-level management, as was the case in the cartels for vitamins, plasterboards, special graphite (COMP/E-2/37.667) and French beer (COMP/C.37750/B2). However, it were the sales directors who were present in the first meetings of the graphite electrodes cartel. Likewise, Ashton and Pressey (2012) emphasise the role of members of the lower-level management for violations of antitrust laws. The OFT (2010, pp. 38–40) recognises the participation of lower-level managers and emphasises that the initiator of collusive conducts needs not be at a specifically high level within a firm's hierarchy.

3.4 Risk Mitigation

This section presents the compliance measures that the participating companies use to mitigate the risk of antitrust law violations. 51 of the firms participating in our survey engage in such measures while 29 of them had been found guilty of violating the competition laws in the past. The following analysis refers to these 51, respectively 29 companies. The participants were asked to express their opinion regarding different measures of risk mitigation. In particular, we were interested in (i) the design and the content of training sessions, (ii) requirements to provide certain information to the compliance or legal department, (iii) measures to restrict disadvantageous discretion in the decision-making power of employees, and (iv) measures to detect and sanction anticompetitive conduct. The participants were presented several measures of risk mitigation, and they were asked: "Is this measure used within your company to mitigate the risks of collusive conduct?" Participants whose firms had been convicted of collusive conduct in the past were also asked: "Was this measure already used the last time when cartel conduct was observed in your firm?"

3.4.1 Training

Providing employees with information about the content and scope of competition laws is an important element of risk mitigation. 97 % of the firms who responded to our questions and actively mitigate antitrust risks provide their employees with information about behaviour that would violate antitrust laws. The information material provided by the companies consists of, e.g. credit-card sized information cards that are supposed to inform about competitive issues and are meant to be carried by all employees. 93 % of the respondents provide antitrust compliance training to inform their employees what conduct violates antitrust laws. They actively inform their employees about the potential monetary (e.g. fines, damages, or litigations costs; 97 %) or non-monetary (e.g. media coverage, loss of reputation; 90 %) losses that accrue to the company. They also inform the employees about the consequences of violations of antitrust laws for the employees themselves (89 %). 100 % of the respondents had issued guidelines concerning ethically and legally relevant behaviour. However, only 69 % informed their employees about the socially detrimental and ethical consequences of collusive conduct.

One observes an upward trend of such measures. At the time of their last infringement of antitrust laws, only about half of the firms conducted such measures. Information about anticompetitive conduct was provided by 53 % of the respondents. 71 % trained their employees in antitrust laws. 50 % informed their employees about the monetary and 53 % about the monetary consequences for the firm. Information about the consequences for the employees themselves was provided by 53 % of the respondents, while 61 % had issued guidelines.

Providing relevant information to employees is important because the literature suggests substantial information deficits. Murphy and Kolasky (2012, p. 63) emphasise the arrogance and hubris of at least some employees who participate in collusive activities. The authors argue that the employees envision themselves as too smart to be detected by the competition authorities. Another body of literature focuses on decisions of poorly informed employees who cannot fully assess the impact of their own behaviour (see e.g. Kaplow 1995).

Information about the consequences of anti-competitive conduct may have a deterrence effect. The literature emphasises the deterrent effect of monetary consequences (Becker 1968). In general, the same is true for non-monetary consequences (e.g. damage to reputation) especially if these are followed by lower cash flows to the firm. Cash outflows from the firm caused by either a damage of a firm's reputation or fines imposed by competition authorities lower the value of an enterprise. However, to the best of our knowledge, empirical investigations about the impact of non-monetary consequences have not been conducted, yet. This topic is discussed in greater detail in Sect. 3.5.

3.4.2 Guidelines: Communication

Beckenstein and Gabel (1986) argue that violations of competition laws can be reduced by a centralisation of the decision-making power within a company. Their line of argument assumes that collusive conduct is rather initiated by employees of the low-level management than by members of the top-level management. To what extent this assumption is justified, is vividly discussed in the literature. However, if one maintains the assumption that employees of the mid- or low-level management initiate collusive activities, violations of competition laws can possibly be diminished or even suppressed by the attempt to centralise decision-making power and/or by the implementation of well-structured behavioural guidelines.

We find a corresponding trend in the responses of the companies participating in our survey. 57 % of the participating companies that use measures to mitigate the risk of violating competition laws require their employees to ask for permission before becoming a member of an industry association. 82 % of these companies have guidelines that put restrictions on the behaviour of their employees before, during and after industry association meetings. 75 % have or aim at a culture of compliance where colleagues and superiors disapprove of conduct that violates antitrust laws.

Behavioural guidelines with respect to meetings of industry associations include the following elements.

- Before the meeting: Obligation to submit the agenda or to contact the legal or compliance department when suspicious topics are on the agenda; legal or compliance department must approve a conference participation; special briefings prior to the meeting
- During a meeting: Chairman of the meeting emphasises the importance of adhering to competition laws; if anti-competitive topics come up employees shall initiate a break, point out the possible violation of competition laws, and leave the meeting
- After the meeting: Submission of the minutes of the meeting to the legal or compliance department; debriefing

The creation of an environment where colleagues and superiors disapprove of violations of antitrust laws is related to the so called *core of compliance* (OFT 2010). Such an environment can be established by means of bilateral communication, i.e., during staff interviews, regular group meetings etc. It can also be established by means of unilateral communication, i.e., issuing zero tolerance policies, requests to report activities that violate antitrust laws. The information flows can be bottom-up (e.g. structured and regular reports about internal checks to the top-level management) or top-down (i.e. top-level management communication). In this context, the practice-oriented literature often refers to the so-called *tone at the top*. Herold (2015) provides a scientific analysis of this concept.

The top-level management must convince other employees of the advantages of law-abiding behaviour. It must make clear that a code of conduct was not only passed because of legal requirements but instead that the adherence to these rules is in the company's very interest. The impact of this signalling function of the *tone at the top* can be analysed by using signalling theory (see Conelly et al. 2011 for an overview and Spence 1973 as a seminal contribution).

Signals have to be observable by the employees. A signal is only credible if it is associated with (opportunity) costs. Therefore, the signal of the top-level management to the employees has to be expensive, or at least it has to be perceived as expensive (or: burdensome). Law-abiding behaviour cannot be established for free if the incentives for violating the law are high. Such an expensive and observable signal can, for example, be sent by obtaining a CMS-certificate that is issued by an audit firm. Note that these signalling costs are not necessarily incurred in monetary terms. The attention paid to the signals by the top-level management causes indirect costs, too. For instance, the discussion of compliance issues at stockholders' meetings creates costs in the form of allocating the available time to these issues rather than talking about, for example, the newest investment projects. Alternatively, an interview of a member of the executive board with a nationwide newspaper regarding a compliance programme may create costs, too. This is because, for example, giving that interview might require the highly productive executive to assign the chairmanship of a strategy meeting to her less productive deputy. In view of the above considerations, efforts to establish the right *tone at the top* can be understood as measures that represent credible signals of the top-level management to the employees to encourage law-abiding behaviour.

3.4.3 Guidelines: Discretion in Decision-Making

The firms participating in our survey had also implemented behavioural guidelines that apply in situations where an employee is afraid his/her decision might constitute a breach of antitrust laws. 82 % of the firms stated that—in this situation—their employees are required to consult in-house or external counsel to obtain information about the legal consequences of their decisions. In the subset of past cartel offenders, only 50 % had such a requirement in place at the time of the last offence.

64 % of the participating firms give their legal department a veto right to stop potentially collusive conduct. 47 % of the former cartel firms did so in the past.

One company stated that the legal department is required to contact the executive board in these cases. This is in line with many firms' objective to spread the decision-making power in questions with importance to competition law issues (four-eye-principle). Such issues are decided by more than one person, often at councils, that also have to disclose the legal relevance of the decision. 48 % of the respondents (as opposed to 31 % in the past) ask their employees to document the decision-making process in writing when a decision might constitute a breach of antitrust laws.

Respondents also mentioned the introduction of centrally determined, binding pricing schemes as a measure meant to prevent cartel conduct by lower-level employees. However, there is ambiguity concerning the question whether such pricing schemes indeed prevent violations of competition laws. For instance, the legal proceedings against the art auctioneers, the producers of medical gases and lysine have shown that overzealous sales staff has tried to subvert the pricing schemes set by the top-level management, which undermined the stability of collusion (Harrington 2006). Therefore, binding pricing schemes might have an adverse impact on the effectiveness of compliance programmes.

3.4.4 Detection and Sanctions

As one element of antitrust law compliance programmes, firms search for and sanction anti-competitive conduct. These measures serve as a deterrent and prevent violations. 88 % of the responding firms sanction infringements of competition laws. Such measures are on the rise because at the time of their last infringement of competition laws only 44 % of the former cartel offenders had already imposed such sanctions. The companies listed four kinds of sanctions:

- Preventive sanctions: The firms warn their employees that sanctions (e.g. dismissal) will be imposed if the code of conduct is violated. This warning is announced in writing and during training sessions.
- Sanctions while maintaining the employment contract: For example, a paid leave from work, a disciplinary warning letter, or the requirement to attend additional training.
- Sanctions while terminating the employment contract (i.e. dismissals)
- Other sanctions: For example, claiming damages from the employee. Some firms named "labour law-related consequences", "disciplinary actions", or a "zero tolerance policy", but did not specify these terms.

The responses show that the implemented sanction mechanisms are fairly diverse and partly unsystematic. This may impede deterrence because at the time of the violation the employees cannot predict the consequences of their behaviour. Hence, the deterrent effect of the sanctions is undermined if the employees underestimate the intensity of the sanctions. Hence, we recommend further harmonisation and specification of the sanctions imposed on violations of competition laws.

Related to sanctions, 42 % of the firms in our dataset rely on internal leniency programmes. Hence, a firm offers its employees who were involved in collusive conduct a reduction of sanctions if they report the infringement to the compliance or legal department. In doing so, the company incentivises employees who broke the law to reveal collusive activities within the firm. Internal leniency programmes may *de facto* be even more prevalent than is indicated by the figure of 42 % because many firms stated that they offer their employees reduced sanction for confessing collusive conduct. Some also offer them legal assistance or reimburse them for the costs of legal defence. However, these measures are applied somewhat unsystematically. They are neither guaranteed nor communicated sufficiently. This poor design is likely to limit the effectiveness of internal leniency programmes. The firms should set up clear leniency policies, communicate them effectively, and apply them consistently. It is important to note that a reduction of sanctions lowers their deterrent effect as collusive conduct becomes more profitable in expectation. Therefore, firms need to balance the detection and the deterrence effects of fine reductions. This is why Aubert et al. (2006, p. 1248) argue that leniency policies are only successful if the otherwise imposed sanctions are sufficiently high and the cartel agreement is utterly fragile.

Besides relying on internal leniency programmes to detect collusive conduct, 73 % of the participating firms actively screen for collusive conduct as part of internal auditing procedures. Such screening measures have, for example, been discussed by Paha and Götz (2015). The responses of the survey participants suggest that screening measures can be distinguished across four dimensions: (i) Independence, i.e., antitrust audits can be integrated in a broader audit programme or being conducted independently. (ii) Occasion, i.e., periodic screenings can be distinguished from screenings conducted randomly or ones based on concrete suspicions. (iii) Predictability, i.e., audits may be expected or unexpected for the audited persons and divisions. (iv) Content, i.e., some companies audit contracts with customers and suppliers, they analyse the minutes being kept during meetings, or they discuss those matters with the employees in the audited divisions. Although 73 % of the companies in our survey state that they screen for anti-competitive conduct, their other responses indicate that these screening measures could be applied more systematically. They could also be targeted more specifically at violations of antitrust laws. One company stated that it detects infringements of antitrust laws only at random as a result of other audits. We suspect that the same is true for more firms.

Complementing leniency and screening, 88 % of the respondents have installed an anonymous whistleblowing hotline (or the like). This measure enables employee B, who has witnessed a violation of the antitrust law of employee A, to notify the conduct to the firm anonymously.

3.5 Discussion

This concluding section discusses how the 'typical' antitrust law compliance programme emerging from our survey might be enhanced. It also gives some indication for promising avenues of future research in particular concerning reputation effects associated with compliance activities.

3.5.1 *Addressees*

Our survey indicates that compliance measures are often targeted at low-level or middle managers. However, the literature (e.g. Ashton and Pressey 2012; Buccirossi and Spagnola 2008; Harrington 2006) indicates that in the past collusive conduct was initiated at all hierarchical levels. Therefore, it is important that compliance measures are targeted at all levels within the hierarchy of a company, i.e., it may appear relevant to also address top-level management more systematically.

In this context, Beckenstein and Gabel (1982) showed on basis of their survey among competition lawyers that in USA the number of infringements that were caused by poorly informed employees dropped between the 1950s and 1970s. The participants of our survey believe that violations due to uninformed employees still occur in Germany, Austria and Switzerland. We expect that the increase in antitrust law compliance efforts (especially effective training) will decrease the number of unintended infringements in these countries as well.

A decrease in the number of infringements that were caused by poorly informed employees implies that compliance programmes should increasingly be targeted at reducing the profitability of planned antitrust law violations. Those compliance measures will become more important that are intended to prevent planned violations of antitrust laws. This includes, for example, screening, whistle-blower systems, internal leniency, and sanctions. Our study suggests that these measures should be designed more systematically than today and that they should be communicated more clearly.

3.5.2 *Screening and Risk Identification*

Our survey indicates that the participants put a lower weight on the identification and mitigation of risks in the economic/business environment of a firm (e.g. changes in demand or profit) than on risk factors in the legal environment (e.g. employees' ignorance of the competition law). Currently, many compliance programmes focus on training employees about the contents of antitrust laws. We deem it helpful to generally think more closely about the relevance of different risk factors. To achieve this goal, it will certainly be helpful if compliance officers obtain further information on competition economics and case evidence. Getting additional advice from competition economists should be helpful in this context.

We suggest that the firms should also strengthen their screening efforts carried out by, e.g., the internal audit department or external forensic services. In this context, it appears important to target screening not only on the detection of misconduct but start much earlier and emphasise the early identification of business risks that facilitate anti-competitive conduct. Then, preventive measures can be carried out even before misconduct occurs. Note that the costs of these measures should be weighed against their benefits. Since both the costs and benefits are firm-specific, the implementation of screening measures has to be conducted accordingly, i.e., firm-specific solutions should be preferred to general solutions. Paha and Götz (2015, p. 1208) suggest that cheaper methods (i.e., the identification of business risks) should be implemented before starting with more expensive methods such as detailed audits or e-discovery. If investment costs of some method are relatively low the firms should carry out the screening in-house. Methods that are more costly to implement should be acquired from external service providers such as auditing firms.

3.5.3 Reputation Effects

The companies in our survey stated that they implemented a CMS to improve their reputation. They referred to a "unique selling point" and other "competitive advantages". In this context, the implementation of an (antitrust law) compliance programme can be seen as an observable signal to stakeholders. Such signals are important in an environment where the stakeholders are imperfectly informed about the characteristics of the firm. In the following, we describe some ideas how compliance programmes may indeed enhance the reputation of a firms. These ideas are meant to serve as a starting point for future research. We hypothesise that compliance efforts may be relevant as a signalling device when a firm does business mainly with middle-sized customers while signalling would be less relevant with regard to small or large customers.

Large customers may not care about abstract signals sent by their suppliers such as the existence of a code of conduct. Due do their size and market power, large customers can require their suppliers to implement specific compliance measures. For instance, the railway operator Deutsche Bahn requires its business partners to obey a code of conduct. Deutsche Bahn also offers training sessions about competition law issues for its suppliers (Deutsche Bahn 2015). Therefore, some unspecific compliance reputation seems to be secondary when dealing with large customers.

We argue that a compliance reputation is not a sales-related criterion for small customers (e.g. private customers), either. It appears unrealistic to assume that, at the point of sale, buyers would check the websites of the producers for the existence of a compliance programme and act accordingly. Our argument should especially hold true when the products account for only a minor share of a household's spending such as sausages, bananas, candy, coffee, shrimps and detergents that have all been cartelised in the past.

The reputation effect is presumably highest if a firm supplies its goods to middle-sized customers such as commercial buyers. Because of their purchasing volume these customers would suffer significant losses when being overcharged. Therefore, it is relevant for these buyers to actively search for firms with a high compliance reputation. However, middle-sized (unlike large) customers are too small to offer training sessions to suppliers or to demand their consent to a code of conduct. Likewise, they are not able to screen the compliance programmes of their suppliers.

A compliance programme may also unfold a reputation effect on the labour market. If job applicants study the attributes of potential employers thoroughly they may also check whether a company has implemented a compliance programme or not. Presumably, this is of special relevance for job applicants who identify with law-abiding behaviour. They do not want to be faced with decisions that involve illegal actions. Moreover, the reputation of an employer could in part be transferred to an employee. For example, working for an employer who was found guilty of violating antitrust laws may have a negative impact on the career prospects of its employees. Such an effect could be anticipated by potential job applicants. This may cause a selection effect where highly qualified job applicants are drawn to companies that have implemented a compliance programme. The literature on corruption suggests the existence of such effects at least with regard to supervisory boards (see Marcel and Cowen 2014). Further research might address employees who work at other levels of the managerial hierarchy. One should also investigate whether these effects can be found for infringements of competition laws, too.

Acknowledgments We are thankful to a number of people and organizations, private and governmental. The questionnaire was designed with the help of members of the German monopolies commission and the competition authorities in Germany and Switzerland. Equally important were the additional comments made by the members of the German Netzwerk Compliance. Our online survey was distributed to the members of, e.g., Netzwerk Compliance, Deutsches Institut für Compliance DICO, Compliance Praxis AT, Compliance—Die Zeitschrift für Compliance-Verantwortliche. Without the assistance of these organisations we could not have conducted this research project. The same is true for our student assistants Stefanie Bartz, Marie Koch, Bastian Krieger, and Maurizio Strazzeri. We very much appreciate the work of the participating companies that spent often more than 45 min to answer our extensive questionnaire. Thank you.

This chapter is supposed to inform the reader about the results of our survey. Although the presentation of these results has been done thoroughly, we cannot guarantee completeness and correctness. In particular, the content of the chapter is neither legally binding nor does it provide any legal advice.

References

Ashton, J. K., & Pressey, A. D. (2012). Who manages cartels? The role of sales and marketing managers within international cartels: Evidence from the European Union 1990–2009. CCP Working Paper No. 12-11.

Aubert, C., Rey, P., & Kovacic, W. E. (2006). The impact of leniency and whistle-blowing programs on cartels. *International Journal of Industrial Organization, 24*(6), 1241–1266.

Beckenstein, A. R., & Gabel, H. L. (1982). Antitrust compliance: Results of a survey of legal opinion. *Antitrust Law Journal, 51*(3), 459–516.

Beckenstein, A. R., & Gabel, H. L. (1986). The economics of antitrust compliance. *Southern Economic Journal, 52*(3), 673–692.

Becker, G. S. (1968). Crime and punishment: An economic approach. *The Journal of Political Economy, 76*(2), 169–217. Cited after: Becker, G. S., & Landes, W. M. (Eds.). (1974). *Essays in the economics of crime and punishment*. New York: Columbia University Press.

Buccirossi, P., & Spagnola, G. (2008). Corporate governance and collusive behavior. In W. D. Collins (Ed.), *Issues in competition law and policy* (Vol. 2, chapter 51, pp. 1219–1240). Chicago: ABA Book Publishing.

Bussmann, K. D., Nestler, C., & Salvenmoser, S. (2013). Wirtschaftskriminalität und Unternehmenskultur 2013. PricewaterhouseCoopers AG and Martin-Luther-Universität, Halle-Wittenberg. Available from: http://goo.gl/Mjnl3S. Accessed 1 September 2014.

Conelly, B. L., Trevis Certo, S., Duane Ireland, R., & Reutzel, C. R. (2011). Signaling theory: A review and assessment. *Journal of Management, 37*(1), 39–67.

Deutsche Bahn. (2015). Compliance business partners. Available from: http://goo.gl/fLspgp. Accessed 1 September 2014.

European Commission. (2016). Cartel statistics. Available from: http://goo.gl/IZshkg. Accessed 22 August 2016.

Grueninger, S., Schoettl, L., & Quintus, S. (2014). Compliance im Mittelstand. Studie des Center for Business Compliance & Integrity. Hochschule Konstanz Technik, Wirtschaft und Gestaltung. Available from: http://goo.gl/5gNsv8. Accessed 1 September 2014.

Harrington, J. E. (2006). How do cartels operate? In *Foundations and trends in microeconomics*. Hannover: Now Publishers.

Herold, D. (2015). Competition law compliance programs as internal signaling devices. Unpublished Working Paper.

Herold, D., & Paha, J. (2016). Predicting cartel formation. Unpublished Working Paper.

Kaplow, L. (1995). A model of optimal complexity of legal rules. *Journal of Law, Economics, & Organization, 11*(1), 150–163.

Marcel, J. J., & Cowen, A. P. (2014). Cleaning house or jumping ship? Understanding board upheaval following financial fraud. *Strategic Management Journal, 35*(6), 926–937.

Miller, N. H. (2009). Strategic leniency and cartel enforcement. *The American Economic Review, 99*(3), 750–768.

Murphy, J., & Kolasky, W. (2012). The role of anti-cartel compliance programs in preventing cartel behavior. *Antitrust, 26*(2), 61–64.

Murphy, K. J. (1999). Executive compensation. In O. Ashenfelter & D. Card (Eds.), *Handbook of labor economics* (Vol. 3 (B), pp. 2485–2563). North-Holland, Amsterdam, chapter 38.

Murphy, K. J. (2001). Performance standards in incentive contracts. *Journal of Accounting and Economics, 30*(3), 245–278.

Office of Fair Trading. (2010). Drivers of compliance and non-compliance with competition law. OFT report 1227. Available from: http://goo.gl/rbfoqr. Accessed 1 September 2014.

Paha, J. (2014). Cooperation and compliance with risk and uncertainty about law enforcement. Unpublished Working Paper.

Paha, J., & Götz, G. (2015). Screening und das Compliance-Risikomodell: Konzepte zur unternehmensinternen Aufdeckung von Verstößen gegen das Kartellverbot. *Wirtschaft und Wettbewerb, 12*, 1198–1210.

Rotemberg, J. J., & Saloner, G. (1986). A supergame-theoretic model of price wars during booms. *American Economic Review, 76*(3), 390–407.
Sokol, D. D. (2012). Cartels, corporate compliance, and what practitioners really think about enforcement. *Antitrust Law Journal, 78*(1), 201–240.
Van Heerden, A., Weller, F., & Weidinger, G. (2013). Wirtschaftskriminalität. Deutschland, Österreich, Schweiz im Vergleich. Wirtschaftskriminalität in Grossunternehmen und dem Mittelstand. KPMG AG. Available from http://goo.gl/MQhPEB. Accessed 1 September 2014.

Cases

European Commission (22.11.2001), Case COMP/E-1/37.027
Zinc Phosphate
Decision of 11.12.2001, Reference number K(2001) 4237
European Commission (30.10.2002), Case COMP/E-2/37.784
Fine Art Auction Houses
Decision of 30.10.2002, Reference number COM(2002) 4283
European Commission (27.11.2002), Case COMP/E-1/37.152
Plasterboard
Decision of 27.11.2002
European Commission (17.12.2002), Case COMP/E-2/37.667
Special Graphite
Decision of 5.12.2001, Reference number K(2001) 3923
European Commission (10.1.2003), Case COMP/E-1/37.512
Vitamins
Decision of 22.11.2001, Reference number K(2001) 3695
European Commission (19.8.2003), Case COMP/C.38.279/F3
French Beef
Decision of 2.4.2003, Reference number K(2003) 1065
European Commission (2.4.2003), Case COMP/E-2/37.857
Organic Peroxide
Decision of 10.12.2003, Reference number K(2003) 4570
European Commission (21.4.2004), Case COMP/E-1/36.212
Carbonless Paper
Decision of 20.12.2001, Reference number K(2001) 4573
European Commission (3.9.2004), Case COMP/E-1/38.069
Copper Plumbing Tubes
Decision of 3.9.2004, Reference number K(2004) 2826
European Commission (29.9.2004), Case COMP/C.37750/B2
French Beer Market
Decision of 29.9.2004
European Commission (29.9.2004), Case COMP/C.37750/B231
Sodium Gluconate
Decision of 29.9.2004, Reference number K(2004) 3598
European Commission (29.9.2004), Case COMP/E-1/C.37.773
Monochloroacetic Acid,
Decision of 19.1.2005, Reference number C(2004) 4876
European Commission (19.9.2005), Case COMP 38.337 PO
Thread
Decision of 19.1.2005, Reference numbers C(2005) 3452, C(2005) 3765
European Commission (21.12.2005), Case COMP/F/C.38.443

Rubber Chemicals
Decision of 21.12.2005, Reference number (2005) 5592
European Commission (20.9.2006), Case COMP/F-1/38.121
Fittings
Decision of 20.9.2006, Reference number C(2006) 4180
European Commission (20.11.2007), Case COMP/38.432
Professional Videotapes
Decision of 20.11.2007, Reference number K(2007) 5469
European Commission (28.11.2007), Case COMP/39.165
Flat glass
Decision of 28.11.2007, Reference number C(2007) 5791
European Commission (5.12.2007), Case COMP/38.629
Chloroprene Rubber
Decision of 5.12.2007, Reference number K(2007) 5910
European Commission (19.10.2013), Case COMP/39.437
TV and computer monitor tubes
Decision of 5.12.2012, Reference number C(2012) 8839

Chapter 4
Reducing Antitrust Violations: Do Codes of Conduct and Compliance Training Make a Difference?

Peter Kotzian, Thomas Stöber, and Barbara E. Weißenberger

Abstract In the light of an increasing severity of antitrust enforcement it is of paramount importance to ensure employees' adherence to competition laws. In many firms, codes of conduct and compliance training are part of intense and widespread efforts to address this issue. Still, violations of antitrust laws occur, making headlines, and causing substantial financial and reputational damages. This raises the questions how effective codes of conduct and compliance training are, and how they must be designed to prevent antitrust incidents best. This chapter answers these questions based on new data obtained from a factorial survey in a European multinational firm. Our results indicate that managers are sometimes unaware that some business situations may constitute a violation of antitrust laws. Codes of conduct along with supplementary compliance training improve this awareness. However, they should be complemented by further compliance measures.

4.1 Introduction

Avoiding antitrust violations is a core element of compliance in management control systems, which is readily understandable when fines, damage claims, and the less tangible costs in terms of lost reputation in the wake of antitrust cases are considered. Nevertheless, these efforts are not fully effective, as some managers still engage in anti-competitive behaviour, exposing their firm to severe risks and dire consequences.[1]

Compliance issues range from small-scale misconduct in the everyday behaviour of employees at the workplace, e.g., the misappropriation of firm property, to large-scale issues, involving behaviour that is clearly unlawful, e.g., launching and

[1]The actual tradeoff between financial gains and the financial and non-financial costs might show that cartels pay off.

P. Kotzian (✉) • T. Stöber • B.E. Weißenberger
Heinrich Heine University Düsseldorf, Düsseldorf, Germany
e-mail: peter.kotzian@hhu.de

J. Paha (ed.), *Competition Law Compliance Programmes*,
DOI 10.1007/978-3-319-44633-2_4

maintaining a cartel, or even criminal.[2] For both, academic research and management practice, this poses a challenge and a limitation. It may simply not be possible to fully deter unlawful behaviour by agents who are bent on breaking norms for personal reasons and simply calculate, for themselves or for their firm, whether "the expected rewards outweigh the anticipated risks" (Jacobs 2010, p. 417; see Becker 1968 for the original argument). Therefore, if managers are already fully aware of the unlawful nature of their doings and behave accordingly,[3] providing them with codes of conduct or compliance training will probably not succeed where law and law enforcement have failed.

However, the straightforward view of deterrence theory as part of the rational choice framework lacks a behavioural dimension. The firm is not a black box responding only to rules and opportunities, rather, the firm consists of actors who are, first of all humans acting rationally but not perfectly so. They are embedded in a firm, with a certain formal setting, at times denoted the "ethical infrastructure" (Tenbrunsel et al. 2003), but also with informal rules and a corporate culture. This aspect becomes evident when one acknowledges that antitrust violation rarely starts with managers acting unlawfully or criminally right away, based on a rational consideration. Rather, as with other forms of criminality, anti-competitive behaviour initially starts out as a small infringement and then escalates. Polite talks are conducted during lunch or at an event, and drift towards certain themes, innocuous information is collected and passed on, subtle hints from competitors are used to coordinate activities with them, in order to make life a little easier for all. Just as with other types of criminal behaviour, antitrust escalates by going down a slippery slope when what is acceptable behaviour for an individual or in a group gets redefined over time; see Sampson and Laub (1995), Keizer et al. (2008), and Ariely (2009). Once established, such a 'status quo' of anti-competitive behaviour patterns might be hard to reverse, as even new employees entering the firm are socialised to the specific set of implicit rules, the "descriptive norms" which apply "here" (Cialdini 2003). For firms aiming to avoid compliance problems in general and antitrust problems in particular, this implies that they should nip things in the bud, ensuring that employees comply in their everyday behaviour, in order to avoid these slippery slopes leading to serious unlawful behaviour later on (Strobel 2001).

---

[2]Violations of antitrust regulations are in Germany unlawful, but not criminal, so criminal law does not apply, which strongly affects the possible sanctions actors would have to face. In the US, antitrust violations are criminal. We chose the term unlawful, to cover both situations.

[3]In the case of the cartel among suppliers of optical disc drives, the EU found that "The companies were aware that their behavior was illegal and tried to conceal their contacts and to evade detection of their arrangements. For example, they avoided naming the competitors concerned in their internal correspondence but used abbreviations or generic names. The cartelists also avoided leaving traces of anticompetitive arrangements by preferring face-to-face meetings and ensured that the competitors' discussions were not revealed to customers. Some of them met in places where they could not be easily spotted, including in parking lots or cinemas." European Commission (2015).

This chapter considers where problems with antitrust issues may occur and what a firm may realistically do to counter them at an early stage. Even though there is a broad range of potential management control instruments to influence employee behaviour in the desired direction, only few of them are feasible in practice, as in decentralised firms, managers must have leeway to act and to make decisions in their areas of responsibility. A promising management control instrument for inducing compliance is the use of formal behavioural regulations, i.e., codes of conduct, combined with supplementary compliance training to assure compliance in general. This raises the question of how successful codes of conduct, henceforth referred to as codes, and compliance training, are in assuring compliance in the domain of antitrust.

Looking at academic research and evidence from practice, one finds that for the effectiveness of both, codes and compliance training, the empirical record is spotty as well as contradictory. In most cases, empirical analyses of the usage and effectiveness of both codes and/or compliance training refer to little more than the mere (non-)existence of a code or compliance training, thus ignoring practical design elements. For example, how is the code presented, what regulations does it contains, or how is compliance training organised? This leads to the supposition that the impact of varying design elements on codes' and/or compliance training have an impact on their effectiveness.

Our study therefore addresses the following research questions: first, are certain populations in firms more at risk of engaging in anti-competitive behaviour? Second, are codes of conduct, which in practice have a broad range of different formal design elements, effective in reducing problematic behaviour in the domain of antitrust? In particular, does the introduction of whistle-blowing matter for compliance, in the sense that it installs a culture of mutual control and supervision? Third, does compliance training work, in particular training aimed at instilling an awareness of antitrust issues?

We answer these research questions by conducting a factorial survey using a large sample of managers from different global regions who are employed by a large European corporation. Our study was part of a larger project on the impact of codes of conduct and compliance training on unethical behaviour. Our results show that there is a need for an ethical infrastructure of codes and training, because even in the light of social desirability issues, there are managers who admit that they (or their colleagues) are susceptible to unethical behaviour in antitrust issues. Our results show significant functional and regional differences in the tendency to behave unethical in this context. Nonetheless, the tendency to behave (un)ethically can be explained only in a very limited way. Codes of conduct matter, and so do their design elements: the existence of whistle-blowing systems, the use of pictures with negative examples as illustration in the code, establishing a boundary system, and the unambiguous formulation as a strict 'code of ethics' help at least in some situations, to bring behaviour in line with antitrust rules. Yet, the effectiveness of these design elements is limited, so that specific compliance training creating the necessary socialisation mechanisms and providing a set of descriptive norms for ethical behaviour are necessary to complement the code of conduct. Our paper contributes by being, to the best of our knowledge, the first to address research questions on whether and how the design elements of firms' "ethical infrastructures" impact on managers' tendencies to behave in an ethical or unethical fashion, by using an experimental research design.

Our chapter is organised as follows: after reviewing the state of the art in terms of codes of conduct and compliance training as a means of countering antitrust issues, we derive some hypotheses on the effectiveness of codes and training. We then describe our study in more detail and present the empirical results concerning propensities for antitrust problems to arise and our hypotheses. The last section concludes with a discussion and some advice for organising effective antitrust compliance in firms.

4.2 What Do We Know About the Effectiveness of Codes of Conduct and Compliance Training?

Antitrust infringements can cause serious consequences for firms, the involved managers and employees, as well as for society at large (e.g., Hüschelrath 2010; Blair and Durrance 2008; Leslie 2006). In the wake of antitrust cases, convicted firms usually suffer from substantial financial damages, and losses of reputation or image (e.g., European Commission 2016; Bundeskartellamt 2013; Damgaard et al. 2011; Sims 2009; Veljanovski 2007). Therefore, in line with the recommendations of the German Bundeskartellamt (OECD Competition Committee 2011), firms now implement ethics and compliance programmes as a formal organisational "ethical infrastructure" (a notion developed by Tenbrunsel et al. 2003). The objective is to ensure that managers, as well as employees, engage only in ethical behaviour and do not violate antitrust regulations (e.g., Ferrell et al. 2015; Kaptein and Bons 2014; Kaptein 2010; Kaptein and De Kiewit 2008; Weber and Fortun 2005; Paine 1994). Usually, these programmes consist at least of codes of conduct in conjunction with compliance training initiatives (e.g., Kaptein 2015; Ruiz et al. 2015; Sokol 2012; Joseph 2002). In addition, these elements are supplemented, amongst others, by accountability policies, whistle-blowing mechanisms, and ethics-oriented performance appraisal (e.g., Kaptein 2015; Ruiz et al. 2015). Furthermore, they are often administered by a compliance (or ethics) officer (e.g., Adobor 2006; Weber and Fortun 2005).

But even though there is a large body of literature in the business ethics domain focusing in particular on the effectiveness of codes of conduct and compliance training (e.g., Lehnert et al. 2015; Craft 2013; Kish-Gephart et al. 2010; O'Fallon and Butterfield 2005; Kaye 1992), applications to the business ethics sub-domain of antitrust issues are relatively scarce (Hemphill 2004). Furthermore, drawing conclusions from the general effectiveness of an ethical infrastructure on effectiveness in specific settings may be erroneous. Our own research in this topic, see Stöber et al. (2015), indicates that the varying effectiveness indicates conditionality: codes may work for some people and in some situations, but not for all. A code may be effective in preventing managers from choosing a problematic supplier, but not from engaging in anti-competitive behaviour or from accepting gifts.

4.3 On the Effectiveness of Codes of Conduct in Achieving Antitrust Compliance

The terms 'code of conduct' (e.g., Nijhof et al. 2003), 'code of ethics' (e.g., Heermance 1924) or 'business code' (e.g., Kaptein 2004), are often used interchangeably to refer to a "distinct and formal document containing a set of prescriptions developed by and for a company to guide present and future behaviour on multiple issues of at least its managers and employees toward one another, the company, external stakeholders and/or society in general" (Kaptein and Schwartz 2008, p. 113). As a part of firms' management control systems (Merchant and Van der Stede 2012), codes are widely used in business practice (e.g., Kaptein 2015; Wieland 2015; Sokol 2012; Singh 2006; Copeland 2000). According to Kaptein and Bons (2014), approximately four out of five of the Fortune Global 200 companies have implemented a code. With regard to their contents, empirical studies reveal that codes cover a wide range of topics and issues (e.g., Bodolica and Spraggon 2015; O'Dwyer and Madden 2006). They concern, for example, issues relating to granting and receiving gifts or entertainment invitations, the environment, shareholder as well as stakeholder relationships, conflicts of interest, insider trading, and the abidance to the law (e.g., Singh et al. 2011; Lugli et al. 2009; Cressey and Moore 1983). This demonstrates that ethics and legal issues are not mutually exclusive, but interconnected (Treviño and Nelson 2014). The aim of a firm is, of course, not only legal behaviour but also ethical, and the idea is implicitly that of prevention: make employees ethical in order to avoid illegal behaviour. Several issues addressed in codes of conduct are related to antitrust or refer directly to it. In this context, Strobel (2001) emphasises the more or less unconsciously risk taken by employees when they are confronted with 'sweetening situations'. Initially, employees receive gifts of minor value followed by objects or invitations of higher value. In exchange, the donor (e.g., customer) asks for favours. Such situations generally constitute serious compliance issues, as they are the first step towards serious antitrust-violations. In a similar vein, a content analysis conducted by Chatov (1980) reveals that some companies link entertainment invitations to antitrust issues, in particular, when events or meetings are attended where competitors may be present. This is especially important, because meetings within trade associations have long been used by cartels to share information (Levenstein and Suslow 2006). On the other hand, encounters with competitors cannot be avoided, and the strict regulations on information exchange, for instance in the EU, are still recent and subject to some uncertainty as to what they really mean in practice. Nonetheless, the message is clear and Sanderson and Varner (1984, p. 29) point out that "antitrust laws have led to the establishment of corporate policy that prohibits entering into, or even discussing, any unlawful arrangement or understanding that affects pricing policies and terms upon which products and services are sold".

In a more refined perspective, Beckenstein and Gabel (1982) distinguish between two types of antitrust violations, namely rational and irrational. Rational violations consist of decisions made by managers that are based mainly on a cost-benefit analysis. In doing so, they expect that the economic gains will outweigh possible legal consequences due to their risk evaluation (Jacobs 2010; Becker 1968). In contrast, irrational violations rather result from the "ignorance of the enforcement environment" (Beckenstein and Gabel 1982, p. 475) and do not entail a rational cost-benefit calculus. In their study, Beckenstein and Gabel (1982) conclude that compliance programmes, which consist, amongst other things, of a formal code, are perceived as being able to effectively reduce irrational antitrust violations. This is due to the fact that, for example, having a code and communicating it makes managers and employees more aware of antitrust issues, governmental and company related enforcement mechanisms as well as of the possible consequences of antitrust violations. This should reduce the likelihood of antitrust violations which occur "in the erroneous belief that it is profitable and surreptitiously desired by the superiors" (Beckenstein and Gabel 1982, p. 476). When comparing irrational and rational violations, coping with rational violations is becoming more and more important and more complex as they do not result from a lack of communication but is rather driven by "a motive of economic gain" (Beckenstein and Gabel 1982, p. 478). Therefore, they emphasise further developing the compliance programme in order to reduce the incidence of rational antitrust violations. The appropriate measures include, for example, implementing antitrust audits as well as providing confidential access to legal counsel services. The proposed measures aim at increasing the probability of detection and sanctions for the individual, imposed by the company, in order to induce a negative expected value for violating antitrust laws.

Empirical research on codes as an effective means of promoting ethical as well as (legally) compliant behaviour has yielded mixed results. Whereas some studies indicate a positive relationship with desired behavioural outcomes (e.g., Hirth and Weißenberger 2013; Kolthoff et al. 2010; McKinney et al. 2010; Valentine and Barnett 2003; Valentine and Fleischman 2002; Adams et al. 2001), others suggest that there is no relationship with ethical or compliant behaviour (e.g., Chow et al. 2009; Cabral-Cardoso 2004; Stevens 2004; Sims and Brinkmann 2003). Some studies even generate equivocal results (e.g., Singh 2006; Rodríguez-Garavito 2005; Adam and Rachman-Moore 2004).

As part of their research design, most of these studies focus on the effectiveness of the mere existence of a code. For example, Hegarty and Sims (1979) conducted a laboratory experiment with graduate business students and find support that the existence of a code increases ethical behaviour significantly. In a further study, Adams et al. (2001) conducted structured interviews in business practice. They reveal that the mere existence of a code leads to a more positive evaluation of the overall ethical climate within the company. Furthermore, participants indicate more frequently that they feel supported by the company in behaving ethically. Moreover, they evaluate "role set members (top management, supervisors, peers, subordinates, self)" (Adams et al. 2001, p. 199) as acting based on high ethical standards. In contrast, Cleek and Leonard (1998) or Ford et al. (1982) do not find that the mere existence of a code leads to a higher level of ethical or compliant behaviour. In an experimental study, Laczniak and Inderrieden (1987) find support that a code can reduce clearly illegal behaviour, but does not prevent not "merely" unethical (but legal) activities.

The equivocal results relating to the effectiveness of codes may, in part, be due to the impact of various different design elements (Adams et al. 2001; Nijhof et al. 2003) and in addition, to situational (e.g., Jones 1991), as well as personal level characteristics (e.g., Lehnert et al. 2015; Craft 2013; Kish-Gephart et al. 2010; O'Fallon and Butterfield 2005; Kaye 1992; Treviño 1986). To shed more light on these issues, some studies have already addressed the effectiveness of various design elements of codes, in order to promote ethical or compliant behaviour (e.g., Erwin 2011; Schwartz 2004; Weaver 1995). Specifically, codes can use a variety of several design elements. For example, the title of the code, the signature of members of the executive board appearing on the code, the length of the document, the provision of examples to clarity specific regulations, and references to a whistle-blowing hotline (e.g., George et al. 2014; Kaptein 2011; Schwartz 2004). Schwartz (2004) surveys the perceived effectiveness of various design elements amongst a group of managers as well as ethics officers. His study reveals that especially examples, tone, length, training, reinforcement and whistle-blowing hotlines are perceived as important design elements for the code's effectiveness. Yet, there is a lack of empirical evidence on whether the perceived effectiveness of these design elements actually holds in business decision-making situations, i.e. affects decisions made.

4.4 On the Effectiveness of Compliance Training in Achieving Compliance with Antitrust Issues

A thorough implementation of a code requires communicating it as well as making managers and employees familiar with its content (Warren et al. 2014; Rottig et al. 2011; Tenbrunsel et al. 2003; Wotruba et al. 2001; Dean 1992; Sims 1991). This is why firms invest substantial effort and resources in compliance training (Palmer and Zakhem 2001). In the literature, compliance training is referred to as a major element of a compliance programme beside the code itself (e.g., Kaptein and Bons 2014; Singh 2011). Compliance training is especially relevant in the case for antitrust legislation as it is a very specific, complex, and extensive issue (Baye and Wright 2011). Therefore, in practice, some companies use additional and highly specific training, i.e., antitrust training to further improve compliance (Lauer 2008). As Pitt and Groskaufmanis (1990, p. 1559) put it, "periodic training sessions are also an effective means of reinforcing the company's seriousness of purpose". A survey conducted by the Ethics Resource Center (2013) shows that in 2013, more than four out of five companies used compliance training.

Empirical evidence on the effectiveness of compliance training supports the notion that they are an effective means of increasing compliance and ethical behaviour (e.g., Ruiz et al. 2015; Warren et al. 2014; Langlois and Lapointe 2010; Rottig and Heischmidt 2007; Stevens et al. 2005; Schlaefli et al. 1985). The meta-analysis by Schlaefli et al. (1985) shows that compliance training, which focuses on the discussion of ethical dilemmas, constitutes one of the most effective training forms. In addition, the meta-analysis also reveals that a training duration between 4 and 12 weeks is necessary to achieve an impact. Moreover, Ruiz et al. (2015) suggest that a compliance training as well as a compliance training accompanied by a further element of a compliance programme, for example a code, can significantly influence the ethical intention to behave in a desired way in a compliance situation. In this regard, the fact that each element of a compliance programme is coherent with the rest of the programme is identified as a major factor influencing the individual's intention to behave in a compliant manner (Ruiz et al. 2015). Furthermore, Kaptein (2015) reveals that compliance training initiatives, as well as communication of standards (e.g., the code) reduce the incidence of organisational members detecting unethical work behaviour. In a longitudinal study assessing the effectiveness of compliance training, Warren et al. (2014) find that compliance training initiatives are effective means in reducing unethical work behaviour and also increase the willingness to use whistle-blowing, with both effects further improving in the long term, i.e., 2.5 years after the initial training.

4.5 Open Questions and Problems in Empirical Research on Compliance and Antitrust

While there is empirical evidence that codes and compliance training are effective, at least to some degree, specific questions remain. For example, compliance training might work as a means of reducing antitrust problems, but the question still remains what we know about how organising compliance training optimally. For instance in terms of frequency (do managers who undergo compliance training more often behave less often problematic?) and its content (does compliance training which specifically addresses antitrust really increase compliance in antitrust issues more than general training aiming at creating an ethical awareness?).

Equivalently, there is evidence that codes of conduct work, but why are codes sometimes found to be working and sometimes not? Further, even a cursory reading of codes of conduct as they are enacted in various firms reveals substantial variation in both their content and design. The latter aspect is of particular interest, as design aspects they are highly accessible aspects, aspects, where the firms are relatively free to adapt the code to their liking. Accordingly, are there simple design elements, which can be implemented easily but which still improve the effectiveness of the code?

Moreover, there are methodological problems arising when studying compliance in the domain of antitrust. Establishing the effectiveness of a code requires an experimental setting, rather than a survey, as the effect of the code and its design on compliance must be studied independently of the corporate culture in the firm to avoid confounding through self-selection.[4] Most experiments on code effectiveness use students, as the pragmatic solution. However, the transferability of results from a student sample to managers in a firm is questionable, even in the case of business students, which poses a risk for the external validity of the insights obtained.

4.6 Organising Effective Compliance for Antitrust Issues: Hypotheses

What firms label as 'compliance' is in fact a complex ethical infrastructure (Tenbrunsel et al. 2003) of interlocking arrangements installed to make managers stick to the rules. Starting from the behavioural basis of deviant behaviour, there are therefore three broad and complementary approaches from which hypotheses on compliance and non-compliance can be derived. As we elaborate in the section on research design, there is a tradeoff between which hypotheses can be tested and the fact that a 'more valid' sample of real managers is used. We thus formulated only hypotheses, which could test in the setting of running an experiment in a real firm.

As a starting point, rational choice theory, beginning with Becker (1968), assumes abidance to and deviance from norms and rules to be a rational consideration, taking into account the advantages of deviating, the costs of punishment, and the probability of being caught. In the setting of compliance and criminology, this is also denoted as the theory of deterrence (Jacobs 2010). For compliance in a firm this implies that the firm's institutional setting in place to control and enforce compliance works by shifting the probabilities, benefits and costs of (mis-)conduct. It follows that a clearly formulated code with sanctions but also with an effective control system, such as whistle-blowing, is much more effective for compliance than to a code which leaves leeway regarding the classification of an action as allowed or forbidden. While codes often stipulate internal sanctions imposed by the firm on the manager, misconduct in the domain of antitrust is sanctioned by law enforcement, which installs a second layer in calculating of the expectable costs and benefits of non-compliance.

[4] A firm with a specific corporate culture may, on the one hand, install a certain code, and on the other hand, attract certain managers as employees, who chose the firm specifically because of its corporate culture, making the causal link between the code and ethically correct behaviour problematic. The code's effectiveness can only be established, if it affects the behaviour of a randomly chosen group of managers.

However, empirically, compliance is typically not the result of a purely rational consideration (Tyler 1990; Scholz and Lubell 1998). This is why other theories have to be considered, in order to derive an understanding of when, and why a firm's ethical infrastructure consisting of a code and/or compliance training should be effective.

Sociological theory, beginning with Durkheim (1938) and Parsons (1937), argues that norms are internalised by socialisation, i.e., into society but also into a specific group, like a working environment, and that they work through their 'grip on the mind' (Elster 1989, p. 100). In other words, people do not permanently consider and evaluate the benefits and costs of compliance in each and every situation they encounter, but comply because this behaviour is assumed to be 'the right thing to do' (March and Olsen 1989). In this vein, codes as well as compliance training can be interpreted as the relevant socialisation mechanisms for indicating appropriate behaviour to managers.

Psychological theory also offers explanations supported by experimental research on the effect of norms on behaviour (Cialdini 2003, 2007; Ajzen 1991). Cialdini (2003, 2007) argues that regardless of the formal normative setting (in our case the code as well as the legal framework of antitrust regulations), descriptive norms are constituted by observed behaviour: how are things really done in this group. Such descriptive norms may be stronger in determining behaviour than formal norms. Applied to a business setting, Cialdini's argument translates in the effect of the corporate culture and the ethical climate, also denoted as 'tone at the top': Regardless of what is written in a firm's code, what really matters for employee decision-making and behaviour is how other employees within the firm's internal environment behave.

Applying these theories to the setting of compliance and antitrust in a real firm, we argue as follows. First of all, we assume that providing managers with a code remind them to consider ethical aspects and the rules in the first place. Second, especially in the light of rational choice theory, we assume that a code which specifies clear limits as to what is acceptable, for instance in terms of the setting a clear value for an acceptable gift, leaves less room for deliberations on the possibility of whether a regulation will be enforced, i.e., a code violation will be sanctioned. We therefore formulate our first two hypotheses, H1 and H2, as follows:

H1: *Codes of conduct matter. Presenting a code before asking managers to make a decision should induce the manager to make decisions that are more in line with the rules stated in the code.*

H2: *Codes of conduct which are formulated more stringent and clear, leaving less leeway for interpretation, are more effective in inducing decisions that are more in line with the rules stated in the code.*

Compliance training can be interpreted in the light of sociological as well as psychological theory, as they serve as a means for socialisation and also create an environment of descriptive norms. This should especially hold for training that is designed in a very specific fashion and addressing distinct real life situations. Therefore, our hypotheses, H3 and H4, are as follows:

H3: *More frequent compliance training leads to decision-making which is more in line with the rules stated in the code.*

H4: *Specific antitrust compliance training (as opposed to general) is more effective at increasing decision-making which is more in line with the rules stated in the code.*

Finally, mutual control in a firm is installed by setting up whistle-blowing systems. The idea of whistle-blowing is that those co-workers, colleagues and/or superiors most closely involved with a manager also keep an eye on the manager's conduct and report misconduct. Whistle-blowing can be organised in various ways. At its most basic, a report can be made to an internal institution or to an external party, such as an independent legal counsel. One can assume that especially the latter may alleviate whistle-blowing as reporting a colleague's or even superior's misconduct is a delicate matter and may, in the case of internal whistle-blowing, rather result in a firm covering up the damage together with severe disadvantages to the whistle-blower himself. Therefore, the perceived expected cost of whistle-blowing to the whistle-blower should be lower in the in the case of externally than internally organised whistle-blowing. Based on a rational choice framework, our next two hypotheses, H5 and H6, thus run as follows:

H5: *Highlighting whistle-blowing in a code raises its effectiveness in inducing decision-making which is more in line with the rules stated in the code.*

H6: *External whistle-blowing is more effective than internal whistle-blowing in inducing decision-making which is more in line with the rules stated in the code.*

4.7 Research Design

Given the problems of external validity discussed above, we decided to conduct an experimental study in the setting of a real firm with real managers. Unfortunately, this raises another problem, namely what can be studied in terms of a code's design elements is limited when a sample of real managers from a firm is used. While there are interesting and important theoretical arguments about what design elements make a code effective, these design elements are oftentimes not something a firm can actually implement in practice for legal reasons. Further, since the firm's agreement is needed to run the experiment with their managers, this imposes strict limits on studies like ours. Thus, on the one hand, a realistic sample limits what can be studied (i.e., manipulated as design elements of the code, questions one may ask) while on the other hand, a typical sample (i.e., students) might not be informative regarding the questions of interest.

Given these constraints, we focus on selected design elements of a code, whistle-blowing, and compliance training as factors influencing compliance in antitrust. Regarding the effectiveness of codes, we focused on those design elements a firm may implement in practice. A further restriction was that the content of the code, it's regulatory content, was also largely fixed, so we kept that constant. With respect to the effectiveness of compliance training, we surveyed how the training, as implemented in this firm in terms of themes and frequency, affects the behaviour of managers. We also surveyed how managers perceive the compliance training, i.e., as being useful or not. Given that the peer-group effect is relevant for unethical behaviour, we also studied how the possibility of whistle-blowing affects decision-making in situations from the antitrust context.

Our study was conducted as a factorial survey (Auspurg and Hinz 2015) in 2015. We contacted a random gross sample of 4659 managers with lower, middle and top management functions employed by a European corporation. Of these, 1778 managers participated in the study, which consisted of several parts. The high participation quota allowed a coverage of the corporation in terms of regions and functions: the managers were located in all global regions, albeit with a focus on Germany (41 %) and Asia/Pacific (34 %), and covered all management functions and organisational units of the firm. The survey was conducted online, using the software Unipark. Participants received an email from a member of the firm's top management, which announced the study. This was followed by an email with a link to the study's website, and an invitation to participate on a voluntary and entirely anonymous basis. On arriving at the study's landing page, managers were randomly assigned to one of the codes of conduct with a given constellation of design elements, specified below, respectively to the no-code group, serving as the control group. This setup allows us to treat the study as an experiment.

All participants were asked to imagine that they work in a fictitious firm, named TenCon. Codes of conduct were given to all participants with exception of the members of the no-code group. The codes contained the identical regulations, formulated in line with the corporation's existing code, but differed in their design. We manipulated features of the presentation, focus, and appearance, using learning theory, information processing theory, and rational choice theory. The first manipulation aimed at making the code more easily accessible and was to include pictures showing either illustrative examples of correct or wrong behaviour. The second manipulation, aiming also at making the code easier to remember and to learn, was to give examples of behaviour. Again, we included positive examples, showing the right behaviour, and negative examples, showing the wrong behaviour. Both manipulations assume that making the code easier to grasp and 'stickier' for the participant increases its relevance. The third manipulation, targeting the chances of getting away with non-compliance, was including whistle-blowing into the code and we did so in two variants. Either, the whistle-blowing was described as being organised internally, stating that employees should contact a person in the firm, or externally, stating that employees should contact a law firm. Each participant in the code condition was randomly assigned to a different type of code created by the combination of the aforementioned design elements, thus creating different experimental groups.

Participants underwent a short training on their code and were then given several vignettes constituting compliance dilemma situations relevant to the corporation's business model. They were then asked how they would decide in this situation. In each vignette, two options were presented: one was the ethically and legally correct, the other one the ethically inappropriate choice. For this chapter, we put the focus on the vignettes involving antitrust issues.

Vignette 1: Conversation on capacities during professional conference

A colleague at TenCon attends a conference which delegates from competitors of TenCon also attend. During lunch, the conversation turns to the overall situation of the industry. In the course of the conversation, the issue of production capacities comes up.

First, the participant was asked, how likely the colleague would be to remain in the room. Second, the participant was asked what his or her own decision would be if put in the situation of the colleague, i.e., how likely is it that he or she would remain in the room.

Vignette 2: Request to gather confidential information about a competitor

A colleague at TenCon is a member of the same fitness club as employees of a major competitor. The line manager instructs the colleague to use his contact to inquire discreetly about the degree of capacity utilization at the competitor. The line manager insinuates that obtaining such information will have a positive effect on the next appraisal interview.

Again, the participant was asked, how likely he or she thought it was that the colleague would follow this instruction. Second, the participant was asked for his or her own decision, i.e., how likely is it that he or she would follow this instruction.

Both vignettes describe behaviour which is ethically problematic, even at first glance, but moreover constitutes the basis for an antitrust case. The first vignette describes a situation which was developed in close cooperation with the compliance office of the corporation where the study was conducted. It is representative of cases obviously occurring on a regular basis and being part of the corporation's antitrust-training. It was also chosen because there are several anecdotal reports of antitrust cases at EU level, where informal talks like the one described were sufficient to launch an antitrust inquiry. The situation is also a difficult one for the person involved, because two norms clearly collide: first, the social norm of courtesy, that one does not leave the table during lunch, second, the legal norm, which demands just that.

The second vignette was chosen, because the situation is by nature an inducement to enter the first stages of an antitrust agreement (the manager might try to exchange information with the manager from the competing firm) but also involves a tradeoff. On the one hand, there is the legal norm that clearly forbids the line manager to giving such an instruction and also forbids managers to comply with such an instruction. On the other hand, there are questions of personal benefit, for instance the chance to get a promotion, but also questions of loyalty to the firm, which is the ultimate beneficiary of the information obtained.

For both vignettes, answers were captured on a 6-point Likert scale, ranging from 1, very unlikely (the "correct, ethical" choice) to 6, very likely (the "incorrect, unethical" choice). The study concluded by asking questions about personal features, such as demographics, values, affiliation to a certain region or department in the firm, and about their participation in and evaluation of the compliance training in the firm. Even though the latter cannot be manipulated by us, participation and evaluation nevertheless varied among managers in the corporation. This concerns, for instance, aspects like compliance training, which different managers attend with different frequency, and also with respect to different attitudes towards the training. Furthermore, there were variations among the functional units of the firm, for instance, different work-cultures in different departments, or at different levels of the management hierarchy.

4.8 Antitrust Issues: Who Is at Risk?

The results of our study provide us firstly with information on the prevalence of antitrust problems by estimating the number of managers for whom the behaviour described constitutes an acceptable course of action. Figure 4.1 shows the distribution of how managers would decide if they personally were involved in the situations created by our two vignettes. Given that we are interested in the prevalence of the problem, we chose only managers who received no code before deciding but were supposed to be familiar with the corporation's existing code of conduct that contains clear and unequivocal regulations on appropriate behaviour in both vignettes. This was based on the argument that those managers are unaffected by the code that freshly draws specific attention to the desired course of action. Furthermore, in real-life situations it is oftentimes not feasible to use the code for reference purposes.

The two measures of antitrust problems, albeit admittedly crude and presumably biased by social conformity,[5] yield two results. First, while many managers behave, on the whole, ethically and in line with the demands of law and the firm's code of conduct, there is a substantial variation in how managers intend to behave. Second, there is also a substantial share of managers who misbehave to some degree and some managers exhibit a stance which is clearly problematic. Further, the correlation between the stated decisions is low: it is not the case that a manager who recognises that leaving a conference because themes arise, which must not be discussed also rejects gathering information illegally and vice versa. There is, it

[5]Social desirability was measured using the Impression Management Scale developed by Winkler et al. (2006), based on earlier work by Paulhus (1984, 1991). Including the measurement indicates persistent and strong effects of social desirability in the study, indicating that controlling for social desirability is obligatory in studies conducted in the workplace setting. Social desirability is, perhaps little surprisingly, much less of an issue in studies using student samples.

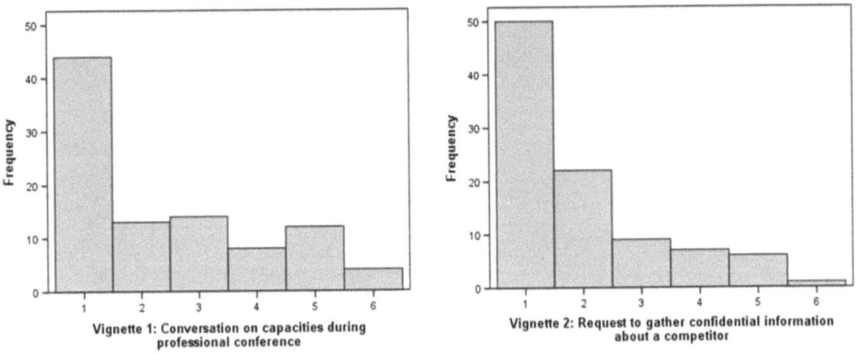

Fig. 4.1 Antitrust problems—how would managers decide? *Notes*: $N = 95$ (managers who did not receive the experimental code of conduct). Dependent variable is the stated likelihood that the manager would behave as described in the vignettes. Likert-type scale; ranging from 1, very unlikely (indicating an ethical stance) to 6, very likely (indicating an unethical stance)

seems, no consistent knowledge or awareness about what is appropriate behaviour or not.

Given the incidence of problematic behaviour, an exploratory question is whether one can identify subgroups of managers more at risk of behaving in a way which constitutes a problem for antitrust. In order to estimate who is at risk, even after taking into account the effect of having received a code, we regress the decision intentions on personal features and occupational background now using all subjects (Table 4.1).

Setting aside the presence or absence of a code of conduct for a moment, we find that there are significant differences in how managers decide in situations with antitrust implications. These differences also occur across the two situations we used, a finding in line with the observation that behaviour in one situation is not really a good indicator of the behaviour in the other (Stöber et al. 2015).

In Table 4.1, we present the results from regressing the intention to behave more or less ethically in both vignettes (dependent variables) on the functional and regional background, as well as personal features (independent variables). The more negative a coefficient in the columns, the greater the tendency to behave ethically with respect to the given situation.

Specifically, looking at management functions, we find that managers in sales and marketing departments are less at risk of slipping into a talk about production capacities, whereas the opposite is true for managers from operations. Looking at regional cultures, the different regions are compared with Germany, which is the baseline reference category. The negative entries found for all regions indicate that the awareness that informal talks during a conference pose an antitrust-issue is lower in Germany and higher almost everywhere else. (The effect for Japan is equally strong, but insignificant due to the small number of participants from this country.) Furthermore, a finding consistent with upper echelons theory (Hambrick

Table 4.1 Factors influencing problematic behaviour in antitrust situations

Variable	Professional conference (vignette 1) Other	Professional conference (vignette 1) Own	Gathering confidential information (vignette 2) Other	Gathering confidential information (vignette 2) Own
Received code of conduct	0.251	0.156	−0.142	−0.277**
Functional background				
Research	0.090	0.163	0.048	0.050
Sales/Marketing	−0.481**	−0.389*	−0.197	−0.114
Operations	0.349**	0.447***	0.266**	0.118
Purchasing	0.302	0.296	0.359	0.108
Finance	−0.081	0.010	−0.017	−0.026
Human Resources	−0.029	0.071	0.232	0.154
Regional background				
Europe w/o Germany	−0.338**	−0.326**	−0.138	−0.059
Asia-Pacific	−0.770***	−0.630***	0.259**	0.169*
Americas	−1.368***	−0.988**	−0.548	0.159
Japan	−1.688	−1.221	−1.523	−0.789
Personal features				
Hierarchy level	−0.091*	−0.189***	−0.042	−0.109***
Sex (Female)	0.076	−0.001	−0.029	−0.181*
Work experience	0.008	0.005	0.001	−0.008*
Impression management	−0.110***	−0.108***	−0.117***	−0.080***
Constant	4.556***	4.241***	4.248***	3.325***
R^2	0.108	0.098	0.075	0.073
R^2_adjusted	0.094	0.084	0.060	0.059
N	1005	1005	1005	1005

Notes: Dependent variable is a Likert-type scale; ranging from 1, very unlikely (indicating an ethical stance) to 6, very likely (indicating an unethical stance). All variables are scaled so that negative coefficients indicate a tendency to decide more ethically. The reference category for the variables indicating the region is Germany, so that, for instance, a negative entry for a region indicates that managers from this region are more ethical in their stated behavioural intentions
Other = expected behaviour of colleagues, own = own behavioural intention
*$p < 0.1$; **$p < 0.05$; ***$p < 0.01$

and Mason 1984) in Table 4.1 is that higher levels of the hierarchy are more aware of antitrust issues and tend to behave accordingly, i.e., more ethically.

Finally, by and large, the stated behaviour of the manager is congruent with the behaviour the manager assumes others in his or her working environment would display. If anything, one's own behaviour is seen as slightly more 'correct' than that assumed of others, which is notably the case for female managers, managers in higher positions and managers who have more working experience. These factors affect one's own behaviour, but are irrelevant for the assumed behaviour of others. Also, as one might have presumed, social desirability, the tendency to answer in a way which the respondent presumes to be the socially desired way, is a strong determinant of the answers. Even so, those background features only explain a small part of variance in ethical behaviours, which is recognisable by the (adjusted) values of R^2, which are relatively low.

4.9 Are Codes of Conduct Effective in Preventing Antitrust Problems?

Based on the finding that there are indeed compliance problems in situations involving antitrust issues, the question arises as to whether giving the managers a code will improve their behaviour in terms of compliance with antitrust rules. Furthermore, an interesting issue is whether, if presenting a code matters, the code's effectiveness can be enhanced by design elements like layout of by highlighting some of its content. Therefore, our following analysis aims at capturing the effects of both the existence of a code, as well as its design. As a firm can use only one code, which is supposed to apply to everybody, we compare only the effects of the code and the variants of the codes *per se* and do not include any functional, regional or personal information on the managers as variables. The results of our analysis are presented in Table 4.2, with the independent variables being design elements of the code and the dependent variables once again being the intention to decide more or less ethically in both vignettes. The more negative the coefficients, the higher the impact of a given design element of a code in reducing unethical behaviour.

Table 4.2 Effectiveness of codes of conduct in antitrust situations

Variable	Professional conference (vignette 1)		Gathering confidential information (vignette 2)	
Received code of conduct	0.103		−0.314**	
External whistle-blowing		0.260		−0.341**
Internal whistle-blowing		−0.037		−0.365**
Pictures with positive examples		0.293		−0.141
Pictures with negative examples		−0.147		−0.361**
Code creating boundary system		−0.116		−0.358**
Code creating belief system		0.193		−0.285
Positive text examples		0.237		−0.178
Negative text examples		0.259		−0.289
Unambiguous code with signature		0.198		−0.349**
Unambiguous code without signature		−0.087		−0.458***
Constant	2.400***	2.400***	1.947***	1.947***
R^2	0.000	0.010	0.006	0.011
R^2 adjusted	−0.001	−0.000	0.005	0.001
N	1005	1005	1005	1005

Notes: Dependent variable is the manager's own behavioural intention. All variables are scaled so that negative coefficients indicate design elements of codes that reduce unethical behaviour
$*p < 0.1$; $**p < 0.05$; $***p < 0.01$

Based on Table 4.2, the central question about the effectiveness of codes can be answered, but the answer is by no means as conclusive as one might wish. Regarding the situation of the professional conference, where the talk turns to production capacities, no code version exerts any significant effect. In our opinion, there are two likely interpretations. First, managers do not see the situation as being a problem at all; it is, for them, not a situation for which the code is applicable. Second, managers, for other reasons, such as compliance training, do either already know or do not know how to behave, and the code does not affect their behaviour.

For the situation of being urged to gather confidential information, codes work. Their effect is significant but limited, in the sense that being given a code shifts the behavioural intention in the right direction, so we can partly confirm hypothesis 1. This effect is not due to all code variants alike, but due to some codes having a strong effect, while others have none. In line with our hypotheses 5, codes emphasising whistle-blowing have a strong effect, but there is no evidence to support hypothesis 6, that external whistle-blowing works better than internal whistle-blowing. Furthermore, regarding the content of a code, a code which offers a recommendation of what to do and how to behave ("beliefs systems", see Simons 1995, p. 33) is ineffective, while a code which states boundaries by emphasising what is forbidden works better ("boundary systems", see Simons 1995, p. 39). This finding is emphasised by the observation that codes stating clear limits and sanctions, leaving thus little or no leeway, i.e., the unambiguous versions, are more effective than others. Issues of layout, for instance with illustrative pictures appealing to the visually minded, or illustrative examples do not matter consistently—there is an effect for negative pictures but not for positive ones, and no effect for codes using examples. In a nutshell, we find that, while codes work, their effectiveness as a means of avoiding problematic behaviour in situations involving antitrust issues is limited. Further, not just any code works. There are options for improving the effectiveness of a code by including those design elements, for which we found a positive impact on effectiveness.

4.10 Compliance Training as a Means of Preventing Antitrust Problems?

Given that presenting codes did little to improve the behaviour in situations with antitrust issues, the question is whether compliance training helps more. Sociological as well as psychological theory suggests just this, as managers are made familiar with the code and its application in their daily work. In our specific study, while all employees of the surveyed corporation were formally required to attend compliance training, there was still substantial variation: most (but not all) employees did attend the obligatory training, and many participated in several training sessions. Furthermore, there was variation in the training subjects. Some sessions were rather general whereas others focused, for instance, specifically on

Table 4.3 Effectiveness of compliance training in antitrust situations

Variable	Professional conference (vignette 1)		Gathering confidential information (vignette 2)	
Received code of conduct	0.217	0.206	−0.294**	−0.296**
Number of compliance training sessions	−0.276***		0.043	
Usefulness of compliance training	−0.185***	−0.186***	−0.062**	−0.062**
Participation in general training		0.124		0.141
Participation in antitrust training		−0.631***		−0.082
Participation in anticorruption training		0.034		0.172*
Constant	3.590***	3.304***	2.120***	2.051***
R^2	0.055	0.072	0.012	0.016
R^2 adjusted	0.052	0.067	0.008	0.011
N	901	901	901	901

Notes: Dependent variable is the manager's own behavioural intention. All variables are scaled so that negative coefficients indicate training features that reduce unethical behaviour
$^*p < 0.1$; $^{**}p < 0.05$; $^{***}p < 0.01$

antitrust issues. To make our experimental design more salient, we formulated our vignettes in close accordance (but not identically) with vignettes that were used in the corporation's antitrust training. Table 4.3 indicates the results of the effectiveness of compliance training, with training features as the independent variable and the tendency to decide more or less ethical in both vignettes being the dependent variable. Again, the more negative the coefficients, the greater the impact of a given training feature in reducing the intention to behave unethically.

As Table 4.3 shows, the effectiveness of compliance training on the intended behaviour in antitrust situations is mixed. Interestingly, compliance training matters in the first situation (professional conference), where codes were found to be irrelevant, but not in the case of following an instruction to gather information quasi-illegally. Furthermore, the way the managers perceive and evaluate compliance training matters for their behavioural intention. Those managers who found compliance training useful behave differently (and more in the intended manner) from those who do not believe so. However, the likely explanation is that the evaluation of compliance training as useful or useless is actually a proxy for general ethical awareness. Managers who are ethically aware are both, more likely to find the compliance training useful and more likely to behave ethically in a difficult situation.

Regarding compliance training in general, the mere frequency of training seems to matter, but a closer look indicates that this effect is due to which training sessions were attended, rather than the frequency. Thus, there is no support for hypothesis 3 but some for hypothesis 4. Looking specifically at which training matters, we observe first that general compliance training does not have any effect, and second, that antitrust training does indeed significantly improve behavioural intentions in the professional conference situation, but that the anti-corruption-training exerts an adverse effect in the case of gathering information. Here, those who underwent this training are even more likely to follow a problematic instruction given to them by their line-manager.

4.11 Summary and Conclusion

In our study, we analysed the effectiveness of codes of conduct and compliance training as a means of avoiding antitrust problems, by conducting a factorial survey with a large sample of managers from a European corporation with global business activities. Our results yield both, good and bad news for organising effective corporate compliance in antitrust issues.

First of all, our descriptive findings indicate that there is a non-trivial number of managers who have no ethical awareness that a certain situation, for instance talking about production capacities during a business conference, may create an antitrust problem or even *per se* already violates antitrust regulation. In particular, in Germany, there are clear deficits which compliance training needs to address. Compared to Germany, managers from all other regions stated a lower likelihood of engaging in problematic behaviour. A German manager is much more likely to stay, when the talk turns to themes like production capacities than managers from other regions. Furthermore, there is also evidence of sub-cultures within the firm, departments and functions, which stand out as problematic in terms of what they think is appropriate conduct in situations involving antitrust issues. On the whole, there is substantial variation in how managers decide, both between managers, and also at the level of the individual manager, who may decide very differently in situations which are equivalent from the perspective of compliance. This variation is due to personal features, and our study, albeit limited in what questions could be asked, was able to identify some of them.

Even when assuming that a lot of variation in behaviour is due to personal features and attitudes, it is likely that both, design elements of the code and of the situation, for which the code's effectiveness was studied, matter in terms of how managers intend to behave. Firms can only control the former element of the equation, the code and to some degree its relevance, via compliance training. Firms may design their code in a particular way, but in doing so, they are constrained in that they need and can implement only one code, which, hopefully, works for most situations occurring in the business context, and also for most managers. A code can neither be tailored to each and every situation, nor to each and every manager. After all, each has a unique combination of traits. Instead, a code must be designed in a way which works best for most managers and across most situations, which will differ in the ethical considerations they require. Concerning a firm's ethical infrastructure of codes and compliance training, the good news is that codes, their design, and compliance training do matter and thus constitute a way to improve compliance. The bad news is that their impact is rather limited.

Regarding the code, the implications of our study are that the firm should aim to be clear and straight, leaving no leeway, and also add a layer of informal control by installing whistle-blowing. Regarding compliance training, our evidence indicates that general training, which is obligatory for all, seems to be too much of a bothersome routine to be effective. Specific training is more effective, in particular in antitrust issues.

Our results are subject to some limitations. For example, the generalisability of our results clearly depends on whether the fact that all managers surveyed belonged to one corporation creates a more or less unique setting. We believe, this may have an impact, but probably rather with respect to the level of observed behaviour and not to the impact directions of our surveyed independent variables. Furthermore, as all managers belong to the same corporation we have no confounding effects created by providing the participants with a fictitious code of conduct that varies more or less from the codes they are subjected to in their business lives. However, to overcome this limitation, we suggest that our study is replicated in other firms to shed more light on this issue.

Apart from the considerations of validity, in our research design, we paid substantial attention to the delicate setting in which our study was conducted. Using a sample of managers imposes constraints on time and content of a study, which are not comparable to conducting an experiment with (paid) students. However, the particular situation of being able to conduct a study with managers from a firm was not only a constraint, but also an opportunity, in that we obtained information about how compliance training works in practice, and how managers react if given a code of conduct with certain properties.

Summing up the implications of our research on ethical infrastructures as a means of resolving antitrust problems, we suggest that when designing a code of conduct, firms should pay attention to issues of layout and content, where it is possible to reap some benefits in terms of compliance at little cost. However, there are clear limits. Therefore, firms should not limit their efforts by aiming at coming to grips with compliance problems by issuing a code of conduct, which is optimised in content, layout and supplementary compliance training. They would do better by identifying groups with given personal features, and also with certain group-values characterising their work environment, which evidently have a lower level of ethical awareness in antitrust problems. Firms can counter this by focusing on increased and specific compliance training of these managers. Because, even if the overall level of compliance may be quite high, there will probably managers who do not have any real ethical awareness and do not behave ethically. Firms would do better identifying such individuals and enhance their 'personal ethical infrastructure' so as to guide their behaviour.

Appendix 1: The Different Types of Codes of Conduct Used in Our Study

We manipulated the design characteristics of codes of conduct, using the same content, oriented at the content of the firm's current code, and manipulated several isolated design elements. The 11 experimental conditions, used for the vignette experiment, for which the effectiveness of the code for decision making was the object, and the survey, for which the effects of the code on the working climate and the relationship between the manager and the firm was the focus, were:

1. Baseline treatment (the participants received no code of conduct; only for the vignette experiment)
2. Code with an external whistle-blowing system
3. Code with an internal whistle-blowing system
4. Code with positive pictures (showing appropriate behavior)
5. Code with negative pictures (showing inappropriate behavior)
6. Code with a foreword and a conclusion that emphasize the commandment not to violate any regulations (boundary system)
7. Code with a foreword and a conclusion that emphasize the company values (belief system)
8. Code with positive text examples (descriptions of appropriate behavior)
9. Code with negative text examples (descriptions of inappropriate behavior)
10. Unambiguous code ('code of ethics') with strict regulations (no room for maneuver) and signed by the management board members
11. Unambiguous code ('code of ethics') with strict regulations (no room for maneuver) and without any signatures by the management board

Appendix 2: Measurement of Independent Variables

	N (valid)	Min	Max	Mean	Std. Dev.
Dummy variables indicating functional background					
Research	1005	0	1	0.35	0.48
Sales/Marketing	1005	0	1	0.07	0.26
Operations	1005	0	1	0.23	0.42
Purchasing	1005	0	1	0.02	0.13
Finance	1005	0	1	0.05	0.23
Human Resources	1005	0	1	0.03	0.16
Dummy variables indicating regional background					
Europe w/o Germany	1005	0	1	0.21	0.41
Asia-Pacific	1005	0	1	0.30	0.46
Americas	1005	0	1	0.02	0.13
Japan	1005	0	1	0.00	0.04

(continued)

	N (valid)	Min	Max	Mean	Std. Dev.
Personal features of participants					
Hierarchy level (1 = lowest, 5 = highest category)	1005	1	5	1.84	1.14
Sex (with 1 = Female and 0 = Male)	1005	0	1	0.24	0.43
Impression management (high values = tendency to answer socially acceptable)	1005	3	18	13.79	2.82
Work experience (total work experience in years)	1005	1	45	18.54	9.25
Participation and evaluation of compliance training					
Number of compliance training sessions attended (total number)	1005	0	4	1.60	0.96
Usefulness of compliance training (high values indicate perceived usefulness)	901	1	6	4.54	1.40
Dummy variables indicating types of compliance training completed					
Participation in general training	1005	0	1	0.83	0.37
Participation in antitrust training	1005	0	1	0.45	0.50
Participation in anticorruption training	1005	0	1	0.29	0.46

References

Adam, A., & Rachman-Moore, D. (2004). The methods used to implement an ethical code of conduct and employee attitudes. *Journal of Business Ethics, 54*(3), 225–244.

Adams, J. S., Tashchian, A., & Shore, T. H. (2001). Codes of ethics as signals for ethical behavior. *Journal of Business Ethics, 29*(3), 199–211.

Adobor, H. (2006). Exploring the role performance of corporate ethics officers. *Journal of Business Ethics, 69*(1), 57–75.

Ajzen, I. (1991). The theory of planned behavior. *Organizational Behavior and Human Performance, 50*(2), 179–211.

Ariely, D. (2009). *Predictably irrational*. New York: HarperCollins.

Auspurg, K., & Hinz, T. (2015). *Factorial survey experiments*. Thousand Oaks: Sage.

Baye, M. R., & Wright, J. D. (2011). Is antitrust too complicated for generalist judges? The impact of economic complexity and judicial training on appeals. *The Journal of Law and Economics, 54*(1), 1–24.

Beckenstein, A. R., & Gabel, H. L. (1982). Antitrust compliance: Results of a survey of legal opinion. *Antitrust Law Journal, 51*(3), 459–516.

Becker, G. S. (1968). Crime and punishment: An economic approach. *Journal of Political Economy, 76*(2), 169–217.

Blair, R. D., & Durrance, C. P. (2008). Antitrust sanctions: Deterrence and (possibly) overdeterrence. *Antitrust Bulletin, 53*(3), 643–661.

Bodolica, V., & Spraggon, M. (2015). An examination into the disclosure, structure, and contents of ethical codes in publicly listed acquiring firms. *Journal of Business Ethics, 126*(3), 459–472.

Bundeskartellamt. (2013). Leitlinie für die Bußgeldzumessung in Kartellordnungswidrigkeitenverfahren. Available from: http://www.bundeskartellamt.de/SharedDocs/Publikation/DE/Leitlinien/Bekanntmachung%20-%20Bu%C3%9Fgeldleitlinien-Juni%202013.html. Accessed 21 January 2016.

Cabral-Cardoso, C. (2004). Ethical misconduct in the business school: A case of plagiarism that turned bitter. *Journal of Business Ethics, 49*(1), 75–89.

Chatov, R. (1980). What corporate ethics statements say. *California Management Review, 22*(4), 20–29.
Chow, W. S., Wu, J. P., & Chan, A. K. K. (2009). The effects of environmental factors on the behavior of Chinese managers in the information age in China. *Journal of Business Ethics, 89*(4), 629–639.
Cialdini, R. B. (2003). Crafting normative messages to protect the environment. *Current Directions in Psychological Science, 12*(4), 105–109.
Cialdini, R. B. (2007). Descriptive social norms as underappreciated sources of social control. *Psychometrika, 72*(2), 263–268.
Cleek, M. A., & Leonard, S. L. (1998). Can corporate codes of ethics influence behavior? *Journal of Business Ethics, 17*(6), 619–630.
Copeland, J. D. (2000). The Tyson story: Building an effective ethics and compliance program. *Drake Journal of Agricultural Law, 5*(2), 305–353.
Craft, J. L. (2013). A review of the empirical ethical decision-making literature: 2004–2011. *Journal of Business Ethics, 117*(2), 221–259.
Cressey, D. R., & Moore, C. A. (1983). Managerial values and corporate codes of ethics. *California Management Review, 25*(4), 53–77.
Damgaard, M. T., Ramada, P., Conlon, G., & Godel, M. (2011). The economics of cartels: Incentives, sanctions, stability, and effects. *Journal of European Competition Law & Practice, 2*(4), 405–413.
Dean, P. J. (1992). Making codes of ethics 'real'. *Journal of Business Ethics, 11*(4), 285–290.
Durkheim, E. (1938). *The rules of sociological method* (S. A. Solovay & J. H. Mueller, Trans, 8th ed.). New York: Free Press.
Elster, J. (1989). *The cement of society: A study of social order*. Cambridge: Cambridge University Press.
Erwin, P. M. (2011). Corporate codes of conduct: The effects of code content and quality on ethical performance. *Journal of Business Ethics, 99*(4), 535–548.
Ethics Resource Center. (2013). *National business ethics survey of the U.S. workforce*. Arlington, VA.
European Commission. (2015). Antitrust: Commission fines suppliers of optical disc drives € 116 million for cartel. Press Release of 21 October 2015. Available from: http://europa.eu/rapid/press-release_IP-15-5885_en.htm. Accessed 25 February 2016.
European Commission. (2016). 1. Cartel statistics (situation as of 27 Jan 2016). Available from: http://ec.europa.eu/competition/cartels/statistics/statistics.pdf. Accessed 4 February 2016.
Ferrell, O. C., Fraedrich, J., & Ferrell, L. (2015). *Business ethics. Ethical decision-making and cases* (10th ed.). Stamford: Cengage Learning.
Ford, R., Gray, B., & Landrum, R. (1982). Do organizational codes of conduct really affect employees' behavior? *Management Review, 71*(6), 53–55.
George, G., Jones, A., & Harvey, J. (2014). Analysis of language used with codes of ethical conduct. *Journal of Academic and Business Ethics, 8*, 1–24.
Hambrick, D. C., & Mason, P. A. (1984). Upper echelons: The organization as a reflection of its top managers. *Academy of Management Review, 9*(2), 193–206.
Heermance, E. L. (1924). *Codes of ethics: A handbook*. Burlington: Free Press.
Hegarty, W. H., & Sims, H. P., Jr. (1979). Organizational philosophy, policies, and objectives related to unethical decision behavior: A laboratory experiment. *Journal of Applied Psychology, 64*(3), 331–338.
Hemphill, T. A. (2004). Antitrust, dynamic competition and business ethics. *Journal of Business Ethics, 50*(2), 127–135.
Hirth, T., & Weißenberger, B. E. (2013). *Ethical dilemmas in management accounting settings*. Paper presented at the 2nd workshop on business ethics, Universidad Complutense de Madrid, 28–29 November 2013.

Hüschelrath, K. (2010). How are cartels detected? The increasing use of proactive methods to establish antitrust infringements. *Journal of European Competition Law & Practice, 1*(6), 522–528.
Jacobs, B. E. (2010). Deterrence and deterrability. *Criminology, 48*(2), 417–441.
Jones, T. M. (1991). Ethical decision making by individuals in organizations: An issue-contingent model. *Academy of Management Review, 16*(2), 366–395.
Joseph, J. (2002). Integrating business ethics and compliance programs: A study of ethics officers in leading organizations. *Business and Society Review, 107*(3), 309–347.
Kaptein, M. (2004). Business codes of multinational firms: What do they say? *Journal of Business Ethics, 50*(1), 13–31.
Kaptein, M. (2010). The ethics of organizations: A longitudinal study of the U.S. working population. *Journal of Business Ethics, 92*(4), 601–618.
Kaptein, M. (2011). Toward effective codes: Testing the relationship with unethical behavior. *Journal of Business Ethics, 99*(2), 233–251.
Kaptein, M. (2015). The effectiveness of ethics programs: The role of scope, composition, and sequence. *Journal of Business Ethics, 132*(2), 415–431.
Kaptein, M., & Bons, F. (2014). The business codes of the Fortune Global 200. KPMG/RSM Erasmus University (Eds.). Available from: http://www.kpmg.com/NL/nl/IssuesAndInsights/ArticlesPublications/Documents/PDF/Forensic/The-Business-codes-of-the-Fortune-Global-200.pdf. Accessed 21 January 2016.
Kaptein, M., & De Kiewit, M. (2008). Business codes of the Global 200. KPMG/RSM Erasmus University (Eds.). Available from: http://www.kpmg.com/cn/en/issuesandinsights/articlespublications/pages/business-codes-global-200-o-200804.aspx. Accessed 21 January 2016.
Kaptein, M., & Schwartz, M. S. (2008). The effectiveness of business codes: A critical examination of existing studies and the development of an integrated research model. *Journal of Business Ethics, 77*(2), 111–127.
Kaye, B. N. (1992). Codes of ethics in Australian business corporations. *Journal of Business Ethics, 11*(11), 857–862.
Keizer, K., Lindenberg, S., & Steg, L. (2008). The spreading of disorder. *Science, 322*(5908), 1681–1685.
Kish-Gephart, J. J., Harrison, D. A., & Treviño, L. K. (2010). Bad apples, bad cases, and bad barrels: Meta-analytic evidence about sources of unethical decisions at work. *Journal of Applied Psychology, 95*(1), 1–31.
Kolthoff, E., Erakovich, R., & Lasthuizen, K. (2010). Comparative analysis of ethical leadership and ethical culture in local government. *International Journal of Public Sector Management, 23*(7), 596–612.
Laczniak, G. R., & Inderrieden, E. J. (1987). The influence of stated organizational concern upon ethical decision making. *Journal of Business Ethics, 6*(4), 297–307.
Langlois, L., & Lapointe, C. (2010). Can ethics be learned? Results from a three-year action-research project. *Journal of Educational Administration, 48*(2), 147–163.
Lauer, S. A. (2008). Director training: What should it cover and who should lead it? *Corporate Secretary's Guide: Corporate Directions, 497*, 753–755.
Lehnert, K., Park, Y., & Singh, N. (2015). Research note and review of the empirical ethical decision-making literature: Boundary conditions and extensions. *Journal of Business Ethics, 129*(1), 195–219.
Leslie, C. R. (2006). Antitrust damages and deadweight loss. *Antitrust Bulletin, 51*(3), 521–567.
Levenstein, M. C., & Suslow, V. Y. (2006). Cartel bargaining and monitoring: The role of information sharing. In Swedish Competition Authority (Ed.), *The pros and cons of information sharing* (pp. 43–82). Stockholm.
Lugli, E., Kocollari, U., & Nigrisoli, C. (2009). The codes of ethics of S&P/MIB Italian companies: An investigation of their contents and the main factors that influence their adoption. *Journal of Business Ethics, 84*(1, supplement), 33–45.

March, J. G., & Olsen, J. P. (1989). *Rediscovering institutions*. New York: Free Press.
McKinney, J. A., Emerson, T. L., & Neubert, M. J. (2010). The effects of ethical codes on ethical perceptions of actions toward stakeholders. *Journal of Business Ethics, 97*(4), 505–516.
Merchant, K. A., & Van der Stede, W. A. (2012). *Management control systems. Performance measurement, evaluation and incentives* (3rd ed.). Harlow, England: Financial Times Prentice Hal.
Nijhof, A., Cludts, S., Fisscher, O., & Laan, A. (2003). Measuring the implementation of codes of conduct. An assessment method based on a process approach of the responsible organization. *Journal of Business Ethics, 45*(1), 65–78.
O'Dwyer, B., & Madden, G. (2006). Ethical codes of conduct in Irish companies: A survey of code content and enforcement procedures. *Journal of Business Ethics, 63*(3), 217–236.
OECD Competition Committee. (2011). Roundtable on promoting compliance with Competition Law: Note by the delegation of Germany. Available from: http://www.bundeskartellamt.de/SharedDocs/Publikation/EN/Diskussions_Hintergrundpapiere/OECD_2011.06.20-Promoting_Compliance_Competition_Law.pdf?__blob=publicationFile&v=4. Accessed 21 January 2016.
O'Fallon, M. J., & Butterfield, K. D. (2005). A review of the empirical ethical decision-making literature: 1996–2003. *Journal of Business Ethics, 59*(4), 375–413.
Paine, L. S. (1994). Managing for organizational integrity. *Harvard Business Review, 72*(2), 106–117.
Palmer, D. E., & Zakhem, A. (2001). Bridging the gap between theory and practice: Using the 1991 Federal Sentencing Guidelines as a paradigm for ethics training. *Journal of Business Ethics, 29*(1), 77–84.
Parsons, T. (1937). *The structure of social action*. New York: McGraw-Hill.
Paulhus, D. L. (1984). Two-component models of socially desirable responding. *Journal of Personality and Social Psychology, 46*(3), 598–609.
Paulhus, D. L. (1991). Measurement and control of response bias. Balanced Inventory of Desirable Responding (BIDR). In J. P. Robinson, P. R. Shaver, & L. S. Wrightsman (Eds.), *Measures of personality and social psychological attitudes* (pp. 17–59). New York: Academic Press.
Pitt, H. L., & Groskaufmanis, K. A. (1990). Minimizing corporate civil and criminal liability: A second look at corporate codes of conduct. *Georgetown Law Journal, 78*, 1559–1654.
Rodríguez-Garavito, C. A. (2005). Global governance and labor rights: Codes of conduct and anti-sweatshop struggles in global apparel factories in Mexico and Guatemala. *Politics & Society, 33*(2), 203–233.
Rottig, D., & Heischmidt, K. A. (2007). The importance of ethical training for the improvement of ethical decision-making: Evidence from Germany and the United States. *Journal of Teaching in International Business, 18*(4), 5–35.
Rottig, D., Koufteros, X., & Umphress, E. (2011). Formal infrastructure and ethical decision making: An empirical investigation and implications for supply management. *Decision Sciences, 42*(1), 163–204.
Ruiz, P., Martinez, R., Rodrigo, J., & Diaz, C. (2015). Level of coherence among ethics program components and its impact on ethical intent. *Journal of Business Ethics, 128*(4), 725–742.
Sampson, R. J., & Laub, J. H. (1995). *Crime in the making*. Harvard: Harvard University Press.
Sanderson, G. R., & Varner, I. I. (1984). What's wrong with corporate codes of conduct? *Management Accounting, 64*(7), 28–35.
Schlaefli, A., Rest, J. R., & Thoma, S. J. (1985). Does moral education improve moral judgment? A meta-analysis of intervention studies using the Defined Issues Test. *Review of Educational Research, 55*(3), 319–352.
Scholz, J. T., & Lubell, M. (1998). Trust and taxpaying: Testing the heuristic approach to collective action. *American Journal of Political Science, 42*(2), 398–417.
Schwartz, M. S. (2004). Effective corporate codes of ethics: Perception of code users. *Journal of Business Ethics, 55*(4), 323–343.
Simons, R. (1995). *Levers of control: How managers use innovative control systems to drive strategic renewal*. Boston: Harvard Business School Press.

Sims, R. R. (1991). The institutionalization of organizational ethics. *Journal of Business Ethics, 10*(7), 493–506.
Sims, R. R. (2009). Toward a better understanding of organizational efforts to rebuild reputation following an ethical scandal. *Journal of Business Ethics, 90*(4), 453–472.
Sims, R. R., & Brinkmann, J. (2003). Enron ethics (or: culture matters more than codes). *Journal of Business Ethics, 45*(3), 243–256.
Singh, J. B. (2006). Ethics programs in Canada's largest corporations. *Business and Society Review, 111*(2), 119–136.
Singh, J. B. (2011). Determinants of the effectiveness of corporate codes of ethics: An empirical study. *Journal of Business Ethics, 101*(3), 385–395.
Singh, J., Svensson, G., Wood, G., & Callaghan, M. (2011). A longitudinal and cross-cultural study of the contents of codes of ethics of Australian, Canadian and Swedish corporations. *Business Ethics: A European Review, 20*(1), 103–119.
Sokol, D. D. (2012). Cartels, corporate compliance, and what practitioners really think about enforcement. *Antitrust Law Journal, 78*(1), 201–240.
Stevens, B. (2004). The ethics of the US business executive: A study of perceptions. *Journal of Business Ethics, 54*(2), 163–171.
Stevens, J. M., Steensma, H. K., Harrison, D. A., & Cochran, P. L. (2005). Symbolic or substantive document? The influence of ethics codes on financial executives' decisions. *Strategic Management Journal, 26*(2), 181–195.
Stöber, T., Kotzian, P., Weißenberger, B. E., & Hoos, F. (2015). *One size fits all – but not all the time: Experimental evidence on the effectiveness of codes of conduct in decision dilemmas.* Paper presented at the 38th EAA Annual Congress, University of Strathclyde Glasgow, 28–30 April 2015.
Strobel, F. (2001). Was bringt ein unternehmensweiter Ethik-Kodex? *Der Schweizer Treuhänder, 75*(5), 413–418.
Tenbrunsel, A. E., Smith-Crowe, K., & Umphress, E. E. (2003). Building houses on rocks: The role of the ethical infrastructure in organizations. *Social Justice Research, 16*(3), 285–307.
Treviño, L. K. (1986). Ethical decision making in organizations: A person-situation interactionist model. *Academy of Management Review, 11*(3), 601–617.
Treviño, L. K., & Nelson, K. A. (2014). *Managing business ethics. Straight talk about how to do it right* (6th ed.). New York: Wiley.
Tyler, T. R. (1990). *Why people obey the law.* New Haven, London: Yale University Press.
Valentine, S., & Barnett, T. (2003). Ethics code awareness, perceived ethical values, and organizational commitment. *Journal of Personal Selling & Sales Management, 23*(4), 359–367.
Valentine, S., & Fleischman, G. (2002). Ethics codes and professionals' tolerance of societal diversity. *Journal of Business Ethics, 40*(4), 301–312.
Veljanovski, C. (2007). Cartel fines in Europe. *World Competition, 30*(1), 65–86.
Warren, D. E., Gaspar, J. P., & Laufer, W. S. (2014). Is formal ethics training merely cosmetic? A study of ethics training and ethical organizational culture. *Business Ethics Quarterly, 24*(1), 85–117.
Weaver, G. R. (1995). Does ethics code design matter? Effects of ethics code rationales and sanctions on recipients' justice perceptions and content recall. *Journal of Business Ethics, 14*(5), 367–385.
Weber, J., & Fortun, D. (2005). Ethics and compliance officer profile: Survey, comparison, and recommendations. *Business and Society Review, 110*(2), 97–115.
Wieland, J. (2015). Ethical codes, professional: Business codes. In J. D. Wright (Ed.), *International encyclopedia of the social & behavioral sciences* (2nd ed., Vol. 8, pp. 21–24). Amsterdam: Elsevier.
Winkler, N., Kroh, M., & Spiess, M. (2006). Entwicklung einer deutschen Kurzskala zur zweidimensionalen Messung von sozialer Erwünschtheit. DIW (Ed.). Berlin. Discussion papers 579. Available from: https://www.diw.de/documents/publikationen/73/diw_01.c.44281.de/dp579.pdf. Accessed 10 January 2016.
Wotruba, T. R., Chonko, L. B., & Loe, T. W. (2001). The impact of ethics code familiarity on manager behavior. *Journal of Business Ethics, 33*(1), 59–69.

Chapter 5
Compliance and Incentive Contracts

Daniel Herold

Abstract In the discussion of competition law compliance programmes it is important to address the internal delegation problems within the firm. Hard core cartels are typically triggered by economic developments having a strong impact on industry profits, and are formed on a higher level of the firm's hierarchy. One way to control managerial behaviour is by designing incentive contracts. This chapter argues that compliance measures such as training programmes or internal monitoring should be complemented by an appropriate design of incentive pay. Insights from the economic literature on agency problems and cartels show that particularly profit thresholds that must be met to receive a bonus and bonus caps have a crucial impact on managerial incentives to engage in collusive activity. Properly designed incentive contracts complement other compliance measures and improve deterrence.

5.1 Introduction

EU and US cartel statistics reveal that the level of fines imposed on firms due to violations of antitrust laws has been rising since about 2005, with the highest fine imposed on a single firm amounting to €715 million in the Carglass case.[1] Competition law compliance programmes are one way for firms to avoid illegal conduct of this kind. The European Commission defines compliance as 'respecting the law. In the competition field, it means business proactively respecting competition rules'.[2] Thus, a compliance programme should involve measures that ensure a firm's law abiding behaviour by avoiding violations of antitrust laws, especially collusive behaviour. To do so, these programmes involve training programmes,

[1]See http://goo.gl/IZshkg.

[2]This definition is taken from the European Commission (DG Comp), see http://goo.gl/8l1lqT (last visit: October 13, 2015).

D. Herold (✉)
Department of Economics, Justus Liebig University Giessen, VWL I - Industrial Organization, Regulation and Antitrust, Giessen, Germany
e-mail: Daniel.herold@wirtschaft.uni-giessen.de

J. Paha (ed.), *Competition Law Compliance Programmes*,
DOI 10.1007/978-3-319-44633-2_5

screening measures such as audits, whistle-blowing hotlines, and top-management dedication (OFT 2010).

These measures are effective in deterring misconduct like information exchange or collusive agreements arising from a deficit in employees' knowledge of antitrust laws. To improve the effectiveness of a compliance programme when it comes to hard core cartels, these measures could be complemented by methods that explicitly target higher level managers. This concerns not only members of the board of directors but also managers of departments such as marketing or sales. Those managers are to a large extent responsible for initiating and controlling hard core cartels (Stephan 2009). One can also expect hard core cartels to be carefully planned as they often arise from developments affecting all firms in an industry. In Sect. 5.2, I review case evidence suggesting that price fixing is a rational business strategy. In the light of this finding, the economic principal-agent literature analysing cartels offers insights on how to improve competition law compliance programmes especially when it comes to controlling the conduct of managers further up in a firm's hierarchy.

A crucial question that arises in this context is whether a cartel pays off for the firm and/or for the parties responsible for managing the collusive agreements. A major driver of a cartel's profitability is the expected level of corporate fines. If fines are expected to be lower than the additional profits realised in a cartel, it will pay off for the firms to engage in collusive conduct. Many cartels raise the firms' profits substantially as average overcharges of cartels are about 30 % (Connor and Bolotova 2006).

It is an open question whether fines are high enough to be deterrent. Connor (2004) argues that fines are too low to effectively deter collusive conduct in the European Union. Veljanovski (2007) supports this finding even after the increase in expected fines that resulted from the update of the fining guidelines in 2006.[3]

Even if one assumes that fines deter collusive behaviour, there will still be a delegation problem. Despite the fact that the firm as a whole might lose from collusion, it can still pay off for the firms' decision makers to engage in collusive activity. These decision makers are typically found on a higher level in a firm's hierarchy (Harrington 2006). They might, for instance, want to save on working effort by colluding with their competitors. And they would not necessarily be deterred by sanctions imposed in the future as they may expect to already have left the firm when the cartel is detected and fined, thus not experiencing the impact of the fines themselves (Stephan 2009). In economics, the resulting delegation problem is referred to as a principal-agent problem. For example, shareholders (the so-called principal) delegate a CEO (the agent) to run the firm. In the present chapter, I will mainly use the terms principal and agent as placeholders. The principal might also be the head of the marketing or human resource department

[3]For an extensive review of fines and other components of the European Commission's decisions, see Carree et al. (2010).

who hires a sales representative (agent). Similarly, a department manager might want to ensure law-abiding behaviour while a sales agent prefers to collude.

This chapter explores the delegation problem described above and reveals potential pitfalls for compliance. In Sect. 5.2.1, I describe the economic circumstances of cartel formation. Section 5.2.2 examines measures currently employed as elements of competition law compliance programmes. An overview of the economic literature on agency problems can be found in Sect. 5.3, where a focus has been put on literature studying cartels. Implications for antitrust law compliance will be derived from economic theory. Section 5.4 concludes.

5.2 Compliance Programmes and Cartel Formation

5.2.1 Drivers of Cartel Formation

Violations of antitrust laws are acts of corporate crime. An individual takes an illegal action that harms society while the wrongdoer is liable for the misconduct. The individual violating the laws might be a manager who colludes with his/her competitors. 'Society' in this case comprises the customers damaged because of higher prices. In the case of cartels, also the firm, i.e. its shareholders and stakeholders may suffer from cartel fines in case of detection. Antitrust law violations are thus related to other types of white-collar crime such as bribery, fraud or forgery.

In economics, the concept of utilitarianism is almost always applied when examining the decision-making process of the individual: the manager tries to maximise his/her utility by comparing the perceived benefits and costs of his respective action. The same rationale applies to illegal actions.

One of the most influential ideas in the field of the economics of crime was developed by Nobel laureate Gary Becker. According to Becker (1968), a manager will break the law if the expected benefits outweigh the expected costs of an illegal action. Costs may include individual fines, reputational damage or foregone bonuses. Benefits might include higher bonus payments in case of non-detection, promotion or lower working effort (see Sect. 5.3). Hence, an individual who is about to decide whether to collude or not faces a problem of uncertainty: he/she might be detected when breaking the law. However, the probability of detection as well as personal fines might be unknown. Furthermore, a manager has to take into account being sued by the firm itself when the violation is detected externally.[4] When evaluating this problem from a compliance perspective, it should be kept in mind that the decision makers might substantially underestimate the probability of detection. This is typically referred to as *hubris* (Murphy and Kolasky 2012). Even if cartel fines are deterrent, a manager might still engage in collusive activity if

[4]In a recent bribery case, Siemens sued a former member of its board for not having stopped and reported internally detected misconduct (see http://goo.gl/zemslQ).

he/she expects not to be caught. Because of the problem of hubris it is important to control managerial behaviour through channels other than fines.

Based on economic theory, a cartel will form if the expected benefit for all persons involved is higher in the cartel than in competition. Not only must the managers of firms *A* and *B* be willing to start illegal communications, but also no subordinate or superior who must have any incentive to blow the whistle or stop the conduct in any other way. For instance, Harrington (2006) describes the problem of sales agents being uninformed about the cartel and, thus, deviating from the agreements by being too ambitious in their efforts to make sales.

Although it is difficult to reconstruct who in a firm was informed about a particular illegal agreement at a specific point in time, Harrington (2006) as well as Stephan (2009) suggest that managers at a high level of a firm's hierarchy are involved. This includes CEOs, Vice Presidents or managers of departments such as sales or marketing.

It is crucial to determine the benefits and costs of the respective individuals involved in the cartel. Knowing about these costs and benefits may help to stop collusive activity already at the formation stage, which effectively prevents the firm from being sanctioned later-on. It will be explained in Sect. 5.3 that managers' remuneration is often connected to a firm's profits because the principal expects that such incentive scheme influences managerial behaviour. Therefore, understanding the economic conditions that affect the firm's profits and thus managers' incentive to collude is crucial for setting up an optimal compliance programme.

From a firm's (i.e., the principal's) perspective, a cartel is profitable if the discounted excess profits generated by the cartel exceed the expected fines, litigation costs and other costs such as reputational damages. Additionally, a cartel will only be stable if no firm has an incentive to deviate from the collusive agreement. For instance, it can secretly undercut the prices set by rivals in the cartel (Stigler 1964). In the short-run, a deviator typically earns higher profits than the other cartel firms. These other firms might decide to never trust the deviator again in a sense that collusion will not be re-established. Therefore, a deviator must take into account earning lower profits after a deviation than in compared to the case when the cartel would still exist. If a firm does not value future profits highly, a cartel will not be stabilised because the temptation to deviate from a collusive agreement is too strong. This problem will be explained in more detail in Sect. 5.3.

To shed light on the firms' expected gains from collusion, I will now examine the circumstances under which cartels are actually formed. Although the theoretical literature on cartel formation in Industrial Organisation is quite scarce,[5] case evidence shows that economic shocks, i.e. unexpected events influencing industry profits, are the most important triggers of collusion. In their case study, Grout and

[5]See e.g. d'Aspremont et al. (1983) and Prokop (1999).

Sonderegger (2005) reveal that in some cases a serious decrease in the firms' profitability preceded a cartel. Reasons for the negative impact on their profitability include demand instability[6] and excess capacities. Cartels may also be established in response to unexpected economic events influencing the firms (Herold and Paha 2015). Interestingly, those events can trigger cartel formation not only if they lower demand but sometimes also if they raise demand. This is because a cartel might be considered the most promising way to benefit from such favourable conditions. The following case is an example for a positive shock that, through different channels, led to a cartel in the industry.

The plasterboards case (COMP/E-1/37.152) illustrates the connection between cartel formation and the firms' profits quite well.[7] By the time the cartel was formed, the suppliers' profitability was low despite an increase in demand (European Commission 2002, par. 52–73). Other things being equal, the latter can be seen as a positive development for the supply side of the industry. However, prior to the cartel, overcapacities resulted from an overestimation of the increase in demand for the product (ibid., par. 72). This expansion of production capacities led to a downward pressure on prices. As a consequence, the firms' profits decreased. According to the official documentation provided by the European Commission (ibid., par. 55–56), a member of the cartel stated that the firms colluded with the objective to stop a 'ruinous price war'. Additionally, this member described a 'bleak outlook' for the industry.

Given this information, one can expect that the firms' managers tried to find ways to improve the situation. One way to seemingly solve problems connected to, e.g. overcapacities or a shrinking demand is to allocate market shares through a cartel. It is a firm's management that in those situations is responsible for finding ways to secure a certain level of profitability. As outlined above, a manager has to figure out whether it will pay off to break the laws by colluding with the firm's competitors, or whether there are other ways to improve a firm's situation. The question is who benefits most from collusion. The important point from a compliance perspective is to make sure that it does not pay off for the manager even if it pays off for the firm. Potentially, a manager has to choose among different alternatives which are all damaging to either one or the other party. As argued above, if his/her income, social status or other benefits are based on the firm's profits, he/she might take illegal actions that harm society with certainty but only have negative consequences for the firm or manager if such conduct is detected by an authority. In this context, it may be questioned whether fines, by the time they are imposed on the firm, have an effect on the manager who might not be working for the firm anymore once the cartel is detected and sanctioned (Stephan 2009).

---

[6]Theoretical findings in the theory of collusion with respect to demand fluctuations are manifold. Some relevant papers are Green and Porter (1984), Rotemberg and Saloner (1986), Haltiwanger and Harrington (1991), Staiger and Wolak (1992), Fabra (2006) and Paha (2013).

[7]See: http://ec.europa.eu/competition/antitrust/cases/dec_docs/37152/37152_72_1.pdf.

5.2.2 Implications for Compliance Programmes

In the light of the findings of Sect. 5.2.1, typical compliance measures may not be sufficient to prevent managers from colluding. In the following, potential weaknesses of training programmes, whistle-blowing hotlines and audits will be addressed.

Antitrust training informs the employees about the Do's and Don'ts of antitrust law. This facilitates the prevention of misconduct resulting from a lack of knowledge about antitrust laws and, in combination with whistle-blowing hotlines, also helps to reveal violations of antitrust laws performed by other employees. Thus, training programmes are an essential feature of compliance programmes (OFT 2010). However, Stephan (2009) describes that those involved in a cartel often know about the illegality of their actions. This can be inferred from their efforts to generate as little evidence of their involvement as possible. This holds true even for employees at lower levels of the hierarchy, e.g. marketing personnel. In their case study, Ashton and Pressey (2012) describe how cartels were trying to camouflage their activities and meetings, and that marketing personnel was involved in these conspiracies. Training programmes might not ensure full compliance with antitrust laws if some wrongdoers already know about the illegality of such conduct but are still not deterred from breaking the law. Therefore, training programmes should be complemented by further measures to prevent illegal activity more effectively.

Auditing, as another pillar of competition law compliance programmes, helps to acquire information that can make leniency applications possible by screening documents and communication devices (emails etc.) of employees who have pricing and sales responsibilities (Stephan 2009). When evidence is found, further steps have to be taken to stop and to report the cartel. However, if violating the laws is in the interest of the firm, an executive having evidence of cartel conduct might not always have an incentive to stop it and to report it to the authorities. Therefore, auditing alone can hardly prevent collusive activities altogether. The same applies to whistle-blowing hotlines. For example, an employee's incentive to report misconduct may be reduced substantially if the employee expects internal or external sanctions (such as dismissal or damage claims) for revealing misconduct (Near and Dworkin 1998).

At this point, an additional problem has to be mentioned that confines the effectiveness of internal fines, screening and incentive schemes, namely the discretion of managers. For instance, Bebchuk and Fried (2003) describe the problem that managers can basically control and regulate themselves rather than being supervised by others. If a high level manager has a chance to avoid any negative internal consequences for himself, he/she may also do so. To overcome this problem, either an official authority has to interfere or there has to be an independent firm-internal entity that can impose sanctions within a firm despite resistance from top-level management. These are organisational and legal problems that need to be solved in the future.

These considerations suggest that the effectiveness of compliance programmes can be improved if the measures just described are complemented by a tool that prevents specifically top-level management from colluding. Appropriately designed payment schemes can be one such tool as they help to align managers' incentives and actions with the incentives and interests of the shareholders.

5.3 Incentive Contracts

One important instrument for controlling managerial behaviour is an incentive contract. In this chapter, I focus on any type of direct and monetary incentive pay based on performance. The payments are not stock-based and do not include other benefits such as promotion unless stated otherwise. I will argue that for managers, the design of incentive payments can have a strong impact on the propensity to collude. The following section captures some basic findings of the literature on incentive pay and agency problems and highlights relevant factors when it comes to cartels. Ross (1973) defines agency problems as follows:

> . . . an agency problem has arisen between two (or more) parties when one, designated as the agent, acts for, on behalf of, or as representative for the other, designated the principal, in a particular domain of decision problems.

Uncertainty about the type of the agent (adverse selection) or actions the agent has taken (moral hazard) typically lead to outcomes where both parties could be better off if they had been fully informed about the type or action. As explained below, these actions may include effort or illegal, collusive behaviour. In this chapter, I focus on moral hazard problems prevalent in a compliance context. Concerning the example just outlined, the agent's choice whether to communicate with a competitor is not perfectly observable to the principal. The principal can control the agent despite the non-observability of his/her actions by designing the agent's remuneration properly.

Although this problem seems to be quite abstract, real-life applications are manifold. For instance, it is impossible for the shareholders of a large enterprise to continuously and perfectly observe managerial effort. A manager even needs some discretion because he/she has to be able to react to unexpected (and uncontracted) events affecting the firm. Aligning the incentives of both parties is difficult and an incentive contract is one way to do so. In the following, I will first give a short literature review on the topic and then turn to some selected works that I consider directly relevant for compliance.

Jensen and Meckling (1976) were among the first to break up the assumption of the firm being a 'black box'.[8] They provide a theory of the firm in the light of the internal conflict arising from the separation of ownership and control. Selected

[8]There is also earlier work analysing the internal operation of a firm and contracts, e.g. Berhold (1971) and the book of Barnard, originally published in 1938 as well as the work of Herbert Simon in the 1950s.

problems in a firm-related context such as exerting optimal effort, choosing the optimal capital structure, insurance problems or breaking the laws, can be broken down to one principal delegating a task to one or more agents. It is thus reasonable to take a closer look at this general theory.

Suppose there is an outcome X that can be increased by the agent's action a, e.g. working effort, but is also subject to external influence outside of the agent's control θ. The principal benefits from higher values of X and the agent's utility decreases for higher values of a, i.e., the agent incurs costs of exerting effort. As the principal can observe neither effort a nor the external shock θ, the agent bears some risk: If payments w are (positively) based on the observable outcome X, a 'bad' realisation of θ that is outside the scope of the agent's efforts would decrease his remuneration substantially although the agent exerted high effort.

In a shareholder-manager relationship, X could be profits and a managerial effort. In the context of compliance, the set of the agent's possible actions not only covers effort but also law violations. The state of nature θ could in this case be market demand or the overall state of the business cycle.[9] Ignoring factors such as potential job loss and intrinsic motivation, paying a fixed wage typically leads to a situation where the agent exerts minimal effort as he/she will not benefit from higher effort levels. On the other hand, leaving the agent with a large share of realised profits is not in the principal's interest who would have to provide high remuneration. Designing the most efficient type of contract given different settings of uncertainty and observability of a and θ as well the risk attitude of both the principal and the agent are the subject of a huge strand of literature in economics.[10]

A central issue in these theoretical papers is to develop a type of contract that generates a solution which is as close as possible to the first-best effort levels that could be contracted upon if effort was observable. Good overviews of the problems, possible solutions and some relevant literature can be found in the textbooks of Laffont and Martimort (2002) and Bolton and Dewatripont (2005).

Now that the basic ideas of principal-agent problems are outlined, I will present the concepts of three papers that analyse hidden action and cartels, namely, Fershtman et al. (1991), Aubert (2009) and Herold (2016).[11] The basic idea of these papers is similar to the one just described. There is an owner of the firm—the principal—who delegates the agent to run the firm. The agent can, among other things, decide whether to collude to compete. The principal cannot directly observe the agent's decision. However, the principal can control it by designing incentive schemes.

---

[9]For instance, Bagwell and Staiger (1997) analyse cartel stability over the business cycle from a firm's perspective. Future research could examine how their analysis translates into a principal-agent relationship.

[10]Some important papers are Arrow (1970), Pauly (1974), Harris and Raviv (1979), Shavell (1979), Holmström (1979), Grossman and Hart (1983) and Innes (1990).

[11]The selected articles do not provide a complete overview of the problem. I refer to these papers due to their relevance for our topic.

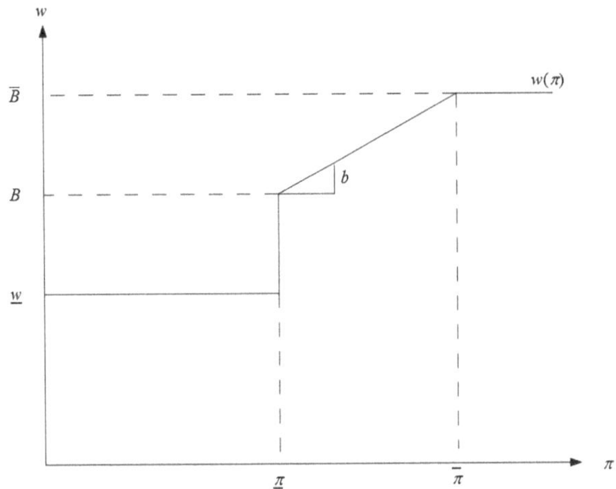

Fig. 5.1 Typical incentive pay according to Murphy (1999)

Before turning to the analysis of collusion and contracts, I will first describe the typical composition of incentive pay which is commonly observed in reality. Managerial compensation normally consists of payments w positively related to the firm's profits π by conditioning wages on accounting values such as, for instance, earnings before interest and taxes or sales (EBIT). The relationship between profits and payments w, however, can be non-linear: wages are constant when profits are below a certain value referred to as the profit threshold $\underline{\pi}$.

Murphy (1999) provides an overview of incentive pay typically employed in large companies. As seen in Fig. 5.1, these schemes consist of three ranges depending on realised profits π. In the range $\pi \in [0, \underline{\pi})$, profits are below the threshold $\underline{\pi}$ and wages are constant at a fixed level $\underline{w}$, referred to as the base wage. When meeting the threshold $\underline{\pi}$, the agent receives a bonus $B - \underline{w}$ which can be seen as the minimum bonus payment. There is a profit cap $\overline{\pi}$. Above this cap, remuneration is constant at $\overline{B}$ which thus constitutes the maximum earnings a manager can achieve in the respective firm. The range from $\underline{\pi}$ to $\overline{\pi}$ is referred to as the incentive zone where bonuses are increasing in π.[12] In Fig. 5.1, the agent earns a percentage $b \in (0,1)$ of profits and remuneration is linear from $\underline{\pi}$ to $\overline{\pi}$. However, one can think of any increasing function $w(\pi)$ in the range $\pi \in [\underline{\pi}, \overline{\pi}]$.

A commonly used application of that scheme is the so-called 80/120 plan where bonuses are paid when 80 % of a certain (profit) target is realised and capped at 120 % of the target (Murphy 1999). As there is a strong connection between the profit target and the threshold $\underline{\pi}$, I use the terms synonymously.

Based on a variant of the scheme outlined above Fershtman et al. (1991) show that internal delegation in combination with a proper incentive scheme solves the cartel's stability problem. To see this stability problem, consider first a situation

[12] One example of a firm that employs a comparable remuneration scheme is ThyssenKrupp, see https://www.thyssenkrupp.com/en/investor/verguetungsbericht.html.

without delegation. Two symmetric and myopic firms 1 and 2 can earn profits C in case of competition. In a cartel, both firms realise profits K with $K > C$. If one firm deviates from the collusive agreement, it will earn profits D. Defection yields the highest possible profits while the other firm gets tricked and earns T only. It holds that $D > K > C \geq T$. In this game, the only Nash Equilibrium is that both firms deviate. They then realise profits C.[13] In the example, if firm 1 chooses to collude with the intent to realise collusive profits K, firm 2 will react accordingly and deviate from the collusive agreement, realising profits $D > K$. Firm 1, in this case, would be tricked and realise profits $T < K$ only. Since firm 1 knows that if it colludes, firm 2 will deviate, firm 1 will never choose to cooperate with firm 2. The same rationale applies to firm 2. The result is a so-called Prisoner's Dilemma: the efficient outcome for the firms, i.e. being in a cartel, cannot be established because the temptation to deviate from the efficient strategy is too strong.[14]

Given the setup just described, Fershtman et al. (1991) break up the assumption that the firm is a 'black-box'. Instead, the owner (principal) hires a manager (agent) to play the cartel game on his behalf. The agent is paid according to an incentive scheme. By introducing a target compensation function comprising a profit threshold of $\underline{\pi} = K$, it is possible that a cartel arises in equilibrium.[15] Given $\underline{\pi} = K$, if profits exceed K the agent will earn a constant total remuneration $B > 0$, otherwise the agent receives a payment of zero.[16] A crucial assumption is that the contracts are common knowledge. Both agents cannot gain from deviation because their payment does not change, anyway, and they know that the other firm's agent will want to hold on to the collusive agreement as well. Hence, by simply delegating the decision to collude to a different person, the firm's owners can commit to the cartel agreement. This model illustrates the idea of how the principal can control the agent's behaviour by a properly designed incentive scheme. Fershtman et al. (1991) show how a cartel can be stabilised. From their framework it is also straightforward to see how to induce the opposite behaviour and to destabilise the cartel: set a positive fixed wage $\underline{w} > 0$ to ensure that the agent accepts the contract and a profit threshold of $\underline{\pi} = D$, as this would turn deviation into the dominant strategy, again.

[13]In a Nash Equilibrium, no player (here: firm) has an incentive to unilaterally choose a different strategy given the other firms play their equilibrium strategies.

[14]The term 'efficient' in this case covers allocative efficiency. In a cartel, both firms realise profits K. Higher profits are only possible if one firm deviates: however, the other firm is worse off in this case. The profits of one firm cannot be increased without decreasing the profits of another firm.

[15]To be more precise, the authors (ibid.) show that collusion is a subgame perfect Nash Equilibrium. Subgame perfection is a refinement of the original Nash Equilibrium concept. If the latter is subgame perfect, it does not contain any non-credible threats. In most games it is important to determine an optimal reaction for every player to any choice of the other players (best response). Subgame perfection requires every possible action to be a best response, even those who are not played (threats).

[16]It also has to hold that $B < K - C$ because otherwise the principal would not have an incentive to offer the contract.

In Aubert (2009), the agent can—in addition to choosing the market strategy—exert effort. This is an important extension of the ideas of Fershtman et al. (1991) because it is one of the actual intentions behind incentive pay to promote the incentives to exert effort. Higher effort levels increase expected profits in all situations, i.e., D, K, C and T are increasing in effort. However, exerting effort is exhausting and, therefore, costly for the agent. As in Fershtman et al. (1991), the agent is paid according to an incentive scheme which in Aubert (2009) is unknown to the competitor. Similar to Fershtman et al. (1991), Aubert (2009) reveals a major problem of the profit threshold $\underline{\pi}$: Originally designed to incentivise agents to exert effort, it also fosters collusion. The reason for this is straightforward: by colluding with his/her competitors the agent can save on working effort. He/she can meet any high profit target by exerting costly effort. Collusion allows the agent to reduce this effort. To avoid cartelisation, the principal has to accept a lower effort level and, thus, set a lower profit target. The downside of lower profit targets or thresholds are decreasing effort levels that lessen internal efficiency.

Herold (2016) also investigates effort incentives and the incentives to engage in illegal activity, e.g. collusion, in a principal-agent model. In the paper, the agent is incentivised according to a simplified version of the Murphy-style incentive contract just described (Murphy 1999). As one important insight, Herold (2016) reveals that not only very high profit thresholds incentivise the agent to collude but also very low profit thresholds. In the model, cartel formation is not necessarily successful. The reason for this assumption is, firstly, that there might be some distrust between the parties involved in the formation process of the cartel (Harrington and Chang, 2009). Secondly, there is empirical evidence provided by Connor and Bolotova (2006, p. 1128) that firms' collusion can be unprofitable. This assumption gives rise to a situation in which the firm remains in a competitive market environment and is exposed to antitrust fines because the agent's choice to collude did not result in a profitable cartel.

Considering how corporate fines can be taken into account when calculating whether the profit target is met helps to see the consequence of this outcome.[17] Suppose a bonus B will be paid when the profit target $\underline{\pi}$ is met, and the agent knows the value of the profit target when deciding whether to collude or to obey the laws. An authority imposes fines F. The probability of detection is ρ. As defined above, a firm's profits in competition are denoted by C and in a (profitable) cartel denoted by K. Assume that expected corporate fines ρF are not high enough to deter collusion, i.e. $C < K - \rho F$ holds. A high profit target in this case would be $\underline{\pi}_{\mathrm{H}} = K - \rho F > C$. Collusion is fostered because, other things being equal, the agent will only receive a bonus payment in a cartel. A medium profit target allows for bonuses in a competitive market environment ($\underline{\pi}_{\mathrm{M}} = C < K - \rho F$). This makes law-abiding behaviour more attractive; now the agent can earn a bonus even without colluding with his

[17] This is a slight modification of the original model which also incorporates a stochastic influence of effort on profits. I abstract from the stochastics arising from the state of nature θ outlined above in order to focus on the intuition. Note that the results in the original paper are less straightforward.

competitors. If cartel formation is not successful, the firm will remain in a competitive market state but is exposed to fines. Expected profits in this case are $C - \rho F$.[18] Compared to a medium target, a low profit threshold $\underline{\pi}_{\mathrm{L}} = C - \rho F < C < K - \rho F$ makes collusion more attractive. With a low target, the agent might decide to collude and expect to always earn a bonus even if cartel formation is not successful. If a medium profit target was in place, the agent could not earn a bonus in case of an unsuccessful cartel. Compared to a medium target, a low target thus provides a 'back-up' option for the agent as he/she can also earn a bonus even if collusion fails to be effective. The best way to deter the agent's misbehaviour, thus, is to have an intermediate profit target in place which is realisable with proper effort in a competitive environment.

From a practitioner's perspective, therefore, it is important to determine the target values with care. One could for example use accounting data to come up with a reasonable estimate of a firm's profits that are realisable with proper managerial effort but without violating the laws. This requires a strong cooperation between different departments of a firm. Firstly, accounting data have to be provided and analysed to estimate potential future profits. Secondly, there has to be a general outlook on the future industry structure which might in turn be influenced by the business cycle. Thirdly, these data and estimates would have to be utilised to culminate in the final incentive contract. Fourthly, the contract should also account for other measures than EBIT or profits in the bonus calculations. For instance, a high number of sales or an increase in market shares could be rewarded separately because these tend to destabilise cartels (see e.g. Harrington 2006).

In both Aubert (2009) and Herold (2016), the role of individual fines are analysed as well, and it is shown that they are a proper tool to deter an agent from violating antitrust laws. Individual fines are consistent with antitrust laws because in many jurisdictions, an individual violating antitrust laws must expect sanctions such as monetary fines as in Germany or even imprisonment as in the US. Another aspect of individual fines is that the firms can potentially cut bonuses.[19]

The problem with fines is that, as on the level of the firms, their amount is crucial. A deterrent level is hard to determine and may strongly vary depending on individuals and firms. This problem could be mitigated if firms were in a position to impose sanctions. Because of their additional knowledge about their employees, they might be able to better determine a deterrent level of fines. This does of course not apply to imprisonment. However, depending on the respective jurisdiction, the firms' ability to punish employees may be limited (Polinsky and Shavell 1993). Additionally, as mentioned above, top-level management has to potentially impose

[18] In the paper, the agent can exert effort. When an attempt to collude failed, it is shown that profits are generally lower than if there was no collusion at all.

[19] For instance, in the LIBOR case bonuses of former bankers were cut or not paid at all. In one case, this process is the subject of lawsuits (see Bloomberg, http://goo.gl/qN43z1). One bank actually plans to use the bonus pool to pay the fines imposed by the authorities (see Financial Times, http://goo.gl/5A6I0z).

sanctions upon itself. Despite these problems, it would be much easier for a firm to ensure law-abiding behaviour of their employees if it was possible to impose deterrent individual penalties (Stephan 2009).

Besides incentive schemes offering direct payments connected to performance, manager's remuneration is often stock-based (Murphy 1999). Spagnolo (2000) offers a comprehensive analysis of the effect of these compensation schemes on the stability of collusion. He shows that many types of stock-based payment stabilise collusive agreements. The intuition behind this result is that if the stock market has perfect foresight, stock prices decrease after a deviation of a firm's manager. Hence, the incentive to deviate is lowered because there is no short-run gain any longer. Cartelisation is a long-term decision—as described in Sect. 5.2, firms have to be patient to stabilise a cartel—and long-term incentive plans, like stock-based payments, can have the perverse side-effect of actually fostering collusion. However, removing stock-based remuneration also loosens the agent's alignment with a firm's long-run performance. As explained above, a cartel can be seen as an illegal long-run investment that might be very profitable if it remains undetected. The question is whether removing stock-based remuneration to deter collusion outweighs the costs of possibly prohibiting other investments that pay off in the long run such as innovations, investments in new technologies or serving new markets.

In another influential paper, Spagnolo (2005) analyses the impact of bonus caps on collusive behaviour. When a bonus cap is chosen carefully, the incentives for a manager to deviate from a collusive agreement can be eliminated and collusion can be sustained more easily. The explanation is that if bonuses are capped at cartel profits $\overline{\pi}=K$, the agent cannot increase his remuneration by deviation. However, if collusion breaks down after a deviation, payments are lower than in a cartel because profits are below K and bonuses below their maximum value. Losses that occur in those periods thus outweigh the gains from deviation which are limited due to the cap.

In summary, both the profit target as well as the profit cap constitute parameters which can be expected to have a substantial impact on a manager's incentives to violate antitrust laws. A high profit target promotes collusive activity. If the target is so high that it can only be met in a cartel, the agent has a clear incentive to collude to receive a bonus payment (Fershtman et al. 1991). However, very low targets can also foster collusion because if cartel formation fails to be effective, the agent is provided with a back up to still earn a bonus (Herold 2016). Profit caps, on the contrary, should be high in order to provide the agent with an incentive to deviate from any collusive agreement and thus destabilise a collusive agreement (Spagnolo 2005). Stock-based payments may also have the negative side effect that they weaken an agent's incentives to deviate from a collusive agreement and, therefore, promote collusion (Spagnolo 2000). Imposing individual fines on the manager generally deters her/him from engaging in any collusive agreement (see e.g. Aubert 2009).

5.4 Conclusion

This chapter has shown the importance to take into account managerial incentives when designing competition law compliance programmes. Past international hard core cartel cases indicate that collusion is likely to be a planned business strategy. If a firm prefers to avoid being involved in a cartel, existing measures such as training programmes, monitoring and whistleblowing hotlines can be complemented by taking into account managerial incentives. This primarily involves the design of incentive pay.

It was shown that common features of managerial contracts originally designed to align the agent's incentives with those of the firm can have negative side effects on a firm's law-abiding behaviour. High profit targets for instance not only provide incentives to exert effort but also to engage in collusive activity and thereby actually saving on working effort (Aubert 2009). Also, profit targets that are too low might be problematic because if cartel formation is not successful or the cartel turns out not to be profitable, the agent can still earn a bonus, thus promoting illegal activity (Herold 2016). One intention of bonus caps is to limit 'excessive' managerial behaviour—however, they also eliminate the gains of deviating from a collusive agreement and thus stabilise collusion (Spagnolo 2000). The same argument applies to stock-based payments. In order to provide long-term incentives for managers, they limit the gains from deviation as stock-prices might decrease because of potential price wars following a cartel's breakdown (Spagnolo 2005).

Future research might offer solutions for incentive pay by dissolving the trade-off between motivating the agent to exert effort and deterring the agent from collusive behaviour and corporate crime in general. Based on the results presented in Sect. 5.3, it is important to determine the bonus thresholds and caps very carefully. As case evidence suggests (see Sect. 5.2), the overall development of the industry has to be taken into account. For instance, setting the same goals as in previous periods when a recession hits the market might put management under pressure and foster illegal actions. This requires a more intense cooperation between different departments in an enterprise, especially between internal accounting, internal auditing and the board of directors.

Moreover, when both the principal and the agent actually benefit from breaking the laws, ways have to be found to misalign the incentives of both parties. The crucial point is to maintain the incentives for agents to exert effort. These factors make it a complicated endeavour to design incentive contracts most appropriately. In the light of increasing corporate fines, the benefits of a rather imperfect contract in terms of effort incentives might still outweigh the costs of a more or less perfect effort contract that in the end fosters illegal behaviour.

References

Arrow, K. (1970). *Essays in the theory of risk-bearing*. Amsterdam: North-Holland Publishing Company.

Ashton, J., & Pressey, A. (2012). Who manages cartels? The role of sales and marketing managers within international cartels: Evidence from the European union 1990–2009. CCP Working Paper November 2012.

Aubert, C. (2009). Managerial effort incentives and market collusion. TSE Working Paper 09-127.

Bagwell, K., & Staiger, R. W. (1997). Collusion over the business cycle. *The RAND Journal of Economics, 28*(1), 82–106.

Bebchuk, L. A., & Fried, J. M. (2003). Executive compensation as an agency problem. *Journal of Economic Perspectives, 17*(3), 71–92.

Becker, G. (1968). Crime and punishment: An economic approach. *Journal of Political Economy, 76*(2), 169–217.

Berhold, M. (1971). A theory of linear profit-sharing incentives. *The Quarterly Journal of Economic, 85*(3), 460–482.

Bolton, P., & Dewatripont, M. (2005). *Contract theory*. Cambridge/London: MIT Press.

Carree, M., Günster, A., & Schinkel, M. P. (2010). European antitrust policy 1957–2004: an analysis of commission decisions. *Review of Industrial Organization, 36*(2), 97–131.

Connor, J. M. (2004). Global antitrust prosecutions of international cartels. Staff Paper No. 04-15, Purdue University.

Connor, J. M., & Bolotova, Y. (2006). Cartel overcharges: Survey and meta-analysis. *International Journal of Industrial Organization, 24*(6), 1109–1137.

D'Aspremont, C., Jacquemin, A., Gabszewicz, J., & Weymark, J. (1983). On the stability of collusive price leadership. *The Canadian Journal of Economics, 16*(1), 17–25.

European Commission (2002). Commission Decision of 27.11.02 relating to a proceeding under Article 81 of the EC Treaty, Case COMP/E-1/37.152 – Plasterboard. http://ec.europa.eu/competition/antitrust/cases/dec_docs/37152/37152_72_1.pdf

Fabra, N. (2006). Collusion with capacity constraints over the business cycle. *International Journal of Industrial Organization, 24*(1), 69–81.

Fershtman, C., Judd, K., & Kalai, E. (1991). Observable contracts: Strategic delegation and cooperation. *International Economic Review, 32*(3), 551–559.

Green, E. J., & Porter, R. H. (1984). Noncooperative collusion under imperfect price information. *Econometrica, 52*(1), 87–100.

Grossman, S. J., & Hart, O. D. (1983). An analysis of the principal-agent problem. *Econometrica, 51*(1), 7–45.

Grout, P., & Sonderegger, S. (2005). Predicting cartels. Office of Fair Trading OFT 773.

Haltiwanger, J., & Harrington, J. F. (1991). The impact of cyclical demand movements on collusive behavior. *The RAND Journal of Economics, 22*(1), 89–106.

Harrington, J. E. (2006). How do cartels operate? In *Foundations and trends in microeconomics*. Hannover: Now Publishers.

Harrington, J. E., & Chang, M. (2009). Modeling the birth and death of cartels with an application to evaluating competition policy. *Journal of the European Economic Association, 7*(6), 1400–1435.

Harris, M., & Raviv, A. (1979). Optimal incentive contracts with imperfect information. *Journal of Economic Theory, 20*, 231–259.

Herold, D. (2016). The impact of incentive pay and internal monitoring on corporate crime. Unpublished Working paper.

Herold, D., & Paha, J. (2015). Predicting cartel formation. Unpublished Working paper.

Holmström, B. (1979). Moral hazard and observability. *The Bell Journal of Economics, 10*(1), 74–91.

Innes, R. (1990). Limited liability and incentive contracting with ex-ante action choices. *Journal of Economic Theory, 52*(1), 45–67.

Jensen, M., & Meckling, W. H. (1976). Theory of the firm: Managerial behavior, agency costs and ownership structure. *Journal of Financial Economics, 3*(4), 305–360.
Laffont, J. J., & Martimort, D. (2002). *The theory of incentives*. New Jersey: Princeton University Press.
Murphy, K. J. (1999). Executive compensation. In O. C. Ashenfelter & D. Card (Eds.), *Handbook of labor economics* (Vol. 3, pp. 2485–2563). New York: Elsevier.
Murphy, K. J., & Kolasky, W. (2012). The role of anti-cartel compliance programs in preventing cartel behaviour. *Antitrust, 26*(2), 61–64.
Near, J. P., & Dworkin, T. M. (1998). Responses to legislative changes: Corporate whistleblowing policies. *Journal of Business Ethics, 17*(14), 1551–1561.
Office of Fair Trading. (2010). Global antitrust prosecutions of international cartels.
Paha, J. (2013). Cartel formation with endogenous capacity and demand uncertainty. MAGKS Working Paper No. 43-2013.
Pauly, M. (1974). Overinsurance and public provision of insurance: The roles of moral hazard and adverse selection. *The Quarterly Journal of Economics, 88*(1), 305–360.
Polinsky, A. M., & Shavell, S. (1993). Should employees be subject to fines and imprisonment given the existence of corporate liability? *International Review of Law and Economics, 13*(3), 239–257.
Prokop, J. (1999). Process of dominant cartel formation. *International Journal of Industrial Organization, 17*(2), 241–257.
Ross, S. A. (1973). The economic theory of agency: The principal's problem. *American Economic Review, 63*(2), 134–139.
Rotemberg, J. T., & Saloner, G. (1986). A supergame-theoretic model of price wars during booms. *The American Economic Review, 76*(3), 390–407.
Shavell, S. (1979). Risk sharing and incentives in the principal agent relationship. *The Bell Journal of Economics, 10*(1), 55–73.
Spagnolo, G. (2000). Stock-related compensation and product-market competition. *The RAND Journal of Economics, 31*(1), 22–42.
Spagnolo, G. (2005). Managerial incentives and collusive behaviour. *European Economic Review, 49*(6), 1501–1523.
Staiger, R. W., & Wolak, F. A. (1992). Collusive pricing with capacity constraints in the presence of demand uncertainty. *The RAND Journal of Economics, 23*(2), 203–220.
Stephan, A. (2009). Hear no evil, see no evil: Why antitrust compliance programmes may be ineffective at preventing cartels. CCP Working Paper 09-09.
Stigler, G. J. (1964). A theory of oligopoly. *The Journal of Political Economy, 72*(1), 44–61.
Veljanovski, C. (2007). Cartel fines in Europe – Law, practice and deterrence. *World Competition, 30*(1), 65–86.

Chapter 6
Antitrust Compliance and Abusive Behaviour

Ulrich Schwalbe

Abstract The economic literature on antitrust compliance has concentrated on cartels as the most serious competition law violation. There are, however, infringements of competition law in form of an abuse of a dominant position which have not yet been considered in detail in the economics literature on antitrust compliance. This chapter examines how a comprehensive antitrust compliance programme should deal with abusive behaviour. In a first step, such a programme should determine whether the firm under consideration holds a dominant position. This requires the definition of the relevant antitrust market and the assessment of the competitive conditions in this market. If the firm is found to be dominant, the second step of a compliance programme has to ensure that no exploitative or exclusionary practices are employed. While for exploitative abuses screens similar to those in cartel cases can be used, no simple and reliable screens for exclusionary behaviour have been devised yet. Instead, the "no economic sense" test that has been suggested as an administrable rule to identify exclusionary behaviour could be applied. Roughly speaking, this test requires that a firm is able to demonstrate that the conduct under consideration is rational for the firm absent a tendency to eliminate competition. In the digital economy particular problems arise with respect to the definition of the relevant market and the determination of dominance. This is mainly due to the two-sided nature of most platform markets. Also, new forms of abusive behaviour can emerge in the digital economy that are related to the user data a platform has collected.

The author is grateful to Georg Götz and Johannes Paha for helpful comments.

U. Schwalbe (✉)
Department of Economics, University of Hohenheim, Stuttgart, Germany
e-mail: ulrich.schwalbe@uni-hohenheim.de

J. Paha (ed.), *Competition Law Compliance Programmes*,
DOI 10.1007/978-3-319-44633-2_6

6.1 Introduction

Antitrust compliance has become an important subject of economic as well as legal research in the last decade. The economic literature on antitrust compliance however, has concentrated almost exclusively on one specific type of competition law infringement, the violation of the ban on cartels.[1] Firms in a cartel agree to limit competition by jointly setting the prices of their products, by assigning output quota or by dividing the market for example by region or with respect to the customer groups the firms serve. This leads to higher prices, lower quantities and also to a reduction of consumer surplus as well as a significant welfare loss. For this type of competition law violation, the literature has suggested several types of qualitative and empirical screens to detect cartels.[2] By using these screens, market conditions that are particularly favourable for the formation of cartels can be identified and the changes in market outcome due to a cartel can be detected. It has been pointed out in the antitrust compliance literature that empirical screens should be employed also within a firm to make compliance programmes robust (Abrantes-Metz et al. 2010).

The screens developed can be classified into structural screens and behavioural screens. Structural screens consider specific features of markets that are particularly favourable for the formation of cartels. Behavioural screens concentrate primarily on the price setting behaviour and the market outcome.[3] For example, an indicator of a cartel are prices above the competitive level where the competitive price level is determined according to suitable comparator markets, e.g. competitive markets in different geographic regions. Also, prices that are less volatile than under competitive conditions could indicate a cartel. A further cartel marker is given if price increases are observed more often than in a comparable competitive market. The economic rationale behind these screens is that cartels have an incentive to increase prices more often than competitive firms. In addition, higher moments of the distribution of the prices can be considered (von Blanckenburg et al. 2012). Also, purely mathematical tests that are based on the distribution of digits, for example Benford's law have been devised. If e.g., the distribution of digits in the bids made at an auction does not satisfy Benford's law, this could indicate that a bidding ring may have been formed.[4]

However, there is a second type of competition law violation that has hitherto not been considered in detail in the economic literature on antitrust compliance but which also can inflict significant damages on competitors, customers, suppliers and

---

[1] See for example the contribution by Abrantes-Metz and Sokol (2013) which, despite the title "Antitrust Corporate Governance and Compliance", only deals with cartels.

[2] See among others Arbantes-Metz (2013a, b), Abrantes-Metz and Sokol (2013), Abrantes-Metz et al. (2006), von Blanckenburg and Geist (2011), Harrington (2010), Sokol (2011).

[3] For a discussion of structural and empirical screens for detecting cartels see Harrington (2010).

[4] See Abrantes-Metz et al. (2013) for an application of Benford's law in the context of the Libor-cartel.

also final consumers. This is the abuse of a dominant position.[5] As abusive behaviour is also heavily fined by competition authorities, it is important for firms to have internal screens to make sure compliance takes place also with respect to this part of antitrust law. But not only a dominant firm itself should be interested in complying with antitrust law, but also firms that compete with dominant undertakings or are customers or suppliers of those firms have an interest in detecting abusive behaviour as they are entitled to claim damages if they suffered losses from this type of anticompetitive behaviour. Thus, for an effective antitrust compliance programme, the existing programmes, screens, and methods employed to detect and prevent cartels as well as other illegal horizontal or vertical agreements between firms should be complemented by screens that are able to detect and avoid all types of abuse of dominance. This would ensure that antitrust compliance programmes cover all types of competition law infringements and would contribute to a lawful behaviour of firms with respect to all aspects of competition law.

While a variety of screens for cartel detection has been devised, methods to detect and prevent abusive behaviour have, to the best of our knowledge, not yet been discussed in the economic literature on antitrust compliance. As there are important differences between the two types of competition law infringement, the methods to detect and avoid abusive behaviour will differ from the screens for detecting cartels.

This paper addresses some approaches to the problem of antitrust compliance with respect to abusive behaviour. The chapter is organised as follows: In Sect. 6.2 the different types of abusive behaviour, exploitative and exclusionary abuse are discussed. In Sect. 6.3, the problems of structural and behavioural screens for abusive behaviour are pointed out. Section 6.4 briefly addresses some aspects that relate to specific problems that arise in the digital economy, where in many cases platform markets have achieved a strong or even dominant market position and where new types of abusive behaviour might arise. Section 6.5 concludes.

6.2 Antitrust Compliance and Abusive Behaviour

In competition theory as well as in competition law, two different types of infringements are considered. First, anticompetitive agreements between firms as e.g. price fixing cartels or vertical agreements like resale price maintenance and secondly, the abuse of a dominant market position. Both types of competition law infringement aim at the reduction of competition to increase the profits of the firms involved in the infringement. Cartels try to directly reduce the competitive pressure that firms in the same market exert on each other. They are based on agreements between firms

[5] Actually, also an abusive behaviour of several firms that are jointly dominant is conceivable, e.g. where the members of a cartel agree to employ an exclusionary strategy to force a firm not participating in the cartel to exit the market. In this chapter the focus is on single firm dominance and abusive behaviour.

to limit competition and thus to increase the profits of the cartel members. Cartels may take different forms depending on the competitive variables that the firms agree upon. The most common forms are price fixing cartels and quota cartels. In the former case, cartels set prices directly while in the latter case, cartel members agree to limit production and thereby increase prices and profits. Other forms of cartels include market allocation cartels or, in case of auction markets, bidding rings. For a cartel, the central problem is to coordinate the behaviour of several firms and to solve the incentive problem to guarantee the internal as well as external stability of the cartel agreement. Cartels usually lead to severe allocative, productive, and dynamic inefficiencies in the form of prices that are significantly higher than in a competitive environment, by keeping inefficient firms in the market that would have to exit under competitive conditions and also by reducing investments in research and development. The latter type of cartel can lead to large welfare losses in particular in markets where firms mainly compete with innovations.

The other form of competition law violation is the abuse of a dominant position. In the economic as well as the legal literature, two different types of abusive behaviour are considered: First, the case of exploitative abuse where a firm charges excessive prices or uses strategies of price discrimination where different types of customers are charged different prices for the same product or service without any objective justification, i.e. higher transport costs for customers at specific locations, different costs of providing the service etc.[6] Here, similarly to a cartel, the dominant firm directly tries to increase its profits by charging excessive prices or to better exploit the willingness to pay by charging different prices to different customers.[7]

The second type of abusive behaviour is known as exclusionary abuse. Here, a dominant firm tries to improve its competitive position by reducing the competitive pressure that is exerted by rivals by weakening their competitive position and not by entering into an agreement with these firms. This objective can be achieved by limiting the growth of competitors, by marginalising them or to force them to exit the market. The practices employed to exclude competitors differ with respect to the strategic variables employed. The literature usually distinguishes between practices that relate to price as the main strategic variable and abusive behaviour that relates to other strategic variables.[8] Price related practices are for instance

[6]Price discrimination can also be present if customers are charged the same price but where the cost of providing the product or service differ.

[7]A well known case of excessive prices is *United Brands* (Case 27/76 *United Brands v Commission* [1978] ECR 207, [1978] 1 CMLR 429). The European Commission found that United Brands was charging unfair (excessive prices for Chiquita bananas in several European countries. This decision, however, has been dismissed by the European Court of Justice. A case of price discrimination is *Irish Sugar* (Case T-228/97 *Irish Sugar v Commission* [1999] ECR II-2969). Here, the dominant firm offered rebates for customers located near the border to Northern Ireland which, besides preventing foreign imports, distorted competition between the dominant firm's customers.

[8]For a comprehensive survey of European cases related to the abuse of a dominant position including the economics background see O'Donoghue and Padilla (2013).

predatory pricing, the use of specific discount systems, for example loyalty rebates, or, in case of a vertically integrated firm, a full or partial input foreclosure. Here, the vertically integrated firm charges excessive prices for an input that a competitor on the downstream market needs to compete with the downstream division of the integrated firm. If there are no close substitutes for the input, the costs of the independent downstream rivals increase and they suffer a competitive disadvantage compared with the downstream department of the integrated firm. They either have to charge higher prices which will reduce their revenue as well as their market shares or their profit margin shrinks. In addition, the integrated firm could at the same time lower the price of the downstream product to squeeze the profit margin of independent downstream competitors from the cost as well as the revenue side. Other forms of exclusionary abuse relate to non-price variables for example bundling and tying to leverage market power from one market to another, building up excess capacities to avoid a market entry of a potential competitor or even a downright refusal to deal by not granting access to an essential facility. Such a refusal to deal could also be present if the price for an input or for the access to an essential facility are so excessive that no equally efficient competitor could profitably operate in this market.

Notice that the two types of abusive behaviour differ in an important aspect as the first type aims directly at increasing the profits by charging higher prices either for all buyers or using a profit-maximising price structure that implies higher prices only for some types of buyers as in the case of price discrimination. The other form of abusive behaviour operates in an indirect way: In a first step the competitive position of rivals is weakened by employing unlawful means and only after these firms have been marginalised or forced to exit the market, prices are increased. This is particularly obvious in case of predatory pricing, where in the predation phase the competitor is weakened and in the recoupment phase the dominant firm charges monopolistic prices and realises monopolistic profits. This is an important difference which has implications for the screens that can be employed in compliance programmes.

6.3 Screens for the Abuse of a Dominant Position

A major difference between anticompetitive agreements and abusive behaviour relates to the market position of the firms concerned. The ban on cartels, for example, is independent of a firm's market position, i.e. even a small firm can violate the ban on cartels. This also holds for other anticompetitive agreements between firms. For a certain business practice to be found abusive, however, the primary condition is that the firm holds a dominant market position. Dominance as defined in *United Brands* "...relates to a position of economic strength enjoyed by an undertaking which enables it to prevent effective competition being maintained on the relevant market by giving it the power to behave to an appreciable extent independently of its competitors, customers and ultimately of its consumers."[9] Dominance usually is determined by a combination of several factors, where the market share of a firm is the most important criterion.

In European competition law for example, a firm is usually not considered as dominant if the market share is below 40 %. Market shares in the range of 40–50 % give neither an indication of dominance nor its absence.[10] Additional factors have to be considered. Market shares between 50 % and 70 % likely raise the presumption of dominance while market shares above 70 % are generally considered as evidence of a dominant position. But even a firm with high market shares is not necessarily dominant if there is for example competitive pressure from potential competitors. Therefore, the competitive conditions in the respective market have to be examined. Important aspects that relate to the competitive conditions are barriers to entry and to expansion.[11]

If entry barriers are low, even a firm with a high market share is constrained in its behaviour as e.g. increased prices would lead potential competitors to enter the market or actual rivals to expand their output. With high barriers to entry, however, the leading firm might find it easier to increase prices or to employ exclusionary strategies (O'Donoghue and Padilla 2013, p. 151). Another aspect that is important for a firm being considered as dominant is the existence of countervailing buyer power, i.e. the ability of buyers to influence the terms and conditions on which they purchase goods (OECD 1998, p. 1). If the behaviour of a firm with a high market share is constrained by the buyers of its product, it should not be considered as dominant.

This implies that a screen for detecting or preventing abusive behaviour has to consist of two parts: The first part checks whether the firm under consideration holds a dominant position while the second part should ensure that no abusive behaviour takes place. There are at least two reasons why an internal compliance programme should provide not only a screen for cartels but also provisions that are able to detect and prevent the abuse of a dominant position. First, it is important to know for a firm if it indeed holds a dominant position because it is legally prohibited to employ certain business practices if this is the case. For example, bundling or tying as well as certain types of discount schemes could be considered as abusive if a firm holds a dominant position. Secondly, depending on the internal structure of the firm and of the incentive and remuneration systems used some managers could have a strong incentive to employ abusive practices to increase their pay-offs.

With respect to the concept of dominance, it is important to notice that a dominant position does not depend on the absolute size of a firm but its size in relation to the relevant antitrust market. Even a firm that is small in absolute size,

---

[9]*Chiquita*, Official Journal 1976 L 223/27, confirmed on appeal in Case 27/76, *United Brands Company and United Brands Continentaal BV v Commission* [1978] ECR 207, para. 65.

[10]In some national competition laws different thresholds are used. For example, in Austria, a firm with a market share of 30 % could be considered as dominant.

[11]For the concept of barriers to entry see McAfee et al. (2004).

i.e. with respect to employment or turnover, can hold a dominant position if the market is sufficiently small.[12] Stated otherwise, the size of the relevant antitrust market determines whether a firm holds a dominant position or not. The relevant antitrust market, in turn, is determined by the definition of the relevant product and geographic market. If the firm implicitly uses a wider concept of the market it operates in than the correctly defined relevant antitrust market, it might consider its position not as dominant because the market share is below the relevant threshold, for example below 40 %, and is therefore allowed to employ certain business practices, for example granting loyalty rebates.[13] The competition authorities, however, could define a smaller relevant antitrust market and would come to the conclusion that the firm actually holds a dominant position and therefore is not allowed to employ certain practices that would raise no concerns in case of a non-dominant firm.

The second reason why it might be useful to complement the compliance programmes with screens to detect and prevent an abuse of a dominant position is the following: In many cases, dominant firms are also large and complex organizations with a differentiated internal structure. In such a complex organization the departments of the firm are often organised as independent profit centres where managers are responsible for a certain group of products or a geographic region. If the salary of a manager depends on the success of the profit centre, i.e. the profits generated, he could have an incentive to engage in abusive business practices without the top management being aware of this behaviour. In comparison to entering a cartel agreement with the competitors, it might even be easier to behave abusively as it does not require any coordination between several firms. Therefore, screens to detect and prevent abusive behaviour should be integrated into compliance programmes. In the next section, structural screens are discussed that could help to determine whether the firm under consideration holds a dominant position.

6.3.1 Structural Screens

The first screen in a compliance programme that is necessary to detect and prevent abusive behaviour is a structural one that identifies whether the firm under consideration actually holds a dominant position. This is usually not immediately clear because the relevant market as seen by the firm could be substantially different from the relevant antitrust market as defined by the competition authority. This may be the case because firms tend to consider a wider variety of products as substitutes to

[12]For example, in the German market for spices the company Fuchs holds a market share of 75 %, despite being only a small or medium sized firm.

[13]This could be the case if a dominant firm has inflated the prices of its products and thus "created" competition by substitute products that would not be considered as substitutes at competitive prices. Here, the firm would have made the mistake of the "cellophane fallacy". See Sect. 6.3.1.

its own products and therefore more firms as competitors than there actually are in the sense of competition law. Stated otherwise, they consider the market as wider than the relevant antitrust market actually is.

One reason for such an incorrect assessment of the relevant market could be that firms are unfamiliar with the hypothetical monopolist test (HMT) that is usually applied to define the relevant antitrust market. The HMT defines the relevant market as the smallest set of products and regions for which a profit maximizing hypothetical monopolist would effect a small but significant and not only temporary increase in price. Therefore, this test is also known as the SSNIP test (small but significant non-transitory increase in price). But even if the SSNIP-test is applied, the given price level may be taken as the starting point from which a price increase is considered. This, however, could lead to a mistake in the definition of the relevant market if the firm under consideration in fact holds a dominant position. This incorrect definition of the relevant market is known as the "cellophane fallacy".[14] The fallacy leads to a market delineation that is too wide because the current price level is already inflated due to the market power of the dominant firm. At these inflated prices, customers consider products as substitutes that they would not have considered as substitutable at the competitive price level. The market shares of the firm given the incorrect definition of the relevant market are too small and the firm may erroneously not be considered as dominant. If, however, the competitive price level would have been taken as the starting point from which a small but significant increase in price is calculated, the market would be defined more narrowly, the market shares were larger and the firm would be considered as dominant. These two reasons could lead a firm that would in fact be dominant under a correct definition of the relevant antitrust market to the conclusion that it does not hold a dominant position and thus may employ business practices that would be considered as violations of competition law and would be fined accordingly.

It could also be the case that the market definition that a firm employs internally is too restrictive. In this case, the firm would consider itself as dominant and therefore would not employ certain business practices that are perfectly compatible with competition law because the firm does not hold a dominant position in the relevant antitrust market.[15] Such an overly narrow definition of the relevant market could lead to social costs in form of over-compliance, i.e. the firm would abstain from business practices that would increase the efficiency of the firm thereby generating social benefits.[16] For example, a bundling strategy would not be used by a firm that considers itself as dominant for fear of violating competition law despite that fact that bundling would save the consumers significant transaction cost and would be in accordance with competition law. Also, a loyalty discount may not

[14]For a discussion of the cellophane fallacy and how to avoid it see e.g. OECD (2012).

[15]Sales managers, for example could consider their firm as a market leader and therefore implicitly use a narrower market definition.

[16]Of course, overcompliance assumes that the staff is informed about the relevant aspects of competition law.

be granted despite the fact that it would generate efficiency gains as for example dealers would exert a higher level of effort to make sure that they will enjoy the discount.

Therefore, the first step of a compliance programme in relation to abusive behaviour has to be the correct definition of the relevant antitrust market and comliance programmes should provide information about how to apply the HMT. In particular, the cellophane fallacy should be avoided. The assessment of the relevant market should be carried out regularly by a firm as the boundaries of the market might change over time. This could imply that a dominant position disappears if the boundaries of the relevant market become wider. In this case, market shares may drop below the 40 % threshold and the firm could employ a broader range of business practices. On the other hand, it could also happen that the boundaries of a relevant market become tighter, the market shares of a firm increase and a dominant position emerges.

After having defined the relevant market, the market share of the firm has to be considered. If it is below 40 % than it is unlikely that the firm under consideration has a dominant position. In this case, a further investigation does not seem to be necessary. In the case of market shares between 40 % and 50 %, additional competitive conditions in the market should be taken into account, primarily barriers to entry and countervailing buyer power.

Barriers to entry are a controversial topic in economics and several definitions have been suggested. In the context considered here, barriers to entry are defined as "factors which prevent or hinder companies from entering a specific market" (European Commission 2002). In practice, competition authorities consider the market specific conditions of entry and the characteristics of the firm under consideration as well as the market behaviour of the firm.[17] Market specific characteristics are legal restrictions if, for example, the firm is a state monopoly or if a licence is necessary to be active in the respective market. Patents or other forms of intellectual property rights constitute further barriers to entry. Secondly, there are economic barriers to entry such as large sunk costs, i.e. cost that cannot be recovered when the firm leaves the markets. Also, economies of scale and scope are a barrier to entry because in these cases it is difficult for smaller firms to compete because they often have to operate with higher average and/or marginal cost. If there are network effects present in the market, entry could also be difficult if the incumbent firm has already achieved a large installed base of customers. This barrier is even more significant if consumers have to bear significant switching cost when changing their supplier. With respect to firm specific conditions for barriers to entry to exist in the market, an important aspect is a privileged access to essential inputs which would give the firm under consideration an advantage over its competitors. This could be the case if a firm is vertically integrated into the upstream market and therefore faces lower transaction costs as compared to

[17]For a detailed discussion of the competitive conditions in the context of single firm dominance see O'Donoghue and Padilla (2014), pp. 143–174.

independent downstream rivals. For example, Scandlines, the owner of the port of Puttgarden and the only provider of ferry services between Puttgarden and Rødby has permanently refused to enable a competitor to use its port in return for an appropriate fee and thereby prevented another ferry service from competing on this particular route. Other firm-specific barriers to entry are excess capacities that could be used to signal to potential competitors that market entry is not worthwhile. Post-entry, the incumbent firm would produce at full capacity, leading to lower prices and rendering market entry unprofitable. Besides these factors, the financial strength of the firm under consideration and its profitability are sometimes also considered as barriers to entry. The importance of these factors, however, seems to be ambiguous.

Therefore, a structural screen as the first part of a comprehensive assessment of dominance is the correct definition of the relevant market which is, particularly in dominance cases, often quite difficult. Therefore, it could be sensible to use external economic expertise or, if time and resources are essential, to employ a conservative approach and define a narrow relevant market. If market shares are above 40 %, additional conditions have to be checked. The most important conditions are barriers to entry and countervailing buyer power. If these conditions are satisfied, i.e. if there are significant barriers to entry and if there is no countervailing buyer power, the probability is high that a competition authority will conclude that the firm holds a dominant position. In this case the second part of the screen has to be applied to assess whether the firm is constrained by competition law to employ certain business practices.

6.3.2 *Behavioural Screens*

If an internal compliance programme has found that the firm actually holds a dominant position, then the firm should refrain from using business practices that would violate competition law. In what follows, we discuss the two types of abusive behaviour, exploitative and exclusionary abuse separately as the methods to detect and to prevent abusive behaviour differ for the two cases.

6.3.2.1 Exploitative Abuse

In case of an exploitative abuse in form of excessive prices, it has to be examined whether the prices charged by the firm under consideration are significantly above the competitive level. Here, screens similarly to those used for the detection of cartels can be employed. In particular, a comparator-based approach can be used where the prices a dominant firm charges are compared to prices in other geographic markets were similar conditions prevail. If it turns out that prices are significantly lower in other markets—taking into account differences in cost, demand etc.—this could indicate excessive prices. Another indicator of excessive prices are reactions to cost changes. It is well known that changes are increasingly passed-on to output prices the higher the competitive pressure in the market is. If reductions in marginal cost are not reflected in price reductions or only to a very limited degree, this could indicate a lack of competitive pressure and thus excessive prices (OECD 2011, pp. 48–53). A further criterion that could be employed by the firm is the price-cost margin that can be determined by using internal cost information.[18] Here, it is important that a suitable measure of cost is used, i.e. marginal cost which are different from variable or average costs. Marginal cost, however, are a theoretical concept and are not included in the accounting records. Therefore, variable cost that can be provided by the accounts department can be used as a substitute.[19] In practice, however, there was only a limited number of cases of excessive prices and firms were rarely sanctioned by competition authorities for this type of infringement. The reason is that it is generally difficult to demonstrate that prices are indeed significantly above the competitive level. To save on time and resources, compliance programmes therefore should focus mainly on price discrimination and exclusionary abuses.

With respect to price discrimination, the economic effects can be welfare increasing or decreasing depending on the specific circumstances of the case at hand. Roughly speaking, price discrimination tends to be welfare enhancing if the output increases due to price discrimination. Nevertheless, price discrimination is considered to be abusive by Article 102 (c) TFEU if dissimilar conditions to equivalent transactions with other trading parties are applied, thereby placing them at a competitive disadvantage. Here, transactions are considered as equivalent if, first, the products or services are identical or similar with respect to their physical or functional properties. Secondly, transactions should take place at approximately the same time and thirdly, they have to take place in a commercially similar context. Dissimilar conditions are present if equivalent transactions lead to different rates of return for the firm under consideration. For example, if the cost of providing a service is the same for two different types of customers or two different geographic regions and the prices are different, dissimilar conditions would be present.[20]

Finally, the condition of competitive disadvantage implies that the trading partners that are treated differently compete with each other.[21] No definite criteria, however, with respect to the magnitude of the necessary competitive disadvantage or the nature of competition have been devised yet.

---

[18]With respect to the magnitude of the price-cost margin, concepts from the economics of regulation could be employed where returns on capital in excess of 20 % are considered as problematic. See e.g. Littlechild (2011).

[19]Additional problems may arise for example with respect to the allocation of common cost in multi-product firms or concerning the appropriate time period because in the short term, most costs are fixed and variable costs are therefore low and vice versa.

[20]This implies that dissimilar conditions are also present if for example the same price is charged in two different geographic regions where the costs of providing the good or service differ.

[21]See e.g. the case of *Irish Sugar* (Case T-228/97 *Irish Sugar v Commission* [1999] ECR II-2969).

Charging different prices to different trading partners is however only an indication of an exploitative or discriminatory abuse. If the dominant firm can provide an objective justification for dissimilar conditions, this would not be considered as abusive behaviour. The most convincing justifications in the eyes of competition authorities are differences in cost of serving different groups of trading partners. For example, if the transport costs are higher for one group, charging a price that reflects this cost difference would not be considered as abusive. Similar arguments hold in the case of taxes or custom duties. Also, if larger volumes can be produced at lower average cost, as in the case of economies of scale, a buyer of a large volume may be charged a lower price as compared to a low-volume buyer. There are also several economic reasons why price discrimination may be pro-competitive and increase welfare. For example, price differences can be used as an incentive scheme if prices are dependent on purchases in the past. These arguments however, will probably not be considered as sufficient to dispel the suspicion of an abusive behaviour.

Therefore, if a firm has found to be dominant and charges different prices in otherwise equivalent transactions putting some trading partners at a competitive disadvantage, this behaviour should be justified by objective and verifiable reasons to ensure that the firm complies with competition law.

6.3.2.2 Exclusionary Abuse

While screens for exploitative abuse can be devised—in case of excessive prices by screens similar to those used for the detection of cartels, and cost-price comparisons in the case of price discrimination—matters become considerably more difficult with respect to the different types of exclusionary abuse.[22]

There are several reasons why it is more difficult to screen for exclusionary abuses as compared to cartels or exploitative abuses. First, most business practices that are potentially abusive have simultaneously pro-competitive as well as anti-competitive effects. Bundling for example lowers transactions cost but may at the same time be employed to leverage market power from one market into another. Secondly, it is often difficult to discriminate between these two effects. For example, if it is observed that prices decrease after a newcomer has entered the market, it is unclear whether this is a normal reaction to increased competition or a predatory pricing strategy directed at forcing the entrant to leave the market. Is a loyalty discount granted by a manufacturer to its retailers to set the right incentives to provide an efficient level of effort or it is used to marginalise the competitors by inducing a suction effect to withdraw demand from the rivals? Thirdly, for many types of potentially exclusionary behaviour, economic theory has so far not devised simple, clear and verifiable criteria to distinguish between those groups of cases

[22] A detailed overview of the different types of exclusionary abuse including the legal aspects is provided by O'Donoghue and Padilla (2013).

where a given behaviour increases competition and those where the anti-competitive effects dominate. Therefore, in cases of exclusionary abuse, the well known problems of discriminating between abusive behaviour on the one hand and competition on the merits on the other reappear. A screening for abusive behaviour is thus considerably more difficult as compared to the detection of cartels. Compliance programmes should therefore raise the awareness to potentially abusive types of behaviour and should encourage staff to inform the legal department and ask for clarification when indicated. Except for the case of predatory pricing, economic theory has not yet developed a set of clear and verifiable conditions that have to be satisfied for e.g. bundling to be pro-competitive.

For the case of predatory pricing, however, some tests have been suggested to determine whether prices are predatory. One well-known test for predatory pricing is the Areeda-Turner-rule stating that prices should be considered as predatory if they are below short-run marginal cost and if the market structure is such that a recoupment for the foregone profits after the exit of the rival is probable.[23]

As marginal costs are difficult to measure, short-run average variable costs are usually taken instead. It has been recognised, however, that prices below short-run average variable cost are neither necessary nor sufficient for prices to be predatory. Therefore, a different test has been suggested that refers to the Long-Run Average Incremental Cost (LRAIC), the sum of the variable and the product-specific fixed cost in relation to the total output of the product considered (European Commission 2009). This cost concept is considered as an appropriate benchmark in particular for industries characterised by high fixed costs. LRAIC is used by many competition authorities as well as regulators and can therefore also be employed as the relevant cost concept in compliance programmes.

But also for prices below LRAIC, objective justifications can be given, for example if the products in question are perishable, if it is a promotional price or if a low price is necessary for market penetration. Another justification could be a meeting competition argument, i.e. a price below LRAIC is necessary to match lower prices of competitors. If objective justifications for prices below LRAIC can be provided, then this pricing behaviour will probably not be considered as predatory.

For other types of abusive behaviour such as bundling, tying, loyalty discounts, exclusive dealing agreements, refusal to deal etc. however, so far no reliable screens have been developed or criteria provided to delineate different groups of scenarios to decide whether in a certain case the pro- or the anti-competitive effects of a certain conduct dominate. Here, more economic research is desirable. Until those criteria are developed, a possible solution in the context of an internal compliance programme to avoid exclusionary conduct could be a positive screen that requires a firm to provide objective justifications or sound and convincing economic arguments or for a certain conduct. This may also be used to find out whether practices already employed by the firm could be considered as

[23]See Areeda and Turner (1975). For predatory pricing see Bolton et al. (2001).

exclusionary. An example of an objective justification in the case of bundling would be significant savings in transaction cost for the firm as well as for the customers as compared to separate selling of the products. With respect to the sound and convincing economic arguments, either in addition or as alternative to an objective justification of a certain conduct, the *no economic sense test* could be used.[24] This test requires that a firm is able to demonstrate that the conduct under consideration makes economic sense and works without marginalizing competitors or forcing them to leave the market. If a firm is dominant, to ensure that its behaviour is consistent with competition law, a comprehensive antitrust compliance programme should not only contain anti-cartel measures but also require that any problematic business practices used by a dominant firm pass the no economic sense test. This implies that objective justifications for the practices employed are provided and it is also demonstrated that the challenged conduct is rational for the firm absent a tendency to eliminate competition (Werden 2006, p. 298).

The *no economic sense test* was developed in the context of the design of an effective and efficient competition law. Here, the main question was whether this test is better able to discriminate between pro- and anticompetitive behaviour as compared to the vague measures that have been used in the past as for example profit sacrifice tests (Werden 2007). If this test would be applied as part of an internal compliance programme, it serves a slightly different objective. In the context of compliance, the *no economic sense test* helps the firm to ensure that there are sound and convincing economic and business arguments for employing a certain conduct. In addition, by using this test, the firm can ascertain that there is no tendency to eliminate competition by weakening rivals or forcing them to exit from the market. In the context of a compliance programme, this test seems to be a reasonable and practicable way to ensure that a dominant firm does not employ exclusionary practices. At the same time, business practices where either an objective justification can be provided and which pass the test and are thus potentially welfare increasing are not prevented. For example, if the firm can demonstrate that bundling products reduces cost and therefore increases profits, i.e. makes economic sense without lessening or eliminating competition, the practice should not be considered as exclusionary. If bundling, however, makes no economic sense but for the tendency to lessen or eliminate competition, the firm should not use this practice as competition authorities might consider it as abusive. When a firm employs only business practices that have passed the *no economic sense test*, it can be reasonably sure that it does not violate competition law. On the other hand, competition is not constrained as this test allows for all business practices that are compatible with competition on the merits. Therefore, employing this test seems to strike a reasonable balance between not being too generous by not

[24]This type of reasoning for discriminating between abusive and lawful behaviour has been suggested by Werden (2006, 2007), and Melamed (2005, 2006). It has been questioned however whether this test can be applied all kinds of exclusionary behaviour in particular to exclusive dealing. See Jacobsen and Sher (2006).

flagging an unlawful conduct and being overly restrictive, i.e. preventing business practices that are perfectly compatible with antitrust law. This test could be implemented in a compliance programme by informing the employees that no business practice should be used that is profitable only if competition is lessened or if competitors are excluded.

6.4 Abusive Behaviour in the Digital Economy

The problem of abusive behaviour of a dominant position is of particular relevance in the digital economy. Firms in this sector of the economy often are two-sided markets or platforms characterised by direct and indirect network effects. Due to the positive feedback effects, firms tend to become larger and markets tend to be dominated by only a few large firms or even only a single firm.[25] For example, in search engine markets, in online auction markets, and also in social media, one firm tends to become significantly larger than its competitors as in the cases of Google, eBay or Facebook. Due to their size in comparison with their competitors and also in relation to the size of the market, it could be suspected that several firms in the digital economy hold a dominant position.

Whether this is indeed the case is, however, often difficult to determine. There are several reasons why it is problematic to establish the market dominance even in the case of a large company. First, as most digital platforms are two-sided-markets, market definition is inherently difficult as both market sides have to be considered simultaneously because there are indirect network effects between the different groups of users on the two sides of the market. If the price for users on one market side is increased, the number of users will usually decline. This, however, has a negative impact on the number of users on the other market side. This has to be considered when employing the HMT in the case of two-sided markets.[26] Secondly, carrying out the HMT in two-sided markets is often problematic as in many markets, for example in the search engine market, or in social media, the users on one market side pay a price of zero. This implies that the HMT in its standard form that usually considers a price increase of 5–10 % cannot be carried out in the same way as in traditional markets. Thirdly, it may turn out that a firm holds a dominant position on one market side, for example with respect to the firms that advertise on this platform, but not on the other side of the market where users either multihome, i.e. are active on several similar platforms or can easily switch to another search engine. Multihoming by users on one market side could exert a competitive pressure on the two-sided platform that is so strong that this platform is not

25 An introduction to the competitive aspects of two-sided markets is provided by Evans and Schmalensee (2013).

26 For discussions of how to apply the HMT in the case of two-sided markets see e.g. Filistrucchi et al. (2012).

dominant despite of a high market share. Therefore, platforms have strong incentives to limit multihoming by using exclusivity clauses (Brühn and Götz 2015).

But not only problems with respect to determine whether a firm holds a dominant position arise in the digital economy but also new aspects might emerge in relation to abusive behaviour. Here, new types of an abuse of a dominant position could occur in the digital economy, in particular with respect to the data that digital platforms collect. For example, data on the purchase history of a customer could be used to condition the price of a good on the purchase behaviour of this customer in the past, a conduct that could be considered as an exploitative abuse in form of price discrimination. Also, the question might arise whether these data are an essential facility. If competition authorities and courts come to the conclusion that the data have to be considered as an essential input for other firms, not granting competitors access to these data or charging an inflated price for access could be considered as an exclusionary abuse of a dominant position. In addition, violations of data protection laws could be an issue and also the question of the relation of competition law and data protection law. This, however, is not directly related to antitrust compliance and is therefore not discussed here.

6.5 Summary and Discussion

To make sure that antitrust compliance programmes are comprehensive, all types of competition law infringement should be covered by such programmes. So far, mainly competition law violations in the form of cartels are analysed in detail and only for this type of infringement effective screens have been devised. However, also abusive behaviour is a violation of competition law and is often heavily fined because it can lead to significant harm to competitors, customers, suppliers and ultimately consumers. Hence, it is appropriate to complement compliance programmes with screens to detect and prevent all types of abusive behaviour.

The first step of such a screen is necessary to determine whether the firm under consideration in fact holds a dominant position because an abusive behaviour is directly related to market dominance. For this assessment, the relevant antitrust market has to be defined preferably by using the hypothetical monopolist test. As the price level could already be inflated if the firm is in fact dominant, the problem of the cellophane fallacy has to be avoided. When the market is defined, the market share has to be calculated. If the market share is significantly higher than 40 %, the competitive conditions in the market, i.e. barriers to entry or countervailing buyer power have to be assessed to determine whether the firm can behave to an appreciable extent independently from its competitors, customers and its consumers.

If a firm is found to be dominant, the second step of a compliance programme is to ascertain that no business practices are used that could be considered as an exploitative or exclusionary abuse. For the exploitative abuse of excessive prices similar screens as in cartel cases can be used, for example prices in comparator markets. With respect to price discrimination, the dominant firm should be able to provide convincing objective justifications and also economic arguments why different conditions are applied in equivalent transactions.

In contrast to cartel screens, no simple and practicable screens have been devised to discriminate between competitive and exclusionary conduct. To deal with exclusionary behaviour, a comprehensive antitrust compliance programme should require that either objective justifications for the conduct under consideration are provided and the conduct passes the "no economic sense" test. This test considers business practices as compatible with competition law if they are rational for the firm absent a tendency to eliminate competition. Particular problems with respect to abusive behaviour arise in the digital economy. Here, the definition of the relevant market is problematic due to the two-sided nature of most platforms. Also, new types of abuse related to data could arise in the digital economy for example if a platform charges prices contingent on the purchase history of a customer or if it blocks competitors from accessing the user data it has collected. The latter conduct could be considered as a market foreclosure in particular if the data are considered as an essential facility by competition authorities. Therefore, compliance programmes for firms in the digital economy should take into account that problems related to the collection and usage of data may emerge.

References

Abrantes-Metz, R. M. (2013a). *Proactive vs reactive anti-cartel policy: The role of empirical screens*. Working Paper.

Abrantes-Metz, R. M. (2013a). Interview: Update on "Screens for Conspiracies and Their Multiple Applications". *Competition Policy International, 8*, 173–176.

Abrantes-Metz, R. M., Bajari, P., & Murphy, J. (2010). *Antitrust screening: Making compliance programs robust*. Working Paper.

Abrantes-Metz, R. M., Froeb, L. M., Geweke, J. M., & Taylor, C. T. (2006). A variance screen for collusion. *International Journal of Industrial Organization, 24*, 467–486.

Abrantes-Metz, R. M., & Sokol, D. D. (2013). *Antitrust corporate governance and compliance*. University of Minnesota Law School. Legal Studies Research Paper Series, Research Paper No. 13-18.

Abrantes-Metz, R. M., Villas-Boas, S. B. & Judge, G. (2013). *Tracking the Libor-rate*. University of California, Berkeley, Department of Agricultural & Resource Economics, CUDARE Working Papers 1108R2.

Areeda, P. E., & Turner, D. E. (1975). Predatory pricing and related practices under Section 2 of the Sherman Act. *Harvard Law Review, 88*(4), 697–733.

Bolton, P., Brodley, J. F., & Riordan, M. H. (2001). Predatory pricing: Strategic theory and legal policy. *Georgetown Law Journal, 89*(8), 2495–2529.

Brühn, T., & Götz, G. (2015). *Exclusionary practices in two-sided markets: The effect of radius clauses on competition between shopping centres*. Joint Discussion Paper Series in Economics MAGKS, No. 28-2015.

European Commission. (2002). Glossary of terms used in competition policy, 17.

European Commission. (2009). Communication from the commission — Guidance on the Commission's enforcement priorities in applying Article 82 of the EC Treaty to abusive exclusionary conduct by dominant undertakings. *Official Journal of the European Union C* 45/7-20.

Evans, D. S., & Schmalensee, R. (2013). *The antitrust analysis of multi-sided platform businesses*. University of Chicago Institute for Law & Economics, Olin Research Paper No. 623.
Filistrucchi, L., Geradin, D., & van Damme, E. (2012). *Identifying two-sided markets*. Tilburg University, TILEC Discussion Paper No. 2012-008.
Harrington, J. (2010). Detecting cartels. In P. Buccirossi (Ed.), *Handbook of antitrust economics* (pp. 213–258). Cambridge, MA: MIT.
Jacobsen, J. M., & Sher, S. A. (2006). The "No Economic Sense" test makes no sense for exclusive dealing. *Antitrust Law Journal, 73*(3), 779–801.
Littlechild, S. (2011). The nature of competition and the regulatory process. *Intereconomics, 46*, 10–17.
McAfee, R. P., Mialon, H. M., & Williams, M. A. (2004). What is a barrier to entry? *American Economic Review, 94*, 461–465. Papers and Proceedings.
Melamed, A. D. (2005). Exclusionary conduct under the antitrust laws: Balancing, sacrifice and refusals to deal. *Berkeley Technology Law Journal, 20*, 1247–1267.
Melamed, A. D. (2006). Exclusive dealing agreements and other exclusionary conduct - are there unifying principles? *Antitrust Law Journal, 73*, 375–412.
O'Donoghue, R., & Padilla, J. (2013). *The law and economics of Article 102 TFEU* (2nd ed.). Oxford: Hart Publishing.
OECD. (1998). Roundtable on buying power of multiproduct retailers. *DAFFE/CLP* (99)21, 18.
OECD. (2011). Roundtable on excessive prices. *DAF/COMP* (2011)18.
OECD. (2012). Roundtable on market definition. *DAF/COMP* (2012)19.
Sokol, D. D. (2011, September). Detection and compliance in cartel policy. *CPI Antitrust Chronicle*, (2), 1–5.
von Blanckenburg, K., & Geist, A. (2011). Detecting illegal activities: The case of cartels. *European Journal of Law and Economics, 32*(1), 15–33.
von Blanckenburg, K., Geist, A., & Kholodilin, K. A. (2012). The influence of collusion on price changes: New evidence from major cartel cases. *German Economic Review, 13*(3), 245–256.
Werden, G. J. (2007). Identifying single firm exclusionary conduct: From vague concepts to administrable rules. In *International Antitrust Law & Policy: Fordham Competition Law 2006*.
Werden, G. J. (2006). Identifying exclusionary conduct under Section 2: The "No Economic Sense" Test. *Antitrust Law Journal, 73*(2), 413–433.

Part III
Criminal Sanctions

Chapter 7
Criminal Sanctions Against Corporations

Andreas Ransiek

Abstract Most European countries impose criminal sanctions on corporations. This article argues that whereas administrative sanctions should be provided for by law to deter offences in the course of business, there is no benefit in criminalising corporate wrongdoing. If administrative sanctions against corporations and other business enterprises apply, the law might forgo the criminal responsibility of natural persons.

7.1 Toward Corporate Criminal Liability in German Law

7.1.1 Traditional Arguments

There are no criminal sanctions against corporations and other business enterprises in German law. They have been discussed in Germany since the 1950s (see Discussion of the 40. Deutscher Juristentag, 1953) but the majority of legal scholars was and still is heavily opposed (cf. Jahn and Pietsch 2015, pp. 1, 3). In 2001, a commission on the reform of the law of criminal sanctions appointed by the Federal Government voted 12 to 1 against the introduction of a criminal responsibility of corporations.[1] Others, however, favour criminal sanctions against corporations for business crimes (Erhardt 1994, p. 215 et seq.). If the damages caused by illegal conduct are severe, e.g. in antitrust or tender cases, they argue that criminal law should apply to clarify the degree of wrongdoing.

The author would like to thank *Gil Miller* and *André Winsel* for their invaluable help to improve the phrasing—all remaining inaccuracies are the author's. A slightly different version of this article has been published in the European Criminal Law Review (EuCLR) 2015.

[1]Bericht der Kommission zur Reform des strafrechtlichen Sanktionenrechts, https://www.bib.uni-mannheim.de/fileadmin/pdf/fachinfo/jura/absclussber-der-komm-strafreform.pdf.

A. Ransiek (✉)
Faculty of Law, Bielefeld University, Bielefeld, Germany
e-mail: andreas.ransiek@uni-bielefeld.de

J. Paha (ed.), *Competition Law Compliance Programmes*,
DOI 10.1007/978-3-319-44633-2_7

The main arguments have not changed much since the 1950s: A corporation or firm is unable to commit a criminal act. And thus, a corporation's personal culpability is inconceivable. There is "no soul to damn and no body to kick" (Coffee 1981, p. 386), vice versa the corporation is not capable to kick itself or to decide on its own to choose the proper or criminal path. There are necessarily humans acting on behalf of the company. They are to blame and thus may be held responsible for their deeds committed in the course of business. The worker opening a valve so that the leaking wastewater poisons a river will be punished for a willful or negligent crime against the environment. If a criminal act was ordered by the head of business or the management they may be held personally responsible as well, either as perpetrators or for aiding or abetting.

In support of this view is an argument based on the interpretation of Article 1 of the German Constitution by the Federal Constitutional Court. This Article protecting human dignity demands that somebody may be held criminally responsible only if he can be blamed for committing the crime. Culpability in the Article's meaning is based on the personal responsibility of man, his ability to act self-determinedly and to choose between right and wrong. Thus, a criminal sanction against somebody not personally blameworthy is a violation of his dignity. This rule is considered to be a sacrosanct imperative of the Constitution's identity (Entscheidungen des *Bundesverfassungsgerichts* BVerfGE 123 p. 267 margin no 364).

7.1.2 New Developments

The topic, therefore, seemed to be dead. But it is on the agenda again. In 2011, the Attorney Generals of the German states supported a proposal by North Rhine-Westphalia (Justizportal Nordrhein-Westfalen 2013) to discuss the issue again in order to fight white-collar crime more effectively. Since November 2013, we have a Model Corporate Penal Code[2] submitted by North Rhine-Westphalia's Attorney General. This model code has been called a "zombie of legal policy" (Schünemann 2014, p. 1), but may become the law in the near future, nevertheless.

In addition, there is a more important player in the field: the Commission of the European Union. For example, European law requires in the case of crimes against the environment that the law of the member states includes rules that hold corporations responsible for such crimes. Article 7 of the directive on the protection of the environment through criminal law states that the necessary measures have to be taken to ensure that legal persons held liable for violations are punishable "by

[2]Https://www.justiz.nrw.de/JM/justizpolitik/jumiko/beschluesse/2013/herbstkonferenz13/zw3/TOP_II_5Gesetzentwurf.pdf. For a discussion of the model code see Mitsch (2014), p. 1 et seqq.; Hoven et al. (2014), pp. 161 et seqq., 201 et seqq., 241 et seqq.; Hoven (2014), p. 19 et seqq.; Schünemann (2014), p. 1 et seqq.; Zieschang (2014), p. 91 et seqq.; Engelhart (2015), p. 201 et seqq.

effective, proportionate and dissuasive penalties". This does *not* mean that these penalties necessarily have to be criminal penalties. But in other fields, in particular in securities law (Schork and Reichling 2012, p. 125 et seqq.; Zieschang 2014, pp. 91, 97), it is quite evident that the Commission favours criminal sanctions. The guess is that for the time being the Commission restrains itself from making criminal sanctions against corporations mandatory because the German Federal Constitutional Court might hold them unconstitutional and therefore inapplicable in Germany.

But the majority of the European countries impose criminal sanctions on corporations and some of them with legal systems similar to the German system have changed their respective criminal laws over the last years (cf. Weigend and Namysłowska-Gabrysiak 2004, p. 541 et seqq.; Partsch 2012, p. 55 et seqq.): Austria, Spain (see de la Cuesta and Pérez Machío 2008, p. 527 et seqq.; Mateu 2011, p. 331 et seqq.; Silva Sánchez 2012, p. 59 et seqq.) and Switzerland (see Heine 2003, p. 24 et seqq.; Heine 2005, p. 17 et seqq.). The United States Supreme Court upheld criminal sanctions against corporations in *New York Central & Hudson River Railroad Co. v. United States* as early as 1909 (221 U.S. 481 [1909]). Thus, it is said that in the meantime Germany almost stands alone in rejecting criminal sanctions against corporations (Frisch 2013, pp. 349, 351). German law might be outdated and it could be only a matter of time that the law will change.

7.2 Administrative Versus Criminal Fines

I have not told the whole story yet. There are no criminal sanctions against corporations according to German law, but legal persons and partnerships may be held liable for infringements of the law by penalties if a director, partner or another person managing the affairs of the enterprise commits a crime or offence (Ordnungswidrigkeit) violating the firm's business duties or acting to enrich the corporation. The penalty is an administrative fine. Thus, the corporation may have to pay when managing employees commit a business crime.

7.2.1 Internal Measures to Avoid the Fine

The quite simple idea behind this is that the corporation will employ internal measures to avoid having to pay the fine and thus will see that the business is conducted in compliance with the legal regulations (cf. Schünemann 2014, pp. 1, 17). Crimes and other offences are deterred. Of course, there is no guarantee that the concept of deterrence actually works in all cases all the time. But that is the same in criminal law as otherwise there would be no crimes. In a business context the assumption seems to be fair that if chances of future gains and losses have to be regarded by the corporation in order to be economically successful, the possibility of having to pay a fine will be taken into account. Some persons acting for the corporation may not realise the looming dangers, they will misjudge risks or take irrational risks, but generally it is not probable that the corporation will intentionally shoot itself in the foot by not avoiding an avoidable fine and thus incurring a financial loss.

So it might be argued that if the corporation fears having to pay a fine and tries to avoid it, it is simply irrelevant if the fine is called criminal or administrative—relevant is only that the corporation has to pay when breaking the law. The deterrent effect depends on the amount of the fine and the probability that it will actually be imposed and not on its nature or name. To put it more bluntly: One might argue that German law is cheating. It contains sanctions against corporations. They taste and smell and work like criminal sanctions, yet they are not called that.

7.2.2 *Deterrent Effects of Criminal and Administrative Sanctions*

North Rhine-Westphalia's Attorney General argues, however, that there is a difference between an administrative fine and a criminal sanction. Administrative sanctions for example are imposed for traffic violations: park in a no parking zone and you get fined 20 euros. This, so the argument goes, is no big deal, whereas a criminal sanction as a consequence for disobeying the law is much more severe because it carries a reproach of wrongdoing. A criminal deed is different from an administrative offence. As an American colleague put it, the subject of criminal law should be "something more than the equivalent of spitting on the sidewalk" (Coffee 1992, pp. 1875, 1881).

I believe that the American colleague is correct, and that the Attorney General is simply wrong. His argument does not hold because the amount of the fine is regardless of whether a crime or an offence has been committed. The picture he paints is not the existing law. Of course, it would be a bad joke if a DAX-corporation were to be fined 20 (or for that matter 2 million) euros for breaking antitrust or environmental laws, maybe hoping to make a huge profit by doing so undetected. But in the case of competition law we have fines up to billions of euros based on Article 15 Council Regulation 17/1962 and its successor Article 23 Council Regulation 1/2003—European law directly applicable in Germany since 1962. In December 2013, six top level banks paid fines of 1.71 billion euros for manipulating key interest rates (Handelsblatt 2013). The Deutsche Bank paid more than 900 million dollars (Protess and Silver-Greenberg 2015). Thus, the fines imposed do *not* have the character of traffic tickets. They are multiple times higher than the highest criminal fine the German Penal Code allows. They only have to be large enough to be effective. It may be necessary to enforce fines against corporations more effectively. This may be granted but it has nothing to do with the fine's nature.

It is argued that there is a special deterring effect connected with a criminal sanction as opposed to other sanctions no matter how much money has to be paid (for details Ransiek 2012a, pp. 285, 288 et seqq.). It is the reproach of wrongdoing expressed by a judge declaring the offender guilty of a crime (Ransiek 2012b, pp. 45, 47; Stree and Kinzig 2014: Vorbem. §§ 38 et seqq. margin no 37 et seq). This argument does not fly either. Suppose there is an administrative fine of 1000 impending for a violation of business rules and assume further that from the corporation's point of view there is a probability of 30 % that the violation will be detected and the fine will actually be imposed. A rational person acting on behalf and in the interest of the corporation will not commit the offence if the corporation's financial advantage by breaking the law is 300 or less. There is no advantage in committing the crime (cf. also Ransiek 2012b, pp. 45, 46 et seq.). As argued above, this is true regardless of the sanction's criminal or non-criminal nature.

Suppose that the corporation's agent still tries to act in the corporation's best interest but he commits the offence nevertheless. His behaviour would then be simply irrational because the impending fine is higher than the benefit he tries to gain for the corporation. He must be nuts. If he is nuts, we would have to believe that the threat of a criminal sanction in contrast to an administrative sanction (that works for rational people but not for him) makes him an individual who is acting rationally again. While that would be nice, I do not believe that the threat of a criminal sanction has this effect. Because the person is acting irrationally, he cannot be deterred by a criminal sanction either. Anyway, a more probable explanation for an employee acting like this is that he intends to damage the corporation by causing the fine to be imposed. But then the offence would no longer be a corporate offence anymore. For deterrence purposes, we would have to look for personal consequences for this person and not for a corporate sanction.

7.3 Imprisonment and Other Sanctions

Only monetary sanctions have been approached up to now. The sanction we associate with criminal law in the first place, imprisonment, seems to be wholly inappropriate in our context. You cannot throw a corporation into jail. On second thoughts, the idea is not that ridiculous. A natural person having to serve a sentence is deprived of his liberty to go where he would like. Legal persons are going nowhere but they may be deprived of their liberty to choose their range of business. Restrictions could apply to do business in certain areas, e.g. arms dealing.

Other sanctions could be specifically invented and enacted for corporate crimes: a corporation involved in crimes more often could be placed under receivership (Schünemann 2008, pp. 429, 446 et seq.); a firm convicted of a crime could lose the right to submit bids for public contracts for a certain time, it could lose public subsidies (cf. *European Court of Justice (ECJ)*, Europäische Zeitschrift für

Wirtschaftsrecht [EuZW] 2012, p. 543 [Bonda]; Lacny and Szwarc 2012, p. 170 et seq.; Ransiek 2012b, pp. 285, 292; Schünemann 2008, pp. 429, 446 et seq.); or vice versa: a corporation in compliance with legal regulations may receive a bonus. And even the "death penalty" is an option: A corporation being involved in crimes over and over again, being a threat to public safety concerns for the future, may be dissolved. All these sanctions are not new; most of them are provided for by existing laws. They are just not criminal sanctions and there is no reason why they should become part of the criminal law. The dissolution of companies by court or by a government agency's decision, e.g., is governed by various German company acts. This has been the law for corporations since 1937, for closed corporations since 1892. Thus, North Rhine-Westphalia's model penal code's idea to enable criminal courts to dissolve corporations is definitely old news.[3] In brief, there is no need for criminal law when special sanctions against corporations are devised.

7.4 Distinguishing Personal Culpability and Corporate Liability

I do not have any doubts that the dissolution of a company is a legitimate measure if there is no other remedy left to eliminate severe dangers for the public good caused by the corporation. It is beside the point that the German Constitution as well as Protocols to the Convention for the Protection of Human Rights[4] explicitly outlaw the death penalty. It is not a cruel and unusual punishment forbidden by the 8th Amendment to the U.S. Constitution if you dissolve a corporation. The protection of human dignity does not apply when a business enterprise is forced to shut its doors forever. A corporation does not have human dignity that could be protected by these prohibitions and rights. Thus, you could inflict criminal sanctions on corporations without violating their human dignity because they do not have human dignity. It is quite clear that there is a difference between humans and legal persons; and because there is a difference, imposing a criminal sanction should be restricted to humans, because only a human can act personally responsible, can be blamed, can be guilty (BVerfGE 123 p. 267 margin no. 413; *BVerfG*, Neue Juristische Wochenschrift [NJW] 2013, p. 1058, 1059).

There is a distinction the law should make if a baker as a sole proprietor of his bakery personally sells a spoiled slice of cake intentionally poisoning and killing his unsuspecting customer eating the cake or if a big bakery corporation is liable for the

[3]Since 1945 no corporation has been dissolved. So § 396 AktG is dead law.

[4]European Treaty Series No. 114—Protocol No. 6 to the Convention for the Protection of Human Rights and Fundamental Freedoms concerning the abolition of the death penalty; European Treaty Series No. 187—Protocol No. 13 to the Convention for the Protection of Human Rights and Fundamental Freedoms, concerning the abolition of the death penalty in all Circumstances.

customer's death because its salesperson intentionally poisons the customer to make a profit for the bakery. If the baker runs a huge bakery with hundreds of branches as a sole proprietor there is a difference if he personally kills his customer or is liable as a business owner for the damages his employees cause in the course of business.

Legal scholars tend to be stubborn folk: Even if the Attorney General's model code becomes the law and both deeds would carry criminal sanctions against the baker, we would claim that the sanctions only share the same name but are still different sanctions (Heine 2011, pp. 127, 128 et seq.; Neumann 2012, pp. 13, 20; Ransiek 2012a, pp. 285, 288 et seq.). Only in the first case, personal culpability is involved.

If criminal sanctions apply it stands to reason or is even mandatory that the procedural safeguards connected with (and restricted to) criminal law are applicable for corporations as well, e.g. the self-incrimination privilege (Krems 2015, pp. 5, 10). If sanctions against corporations are not criminal sanction, then this is not the case. Both the European Court of Justice (see *ECJ*, 18.10.1989, case 374/87 (*Orkem/Commission*), [1989] ECR 3283; ECJ, 10.11.1993, case 60/92 (*Otto/Postbank*), [1993] ECR I-5683) and the German Constitutional Court (see BVerfGE 95 p. 220, 242) held that the privilege does not protect corporations (cf. also Minoggio 2003, pp. 121, 125; Schohe 2002, pp. 492, 493; for details Kempf 2012, p. 347 et seqq.). Summarizing: criminal sanctions against corporations are a bad idea.

7.5 Sanctions Against Corporations at All?

The most important question remains. It is not criminal versus non-criminal sanctions against the corporation but whether there should be sanctions against companies at all. Since corporations cannot act without human beings acting for them, these human acts and omissions are either considered as acts or omissions of the corporation itself or they are ascribed to the corporation so that it is liable for someone else's fault (Schmidt 1990, pp. 130, 133). Some scholars argue that it is hardly justifiable to impose sanctions on both the corporation and the offending natural persons and wonder if this constitutes double jeopardy (Engisch 1954; cf. also Schünemann 2014, pp. 1, 11 et seqq.; Schünemann 1979, p. 242 et seqq.). It is stressed as well that when a corporation is fined, the consequences of this fine have to be borne by wholly innocent people, the shareholders and employees of the corporation (Schünemann 2015, pp. 274, 279; cf. Ransiek 2012b, pp. 45, 48).

Taking a side glance at tort law, it is quite clear that mainly the corporation not the corporation's employees is liable for its products and has to compensate for resulting damages. If a motor vehicle is faulty, e.g., the company is responsible for the product. As early as 1915, the German Reichsgericht held a manufacturer of table salt liable for damages caused by splinters of glass contaminating the product regardless of whether the plaintiff could prove how or by whom the splinters got into the salt (Entscheidungen des *Reichsgerichts* in Zivilsachen RGZ 87 p. 1, 3). It meets no concerns that corporations can be liable in private law. Therefore, it meets no concerns either if they are potential addressees of fines or other sanctions for violating legal rules, e.g. safety standards for their products. If corporations or other business partnerships are granted their own rights by law, especially the right to make a profit, the law may vice versa establish legal obligations for the corporation, conditions that have to be met in order to do business. If a "statute requires all persons, corporate or private, to refrain from certain practices, forbidden in the interest of public policy", it would be unjustifiable if only the private person could be subjected to a fine for violating the statute (*New York Central & Hudson River Railroad Co. v. United States*, 221 U.S. 481, 495 [1909]). It would not be justifiable if the private person's fine would be determined by his enterprise's income, but in the case of a corporation by the acting person's income.

In brief, if the law creates rights in favour of the corporation it may create obligations also. The legal person is a creature of law. Thus, by law, the legal person, not its shareholders or employees, is assigned its own duties which can be enforced by imposing sanctions. The U.S. Supreme Court held the same for criminal sanctions in *New York Central & Hudson River* in 1909: "Congress can impute to a corporation the commission of certain criminal offences and subject it to criminal prosecution therefor." (See *New York Central & Hudson River Railroad Co. v. United States*, 221 U.S. 481 [1909]).

7.6 Sanctioning Offences in the Course of Business

This does not mean that a corporation, partnership, or private manufacturer should automatically be liable for everything going wrong and causing damages in the course of business. The corporation is liable only for business offences, offences in the scope of the acting person's employment, not for all crimes committed on its premises. If an employee steals something from his co-worker or intends to damage the corporation by opening all the valves so that poisonous wastewater runs into a river, the corporation's duties are not involved. Usually, it is irrelevant where a theft takes place. It is a private crime. Nevertheless, the distinction between crimes in the course of business and "private" crimes of employees may be difficult. If the wastewater is extremely dangerous it may be negligent to let one single person be in charge of it. If the employee opens the valves negligently without the intent to damage the corporation he acts in the course of his employment. The German Federal Criminal Court, e.g., had to decide, whether mobbing of a mentally handicapped person by his co-workers was a risk sufficiently related to business activity (Entscheidungen des *Bundesgerichtshofs in Strafsachen* BGHSt 57 p. 42).

Looking at the Reichsgericht case again, imposing a fine for selling contaminated salt is only reasonable if either the contamination itself or the sale of the contaminated salt was avoidable by reasonable means, e.g. by controlling the purity of the salt before selling it. Threatening somebody to impose a fine for undesired consequences is useless if there is no way to eliminate these consequences. An impending fine cannot induce the manufacturer to take means to avoid the consequences if no such means are available. Thus, there is no preventive effect and the fine is useless. In the Reichsgericht case: If there were nothing one could do to ensure that only uncontaminated salt were put on the market, the only way out would be to shut down the business altogether.

Therefore, the corporation should only be liable if it did not take the adequate and reasonable steps to prevent the violation. By whom these steps had to be taken is irrelevant if the corporation is understood as a unity encompassing all its facilities, equipment, and persons working for the corporation.[5] Thus, the question which single person, a regular employee, a midlevel manager or a board member, actually caused the violation by his or her act or omission should be irrelevant. Relevant is alone if the corporation as a whole, through all its members, could avoid the violation (see also Ransiek 2012b, pp. 45, 50 et seq.; Ransiek 2012a, pp. 285, 299 et seq.). If the corporation took all the reasonable and adequate steps to comply with the law, there is no corporate liability.

The devil is, of course, in the details because it has to be decided what the necessary and reasonable steps are (see Beulke and Moosmayer 2014, pp. 146, 151 et seq.: selection and instruction of employees; determination and assessment of risks and dangers; express instructions and education). To cite the 9th Circuit's Hilton Corporation case (*United States v. Hilton Hotels Corporation*, 467 F.2d 1000 [1972]) as an example, an employee is still acting within the scope of his employment even if he acts contrary to direct orders of his superior and to guidelines by the hotel group's management. If, however, there were not only orders but a system to enforce them as well, it can be argued that these are sufficient steps to prevent the violation. The employee circumventing these measures acts outside the scope of his employment.

When it comes to sentencing German criminal law is quite clear and all arguments are in favour of applying these rules to sanctions against corporations as well. It is a mitigating factor if the corporation newly installs or improves an existing compliance system in order to prevent future violations (see Moosmayer and Gropp-Stadler 2012, pp. 241, 242; this does not mean that the mere existence of a compliance programme that could not prevent the violation is a mitigating factor. See Krebs et al. 2011, p. 213 et seqq.; Engelhart 2015, pp. 201, 207). The Attorney General's model code provides an express section (§ 5) allowing to abstain from fining the corporation in this case.

[5]In principle, the approach of German law is different: Originally, only board members and CEOs could trigger a fine against the corporation. The position presented here is the view of U.S. law, *New York Central & Hudson River Railroad Co. v. United States*, 221 U.S. 481, 491, 495 et seq., and European antitrust law, *ECJ*, 07.06.1983, case 100/80 (*Musique Diffusion francaise et al./ Commission*) [1983] ECR 1825, 1903. Since German Law now includes midlevel managers and compliance officers, differences are small at best.

7.7 Corporate Versus Personal Liability

A closing remark: If a corporation or partnership is regarded as a unity and is held liable for business violations, the law can forgo personal criminal liability of the wrongfully acting or omitting persons. For example, in European antitrust law only corporations (undertakings) are liable, not the acting humans. The enterprise has to comply with antitrust law but the acting persons are of no interest. Likewise, it is a better idea to hold responsible, and fine, ship owners for polluting the sea by releasing used oil than threatening single sailors with a criminal sanction. An even better idea is to have no fine or criminal sanction at all but just enough tanks in all harbours, taking care of the oil with little or no cost for the owner. This is not European law, however; European law is: The sailor is to be held criminally liable to protect the environment (Article 4 Directive 2009/123/EC of 21 October 2009 amending Directive 2005/35/EC on ship-source pollution and on the introduction of penalties for infringements). To date, nobody has been found who has been convicted. Thus, from a procedural perspective one should think twice before introducing criminal sanctions against board members or employees of a corporation in antitrust cases (cf. Busse 2015).

References

Beulke, W., & Moosmayer, K. (2014). Der Reformvorschlag des Bundesverbandes der Unternehmensjuristen zu den §§ 30, 130 OWiG – Plädoyer für ein modernes Unternehmenssanktionenrecht –. *Corporate Compliance Zeitschrift (CCZ)*, 146 et seqq.

Busse, C. (2015). Haftstrafen für Manager. *Süddeutsche Zeitung 25.10*. Available from: http://www.sueddeutsche.de/wirtschaft/kartellrecht-haftstrafen-fuer-manager-1.2707171. Accessed 19 March 2016.

Coffee, J. C. (1981). 'No Soul to Damn: No Body to Kick': An unscandalized inquiry into the problem of corporate punishment. *Michigan Law Review, 79*, 386 et seqq.

Coffee, J. C. (1992). Paradigms lost: The blurring of the criminal and civil law models, and what can be done about it. *Yale Law Journal, 101*, 1875 et seqq.

de la Cuesta, J. L., & Pérez Machío, A. I. (2008). Auf dem Weg zu einem Strafrecht für juristische Personen – das spanische Strafrecht. In U. Sieber, et al. (Eds.), *Festschrift für Klaus Tiedemann* (p. 527 et seqq.).

Engelhart, M. (2015). Verbandsverantwortlichkeit – Dogmatik und Rechtsvergleichung. *Neue Zeitschrift für Wirtschafts-, Steuer- und Unternehmensstrafrecht (NZWiSt)*, 201 et seqq.

Engisch, K. (1954). Verhandlungen des 40. Deutschen Juristentages. BD II, Teil E, S. E. 38.

Erhardt, A. (1994). Unternehmensdelinquenz und Unternehmensstrafe.

Frisch, W. (2013). Strafbarkeit juristischer Personen und Zurechnung. In *Festschrift für Jürgen Wolter* (p. 349 et seqq.).

Handelsblatt. (2013). EU lässt Banken für Zins-Manipulationen bluten. Available from: http://goo.gl/NH5c6I. Accessed 4 December 2013.

Heine, G. (2003). Das kommende Unternehmensstrafrecht. *Schweizerische Zeitschrift des Strafrechts (ZStrR), 121*, 24 et seqq.

Heine, G. (2005). Praktische Probleme des Unternehmensstrafrechts. *Schweizerische Zeitschrift für Wirtschafts- und Finanzmarktrecht (SZW), 77*, 17 et seqq.

Heine, G. (2011). Reform des Kartell(straf)rechts in der Schweiz – Anstöße für Deutschland. In *Festschrift für Hans Achenbach* (p. 127 et seqq.).

Hoven, E. (2014). Der nordrhein-westfälische Entwurf eines Verbandsstrafgesetzbuchs – Eine kritische Betrachtung von Begründungsmodell und Voraussetzungen der Straftatbestände. *Zeitschrift für Internationale Strafrechtsdogmatik (ZIS)*, 19 et seqq.

Hoven, E., Wimmer, R., Schwarz, T. & Schumann, S. (2014). Der nordrhein-westfälische Entwurf eines Verbandsstrafgesetzes – Kritische Anmerkungen aus Wissenschaft und Praxis. *Neue Zeitschrift für Wirtschafts-, Steuer- und Unternehmensstrafrecht (NZWiSt)*, 161 et seqq., 201 et seqq., 241 et seqq.

Jahn, M., & Pietsch, F. (2015). Der NRW-Entwurf für ein Verbandsstrafgesetzbuch – Eine Einführung in das Konzept und seine Folgefragen. *Zeitschrift für Internationale Strafrechtsdogmatik (ZIS)*, 1 et seqq.

Justizportal Nordrhein-Westfahlen (Justiz-online). (2013). TOP II.5: Unternehmensstrafrecht. Available from: https://www.justiz.nrw.de/JM/leitung/jumiko/beschluesse/2013/herbstkonferenz13/zw3/TOP_II_5.pdf. Accessed 20 March 2016.

Kempf, E. (2012). Die Beschuldigtenrechte in einem Strafverfahren gegen Unternehmen. In E. Kempf, K. Lüderssen, & K. Volk (Eds.), *Unternehmensstrafrecht* (p. 347 et seqq.).

Kommission zur Reform des Strafrechtlichen Sanktionensystems. (2000). Abschlussbericht der Kommission zur Reform des Strafrechtlichen Sanktionensystems. Available from https://www.bib.uni-mannheim.de/fileadmin/pdf/fachinfo/jura/absclussber-der-komm-strafreform.pdf. Accessed 15 March 2016.

Krebs, P., Eufinger, A., & Jung, S. (2011). Bußgeldminderung durch Compliance-Programme im deutschen Kartellbußgeldverfahren?. *Corporate Compliance Zeitschrift (CCZ)*, 213 et seqq.

Krems, K.-H. (2015). Der NRW-Entwurf für ein Verbandsstrafgesetzbuch – Gesetzgeberische Intention und Konzeption. *Zeitschrift für Internationale Strafrechtsdogmatik (ZIS)*, 5 et seqq.

Lacny, J., & Szwarc, M. (2012). Legal nature of European Union agricultural penalties. *The European Criminal Law Associations' Forum (eucrim)*, 170 et seqq.

Mateu, C. (2011). Die strafrechtliche Verantwortlichkeit juristischer Personen: Überlegungen zur 'Dogmatik' und zum System der Reform des spanischen Strafgesetzbuchs 2010. *Zeitschrift für die gesamte Strafrechtswissenschaft (ZStW), 123*, 331 et seqq.

Minoggio, I. (2003). Das Schweigerecht der juristischen Person als Nebenbeteiligte im Strafverfahren. In *Zeitschrift für Wirtschafts- und Steuerstrafrecht (wistra)* (p. 121 et seqq.).

Mitsch, W. (2014). Täterschaft und Teilnahme bei der Verbandsstraftat. *Neue Zeitschrift für Wirtschafts-, Steuer- und Unternehmensstrafrecht (NZWiSt)*, 1 et seqq.

Moosmayer, K., & Gropp-Stadler, S. (2012). Der Diskussionsentwurf des Bundesmininisteriums der Justiz zur Änderung der §§ 30, 130 OWiG: Ein Zwischenruf. *Neue Zeitschrift für Wirtschafts-, Steuer- und Unternehmensstrafrecht (NZWiSt)*, 241 et seqq.

Neumann, U. (2012). Strafrechtliche Verantwortlichkeit von Verbänden – rechtstheoretische Prolegomena. In E. Kempf, K. Lüderssen, & K. Volk (Eds.), *Unternehmensstrafrecht* (p. 13 et seqq.).

Partsch, C. (2012). Hundert Jahre Erfahrung mit einem Unternehmensstrafrecht in den USA. In E. Kempf, K. Lüderssen, & K. Volk (Eds.), *Unternehmensstrafrecht* (p. 55 et seqq.).

Protess, B., & Silver-Greenberg, J. (2015). Deutsche Bank nears plea deal over Libor manipulation. *New York Times*, 09.04.2015. Available from: http://goo.gl/15RMK1. Accessed 17 March 2016.

Ransiek, A. (2012a). Überlegungen zur strafrechtlichen Verantwortung des Unternehmensträgers. In E. Kempf, K. Lüderssen, & K. Volk (Eds.), *Unternehmensstrafrecht* (p. 285 et seqq.).

Ransiek, A. (2012b). Zur strafrechtlichen Verantwortung von Unternehmen. *Neue Zeitschrift für Wirtschafts-, Steuer- und Unternehmensstrafrecht (NZWiSt)*, 45 et seqq.

Schmidt, K. (1990). Zur Verantwortung von Gesellschaften und Verbänden im Kartell-Ordnungswidrigkeitenrecht. *Zeitschrift für Wirtschafts- und Steuerstrafrecht (wistra)*, 130 et seqq.

Schohe, G. (2002). Muss die Berufung auf Grundrechte zweckmäßig sein? Zur Aussageverweigerung im europäischen Kartellrecht. *Neue Juristische Wochenschrift (NJW)*, 492 et seq.

Schork, A., & Reichling, T. (2012). Neues Strafrecht aus Brüssel? – Europäische Komission forciert Verschärfung des Kapitalmarktstrafrechts und Einführung eines Unternehmensstrafrechts. *Strafverteidigerforum (StraFo)*, 125 et seqq.

Schünemann, B. (1979). Unternehmenskriminalität und Strafrecht.

Schünemann, B. (2008). Strafrechtliche Sanktionen gegen Wirtschaftsunternehmen?. In U. Sieber, et al. (Eds.), *Festschrift für Klaus Tiedemann* (p. 429 et seqq.).

Schünemann, B. (2014). Die aktuelle Forderung eines Verbandsstrafrechts – Ein kriminalpolitischer Zombie. *Zeitschrift für Internationale Strafrechtsdogmatik (ZIS), 9*, 1 et seqq.

Schünemann, B. (2015). Schuldprinzip und Sanktionierung von juristischen Personen und Personenverbänden – Lehren aus dem deutsch-spanischen Strafrechtsdialog. *Goltdammer's Archiv für Strafrecht (GA)*, 274 et seqq.

Silva Sánchez, J.-M. (2012). Die Strafrechtliche Haftung von juristischen Personen nach spanischem Strafrecht. In E. Kempf, K. Lüderssen, & K. Volk (Eds.), *Unternehmensstrafrecht* (p. 59 et seqq.).

Stree, W., & Kinzig, J. (2014). In A. Schönke & H. Schröder (Eds.), *Strafegesetzbuch StGB 29th ed.*

Weigend, E., & Namysłowska-Gabrysiak, B. (2004). Die strafrechtliche Verantwortlichkeit juristischer Personen im polnischen Recht. *Zeitschrift für die gesamte Strafrechtswissenschaft (ZStW), 116*, 541 et seqq.

Zieschang, F. (2014). Kritische Anmerkungen zu dem Entwurf eines Gesetzes zur Einführung der strafrechtlichen Verantwortlichkeit von Unternehmen und sonstigen Verbänden. *Goltdammer's Archiv für Strafrecht (GA)*, 91 et seqq.

Chapter 8
Compliance and Individual Sanctions in the Enforcement of Competition Law

Florian Wagner-von Papp

Abstract This chapter describes the status quo of criminal enforcement in selected Member States of the European Union and discusses the desirability of criminal enforcement of competition law from a policy perspective. It concludes that at least in Germany the introduction of a criminal offence for horizontal hardcore cartels beyond the existing bid-rigging offence would be desirable, provided an automatic criminal immunity provision for immunity recipients under a leniency programme within the European Competition Network is introduced and the Bundeskartellamt is involved in the criminal prosecution. The introduction of effective criminal enforcement would make compliance training both more important and more effective. Criminalisation makes compliance more important because compliance training helps to spread knowledge about the criminal offence—and only a known threat can deter. Criminalisation makes compliance training more effective because the participants of compliance sessions are motivated to pay attention to avoid criminal liability.

8.1 Introduction

Compliance training can be exhausting for the participants. Managers and employees sit through the first presentation telling them how important it is to comply with product safety standards.[1] The next speaker stresses that the most important thing in the world is to comply with anti-corruption laws.[2] The following

[1]Think of recent recalls, e.g., for Takata airbags (Tabuchi and Ivory 2016); for the defect in the ignition switch for GM vehicles, which resulted in a criminal penalty of $900 million and private settlements of at least a further $600 million (Wright 2015) in addition to a large-scale recall (Vlasic and Stout 2014); or for the defect leading to uncontrolled acceleration in Toyota vehicles, resulting, inter alia, in a financial penalty of $1.2 billion (see Department of Justice 2014a).

[2]See, e.g., the Siemens scandal (on the consequences for compliance, see, e.g., Sindhu 2009). Good relations to the government may help, *cf* Adams and Boxell (2006) on the attorney-general's intervention in the investigation by the Serious Fraud Office (SFO) into alleged corruption of BAE in Saudi Arabia.

F. Wagner-von Papp (✉)
Faculty of Laws, University College London (UCL), London, UK
e-mail: f.wagner-von-papp@ucl.ac.uk

J. Paha (ed.), *Competition Law Compliance Programmes*,
DOI 10.1007/978-3-319-44633-2_8

presentation highlights that *actually* the most important thing in the world is to comply strictly with money-laundering statutes.[3] Shortly before the next presenter can impress the importance of compliance with environmental standards upon the captive (but not captivated) audience, the managers and employees of certain German car manufacturers have dozed off (*cf* Department of Justice 2016). By the time competition law is discussed, only those who secretly answer e-mails or play games on their mobile devices are still awake.

It is challenging enough for law students who have chosen to specialise in any of these subjects to stay alert for a prolonged period of time. Why should managers and employees who have chosen a different career path, and perceive compliance training as an irritating distraction that keeps them from doing their "real work", be any more focused?

In order to get an audience's attention, it is necessary to avoid abstractions and focus on the personal incentives for members of the audience. Attention in the sleepiest school classroom becomes rapt as soon as the word "exam" is dropped. This word focuses students' attention on extrinsic incentives. Likewise, attention in a compliance seminar becomes suddenly extraordinarily focused once the members of the audience are told that "if you fix prices, you go to prison".

The same effect cannot be achieved by saying that "your undertaking may be hit by a high fine". As Part 2 describes in more detail, on the level of the European Union there are growing incentives for undertakings to refrain from entering into cartels. However, to paraphrase the National Rifle Association: undertakings do not form cartels, people form cartels (*cf* Snyder 2016). If the goal is to prevent cartelisation, the message has to get through to the individuals who may actually interact with competitors. That competition authorities may impose a multi-million euro fine on the undertaking does not directly concern these individuals' incentives; there is a principal-agent problem. Individual sanctions, and in particular criminal sanctions, would address this principal-agent problem (Wils 2003, p. 434; 2008: § 559; Wagner-von Papp 2010a, pp. 292–293; 2010b, pp. 270–271).

Many Member States in the European Union have picked up on this problem and have introduced individual sanctions in the form of criminal or individual administrative sanctions. Part 3 of this chapter describes some of these approaches, the level of individual enforcement in selected Member States, and some of the problems such enforcement faces or creates on the Member State level.

In Part 4, I examine the arguments for and against criminal enforcement against individuals for competition law infringements. Whether criminalisation is desirable crucially depends on the institutional framework of the jurisdiction in question and the form the criminal provision takes (Kovacic 2006, 2016). The question whether criminalisation of competition law infringements is desirable can therefore not be answered in the abstract. Specifically in the German context, however, the reasons for introducing further criminal sanctions for horizontal hardcore cartels outweigh the reasons against criminalisation. Some of the remaining institutional arguments

[3]See, e.g., the HSBC case (Department of Justice 2012).

against criminalisation do carry a certain weight, but can be addressed in a broader reform that would introduce criminal sanctions but also modify existing institutions.

It is important to recognise that such an institutional reform would indeed be a necessary complement to the introduction of criminal sanctions. It would be a mistake to insert a criminal prohibition provision into the criminal code or competition legislation and hope that this in itself deters anyone and does not result in unintended consequences. In particular, institutional reforms are required to optimise the interaction between criminal sanctions and leniency programmes, and the cooperation between competition authorities and prosecutors. The introduction of criminal sanctions, after all, is not an end in itself. Its goal is to achieve greater deterrence on the individual level. In order for criminal sanctions to be effective, the offence has to be integrated into the antitrust enforcement system, and criminal sanctions have to be accompanied by a procedural framework that allows effective and transparent enforcement, both nationally and internationally.

In Part 5, I discuss international aspects of the criminalisation debate. Part 6 concludes.

8.2 Rising Sanctions on Undertakings and Their Inadequacy

It is no secret that fines on undertakings for competition law infringements under Article 23 of Regulation (EC) 1/2003 have sharply increased over the past 3 decades. Over each of the 5-year periods from 1990 to 1994, and from 1995 to 1999, the European Commission imposed fines of about €300 million in total.[4] In the 5-year period from 2000 to 2004, this increased tenfold to about €3 billion.[5] From 2005 to 2009, this sum rose again by a factor 2.5 to some €8 billion, where it stayed for the 5-year period from 2010 to 2014.[6]

This sharp rise in total fines is not so much driven by an increase in the number of fined undertakings; that number stayed remarkably stable (with the exception of the period from 1995 to 1999) at around 150–200 undertakings per 5-year period.[7] The rise is partly attributable to a larger number of cartel cases, which rose from about 10 cartels in each of the two 5-year periods in the 1990s to about 30 cartels in each of the three 5-year periods since 2000, arguably due to the introduction of the leniency programmes.[8]

[4]See European Commission, Cartel Statistics, https://perma.cc/KP5P-4GGJ, Table 1.4 (court adjusted) (at the time of writing last changed on 6 April 2016; for periodically updated statistics see http://ec.europa.eu/competition/cartels/statistics/statistics.pdf).

[5]Ibid. The amounts do not seem to be adjusted for inflation, however.

[6]Ibid.

[7]Ibid, Table 1.8 (at the time of writing last changed 6 April 2016).

[8]Ibid, Table 1.10 (at the time of writing last changed 6 April 2016). The number of immunity recipients was 20, 25, and 21, for the three 5 year periods from 2001 to 2005, 2006 to 2010, and

Mostly, however, the rise seems driven by higher average fines per undertaking. The average fine per undertaking rose from below €2 million (1990–1994) to approximately €6 million (1995–1999), €20 million (2000–2004), and eventually approximately €40 million for the latest two full 5-year periods (2005–2009 and 2010–2014).[9] The distribution of cartel fines per undertaking is heavily skewed: the 11 largest cartel fines per undertaking range from €320 million to €715 million.[10] For about 10 % of all fined undertakings the fine makes up about 8–10 % of their global annual turnover.[11]

What do these figures tell us about the effectiveness of relying on fines on undertakings alone? Two possible scenarios have to be distinguished: in the first scenario, the expected fine on the undertaking exceeds the expected benefits from the cartel: fines are optimal. In the second scenario, the expected benefits from the cartel exceed the expected fine on the undertaking: fines are sub-optimal.

Let us first assume that the current fines for the undertakings have already reached an optimal level. If that is the case, cartels "do not pay" for the undertaking, and the undertaking would want their agents to refrain from entering into cartels. Incentives for the manager or employee in question can, however, diverge. Entering into a cartel can still be attractive for these individuals, who may hope to boost their division's sales and so keep their jobs, get a performance bonus, or even be promoted. The fine imposed on the undertaking does not directly affect these incentives. There is a principal-agent problem.

Ex ante screening for managers and employees that will not enter into cartels is not realistically possible.[12] Nor is it practically feasible for the principal (the undertaking) to monitor its agents (managers and employees) perfectly, at least in larger undertakings. This leaves aligning the incentives as a remedy for addressing the principal-agent problem.

The undertaking may indeed take some steps to align the incentives of the undertaking and its managers and employees. The undertaking could pass on some of its displeasure about fines and damages payments to the responsible managers or employees in the form of termination of employment, clawing back bonuses, or perhaps even by seeking indemnification for competition fines or damages.

2011 to 2015, respectively (see Wils 2016), thus accounting fairly precisely for the jump to around 30 cartel cases in each of these periods from the baseline of about 10 cartel cases per 5-year period before 2000.

[9]See Lianos et al. (2014, p. 129) (the average fine for the full period from 2010 to 2014 is only about €41 million, as opposed to the €50 million reported in that report, because the report was published in May 2014 and could not take into account later events, which included both the downward court adjustment of cartel fines and a number of lower fines imposed in 2014).

[10]European Commission, n. 4, Table 1.6 (at the time of writing last updated 6 April 2016).

[11]Ibid, Table 1.11 (at the time of writing last updated 31 December 2015).

[12]Employing risk averse, civic-minded bureaucrat-type personalities would arguably reduce the danger of cartels, but may be suboptimal in terms of vigorous competition.

Contrary to occasional assertions, generally by opponents of criminalisation (Ost 2014, pp. 134–135; Dreher 2011, pp. 242–243; Twele 2013), these indirect internal sanctions are, however, not an effective deterrent if used as an *alternative* to criminal sanctions (Monopolkommission 2014, p. 146). They are unlikely to be imposed by the undertaking for several reasons.

First, even where the undertaking does not wish its agents to engage in cartels, it may be reluctant to terminate the employment in every case in which an infringement occurs. Ditching employees too readily may make future recruitment more difficult. Employment law may be, or be perceived as, an obstacle. A "zero tolerance" policy may even be counterproductive from a compliance angle: The fear of termination of employment may prevent employees that have contributed to a cartel from "owning up", thereby preventing an early and successful leniency application. The individual's continuing cooperation may be important for the success of a leniency application, and a zero-tolerance policy may deter the individual from admitting her own contribution.

Secondly, even to the extent an undertaking should be willing to commit to a "zero tolerance" policy, this is not necessarily a sufficient disincentive for the agents. In some cases, the incentive for the individual to enter into a cartel is that they are falling behind performance targets and fear immediate termination of employment. In these cases, the temptation to boost sales by entering into a cartel will hardly be offset by the remote possibility that the employment will eventually be terminated if and when the cartel is uncovered—even if this contingency materialises, termination would still be delayed, probably by several years. Furthermore, given that the average cartel duration even of detected cartels is approximately 5–7 years[13] and investigations and prosecutions take additional time, chances are good that the employee or manager is no longer employed by the same undertaking by the time that undertaking could seek termination or other remedies against the individual in question (Wils 2003, pp. 429, 434; 2008: § 559). In contrast, for the imposition of criminal sanctions the fact that the individual has

[13]Levenstein and Suslow (2011, pp. 462–463) look at 81 cartels with participants from at least two jurisdictions ("international cartels") that were prosecuted in the US or the EU with start dates from 1990; they find a mean duration of 8.1 years (standard deviation s = 5.8 years) and a median of 7 years (see also ibid, pp. 463–464, citing older studies that report similar means of between 5.3 and 8.3 years). Combe and Monnier (2011, p. 243) consider a sample of 64 European cartels between 1975 and 2009 and find a mean duration of 7 years. Bryant and Eckard (1991) look at a sample of 184 detected cartel cases (US Department of Justice cases from the period between 1961 and 1988) and find a mean duration of between 5.2 and 7.3 years (with a median of between 3.6 and 5.8 years) (the ranges indicate the lowest and highest duration estimates, respectively). See also Harrington and Wei (2015), who argue that the estimated duration derived from the average duration of *detected* cartels is only mildly biased because of two countervailing effects: on the one hand, when cartels are detected, their lifetime is cut short, and so for that reason they may have a shorter duration than those cartels that are not detected, and additionally, the probability of dying cartels to be detected may be higher (in particular because this transforms the stag-hunt-game of leniency programmes into prisoners' dilemmas); on the other hand, longer cartels may be overrepresented in the sample of detected cartels because they are more likely to be detected at some point in their lifetime.

moved on is irrelevant; the only question is whether prosecution is barred by a statute of limitations.

The danger of the undertaking seeking indemnity for the fine is even more remote. First, at least in the United Kingdom and Germany, courts have rejected claims brought by undertakings for indemnification.[14] Secondly, there are de facto obstacles. In particular where board members were involved in the infringement, there is an obvious principal-agent problem between the board as an agent, which decides on whether to initiate an action, and the interest of the shareholders as principals. In Germany, this principal-agent relationship should be attenuated where the firm in question is governed by a two-tiered board; but even there the supervisory board may be personally attached to the members of the executive board. The principal-agent problem is theoretically also attenuated by the possibility of derivative shareholder actions; but these have high procedural and evidentiary hurdles, show little promise in the antitrust sector even in the United States, and play practically no role in the antitrust context in Europe. At any rate, such claims would be limited to purely financial consequences for the individual and are capped at the level of consumer insolvency.[15] This cap for recovery will prevent many undertakings from even trying to recover from individuals. Similar arguments prevent the possibility of victims bringing damages actions against the responsible individuals directly from being an effective deterrent (see Eden 2014).

Therefore, in the scenario in which sanctions on undertakings are optimal, direct individual sanctions are necessary to overcome the principal-agent problem.

---

[14]In the United Kingdom, it was held that the *ex turpi causa* doctrine prevented the undertaking from seeking indemnification from employees and directors, because the Chapter I prohibition and Article 101 TFEU are addressed to the undertaking itself. *Safeway Stores Ltd and others v Twigger and others*, [2010] EWCA Civ 1472, [2011] Bus. L.R. 1629 (for a discussion, see, e.g., Kapp and Hummel 2011). The UK Supreme Court has recently indicated that it may not unreservedly stand behind *Safeway v Twigger*, see *Les Laboratoires Servier and another v Apotex Inc and others*, [2014] UKSC 55, [2015] A.C. 430, 451 [45]: "[T]his is not a case in which any question arises as to the correctness or otherwise of a decision such as that of the Court of Appeal in *Safeway Stores Ltd v Twigger* [. . .], which held that a company could not recover from directors or employees who had by involving the company in acts contravening the Competition Act 1998 caused it to incur a 'personal' liability for penalties imposed under that Act." In Germany, the Landesarbeitsgericht Düsseldorf reached the same result by a similar route: indemnification was held to run counter the purposes of the fine imposed on the undertaking; this was considered to be in particular the case where the fine incorporates elements of disgorgement of illegal gains; and the possibility of imposing fines on the undertaking and the individual was considered to preclude the possibility for the undertaking to seek indemnification from the responsible individuals, both individuals in management (LAG Düsseldorf, 20 January 2015, 16 Sa 459/14, *Neue Juristische Online-Zeitschrift* 2015, 782, 789 ff.; the court below had considered capping the damages claim at the maximum amount for the individual fine) and employees (LAG Düsseldorf, 27 November 2015, 14 Sa 800/14, *BeckRS* 2016, 65558, para 164 (*obiter*, because the court considered the employee's participation in the cartel not to be proven, ibid, paras 180 ff.)).

[15]While Director & Officers' Insurance could lead to deeper pockets, D&O Insurance will not cover willful law infringements.

The analysis is complicated by the fact that we simply do not know whether the sanctions on undertakings are indeed optimal.[16] Fines have admittedly skyrocketed over the past 2 decades and look very high in absolute terms. It is, however, still not clear whether the expected fines are higher than the expected benefits from the cartel. Calculating the optimal fine in the real world meets with several difficulties. Even at an aggregate level, it is difficult to calculate (average) cartel profits. One of the most problematic issues is that it is nearly impossible to determine the rate of detection. The 15–17 % figure that is often bandied about derives from a sample of detected cartels, and the authors of that study were careful to explain that for the population of undetected cartels, this is an *upper bound* for the detection probability, and the detection probability for that population could be lower (Bryant and Eckard 1991). Leniency programmes have probably increased the detection probability, but again the effect is nearly impossible to quantify empirically (Marvão and Spagnolo 2015).

If fines are in reality sub-optimal, then two problems compound each other. First, agents may have their own selfish motives for entering into the cartel, for example, meeting sales targets for bonuses, continued employment or promotions, just as in the case of optimal fines that was discussed above. Secondly, the undertaking in this scenario does not have an incentive to discourage its agents from entering into cartels. On the contrary. If fines are suboptimal, the undertaking does not mind the agents entering into cartels; it only minds them getting caught. The internal sanctioning mechanisms discussed above that are at least theoretically possible—such as terminating the employment, clawing back bonuses, or seeking indemnities—would therefore likely not be used by the undertaking. Theoretically, the undertaking would even have no interest *at all* in employing any of these measures because this would deter other employees from entering into profitable cartels. In practice, it is possible that the undertaking would nevertheless employ some of the measures, for example sacrifice the responsible employees, to create the perception that the undertaking distances itself from the infringement (*cf* Ransiek and Hüls 2009, p. 160). It could even be that the detection of the first cartel makes future cartels unprofitable, either because the probability of detection becomes higher, for example, because the competition authorities keep a closer eye on the activities of a previous offender, or because the fine increase for recidivism is sufficiently high. Where fines on the undertaking are sub-optimal, the introduction of criminal sanctions creates an incentive for individuals to withstand suggestions or pressure from the undertaking to engage in prohibited conduct (Jones and Harrison 2014).

[16]See on the one hand Combe and Monnier (2011), pp. 267–268 (finding that in about half of the cases the fines did not even skim off the gains, so that they would not even be deterrent if the detection probability were 100 %) and on the other hand Allain et al. (2013) (finding that between 30 and 80 % of the fines imposed from 2005 to 2010 were deterrent, depending largely on the assumptions about the competitive mark-up in the counterfactual, about the cartel overcharge, and about the demand elasticities).

One can, of course, make the argument that if fines on undertakings are still sub-optimal, one should first raise the fines on undertakings even further before turning to individual sanctions. However, there are limits to this approach (Monopolkommission 2014: § 148).

First, as mentioned above, approximately 10 % of fined undertakings are fined at a level that approaches the statutory cap of 10 % of the annual global turnover (Article 23(4) of Regulation 1/2003). Unless this statutory cap is raised, increasing fines for these undertakings more than trivially is impossible.

Secondly, raising the level of fines in such a way that a greater proportion of infringers is fined at the statutory cap level risks creating perverse incentives because of a loss of marginal deterrence. Consider the extreme case that fines are raised to a level such that all cartels are fined at the 10 % cap. In this case, cartels could nearly costlessly extend their scope or duration, or engage in any other conduct that would usually constitute an aggravating factor under the Fining Guidelines, such as instigating and leading the cartel, coercing others into the cartel, or becoming a recidivist.[17]

Thirdly, the fines calculated under the Fining Guidelines are already reduced in some cases to avoid an inability to pay.[18] Putting firms out of business in cartelised markets, which tend to be concentrated anyway, is not a particularly good idea, and so, in addition to the statutory cap in Article 23(4) Regulation 1/2003, there is a de facto cap for fines on undertakings at the solvency level.

Fourthly, unless courts can be persuaded that the high fines are necessary to skim off the gains from cartels, they may be unwilling to go along with further increases of the fines. Up to now, the courts have been willing to defer to the competition authorities' assessment that fine levels needed to be raised to be dissuasive. Persuading them of the need for ever higher fines may, however, not be easy given the problems in quantifying the optimal fine based on robust empirical evidence.

Apart from these legal and de facto limits on raising fines on undertakings even further, higher fines on undertakings would not address the principal-agent problem identified above. Alternatively or cumulatively to raising the fine level, one could increase the expected fine by raising the probability of detection (Dreher 2011, p. 240). This, however, would also fail to address the principal-agent problem. Of course, any unused potential to raise the detection probability efficiently should be tapped. The suggestion that deterrence can be substantially increased by this route implies, however, that competition authorities are currently not using the full potential of their powers. They are arguably doing the best they can with their

[17]I say only "nearly costlessly" because any extension of scope or duration of the cartel or intensification of cartel activity would increase the probability of detection of the cartel, so that the expected fine would rise. Nevertheless, if the cartel is considered to be profitable in the first place, it is likely that the marginal increase in the detection probability would be lower than the marginal increase in cartel profits where, for example, the cartel duration is extended.

[18]See point 35 of the Fining Guidelines. See also Almunia and Lewandowski (2010); Monopolkommission (2014), § 148.

present powers; the low-hanging fruit has been picked. A way to increase the detection probability further would be to increase the authorities' powers—and one way to do this is to give them the powers that are available only in criminal investigations, such as wiretapping (below Sect. 8.4.3, sixth argument). Some other additional powers, such as offering rewards for whistleblowers (Monopolkommission 2014: §§ 199–209; Zimmer 2016; see also Stephan 2014a), could arguably even be introduced without criminalising cartels, but are similarly controversial (and criminalisation and these measures are, in any case, not mutually exclusive).

Another suggestion, and one which would go some way to addressing the principal-agent issue, has been to make managers or board members of the infringer directly liable to the victims of cartels for private damages, either as an alternative (eg, Dreher 2009 and 2011; Twele 2013, pp. 229–232) or possibly cumulatively (Eden 2013, pp. 59–60) to criminal sanctions. Whatever the other merits of this proposal may be de lege lata or de lege ferenda, it will be much more difficult to coordinate public enforcement with this form of private enforcement than with criminal enforcement (in particular with regard to leniency programmes); in contrast to criminal sanctions, it would arguably not be possible to limit such extraneous private liability to horizontal hardcore restrictions; and therefore the chilling effects from potentially unlimited private liability (against which insurance is impermissible) is at least as high as that of criminal sanctions. In other words, if the arguments against criminal enforcement were compelling, they would largely apply a *fortiori* to direct liability of managers or board members for private damages.

8.3 Individual Sanctions on the Member State Level

While there are no individual sanctions on the European Union level, a majority of Member States have introduced individual sanctions of some sort, often criminal sanctions.[19] When it comes to sanctions against individuals, some Member States,

---

[19]At least the following EU jurisdictions provide for criminal sanctions for cartels (or, where noted, only bid rigging): Austria (bid rigging only, Ablasser-Neuhuber and Neumayr 2015, p. 19); Belgium (Lebrun and Bersou 2015, p. 25: 'Bid rigging is the sole cartel activity which is likely to lead to criminal sanctions'); the Czech Republic (Fiala 2015, p. 65); Denmark (since 2013, Rung-Hansen 2015, p. 71); France (Viros 2016); Germany (bid rigging; Wagner-von Papp 2011; Wagner-von Papp 2016; Zimmer 2016); Greece (Papadopoulos and Lovdahl Gormsen 2015, p. 107); Hungary (bid rigging; Szabó 2015, p. 120); Ireland (Andrews and Collins 2015, pp. 137–138; for more detail see Massey and Cooke 2011, p. 105); Italy (Caiazzo and Costantini 2015, p. 154); Poland (bid rigging only, Hansberry-Bieguńska and Krasnodębska-Tomkiel 2015, p. 214); Romania (separate provisions for cartels and bid rigging, Rădulescu and Iacob 2015, p. 229); Slovenia (Pipan Nahtigal and Lahovnik 2015, pp. 247–248); UK (for the amended cartel offence, see Stephan 2014; Gilbert 2015; for the 2002 version, see Stephan 2008; Joshua 2011, p. 129). This does not even include criminal sanctions for procedural offences, such as in Cyprus or Finland. Finland, and Sweden (and in the EFTA Switzerland) considered, but eventually rejected

such as Germany, the Netherlands, Poland and Spain, rely (mostly or exclusively) on administrative sanctions, sometimes complemented by more limited criminal provisions in particular for bid rigging.[20] Others use primarily criminal sanctions to the extent they hold individuals liable. The most prominent examples of this approach are the United Kingdom and Ireland, but several continental Member States, such as France or Italy, also fall into this category, even though the requirements for criminal liability in these latter Member States tend to be more restrictive.

8.3.1 United Kingdom

The experience in the United Kingdom is well publicised, and I will only briefly summarise it here.

The criminal cartel offence was enacted as s 188 in the Enterprise Act 2002 (EA 2002), which went into effect on 20 June 2003; it was amended by s 47 of the Enterprise Regulatory Reform Act 2013 (ERRA 2013), which went into effect on

criminalisation. In the EEA, Norway has also criminal sanctions (Sando and Hageler 2015, p. 208). For a global overview of criminalisation see Campbell 2015; Shaffer, Nesbitt and Weber Waller (2015). To be sure, in many of these jurisdictions this is pure law in the books without any significant enforcement. Yet even this law in the books may become relevant when it comes to extradition, see below Sect. 8.5.

[20]For example, the following Member States provide for administrative sanctions for individuals (such as fines and/or director disqualifications), either in addition or as an alternative to criminal sanctions. Germany provides for individual fines of up to €1 million for all intentional or negligent competition law infringements, in addition to the criminal bid-rigging offence (see below Sect. 8.3.2). The UK provides, in addition to the criminal cartel offence, for director disqualification orders (see below Sect. 8.3.1). Greek law provides, in addition to the criminal cartel offence, for individual administrative fines of between €200,000 and €2 million (Papadopoulos and Lovdahl Gormsen 2015, p. 107). Slovenia, also in addition to its criminal cartel offence, provides for individual administrative fines of between €5000 and 30,000 (Pipan Nahtigal and Lahovnik 2015, p. 248). Lithuania, while not providing for criminal liability, provides for individual fines and director disqualifications (Kolesnikovas 2015, p. 176). The Netherlands considered re-criminalising cartels, but eventually decided against it (Frese 2014, pp. 222–224), but Dutch law does provides for individual administrative fines of up to €450,000 (de Pree and Molin 2015, p. 197; Frese 2014, pp. 202–208). Portugal provides for administrative fines on individuals, albeit of a very low magnitude (between approximately €1000 and 5000, Marques Mendes and Vilarinho Pires 2015, pp. 222–223). Article 63.2 of the Spanish Competition Act provides for administrative fines of up to €60,000 for individuals (see Jiménez-Laiglesia et al 2015, p. 262). Swedish law provides for "injunctions against trading" similar to director disqualifications (Pettersson et al. 2015, p. 269). With effect from January 2015, Poland introduced administrative fines on individuals of up to 2 million Polish zlotys (at the time of writing: approximately €455,000) (Motyka-Mojkowski 2015, pp. 1109–1111; Hansberry-Bieguńska and Krasnodębska-Tomkiel 2015, p. 214). There are special criminal prohibitions against bid rigging, for example, in Germany, Austria, Hungary, and Poland.

1 April 2014. The Competition and Markets Authority (CMA) has summarised the provision as follows:

> a person commits the offence if he or she agrees with one or more other persons that two or more undertakings will engage in certain prohibited cartel arrangements, namely price fixing, market sharing, bid-rigging, and limiting output. The offence is subject to certain exclusions and defences. The maximum penalty on conviction on indictment is five years imprisonment and/or an unlimited fine.[21]

In England, Wales and Northern Ireland, the prosecution is brought by the Director of the Serious Fraud Office (SFO), or by or with the consent of the CMA (formerly: OFT). In Scotland prosecutions are brought by the Crown Office and Procurator Fiscal Service (COPFS) on behalf of the Lord Advocate. The Enterprise Act 2002 provides that the CMA may issue a no-action letter that prevents a prosecution in England, Wales and Northern Ireland.[22] The OFT has declared that such no-action letters will be issued to Type A leniency applicants on a blanket basis, and may be issued on a discretionary basis to Type B or C applicants (OFT 2013).

With regard to cartels in Scotland, immunity is not automatic, however. Where the criminal investigation falls into the remit of COPFS, the Memorandum of Understanding between the CMA and COPFS of July 2014 governs the interaction between these authorities (CMA and COPFS 2014). With regard to leniency applicants, the Memorandum of Understanding requires consultation between CMA and COPFS (CMA and COPFS 2014: § 13). Where the CMA recommends criminal immunity for the leniency applicant, the COPFS "will accord such a recommendation serious weight", will "take cognisance of the CMA's own rules on leniency", and will "where possible" give an early indication whether criminal immunity will be granted before the identity of the leniency applicant is disclosed (CMA and COPFS 2014: §§ 14–16).

At the time of the introduction of the cartel offence, about 5–7 prosecutions per year were expected. Actual enforcement lagged significantly behind these predictions. Overall, there have been criminal prosecutions in three cartel cases to date: the *Marine Hose Cartel*, the *Fuel Surcharges Cartel*, and the *Galvanised Steel Tank Cartel*.

The first prosecutions were those against three individuals in the *Marine Hose Cartel*. They had been apprehended in the United States, and their US American plea agreements de facto ensured that they had an interest not only in pleading guilty before the Southwark Crown Court, but even in not contesting any prison sentences in so far as they did not exceed 20 months (David Brammar), 24 months (Bryan Allison) and 30 months (Peter Whittle) respectively.[23] While Judge Rivlin imposed higher sentences than these (namely: 36 months for Peter Whittle and

[21]CMA (2014: § 1.3). Until s 47 of the ERRA 2013 came into force on 1 April 2014, the conduct had to be shown to be "dishonest".

[22]s 190(4) EA 2002.

[23]*R v Whittle and others*, [2008] EWCA Crim 2560, [25]–[28].

Bryan Allison, and 30 months for David Brammar), the Court of Appeal eventually reduced the sentences to the 20, 24 and 30 month minimum sentences anticipated in the US American plea agreements.[24] The Court of Appeal indicated that it might have reduced the sentences even further if the defendants had only sought such a further reduction.[25]

While the defendants in the *Marine Hose Cartel* received incarceration sentences, the case was widely seen as atypical: the result had been largely predetermined by the US plea agreements, and because of the defendants' guilty pleas the criminal cartel offence remained untested in trial.

The second prosecution for an infringement of the cartel offence, and the first attempt at a contested trial, was the *BA Fuel Surcharges Cartel* (*R v Burns*), in which Virgin Atlantic had been the leniency applicant receiving immunity. Interestingly in our context, one of the reasons for selecting this case for criminal prosecution was that it allegedly involved "members of senior management, including a BA board member, most of whom had received competition compliance training" (OFT 2010, p. 10). On the first day of trial, the prosecution had to admit that several thousand e-mails that had previously been thought to have been corrupted were recoverable and should have been disclosed to the defendants. The judge refused to grant more time for the prosecution to remedy this defect, and so the prosecution offered no evidence (OFT 2010).

After this debacle, it was doubted whether the cartel offence could ever be revived (Joshua 2011). The collapse of the prosecution left the question unanswered whether a jury could ever be persuaded that cartel members acted "dishonestly" under the applicable Ghosh test (*R v Ghosh* [1982] EWCA Crim 2). This question had been raised in the literature soon after the cartel offence had been introduced in 2002, and the discussion by the House of Lords in the Ian Norris case under what circumstances cartel agreements constituted the common law offence "conspiracy to defraud" increased this uncertainty.[26]

In 2015, the Competition and Markets Authority (CMA) initiated prosecutions in the *Galvanised Steel Tank Cartel*.[27] One defendant (Mr Nigel Snee) pleaded guilty, and was later sentenced to a suspended 6 month prison sentence plus 120 hours of community service. In sentencing, the judge considered a 2-year prison sentence as the appropriate starting point, but reduced the sentence because of the substantial cooperation of the defendant (CMA 2015b). Two other defendants did not plead guilty and were acquitted at trial—because the jury did not find the "dishonesty" requirement in the then applicable version of s 188 Enterprise Act 2002 to be proven (CMA 2015a). It is difficult to say whether this vindicated the prediction in the legal literature that had warned that this element could be difficult

---

[24] *R v Whittle and others*, [2008] EWCA Crim 2560.

[25] Ibid [31].

[26] *Norris v Government of the United States of America* [2008] UKHL 16, [2008] 2 WLR 673 (HL (E)).

[27] For a summary, see Blake 2015.

to prove, or whether this literature became a self-fulfilling prophecy: the defence could rely on literature written by antitrust practitioners and academics that cast doubt on whether the requirement was met.

The unsuccessful prosecution against the two defendants who had not pleaded guilty in the *Galvanised Steel Tank Cartel* is not, however, necessarily indicative for the probability of success in future prosecutions. The Enterprise Regulatory Reform Act 2013 (ERRA 2013) had already removed the dishonesty requirement before the *Galvanised Steel Tank Cartel* case was decided, and had replaced the dishonesty requirement with a number of exceptions and defences; it was just that these modifications were not yet applicable to the *Galvanised Steel Tank Cartel*.

The modified cartel offence is not committed where the counterparty is sufficiently informed about the arrangement in advance.[28] It is now a defence to the cartel offence that the individual did not intend to conceal the nature of the arrangement from the CMA or from customers.[29] It is also a defence that "he or she took reasonable steps to ensure that the nature of the arrangements would be disclosed to professional legal advisers for the purposes of obtaining advice about them before their making or (as the case may be) their implementation".[30]

It remains to be seen whether criminal prosecutions under this regime will be any easier and whether criminal prosecutions will become more prevalent (see Gilbert 2015; Stephan 2014). I remain sceptical (similarly Nikpay and Taylor 2014, p. 284). The main problems with criminal prosecutions in the United Kingdom are arguably not so much a function of the formulation of the cartel offence but of the enforcement institutions. Enforcement concerning white collar criminality generally, not only in competition law, has seen a string of failures in the United Kingdom (*cf* Wardaugh 2014, pp. 276–277). Criminal prosecutions are extremely expensive in the United Kingdom. Procedural errors may result in acquittal or mistrial. While the extensive rights of defence exist not only in white collar crime but also in blue collar crime, white collar criminals can more easily afford an expert defence team that ferrets out procedural missteps by the prosecution. As Roscoe Pound wrote as early as 1910, after describing the law in the books protecting the defendant in the United States:

> But prosecuting attorneys and police officers and police detectives do not hesitate to conduct the most searching, rigid and often brutal examinations of accused or suspected persons, with all the appearance of legality and of having the power of the state behind them. It is true, no rich man is ever subjected to this process to obtain proof of violation of anti-trust or rebate legislation and no powerful politician is thus dealt with in order to obtain proof of bribery and graft. The malefactor of means, the rogue who has an organization of rogues behind him to provide a lawyer and a writ of habeas corpus has the benefit of the law 'in the books'. (Pound 1910, p. 17).

Of course, this is not a feature specific to the common law—in all jurisdictions wealthier defendants will be able to afford better lawyers and benefit from more

[28] s 188A EA 2002, as amended by s 47(5) ERRA 2013.

[29] s 188B(1), (2) EA 2002, as amended by s 47(6) ERRA 2013.

[30] s 188B(3) EA 2002, as amended by s 47(6) ERRA 2013.

expert knowledge. It is, however, the case that procedural defects in civil law jurisdictions are often treated less absolutely than they are in common law jurisdictions. A German court would not have let the trial in *R v Burns* collapse; it would have granted an extension to remedy the procedural defect.

Another factor is arguably the high staff turnover and the institutional inconsistency over time in the UK. It is difficult to keep track of the names, acronyms and initialisms, competences and constitution of investigating and prosecuting bodies—in the competition sector, for example, DGFT, OFT, CC, CAT, CMA, and SFO, and when it comes to economic regulation and crime more generally, FSA, FCA, Prudential Authority, and NCA. Continental institutions tend to be nearly set in stone, sometimes guaranteed in the constitution, and staffed by career officials that for the most part stay for life. While the higher staff turnover in the UK institutions allows for more injection of fresh ideas and for less ossified bureaucracy, it is also associated with less accumulated institutional knowledge and esprit de corps. The National Audit Office (2016, para 9) noted the disruption and additional cost of the transformation of the OFT and CC into the CMA. The higher staff turnover may be part of the reason why the British competition authorities are at the cutting edge when it comes to policy papers, but rank rather badly when it comes to enforcement.[31]

Overall, then, the much discussed UK cartel offence has a track record of four guilty pleas, resulting in three prison sentences (of 20, 24 and 30 months, plus criminal fines and director disqualification orders) and one suspended 6-month sentence, in more than a dozen years of its existence, with no convictions in contested prosecutions at all. The removal of the dishonesty requirement may make prosecutions easier in the future, although the new exceptions and defences also raise difficult issues to be resolved (Stephan 2014; Gilbert 2015).

In addition to the criminal cartel offence, the Enterprise Act 2002 also introduced the power for courts to disqualify directors for infringing what is today Articles 101, 102 TFEU or their UK equivalents, the Chapter 1 or Chapter 2 prohibitions of the Competition Act 1998, and the power for the OFT (now the CMA) to accept equivalent undertakings.[32] The Director Disqualification Order (DDO) or the equivalent undertaking prevent the individual from acting as a director (or receiver or insolvency practitioner), or from "directly or indirectly" promoting, forming or managing a company. The advantage of these procedures is that the provisions do not require a criminal conviction; they provide for an administrative sanction (for a discussion of DDOs see Stephan 2011).

[31]Wils (2013). The National Audit Office (2016) noted: "The low caseflow we identified in 2010 has continued, with the Office of Fair Trading and the CMA making 24 decisions and the regulators just eight since 2010. The UK competition authorities issued only £65 million of competition enforcement fines between 2012 and 2014 (in 2015 prices), compared to almost £1.4 billion of fines imposed by their German counterparts. The CMA faces significant barriers in increasing its flow of competition cases, although recent activity means it now has 12 ongoing cases."

[32]s 204 EA 2002, amending the Company Directors Disqualification Act 1986 (c. 46) and inserting ss 9A–9E into that Act.

The OFT considered making increased use of DDOs, but has not yet followed up on this announcement. The only Competition DDOs that were imposed were the ones imposed against the three defendants in the Marine Hose Cartel cases.

8.3.2 Germany

Despite some early precursors in Germany that rendered certain forms of bid-rigging criminal offences, for example, in Prussia, and despite the criminal sanctions in the Allied Decartelisation ordinances, the drafters of the Gesetz gegen Wettbewerbsbeschränkungen (GWB), the German Act against Restraints of Competition, decided against the inclusion of criminal sanctions—at least on a temporary basis, until the spirit of competition had been internalised by the business community (Wagner-von Papp 2010a, pp. 275–282; 2011, pp. 160–164). Instead of continuing the categorisation as criminal offences in the Allied Decartelisation ordinances, competition law infringements in the GWB were qualified as "administrative offences" (Ordnungswidrigkeiten), although the drafters indicated that this qualification could be changed to genuine criminal offences once the business community had internalised the new competition norms.[33] However (unlike on the EU level today), it is not only undertakings that are subject to administrative fines, but also—and primarily—individuals. These administrative sanctions on individuals will be discussed below Sect. 8.3.2.1. In 1992 courts began to apply the general fraud offence to bid-rigging arrangements, and in 1997, the legislature added a criminal bid-rigging offence, § 298 of the Criminal Code (Strafgesetzbuch, StGB). This will be discussed below Sect. 8.3.2.2.

8.3.2.1 Individual Administrative Fines

§ 81(1), (2) GWB provides that a number of substantive and procedural infringements of European and German competition law constitute administrative offences. While the substantive competition provisions are mostly addressed to "undertakings" (or associations of undertakings), the German law on administrative offences provides for the primary liability of the individual. For these purposes, the characteristic "undertaking" is notionally attributed to an individual tasked with representing the undertaking (§ 9 OWiG). The undertaking itself is then derivatively liable (§ 30 OWiG), although a fine can be assessed against the undertaking even where the individual as the primary offender is not prosecuted (§ 30 (4) OWiG). Where the proprietor has at least negligently failed to take the necessary precautions to prevent infringements of the undertakings' duties, the proprietor may additionally be liable under § 130 OWiG.

[33]Bundestags-Drucksache 1/3462, Annex 1, 21–22 and Bundestags-Drucksache 2/1158, Annex 1, 27–28, quoted in Wagner-von Papp (2010a, p. 281; 2011, p. 164).

As the offences are administrative ones, the prosecuting authority—here, the competition authorities, in particular the Bundeskartellamt (§ 81(10) no 3 GWB)—have discretion whether or not to prosecute.[34] This prosecutorial discretion has allowed the Bundeskartellamt to publish a leniency notice addressed to individuals (as well as to undertakings and associations of undertakings), which promises automatic immunity provided the conditions for immunity are met, and a discretionary reduction of up to 50 % if the applicants makes a "significant contribution to proving the offence" and the other leniency conditions are met.[35]

The maximum statutory fine for individuals is €1 million.[36] Detailed statistics on the actual practice on setting individual fines are difficult to come by.[37] The Bundeskartellamt has revealed in a case before the Federal Constitutional Court that in the period from 1993 to 2010 it had fined 510 individuals and 563 legal entities for competition law infringements—approximately one individual per legal entity.[38] The average fine per individual in that period was €56,000.[39] This average, however, includes not only horizontal cartel cases (for which fines are arguably on average higher than for other cases), and the maximum fine was doubled from €500,000 to €1 million in 2005 without retrospective effect, so that most of the fines in the sample will have been based on the lower maximum. Both these effects mean that today the average individual fine for hardcore horizontal cartels is probably higher than €56,000.

There are some indications that in larger cartel cases, typical individual fines are in the order of magnitude of €200,000–250,000. In the beer breweries cartel, 14 individuals were fined a total of approximately €3.6 million.[40] Even if this amount were uniformly distributed among all these 14 individuals, the fine for each of these 14 individuals would be approximately €257,000. Since a skewed

---

[34] § 47 Gesetz über Ordnungswidrigkeiten (OWiG). The *Bundeskartellamt* is empowered to publish guidelines in particular on the setting of the fine, and has done so as far as fines for undertakings and associations of undertakings are concerned. The latest version are the 2013 Guidelines. *Bundeskartellamt*, Guidelines for the Setting of Fines in Cartel Administrative Offence Proceedings, 25 June 2013, https://perma.cc/T3L5-WDHD.

[35] *Bundeskartellamt*, Notice no 9/2006, Notice no. 9/2006 of the Bundeskartellamt on the immunity from and reduction of fines in cartel cases—Leniency Programme—of 7 March 2006, https://perma.cc/LNS9-NZ8Q.

[36] § 81(4) GWB. Theoretically, this maximum could be exceeded where this is necessary to skim off illegal gains, § 17(4) of the Gesetz über Ordnungswidrigkeiten (OWiG), which applies with the modification in § 81(5) GWB.

[37] The following paragraph partially replicates what I wrote in Wagner-von Papp (2016), § 15.

[38] BVerfG, 19 December 2012, 1 BvL 18/11, WuW/E DE-R 3766, paragraphs 52, 60—Verzinsungspflicht, available at http://www.bverfg.de/entscheidungen/ls20121219_1bvl001811.html (in German).

[39] Ibid., paragraph 60.

[40] Bundeskartellamt, 2 April 2014, Fallbericht Bußgelder gegen Brauereien (Summary Case Report on the decisions of 27 December 2013 and 31 March 2014, Case B10-105/11), http://www.bundeskartellamt.de/SharedDocs/Entscheidung/DE/Fallberichte/Kartellverbot/2014/B10-105-11.pdf?__blob=publicationFile&v=1.

distribution seems more probable than a uniform distribution, the highest fine is likely to have been higher—possibly substantially higher—than that. Similarly, individual fines of €250,000 and 200,000 were reported in the Wholesale Paper[41] and Grauzement[42] cases, respectively. However, the quantification of the fine depends on multiple factors, among others the wealth and income of the person fined.[43] Accordingly, individual fines even in cartel cases can be substantially lower than the previous numbers suggest.[44]

At first sight, individual administrative fines could appear to address the principal-agent problem. However, there are two conceptual problems with individual administrative fines in general, and one problem specifically with the implementation in Germany.

First, an administrative fine is akin to a speeding fine: it carries no moral opprobrium—it is a "price", not a "sanction". Provided the potential perpetrator is willing to pay this price for being paid a bonus, being promoted, or not being let go for failing to reach performance targets, the administrative fine does not hold much terror. The price is the subjectively expected fine. Objectively, this would be the discounted expected fine—assuming a 20 % detection probability and a €100,000 fine and a duration of some 5–10 years before the infringement is actually sanctioned, this would be substantially less than €20,000. Subjectively, it is likely that cartel participants are overconfident and so underestimate the probability that they are going to be detected. In contrast, a criminal offence would threaten a criminal conviction with a possible entry into the federal criminal register, and at least a potential incarceration term. In addition to the legal sanctions foreseen in the criminal offence, a criminal conviction may also have indirect but severe implications for future employability and the social standing of the perpetrator (see also below Sect. 8.5). These imponderables make the potential infringer's "hedonistic" calculus between the short-term gains and the potentially devastating long-term consequences nearly impossible, and are likely to be conceived as a real "sanction" to be avoided rather than a "price" to be paid.

The second problem is closely related to the first one: Because the administrative individual fine is just a "price", it can be completely compensated ex post or ex ante by the undertaking (Wils 2003, p. 438; 2008: §§ 579, 580; Monopolkommission

[41]BGH, 19 June 2007—KRB 12/07, NJW 2007, 3792, WuW/E DE-R 2225, § 10—Papiergroßhandel (Wholesale Paper).

[42]In the Cement case, the individual fine of €200,000 imposed on the individual "Ed. Sch." was reduced by 5 % (€10,000) on appeal because of the long duration of the appeal procedure, BGH, 26 February 2013—KRB 20/12, WuW/E DE-R 3861, §§ 1, 87–91—Grauzement (Cement).

[43]Second sentence of § 17(3) of the Administrative Offences Act (OWiG).

[44]E.g., in the Cement case, the lowest of the fines for nine individual appellants was only €6000, BGH, n. 42. In another cartel case, the Higher Regional Court Düsseldorf set a fine of some €40,000 for one of the individuals, OLG Düsseldorf, 29 May 2015, V-2 Kart 1+2/13 (OWi), NRWEntscheidungen. For a discussion of the factors influencing the setting of the individual fines in an information exchange case, see OLG Düsseldorf, 29 October 2012, V-1 Kart 1–6/12 (OWi) §§ 140–96, NRWEntscheidungen—Silostellgebühren.

2014: § 152; Zimmer 2016: § 17). It is unlikely that such compensation would be made explicit. First, if sanctions on the undertaking should already be optimal, then it would not be in the undertaking's interest to compensate the individual. Second, in some jurisdictions an explicit compensation for fines may be illegal, either because it undermines the individual sanction's effects, or because it uses the undertaking's resources for purposes not in the undertaking's interests and so breaches fiduciary duties. Third, the undertaking would arguably not want to be seen to encourage illegal conduct.

Nevertheless, it does seem likely that there is implicit compensation. Indeed, the incentives just described (of getting a promotion, a pay raise or a bonus, or of not being fired) serve as implicit ex ante compensation. What is more, undertakings could provide further incentives to compensate implicitly ex post: if fines are still suboptimal, there is an interest in encouraging the conduct; and even if fines are already optimal, it is likely that the undertaking wants to send out a more general signal to managers and employees that those who go to the limits to increase profitability are not left hanging even if they have overstepped the mark. It is likely that the undertaking wants to encourage risk-seeking conduct, even if it does not want to encourage law-breaking.

The third problem is not one that attaches to administrative fines generally, but specifically to the way they are implemented in Germany. Two important functions of sanctions are the deterrence of infringements and the reinforcement of law-abiding conduct. These functions require that the sanctions are *seen* to be imposed. While it is understandable and in keeping with Continental privacy standards that the Bundeskartellamt does not publish the names of the individuals on whom fines have been imposed, there is no good reason not to publish the (approximate) amount of fines that are imposed on (anonymised) individuals. Even the data published in the biennial reports of the Bundeskartellamt (Tätigkeitsberichte) do not allow the calculation of the mean, median, spread or skewness of the distribution of individual fines—hence the reliance above on the data that were submitted to the Federal Constitutional Court as a "one off", and on the anecdotal glimpses into actual fining practice provided by appeal court judgments or selective Bundeskartellamt press releases. It is unclear whether the opaqueness of the individual fine levels is deliberate policy, because the fine levels would actually not be deterrent if they were known, or whether it is due to neglect or a misconceived fear that the publication could raise privacy concerns.

8.3.2.2 Criminal Sanctions

Discussions in Germany about criminalising cartel conduct (or possibly even other competition law infringements) have been going on since the inception of the GWB. Up to now, calls for the introduction of a cartel offence have not resulted in reforms that include a general cartel offence. However, in 1997, the legislator inserted a provision specifically for bid rigging (§ 298 StGB). Criminal liability attaches to cartel conduct only where the general fraud provision is infringed, or where the new bid rigging provision is infringed.

Cartel conduct comes at least close to committing fraud (§ 263 StGB). The elements of the fraud offence in Germany are deceptive conduct (*Täuschung*) on part of the perpetrator, an induced mistake (*Irrtum*) on the part of the victim that causes the victim's decision to make a transfer of value (*Vermögensverfügung*) which results in harm (*Schaden*). Traditionally, the argument has been that if the price is fixed by a cartel, there is no deceptive conduct vis-à-vis the direct customer because there is said to be no tacit assumption that the price is set independently and therefore there is no deceptive conduct or induced mistake. It may also be difficult to establish that the victim suffered harm with the certainty required for a criminal conviction.

In 1992, the Federal Court of Justice distinguished earlier precedent (BGHSt 16, 367) and held in the *Rheinausbau I* decision that as far as bid rigging is concerned, the elements of the fraud offence may be satisfied (BGHSt 38, 186). Where goods or services are procured through a tendering process or auction, it is clear to those participating in the bidding process that the issuer of the call for bids assumes that the entered bids are arrived at independently. This means that submitting a bid based on an agreement between independent bidders amounts to deceptive conduct which results in an induced mistake. While it may be difficult to prove harm because of the difficulties in establishing the counterfactual price with sufficient certainty, the Federal Court of Justice considered it sufficient that the trial judge be able to form a conviction on the basis of circumstantial evidence showing a high probability that the price would have been lower but for the agreement (BGHSt 38, 186, part III.4.). The Court pointed, inter alia, to statistical analyses on cartel overcharges. The Court even seemed to suggest that the very fact of the existence of the agreement showed that the price was higher than it would have been, because otherwise the agreement would not have been sustainable. However, the Court additionally pointed to cross-payments between conspirators.

Some authors have suggested that not only bid rigging, but cartel conduct more generally may constitute fraud (Baumann and Arzt 1970, p. 35; Lampert and Götting 2002). While it is true that customers do not have a legitimate expectation that the price for any given good or service be "just" or "adequate", it is not easy to justify why in today's well-established market economies customers should not have a legitimate expectation that prices are set independently. Indeed, a recent survey shows that 64 % of the 2648 German respondents agreed or strongly agreed that prices were set independently, as opposed to 27 % that agreed or strongly agreed with the position that businesses do not set their prices independently from competitors (Stephan 2015: Table 3). Even if this were not the de facto empirical assumption, one can make the case that the existence of Article 101 TFEU and § 1 GWB show that independent price setting is the normative standard (Lampert and Götting 2002). Given such an empirical or normative baseline, an offer may be seen as an implicit assertion that it complies with this standard. In other contexts, German courts are quite willing to imply statements: for example, impecunious persons who order food or beverages in a restaurant or bar, or who order goods online or via mail order, are considered implicitly to assert their ability and willingness to pay; they are convicted of criminal fraud.[45] In the cartel context, one could equally well imply the assertion that prices have been set independently. Indeed, the argument for finding actionable misrepresentation and induced mistake is even stronger in the cartel context: the cartel is antecedent illegal conduct (§§ 1, 81 GWB, Article 101 TFEU), which may be considered to give rise to a duty to disclose ("*Ingerenz*"), so that the failure to disclose could in itself amount to fraudulent conduct by omission. However, up to now criminal courts have not applied this reasoning to cartels outside the bid-rigging context. For cartels such as price fixing, market or customer allocations other than through bid rigging, courts do not find an implied statement that the terms of the offer has been arrived at independently (accord Twele 2013, p. 220).

With regard to the additional fraud element of "harm", it is true that harm may be difficult to prove in the price-fixing scenario, because one would need to establish the counterfactual price to show harm. However, this element could be established by the same methods which BGHSt 38, 186 applied in the bid rigging scenario. Accordingly, it does not seem impossible or even particularly far-fetched to qualify all or nearly all cartels as fraud. However, this is not what the courts actually do outside the bid rigging context, and so this theoretical possibility is irrelevant for the "law in action" of interest here. In the law in action, the general fraud provision is only of relevance when it comes to bid rigging.

In 1997, the legislature chose to insert a separate bid-rigging offence into the Criminal Code, punishable by a criminal fine or a prison sentence not exceeding 5 years. While, as just described, bid rigging was already considered to be criminal conduct since 1992 to the extent that there was sufficient circumstantial evidence that the counterfactual competitive price would have been lower, the new provision does not require a showing of harm and therefore is easier to prosecute.

Where the elements of the general fraud prohibition are satisfied as well as those of the bid rigging provision, there is concurrent liability; the fraud offence protects the wealth of other persons, the bid-rigging offence competition as an institution, although some argue that the wealth of other persons is protected by the bid rigging prohibition as well. This concurrent liability may become particularly relevant where the conditions for *aggravated* fraud are met, which includes cases of fraud committed in an organised gang, fraud that is committed "professionally", and fraud that results in a large loss (§ 263(3), (5) StGB). In these cases, the law provides for increased minimum sentences (of 6 months imprisonment in the case of § 263(3) StGB, and 1 year imprisonment in the case of professional fraud committed as a member of an organised gang, § 263(5) StGB, in which case the offence becomes a felony, § 12 StGB) and an increased maximum sentence of 10 years, which exceeds the 5-year maximum sentence for bid rigging.

The introduction of the bid-rigging provision § 298 StGB was accompanied by a number of ancillary provisions. § 82 of the GWB ensures that the competition authority retains its competence to prosecute the undertaking for the administrative

[45] See, for example, OLG Hamm, 5 June 1996, 4 Ss 60/96. Further references in Mayer Lux (2013, p. 224 ff.).

offence even where individuals are prosecuted criminally. The two procedures are separate, so that the efficiency *vel non* of the criminal prosecution of the individual does not have an effect on the prosecution of the undertaking. A provision in the Guidelines on Criminal and Administrative Offence Procedures requires early cooperation between prosecutors and competition authorities (RiStBV No 242). § 100a(1), (2)(r) of the Criminal Procedure Code (Strafprozessordnung, StPO) provide that telecommunications may be intercepted where there is an evidence-based suspicion that the bid-rigging offence was committed.

Actual enforcement of the bid-rigging offence seems to compare favourably to the situation in the United Kingdom. It is difficult to get exact statistics on enforcement. The official statistics of the Statistisches Bundesamt report 297 convictions and 42 suspended prison sentences for bid rigging from 1998 to 2013 inclusive (Statistisches Bundesamt 1999–2015; Wagner-von Papp 2016: §§ 13, 14; see also Wagner-von Papp 2010a, pp. 285–286, 302; 2011, pp. 167–168, 182; Zimmer 2016: § 5). To dispel a misunderstanding: these are not cases "where Section 298 of the German Criminal Code has been cited" (Ost 2014, p. 134); they are cases in which bid rigging was the *most serious* of the offences for which the defendant was convicted (Statistisches Bundesamt 2015, p. 13).

As I have explained elsewhere in greater detail (Wagner-von Papp 2010a, pp. 285–286; 2011, pp. 166–170), these official statistics are underinclusive, because they systematically omit cases in which defendants are additionally sentenced for aggravated fraud or other offences that carry a higher maximum sentence than the 5 years imprisonment for bid rigging due to the coding of the data. These cases are instead reported in the statistics for aggravated fraud etc. Anecdotally, there are by now at least three convictions to unsuspended incarceration sentences which are not reflected in the official statistics. The first is the conviction of a Member of the German Parliament, who voted for the introduction of the bid rigging offence of § 298 StGB and was later convicted for aiding and abetting bid rigging and sentenced to prison (BGHSt 49, 201; Wagner-von Papp 2011, pp. 168–169). In the second case of a conviction to a prison sentence to be served, the defendant had previously participated in a European cartel, which was uncovered and the defendant's undertaking fined by the European Commission; while the appeal against this Commission decision was still pending before the European courts, the defendant re-established the bid rigging cartel within Germany. He was criminally prosecuted for this second cartel and sentenced to 2 years and 10 months in prison.[46] The third case was decided in 2015 by the Federal Court of Justice, where "defendant E." was sentenced to 2 years and 4 months for bid rigging and other corruption charges.[47]

Despite this active enforcement of the bid rigging provision, it is difficult to describe the German experience with the bid rigging offence so far as an unqualified success story.

[46]LG Munich II (2006); Wagner-von Papp (2011), pp. 169–170.

[47]BGH, 29 April 2015, 1 StR 235/14, BeckRS 2015, 12466; Wagner-von Papp (2016), § 14.

The most urgent issue is the lack of clarity regarding criminal immunity for leniency applicants. The competition authority has discretion whether or not to prosecute administrative offences (§ 47 OWiG), and the leniency policy of the Bundeskartellamt is a self-binding policy that exercises this discretion in favour of the immunity recipient. In contrast, the public prosecutor is, at least in principle, obligated to prosecute criminal offences ("principle of legality", § 152(2) StPO). There is no criminal immunity provision specifically for leniency applicants. The Bundeskartellamt's leniency policy explicitly states that it must refer proceedings, even as far as the immunity recipient is concerned, to the public prosecutor where § 298 StGB or another criminal prohibition is infringed (Bundeskartellamt 2006: § 24).

As a practical matter, it seems very likely that the public prosecutor would close cases against immunity recipients, and most likely even leniency recipients. Statutory amendments have long made heavy inroads that put the principle that the public prosecutor must prosecute every crime into perspective. In reality, the prosecutor has a great deal of discretion how to allocate its resources under §§ 153–154f StPO. Indeed, the legislator of a recent amendment assumed that an investigation would generally be closed against suspects who helped uncover a crime listed in § 100a StPO where the suspected offence did not carry a minimum prison sentence; both criteria are fulfilled by § 298 StGB.[48] However, all these provisions allow the exercise of discretion not to prosecute or to reduce or abstain from sanctioning only *in individual cases*. Under the current rules, it is therefore not possible to guarantee automatic criminal immunity to a leniency applicant in competition cases. This would not, however, prevent the introduction of a criminal immunity provision de lege ferenda, just as there is a criminal immunity provision in § 371 of the Tax Code (AO).

Another problem is that criminal enforcement is not well publicised in Germany (Kartte and von Portatius 1975, p. 1171; Wagner-von Papp 2010a, p. 288; 2011, pp. 170–172; 2016: § 10). Neither prosecutors nor the Bundeskartellamt have systematic knowledge of convictions or sentences imposed (*cf* Ost 2014, p. 134). Nor, one may infer, have potential perpetrators that are meant to be deterred by criminal enforcement.

A first factor resulting in this poor publication are privacy concerns. The naming and shaming that occurs in many common law jurisdictions, often even before a guilty verdict, is anathema to continental jurisdictions. This would not, however, prevent reporting on an anonymised basis after conviction. The second obstacle to better publication of prosecutions and convictions is the decentralised enforcement through local or regional public prosecutors before regional courts (Wagner-von Papp 2016: § 22).

[48]Where the suspected offence carries a minimum prison sentence, § 49b StGB applies, and the court may either reduce the sentence under § 49 StGB or may abstain from imposing any sentence. This could become relevant for our context where a leniency applicant committed aggravated fraud.

A related problem is that the criminal enforcement of the bid rigging offence is not well coordinated with the competition authorities. As mentioned above, Guideline RiStBV No 242 requires an early and close cooperation between prosecutors and the competition authorities. As I mentioned in 2010, this provision seems to be honoured more in its breach than its observance, and so joint working groups between competition authorities and prosecutors would be helpful (Wagner-von Papp 2010a, pp. 288, 289; see also 2016: § 20). From 2012 onwards, the Bundeskartellamt sought to remedy this by inviting prosecutors to annual meetings.[49] Nevertheless, the information flow appears incomplete.

At least equally important is that the competition authorities are not involved in the criminal prosecution at all, even though their expert knowledge could help the courts, for example, understand the relevant issues and the likely harm inflicted by the cartel. In the proceedings concerning administrative fines, § 82a GWB allows the Bundeskartellamt to put questions to the accused, witnesses, and expert witnesses. Similarly, in private enforcement actions, the court has to inform the competition authorities, which can then make representations, point the court to evidence, and ask questions to the parties, witnesses and expert witnesses (§ 90 GWB). There is no such involvement when it comes to criminal proceedings. And even the participation rights in the GWB fall short of the powers that are given to tax authorities when it comes to the prosecution of tax crimes (Biermann 2007, p. 43; Federmann 2006, pp. 518–520; Raum 2014: paragraph 3; Wagner-von Papp 2016: § 23). There is no reason to deny the competition authorities in criminal competition cases the rights which the tax authorities have in criminal tax cases. Again, this is something that can and should be fixed.

The fourth problem is that the decentralised enforcement makes the appropriate case prioritisation nearly impossible. A busy prosecutor may have an incentive to close a large-scale complex case, perhaps extracting a payment under § 153a StPO, in order to save scarce resources that would be needed to investigate the complex arrangements. Meanwhile a small-scale amateurish bid-rigging attempt between local plumbers may be easy to prove and therefore be prosecuted. In other words, the private incentives for the prosecutor in the case selection may differ from a societal perspective.

The fifth problem is that § 298 StGB singles out bid rigging and subjects it to a regime completely different from that governing other hardcore cartels.

There are admittedly several reasons why bid rigging may be "special" (see Kovacic 2006, p. 52). First, the connection between the cartel and the resulting harm is particularly evident in bid rigging cases, making it particularly clear that this is not a "victimless crime". Second, the evident deception, induced mistake, transfer of value and resulting harm moves bid rigging particularly close to traditional fraud, a fact acknowledged by German courts since the Rheinausbau decisions described above. Third, bid rigging often occurs in organised form such as bid rotation cartels, which depend on repeated rigged bids so that every conspirator can "take their turn". Fourth, bid rigging often affects public procurement and occurs

[49] Bundeskartellamt, Press Releases of 10 February 2012, 15 April 2013, and 3 June 2014.

concurrently with other corruption offences, such as bribery; indeed, § 298 StGB was introduced into the criminal code as part of a legislative package addressing corruption (Dreher 2011, p. 235). Fifth, because of the occurrence of bid rigging in public procurement, it is "the tax payers' money" that is affected, and the perpetrators' prioritising their own private gain over the public good, which the affected project sought to advance, may be considered particularly selfish, anti-social and immoral. Sixth, where bid rigging affects auctions of foreclosed properties, victims may belong to the poorest members of society; while this argument may sound as if it were tailor made to the cases in the United States after the 2008 financial crisis, it was raised in nineteenth century Germany in the debates about the introduction of a bid rigging offence into the Federal Criminal Code, modelled on the Prussian provision (German Reichstag, Document no 54, Volume III, 155, 182; von Sybel 37th Session, 7 April 1870, protocol: 726). For some or all of these reasons, bid rigging has historically often been singled out for special treatment: from the Prussian royal decree of 1797, the Napoleonic Code pénal of 1810, the Prussian Criminal Code of 1851, to § 298 StGB enacted in 1997.

Even though all these factors make bid rigging particularly well-suited to criminalisation, they may or may not be present in any given bid-rigging case, and they may or may not be present in other hardcore cartel cases. It is difficult to justify why someone who participates in a global price-fixing cartel that resulted in harm amounting to billions of euros gets away with an administrative fine, while a local builder who talks with a competitor about prices over a pint of beer is criminally liable. It does not make sense from either a consequentialist perspective (in how much harm does the infringement result?) or a moral perspective (how much "criminal energy" do the perpetrators manifest in their conduct? How culpable are they?) to use as the distinguishing criterion the mechanism by which goods or services are allocated, whether by tender, auction bid, negotiations, or posted prices.

8.3.3 Ireland

The spectrum of criminalisation in the EU reaches from no individual liability at all to potential criminal liability for any infringement of anti-competitive agreements or abuses of dominant positions in Ireland.

In Ireland, any infringement of sections 4 or 5 of the Competition Act 2002 can be prosecuted criminally under sections 6 to 8 of the 2002 Act (see Massey and Cooke 2011). Prison sentences are, however, confined to hardcore cartels relating to price-fixing, output or sales limitation, or customer and market sharing arrangements (s 8 with s 6(2) of the 2002 Act); for other infringements, only criminal fines may be imposed. There is no provision for administrative or civil fines; while there is the possibility to institute civil proceedings, they can only result in declaratory or injunctive relief.

The maximum prison sentence for hardcore cartels was initially 5 years. This was raised to 10 years by the Competition (Amendment) Act 2012. Director disqualification will follow a criminal conviction automatically.

Some 20 individuals have been convicted to date, but no defendant has served time in prison. The sanctions have been either criminal fines or suspended prison sentences (Massey and Cooke 2011). The fact that all prison sentences to date were suspended has often been criticised, and the Judge in the Duffy case, Mr Justice McKechnie, was on the verge of imposing an unsuspended prison sentence, refraining from doing so only to prevent unequal treatment compared to other defendants in the same cartel, who had previously received milder sentences (*Director of Public Prosecutions v Patrick Duffy and Duffy Motors* 23 March 2009: §§ 35 *et seq*). The 2012 Act removed the possibility of applying section 1 (1) of the Probation Act 1907 to offences under sections 6 and 7 of the 2002 Act, but no cases to which the 2012 Act applies have been brought yet.

8.3.4 France

In France, there is provision for criminal sanctions for individuals under Article L. 420-6 of the Code de Commerce. In addition to a competition infringement under Article L. 420-1 (anti-competitive agreements) or L. 420-2 (abuses of dominant positions), it must be shown that the individual was "personally and decisively" involved in the infringement's conception, organisation, or implementation, and acted "fraudulently". The need for "personal" involvement restricts the criminal provision to those who actually acted, potentially excluding persons higher up in the hierarchy who may have known about the infringement (*cf* Blaise 2013: § 10; Viros 2016: § 10). The need for "decisive" involvement has been described as "obscure" (Blaise 2013: § 10); at a minimum, the individual must have played an "active" role, but it is less clear whether more is required, such as being the ring-leader or main persona of the infringement (Blaise 2013: § 10; Viros 2016: § 11 (stating that activity by mere "presence" would be insufficient)). "Fraudulence" has been said to require a "bad faith" element (Viros 2016: § 12; also *cf* Blaise 2013: § 10), reminiscent of the former "dishonesty" requirement in the UK cartel offence (Jenny 2013: § 68), but it has also been said that some decisions appear to let it suffice that the individual was conscious of the illegality of the conduct (Blaise 2013: § 10). Where the cumulative requirements of personal, decisive and fraudulent involvement are met, the individual is criminally liable for a fine of up to €75,000 and a prison sentence of up to 4 years.

As in Germany, telecommunications may be intercepted in criminal investigations (Articles 100 to 100-7 of the Criminal Procedure Code), and these provisions have been used in practice (Viros 2016: § 20).

While the cumulative requirements of personal decisive involvement and fraudulence, which requires "bad faith" conduct, are difficult to prove, there have been a number of prosecutions and convictions. David Viros reports that over the first 2 decades of the existence of the provision, the rate was approximately two convictions per year (Viros 2016: § 13). The Rapport Coulon reports even higher numbers, namely 124 convictions in the 9 years between 1998 and 2006 inclusive

(Coulon 2008, p. 116), but at that time the provision applied to legal persons as well as individuals. While most convictions of individuals were for criminal fines or suspended prison sentences, there have been at least five prison sentences that were not suspended (Viros 2016: § 13).

Problems that have arisen in French criminal competition law enforcement are mostly reminiscent of those encountered in the UK and Germany.

The difficulties of proving personal, decisive, and fraudulent involvement are not unlike the problems that the "dishonesty" requirement created in the former UK cartel offence before the element was removed. This development in the UK has led to calls for removing the restrictive requirements in the French provision as well (Jenny 2013: § 68).

As in Germany, the scope of the criminal provision is problematic. Whereas the bid rigging offence in Germany is arguably too narrow, the problem with Article L. 420-6 Code de Commerce is that it is too broad (Blaise 2013: §§ 15, 23–29). The criminal provision, by referring to Articles L. 420-1 and 420-2 in their entirety, comprises theoretically all anti-competitive agreements and abuses of dominant positions. This wide scope is undesirable for three reasons. First, it may lead to a chilling effect that deters procompetitive conduct. Secondly, it imports the need to consider economic evidence into the criminal trial, where it seems problematic because of the principle of legal certainty in criminal law (Blaise 2013: §§ 15, 25). Thirdly, the excessive scope of the offence may make courts reluctant to punish criminally what seems like a mere regulatory provision that does not make any distinction according to the seriousness of the infringement and does not fit well with the conception of criminal law as a remedy of last resort (see Blaise 2013: §§ 7, 23–26).

As in Germany, the offence is prosecuted not by the competition authority but by local public prosecutors before local courts (Viros 2016: § 12), resulting in little press coverage and public awareness, although Article L. 420-6 Code de Commerce provides that the sentence can be published at the defendant's expense.

As in Germany, the French criminal provision does not sit easy with the Autorité de la Concurrence's leniency programme. The Autorité de la Concurrence has announced in its leniency notice that it will not communicate its file on its own motion to the public prosecutor as far as the leniency applicant is concerned (Autorité de la Concurrences 2015: § 53). However, this is no guarantee that public prosecutors will refrain from initiating criminal investigations on their own motion, and so leniency applications may be deterred by the threat of potential criminal liability (Blaise 2013: § 13). It is also unclear on what legal basis the Autorité de la Concurrence could currently withhold evidence from the prosecutor (Coulon 2008, p. 65; Blaise 2013: § 13). While a reform proposal in the Rapport Coulon suggested the introduction of a model similar to the no-action letter in the UK based on consultation between the competition authority and the prosecutor or the judge, this suggestion has not (yet) been acted upon (Coulon 2008, pp. 64–65, 106 (recommendation no 19); see also Blaise 2013: § 28).

French law has taken some steps to improve the involvement of the competition authority in criminal proceedings. Like German competition authorities, the Autorité may refer cases to the prosecutor. Pursuant to Article L. 450-1-II*bis* of the Code de Commerce, a provision inserted in 2014, the investigating judge may request by letter rogatory support from a representative of the Autorité de la Concurrence. The investigating judge may also request the opinion by the Autorité de la Concurrence under Article L. 462-3 Code de Commerce.

8.4 Pros and Cons of Criminalisation

The views on whether there should be criminal liability for competition law infringements are extraordinarily divided. There are fervent supporters and equally fervent opponents. There are various reasons for the divisiveness on the topic.

8.4.1 Objectives of Criminal Law

There are already diverging opinions on the fundamental question what the objectives of criminal law are, and what conduct should accordingly be criminalised in the first place. General deterrence, reinforcement of law-abiding conduct, individual deterrence, rehabilitation, retribution, and incapacitation are some of the contenders as objectives. It seems unlikely—although, as the "King of the Pipes" case (footnote 47) showed, not impossible—that one and the same individual will be a cartel recidivist. Individual deterrence, rehabilitation and incapacitation therefore play at best a minor role in our context. Those who consider—like Franz von Liszt—individual deterrence, rehabilitation and incapacitation the only or predominant legitimate objectives of criminal law will therefore be less inclined towards the criminalisation of competition law.

In contrast, those who consider general deterrence and the positive reinforcement of law-abiding conduct as the main objectives may be more favourably inclined towards criminalisation. As far as general deterrence is concerned, competition law infringements are generally not committed in the heat of the moment, but are deliberate and calculated acts that are particularly amenable to a "cost-benefit analysis" by the potential perpetrator.

Additionally, white collar criminals often start from a social position fairly high up the ranks. The prospect of a prison sentence, even a relatively short one, is particularly deterring because a conviction often means a loss of acquired social capital and chances of future employment in addition to the direct sanctions imposed (Monopolkommission 2014: § 156; 2015: § 198; Wagner-von Papp 2010b, p. 273; Werden and Simon 1987, pp. 935–936). Potential cartelists are usually moving in social circles that disapprove of associating with "criminals". One participant of the Marine Hose cartel who was extradited (see below Sect. 8.5.1) to the United States, pleaded guilty and served 8 months in prison there, summarised his experience as follows: "'I am totally ruined,' Pisciotti says wearily during an interview in his home north of Milan. 'They destroyed me, my bank account, my family, my career. Everything.'" (Crofts 2015). While some of these effects would arguably be attenuated in the criminal justice systems in most European jurisdictions, any argument that the threat of incarceration would not have a substantial additional deterrent effect is simply implausible (Monopolkommission 2014: § 156).

Opponents of criminalisation sometimes claim that criminal sanctions would not increase deterrence because criminal enforcement would be less rigorous (Bundeskartellamt 2015a, p. 13; Twele 2013, p. 229) or at least that there is no "systematic" evidence for increased deterrence (Kartte and von Portatius 1975, p. 1170; Dreher 2011, p. 238). There are several problems with this argument.

First, it should be remembered that the administrative prosecution against the undertaking is unaffected by the question whether the individual offence is an administrative offence or a criminal offence, so that any argument based on the idea that criminal prosecutions against individuals would lead to a reduction in deterrence on the corporate level fails the mark.

Second, for the reasons outlined above, it is implausible that criminal sanctions should not be more deterring than administrative fines for individuals (Monopolkommission 2014: § 156). The answer by opponents of criminalisation is that criminal sanctions would be less vigorously enforced, and that therefore overall deterrence would fall (Bundeskartellamt 2015a, p. 13; Twele 2013, p. 229). It is of course true that the deterrence is a function not only of the severity of the sanction, but of the expected sanction, which also depends on the probability of prosecution and conviction. Nevertheless, the argument that there is no increase in deterrence in the case of the introduction of a criminal offence lacks merit. Even disregarding for the moment the possibility of enforcing criminal provisions effectively and efficiently by improving the institutional framework and procedures, the argument simply overlooks that even in cases in which the public prosecutor decides not to prosecute the criminal offence, it will transfer the case to the administrative authority (here, the competition authority) under § 43 OWiG for the prosecution of the administrative offence (as Twele himself sees when describing the situation de lege lata, 2013, p. 223). In other words, the introduction of an additional criminal offence need not impair the effectiveness of the existing enforcement scheme one *iota*. The claim that there is no additional deterrence would therefore have to be that the expected probability of conviction for the criminal offence would be not only low, but zero.

Third, contrary to the assertion, there *is* systematic evidence as to the deterrent effect of criminal sanctions. The OFT (2007) commissioned a survey from Deloitte, which asked lawyers and companies to say how important they considered various sanctions for deterrence.

Among the 214 UK and Brussels competition lawyers asked, 141 (66 %) considered criminal sanctions "very important" and an additional 40 (19 %) considered them "important" for deterrence. For comparison: for fines, the respective numbers were 101 (48 %) and 81 (37 %), for private damages actions 39 (18 %) and 64 (30 %), and for director disqualifications 80 (37 %) and 75 (35 %) (OFT 2007, pp. 105–106).

When asked an open-ended question what could be done to improve deterrence, the second most frequently mentioned aspect was "More criminal prosecutions for cartels" (33 mentions, following "encourage private damages actions" with 35 mentions; OFT 2007, p. 109).

Perhaps even more significantly, among the 202 companies, 127 (63 %) considered criminal penalties for cartels "very important", and an additional 47 (23 %) considered them "important"; for fines, the respective numbers were only 74 (37 %) for "very important" and 87 (43 %) for "important".

The OFT summarised these result as follows:

> Both lawyers and companies agreed that criminal penalties were the most important sanction and private damages actions the least. There was some difference in the ranking of fines: while companies considered director disqualification and adverse publicity more important than fines, lawyers did not. (OFT 2007: § 5.58)

The OFT concluded that "[t]hese results highlight the importance of sanctions which operate at the individual, rather than corporate, level." (OFT 2007: § 5.59). These results were obtained, by the way, at a time when there had not yet been a single criminal prosecution in the UK.

Fourth, as even opponents of criminalisation concede (Dreher 2011, p. 238), there is additionally anecdotal evidence that cartels try to avoid and carve out the United States. I have pointed out elsewhere that this is no conclusive proof of the deterrence effect of a criminal offence, because it could also be due to the more effective private enforcement in the United States. Nevertheless, it is very likely that the outlook of being prosecuted criminally plays an important role in the actors' decision to avoid the United States.

Another important function of criminal law is the reinforcement of law-abiding behaviour. There are two distinct aspects to this. First, where the conviction of others' is publicised, those engaging in economic activity but not in anticompetitive conduct are reinforced in their conviction that they have chosen the right path. As far as this argument is concerned, one may, however, wonder whether the marginally higher "satisfaction" (or should I say "Schadenfreude"?) that comes from hearing about the criminal convictions of others as opposed to hearing others receiving a high administrative fine counts for much.

Nevertheless, the reinforcement of law-abiding behaviour is important in another sense. Hardcore cartels are essentially fraudulent conduct, even if one can debate whether they can be technically subsumed under the fraud offence. While it is sometimes claimed that cartels are "victimless" crimes, this is patent nonsense—sometimes the harm stays concentrated with specific victims and sometimes it is spread across a large number of victims, but this does not make the harm disappear. When it comes to general or computer fraud offences, dispersion of harm across many victims does not matter for the question whether a crime is committed—think of those who defraud bank customers by deducting one penny from many accounts. If no individual victim suffers a significant loss, this may be considered in the sentencing, but that is a separate matter. The difference between a cartel and a garden variety fraud is mostly that the sums in question are usually much higher in cartel cases, sometimes in the millions of euro, that the perpetrators come from a white collar background, that the infringement is committed by conspiring with others often over an extended period of time, and that the level of the organisation and attempts at concealment are often very elaborate. All these factors, except for the white collar element, would tend to make the offence more instead of less serious. Treating cartel conduct as an administrative offence—in the same category as a minor traffic infraction—, while small-scale fraud and theft are treated as criminal offences without any de minimis limitation may well create the impression in the populace that the legal system "only goes after the little guy". Such a perception may undermine trust in the legal system and legal compliance.

8.4.2 *What Is the Correct Comparator?*

One problem in the discussion is that the question whether criminalisation of competition law infringements is desirable cannot be answered in the abstract. As in any comparison, it is important that the states to be compared are well-defined. The general discussion about criminalisation of competition law infringements is sometimes distorted by strawman arguments. Of course a badly drafted criminal provision without ensuring effective enforcement and embedding criminal enforcement in the overall antitrust enforcement system would be a bad idea. The real question is whether criminal enforcement of competition law infringements, if well implemented, would be desirable or not. So, what are the two states to be compared?

8.4.2.1 What Conduct Should Be Criminalised?

There is sometimes debate (or confusion) as to what conduct should be criminalised. Opponents of criminalisation sometimes decry the problems that would arise if all competition law infringements, such as vertical restraints and abuses of dominant positions, were subjected to criminal sanctions. This is largely a strawman argument.

It is true that some legal regimes have gone for such "wholesale" criminalisation, in which all competition law infringements including vertical restraints and abuses of dominant positions are made criminal offences, at least on the level of statutory law: this is true, for example, for the United States, France and Ireland.

However, in the United States there is today a consensus that criminal sanctions should be reserved for horizontal hardcore restraints (price-fixing, output or sales limitation, bid rigging as well as customer and market sharing arrangements); there has not been any criminal enforcement against vertical restraints or monopolisation for decades, and the Department of Justice is clear in its communications that it will only employ criminal law against hardcore cartels.

In Ireland, the "wholesale criminalisation" should be taken with a pinch of salt: custodial sanctions are only available for the hardcore infringements price-fixing, output or sales limitation, or customer and market sharing arrangements (section

8 with section 6(2) of the Competition Act 2002), and other infringements are not prosecuted criminally as a matter of prosecutorial discretion.[50]

In France, the overbroad criminal provision is one of the problems for criminal enforcement (see especially Blaise 2013), but especially the requirement that the offence must have been committed "fraudulently" would arguably prevent a successful prosecution of non-hardcore competition infringements.

The prevailing view in competition circles is that criminalisation should only be considered for horizontal hardcore infringements, namely price-fixing, output or sales limitation, bid rigging, and customer and market sharing arrangements (Monopolkommission 2014: §§ 120–123; Wils 2003, pp. 442–443; 2008: §§ 575–577; Wagner-von Papp 2010a, pp. 291, 297–298; 2010b, pp. 277–278, 2011; see already Kartte and von Portatius 1975, p. 1172, conceding that "qualified infringements of competition law, such as ... price fixing, indeed deserve criminal punishment", but fearing a slippery slope to the criminalisation of other infringements). For all practical purposes, this is the position in the United States, and it is the statutory position in the United Kingdom. While some contributors to the German debate would go further (Biermann 2007, pp. 33–34, noting that this should be part of the discussion; Baumann and Arzt 1970), such an extension would risk a chilling effect for pro-competitive conduct and the danger of false positives.

The following discussion proceeds on the basis that a criminal provision would be narrowly drafted to include only horizontal hardcore restraints, namely price-fixing, output or sales limitation, bid rigging, and customer and market sharing arrangements.

One could consider limiting the scope even further. One way to avoid the system being overburdened by de minimis cases with relatively low social harm would be to require a minimum threshold, for example, in terms of the affected turnover (for various solutions see Tiedemann 1976, pp. 152–158); those cartels falling below such a threshold could continue to be dealt with as an administrative offence. Of course, such a de minimis threshold would have to be formulated in such a way that it does not create insurmountable obstacles in the criminal process; asking for a minimum harm or overcharge, for example, would arguably make the offence impossible to prosecute.

8.4.2.2 How Can False Positives and a Chilling Effect on Legitimate Horizontal Cooperation Be Avoided?

Even with a cartel offence that is limited in its scope to horizontal hardcore cartels (Sect. 8.4.2.1 above), there remains a delimitation issue. There is a danger that the formulation of the cartel offence could encompass some legitimate horizontal

[50]In 2012 Ireland considered the decriminalisation of non-hardcore offences, but this was given up when its Attorney General advised that substantial civil fines could raise constitutional concerns under Article 38 of the Irish Constitution.

cooperation, or that some individuals at least fear that legitimate horizontal cooperation could be caught.

This is the issue that the "dishonesty" requirement in the original UK cartel offence was meant to solve and that the exceptions and defences in the new UK cartel offence are meant to address.

The practical significance of the issue is fairly limited. Cartels that have been prosecuted so far in countries that have criminal cartel offences were hardly forms of cooperation that could potentially be justified by pro-competitive reasons. Even a hardcore horizontal cartel is difficult enough to prosecute, so that prosecutors and criminal courts for practical reasons would not want to go near cases that are borderline legitimate cooperation.

Additionally, in reality many other criminal offences are much more open textured than a cartel offence aimed at horizontal hardcore cartels would likely be. Consider, for example, § 266 StGB or environmental offences—and yet managers are usually not deterred from engaging in profitable conduct even if there is some risk of criminal liability in the background.

The assertion, made by some opponents of the criminalisation of cartel conduct, that it is effectively impossible to define criminal cartel conduct with sufficient certainty and precision, appears to assume that criminal offences must be so precise as to require no interpretation or delimitation of borderline conduct at all (see, e.g., Dreher 2011, pp. 240–241; see already Kartte and von Portatius 1975, p. 1171). This is simply not true of *any* criminal offence. The current bid-rigging provision merely refers to making a bid 'based on an illegal arrangement', and yet this has not led to any substantial problems in practice. Indeed, the Federal Constitutional Court has explicitly held the provision not to be so vague as to be unconstitutional (BVerfG 2 April 2009, 2 BvR 1468/08). If the meaning of all criminal provisions were self-evident and did not require interpretation, most literature on criminal law would be superfluous. Furthermore, if it were truly impossible to craft a criminal offence, and if the current formulation of the competition law provisions were constitutionally too vague, then it would be impermissible to impose administrative fines in the tens of millions of euro (on undertakings) and tens or hundreds of thousands of euro (on individuals), because—as Dreher concedes (2011, p. 240)—the principle of legal certainty (*nullum crimen, nulla poena sine lege certa et scipta*) applies to administrative offences as well. It is one thing to demand that a criminal provision be narrowly tailored and well drafted; it is quite another thing to demand infeasibly high standards. The mere fact that any wording in a criminal cartel provision will require interpretation cannot be seen as an insurmountable obstacle.

Nevertheless, it is of course better to make the delimitation between legal and illegal conduct as clear as possible. Elevating the subjective (mens rea) elements of the offence, such as requiring an additional element of "dishonesty" or Absicht (e.g., "with the purpose of distorting competition") would be one way to go. However, as the dishonesty requirement in the old UK cartel offence has shown, this may result in obstacles to the prosecution even of genuine hardcore cartels. The new UK regime partially also relies on additional "intent" requirements (e.g., as to the concealment of the arrangement from the competition authority) in the new defences to the cartel offence.

Another possibility would be to give undertakings the opportunity to lodge their agreement with the competition authority in advance, and to guarantee the non-application of the criminal offence to the extent that the implementation does not exceed what is contained in the registered agreement (similar to the new UK cartel offence and the suggestion by Biermann 2007, p. 32; however, Dreher 2011: fn 99 considers this approach "impracticable" without elaborating). One could object that this would, in essence, replicate to some extent the old notification system under Article 101(3) TFEU. However, most of the costs of the old notification system can be avoided. First, there would be no need for the competition authority to "clear" the agreement. The lodging of the arrangement itself could be enough (similar to the former "*Widerspruchskartelle*" under German law), because it would only affect the applicability of the criminal offence—similar to the non-application of fines under the old notification system once the agreement was notified. Nor would there be an obligation to notify for anyone—notification would be purely optional, so that no-one would have to incur costs if they were sufficiently certain their arrangement did not fall under the criminal offence. Nor would competition authorities be required to spend significant resources on the scrutiny of the notified arrangements—first, hardcore cartels would be unlikely to notify in the first place even if there were known to be only occasional scrutiny, and second, even if a cartel slipped through the net, administrative sanctions could still be imposed.

The new cartel offence in the UK reaches a similar result by including a defence that the arrangement was not intended to be concealed from the competition authority or the counterparty.

In Germany, the Monopolkommission (2015: § 204) has recently submitted a concrete proposal for a criminal cartel provision; this may serve as a starting point for the discussion. In my view, a provision less directly based on the wording of Article 101 TFEU may be preferable, in order to avoid a direct application of the broad interpretation of the wording necessary in the administrative enforcement to criminal enforcement, for example when it comes to "indirectly" fixing prices. A combination of the Monopolkommission's recommendations—especially as to the definition of the personal scope of the offence, including the acting employee as well as management involved in the conduct—with the older recommendation by the Expert Commission to Fight White Collar Crime 1975 in § a (Tiedemann 1976, pp. 204–205) will capture most of the relevant aspects of the offence. It may be worth exploring whether the new UK cartel offence with its exceptions and defences, in particular with regard to a voluntary notification, could give inspiration to draft a sufficiently narrow offence.

8.4.2.3 Increased Defence Rights: A Marginal Issue

Arguments made in the international discussion are in particular that criminal trials are more expensive and require a higher standard of proof than non-criminal sanctions, and that the defendant has increased defence rights (e.g. Dreher 2011, p. 235). These may be compelling arguments in jurisdictions in which administrative or civil fines can currently be imposed with less judicial scrutiny and defendants have fewer defence rights than in criminal proceedings.

In Germany, however, even the current administrative fines are in principle subject to proceedings with criminal procedure standards (§ 46(1), 77(1) OWiG; Monopolkommission 2014: § 173). It is true that some aspects of the strict requirements of criminal procedure can be relaxed by the court under §§ 77–78 OWiG. In particular, it is marginally easier for the court to reject an application to take evidence once the court is already convinced that a certain fact has been established (§ 77(2) OWiG). This relaxation is meant to be a compromise between the defendant's rights of defence and the resources spent on minor offences. It has to be borne in mind, however, that the paradigm cases of administrative offences concern small fines for minor traffic infractions—the general range of administrative fines is between €5 and 1000 (§ 17(1) OWiG). In such cases of small fines, it may well be disproportionate to spend enormous resources in order to protect the defendant against the small probability of wrongful conviction associated with the rejection of such an application to take evidence, given that the consequence even of a wrongful conviction is usually no more than payment of a relatively low administrative fine without substantial further consequences. In competition cases, however, the fine is likely to exceed the general range of administrative fines substantially. The second sentence of § 77(1) OWiG provides that the court has to take account of the import of the case in deciding on the extent to which it takes evidence. Given the high administrative fines in competition cases—even on average they exceed the general maximum of § 17(1) OWiG by a factor of 56—, the second sentence of § 77 (1) OWiG already requires the application of criminal procedure standards even in the administrative fines procedure.

The situation should be similar in other European jurisdictions in which fines are imposed on individuals: substantial individual fines of the sort imposed for competition law infringements are to be classified under the *Engel* criteria as "criminal sanctions" for purposes of the European Convention for the Protection of Human Rights and Fundamental Freedoms (ECHR) anyway. For fines on undertakings, this has been decided in the *Menarini* case; for fines on individuals, this applies a fortiori. Procedures in cases in which fines against individuals have been imposed therefore have to comply at least with the standards required by Article 6 ECHR.

This means that the marginal increase in defence rights and the complexity of litigation is not a very strong argument in jurisdictions that already impose significant sanctions against individuals—certainly not in Germany.

In Germany, some contributors—including the current Vice President of the Bundeskartellamt—suggest, on the contrary, abolishing individual sanctions completely, on the assumption that the quasi-criminal procedure standards, which currently also apply to fines imposed on undertakings, could then be removed in favour of curtailed judicial review in a quasi-administrative procedure (Bundeskartellamt 2015b; Ost 2014, p. 134).

If this were the counterfactual scenario against which individual criminal sanctions would have to be compared, the marginal difference of defence rights would indeed be greater. However, for reasons of German constitutional law and ECHR case law, there are limits to the curtailment of the judicial review of fines as high as those imposed in competition law even if the sanctions are imposed exclusively on undertakings (Bundeskartellamt 2015b). In addition, the approach would make the Principal-Agent problem even worse.

What is true, however, is that some of the traditional guarantees in the German criminal and quasi-criminal procedure are unnecessarily cumbersome without actually strengthening the rights of defence (see Bundeskartellamt 2015b). In so far as this is the case, the criminal procedure should be overhauled and simplified (Bundeskartellamt 2015b; Ost 2014). These reforms, however, mostly apply to the criminal and quasi-criminal (administrative offence) procedure alike, and are therefore necessary or at least desirable, completely independently of the decision to criminalise cartel conduct.

The introduction of criminal sanctions would not make the procedure for individual sanctions substantially more burdensome when compared to the status quo.

8.4.2.4 Criminal Immunity

The discussion of the criminal provisions in the UK, France and Germany has shown that one of the most problematic aspects is interference with leniency programmes. While it may be difficult to quantify the success that these programmes have had, and while one must be careful not to rely too heavily on leniency programmes lest they lose their effectiveness, there is very little doubt that for all practical purposes they have been very successful instruments for the detection and prosecutions of cartels indeed. Opponents and proponents of criminalisation agree that criminalisation should not come at the price of impairing leniency programmes (Wagner-von Papp 2010b, pp. 275–276, 282; 2014; Biermann 2007, pp. 45–46; Dreher 2011, p. 242; Monopolkommission 2014: §§ 175–181).

There is, then, the question whether leniency programmes can be effective in the presence of criminal sanctions. If there is no coordination between the leniency programme and the threat of criminal sanctions, then criminal sanctions are likely to be detrimental to leniency programmes: where a potential applicant faces possible imprisonment or other criminal sanctions, the prize offered of immunity for administrative fines will not be particularly tempting. This, it should be recalled, is the current situation for bid-rigging in Germany and all infringements in France, even though in both countries the probability of actual enforcement of criminal sanctions on the successful leniency applicant is arguably low.

However, this is not a logically necessary consequence of the introduction of criminal sanctions. It is possible to introduce criminal sanctions and provide for criminal immunity for the successful immunity recipient. This is the situation in the United States and in England, Wales and Northern Ireland. If there is criminal immunity, leniency programmes are significantly strengthened: the differential between the consequences of applying for leniency and being caught becomes greater than it was without criminal sanctions. What is more, it multiplies the number of players in the leniency game, and so increases the mutual distrust that results in the effectiveness of leniency programmes.

The question is therefore only whether there are any legal obstacles to the introduction of criminal immunity for immunity recipients under the leniency programme in the jurisdiction for which criminal sanctions are considered. In France, this does not appear to be the case; the Rapport Coulon (2008) explicitly suggested the introduction of immunity. In Germany, constitutional reservations are sometimes voiced in the context of criminal immunity. However, the criminal immunity provision in § 371 of the Tax Code (Abgabenordnung, AO) has hardly presented constitutional problems (see Bundesverfassungsgericht, 28 June 1983—1 BvL 31/82; Monopolkommission 2014: § 179). It is unclear why an equivalent provision for immunity recipients under a competition leniency policy should be any different in this regard. The Monopolkommission (2015, p. 210) has made a concrete proposal for an immunity provision.[51] In other jurisdictions, the situation may of course be different, depending on the relevant constitutional provisions.

Any remaining constitutional doubts would, in any case, be removed in the European Union if EU legislation provided for a prohibition of individual sanctions where they would interfere with leniency programmes. The current consultation may result in such EU legislation (see below Sec. 8.5.2).

8.4.3 *Utilitarian Arguments*

Arguments for and against criminalisation can be subdivided into utilitarian or pragmatic arguments on the one hand, and moral arguments on the other.

Utilitarian or pragmatic arguments in favour of criminalisation can be summarised as follows (see already Wils 2003, pp. 432–442; 2008: §§ 547–574; Wagner-von Papp 2010a, pp. 292–296; 2010b, pp. 270–277; Monopolkommission 2014: §§ 154–166):

1. Individual sanctions are needed to overcome the principal-agent problem that arises when only undertakings are sanctioned.
2. Individual sanctions other than criminal sanctions can be factored into the calculation as a price rather than a sanction, because they lack the moral

[51] The recommendation awards criminal immunity to perpetrators where the competition authority awards immunity from fines to the undertaking, but excludes immunity for the sole instigator and coercers. A debate is to be had whether this should not be reduced to excluding at most coercers, so as not to deter leniency applications from instigators; otherwise, especially cartels with only two members would be stabilised. More importantly, the recommendation would have to be amended to take account of individual leniency applications.

opprobrium and extra-legal (social) consequences associated with a criminal conviction.

3. Criminal sanctions are a particularly deterrent sanction especially for white collar perpetrators because of the additional cost of social capital, and because of the higher opportunity costs if custodial sanctions are imposed, or in case the criminal conviction forecloses future employment opportunities. The argument that there is a lack of empirical evidence for this increased deterrent effect has been rejected above.
4. Criminal sanctions are an effective deterrent because white collar criminality is usually the result of rational deliberation rather than hot-tempered spur-of-the-moment decision making (Coffee 1980, p. 424; Cseres et al. 2006, p. 7).
5. Criminal sanctions reinforce and spread the message that cartel conduct is prohibited.
6. Criminal sanctions would allow the prosecuting authority to make full use of the investigatory tools that are not available in the procedure for administrative offences (see, eg, § 46(3) OWiG).
   In particular, it is to be expected that a criminal cartel offence would also be listed in § 100a StPO, as is already the case for § 298 StGB (§ 100a(2)(r) StPO), which allows the interception of telecommunications without the knowledge or consent of those communicating. Such wiretapping has been used to good effect in competition cases, for example, in France and Chile; in the United States, the possibility for wiretapping where there is a suspicion of antitrust offences was introduced in the Antitrust Criminal Investigation Improvement Act 2005. In addition, the inclusion in the catalogue of § 100a StPO would also allow recordings outside of a residential home under § 100f StPO.
7. Provided the criminal offence takes criminal immunity into account, leniency programmes will be strengthened. The differential between the payoffs for applying for leniency and for being detected or reported by the other cartelist becomes greater.

Utilitarian or pragmatic arguments against criminalisation can be summarised as follows (see in particular Dreher 2011, pp. 240–243; Möschel 1980, pp. 49–52; and the discussion in Wagner-von Papp 2010a, pp. 297–300; 2010b, pp. 277–281):

1. An overbroad definition could result in overdeterrence and a chilling effect. This issue has been discussed above. For a criminal offence restricted to horizontal hardcore cartels, namely price fixing, market sharing, bid rigging, and limiting sales or output, especially if combined with the possibility of registering the agreement with the competition authority to avoid criminal sanctions, the argument is unconvincing.
2. A major problem in France and Germany is the shift in the prosecuting institutions once an offence is a criminal one from the competition authority to (often local or regional) public prosecutors and the criminal courts. Such a shift is undesirable for several reasons: general public prosecutors cannot match the competition authorities' expertise on and dedication to competition law and policy; resources of local and regional prosecutors are scarce, and

non-competition matters that consume less resources will be prioritised; local or regional enforcement leads to fragmented enforcement and may so impair a consistent case prioritisation (possibly leading to the closing of complex, high-stake cases, and the prosecution of low-stake, but easy-to-prove cases); general criminal courts may lack the expertise regarding competition law that the courts dealing with the administrative cartel offences have acquired; and criminal cases tried in local or regional courts are generally not well publicised.

It is to be noted, however, that there is nothing inevitable in shifting the prosecution from the competition authority entirely to the general public prosecutor once an offence is made a criminal one. At a minimum, the coordination between the competition authority and the general prosecutor could be improved along the lines of the fiscal authorities when it comes to the prosecution of tax crimes (Biermann 2007, p. 43; Federmann 2006, pp. 518–520; Raum 2014: paragraph 3; Wagner-von Papp 2016: § 23). A federal or at least more strongly coordinated regional specialised prosecutor for economic crime has been debated for decades (Emrich-Katzin 2013). And while it is true that the "Monopoly for Prosecutions" currently lies with the public prosecutor (with narrow exceptions for private prosecutions), this is not a constitutionally required state of affairs (Bundeskartellamt 2015b, pp. 31–33). Similarly, there is no reason not to task the courts that currently deal with administrative cartel offences with dealing with criminal cartel offences as well; indeed, this was one of the recommendations made more than 40 years ago by the Expert Commission on White Collar Crime 1975 (Tiedemann 1976, p. 208).

3. If there is no accompanying criminal immunity provision (and there currently is none for bid rigging in Germany, and none in France), then the introduction of (further) criminal sanctions may negatively affect the rate of leniency applications. If the choice is between a system with an effective leniency programme without criminal sanctions, and one with criminal sanctions but no effective leniency programme, then it is very likely that the former system is more effective in deterring cartels. The most effective system, however, would most likely be one with criminal sanctions and an immunity prize.
4. Opponents argue that criminal prosecutions would be too complex and costly. As explained above, current prosecutions under the administrative offence in Germany are already quasi-criminal, so that the marginal increase in the burden for the justice system would not be high. Furthermore, in a typical year the Bundeskartellamt imposes individual fines on some 100 individuals. Criminal prosecutions under a cartel offence would arguably be in a similar order of magnitude (in the United States, the Department of Justice has filed charges on average against 54 individuals per year in the 10 years from 2005 to 2014, Department of Justice (2014b)). It seems incongruous that the criminal justice system should be able to prosecute, as was for example the case in 2013, more than 6000 aggravated fraud cases, more than 3000 computer fraud cases, some 2000 cases of embezzlement, and more than 1700 insolvency crimes under the criminal code plus 2000 under the Insolvency Code (Insolvenzordnung, InsO) (Statistisches Bundesamt 2015, pp. 38–54)—and yet break down if it were

tasked with prosecuting 100 cartelists per year criminally instead of in quasi-criminal proceedings.

5. Sometimes the question of marginal deterrence is raised in the context of the criminalisation debate: would cartelists commit additional crimes if they are 'criminally liable' anyway, perhaps to conceal the crime or to avoid prosecution (Spagnolo 2006, pp. 143–146)? The answer to this question is likely no. Sentences for a criminal cartel offence would, in most cases, be expected to be low for first time offenders. Even in the supposedly draconian United States, the average sentence has been 24 months in the fiscal years between 2010 and 2015 (Snyder 2016), and the highest sentence ever imposed in the United States was 5 years imprisonment (United States v. Frank Peake, No. 14–1088 (1st Cir, 14 October 2015); Snyder 2016). Any additional crimes that could be committed to conceal the antitrust offence could therefore be taken into account in sentencing, so that marginal deterrence is not a real issue (see already Werden and Simon 1987, p. 935).
6. Similarly, any concerns that criminalisation could induce cartels to take additional measures to conceal the cartel and therefore make detection harder are unwarranted. The existing level of enforcement already provides a strong incentive to conceal, and it is unlikely that criminalisation would lead to a large marginal increase in resources spent on avoiding detection. The only realistic problem that could occur here is that criminal sanctions could deter leniency applicants from disclosing the cartel; but this would only be the case if a successful leniency application did not result in criminal immunity. This only reinforces the point, made several times above, that it is indispensable to introduce a criminal immunity provision—something that needs to be done in Germany (and France) even at the current level of criminalisation.

The most compelling utilitarian argument against criminalisation is that it could weaken leniency programmes if the law does not provide for criminal immunity; but this is an argument in favour of providing for a criminal immunity provision, not one against criminalisation. Only if there were insurmountable obstacles to a criminal immunity provision would this be different. At least in Germany, this is not the case. What is more, the need for a criminal immunity provision exists anyway because of the existence of the bid rigging provision.

The second utilitarian argument that has some validity at first sight is that a criminal offence could be less effectively enforced than the current administrative offence. However, if the current administrative offence (§ 81 GWB) is retained, and a narrower criminal provision were added, then the worst that could happen would be that public prosecutors would refer these cases back to the competition authorities for the prosecution of the administrative offence (§ 43 OWiG). In addition, if the legislator is willing to give the competition authorities a greater role in the prosecution of the criminal offence, which would be very desirable, then it is unclear why prosecution of the criminal offence should be less vigorous.

Overall, the greater deterrence that would result from the introduction of a criminal offence, and the increased effectiveness of the leniency programme if such a criminal offence were combined with a criminal immunity provision (resulting from increased distrust between cartel participants and leading to a higher probability of detection) arguably dominate.

8.4.4 *Moral Argument*

Criminal offences differ from administrative offences largely in the degree of moral opprobrium. The question from this perspective is whether horizontal hardcore cartel offences justify as much moral opprobrium as is necessary for criminalisation.

This may be discussed at an abstract level—what moral norms have been infringed (see in particular Whelan 2014; see also Stucke 2006), and whether cartel conduct is *malum in se* (as the Irish judge in *Duffy* assumed) or merely *malum prohibitum*. Such a discussion mostly assumes that there is an objective cut-off point, if not a bright line for determining whether conduct deserves criminal punishment (for a criticism of an abstract and static classification into *mala in se* and *mala prohibita* see Stucke 2006, pp. 489–490). In the German discourse, it is uncontroversial that the legislature has, outside a certain core of criminal offences such as violent crime, a large degree of discretion in categorising offences as criminal or administrative in nature. Nevertheless, the categorisation should be consistent with comparable offences. For decades, even before cartels were labelled as the "supreme evil of antitrust" and sanctioned with multi-million euro fines, the categorisation of cartels as mere administrative offences has been the outlier in the set of administrative offences.

The two factors that are decisive for the categorisation are the degree of the "harm" inflicted (Erfolgsunrecht, below Sect. 8.4.4.1) and the degree of "criminal energy" manifested in the deed (Handlungsunrecht, below Sect. 8.4.4.2). Opponents of criminalisation often add a third criterion: public opinion (below Sect. 8.4.4.3).

8.4.4.1 Harm Inflicted

With regard to the first element (Erfolgsunrecht), few commentators deny that the social harm inflicted by cartel conduct is considerable. First, one can argue that the harm inflicted on the institution "competition" is sufficient to justify criminalisation (for this line of argument, see in particular Wardaugh 2014, pp. 43–51; see also Tiedemann 1976, pp. 102–106; 2001). Second, even if one looks for more concrete harm to the wealth of victims, the case for criminalisation is strong. By its nature, it is very difficult to quantify the harm inflicted even by detected cartels, not to mention that caused by undetected cartels. The European Commission estimated the annual harm inflicted by cartels on the EU economy to be in the range between €16.8 billion and €261.2 billion (Ashton and Henry 2013, p. 211, § 8.002). The Bundeskartellamt estimates that its cartel enforcement brings benefits in the order of magnitude of between €500 million and €750 million annually

(Bundeskartellamt 2011, pp. 15–16), and that does not even include the benefits for German markets derived from the EU Commission's enforcement. Overall, there can be little discussion that the social harm inflicted by horizontal hardcore cartels is of a magnitude that justifies the use of criminal sanctions (see already Tiedemann 1976, pp. 106–120).

8.4.4.2 Criminal Energy Manifested

With regard to the criminal energy exerted (Handlungsunrecht), many cartels build up an elaborate organisation. Not infrequently, the cartel organisation consists of a hierarchical organisation with coordination on various levels of management. In the German *Railway Track Cartel*, for example, there were two-tiered meetings of the participants, with high-level coordination by executive managers and detailed coordination by mid-level managers (Bundeskartellamt 2012).

Cartels also take great pains to conceal their conduct (Stucke 2006, p. 494). In the German *Railway Track Cartel*, for example, the participants coordinated their telecommunications via prepaid telephone cards (Bundeskartellamt 2012). The amount of criminal energy spent in cartel activity becomes even clearer when looking at the secret video and recordings of telecommunications which the Federal Bureau of Investigation made of the *Lysine Cartel*.[52] The participants among other things joke about attendance of the FBI at the meeting, deliver the memorable line that "our competitors are our friends, the customers are the enemy", and discuss the dangers of meeting on US American soil because of its strict antitrust laws. Because they show the criminal intent of the participants so clearly, the Lysine Tapes have been called "the single greatest antitrust compliance tool ever created." (O'Brien 2015, p. 24).

Some cartels even resort to threats, violence or other means associated with traditional criminal organisations. The "*Dutch Construction Cartel*" allegedly involved many such features, including threats of physical violence, bribery and other corruption offences (van Bergeijk 2008; van Duyne 2007; Zembla 2001–2006). The criminal court in the German *Pipes Cartel*, LG Munich II (2006), also found threats as an aggravating factor. Threats and violence were also used in the *French Beef Cartel* (European Commission, [2003] OJ L209/12 § 173).

8.4.4.3 Public Opinion

Nevertheless, opponents argue that that there is no wide-spread recognition in the German population that cartel conduct is criminal conduct. This was the argument that kept the legislator of the German Act against Restraints of Competition in 1958 from inserting a criminal offence instead of the administrative offence, and it is an

[52] Links to the transcripts are contained in Hammond (2005); the videos themselves are available on Youtube.

argument still made today (Dreher 2011; Ost 2014). Dreher has also made the argument that this is a crucial difference to the United States, because the public there perceived cartels as criminal conduct and immoral (Dreher 2011).

The argument has long been challenged as asking the wrong question, because the population's understanding whether conduct deserves criminal punishment often follows the legislature's decisions to criminalise or decriminalise conduct. The legislature may shape public opinion; it is not confined to following it (Baumann and Arzt 1970; Wagner-von Papp 2010a, pp. 281–282; 2010b, p. 274; Monopolkommission 2014: § 165).

Even assuming for the sake of argument that the legislature should follow public opinion rather than shape it, however, there is now evidence that shows that the public is not as indifferent to cartel conduct as has been assumed without empirical basis by many (myself included, Wagner-von Papp 2010b, p. 274; Dreher 2011; Wardaugh 2014, p. 308). Stephan (2015, 2016) reports on surveys conducted in the United Kingdom, Germany, Italy and the United States (for the United States see also Stucke 2006, pp 500–502). The survey for Germany, which was conducted by YouGov and included a representative sample of 2648 panel members, found that:

- 75 % of those surveyed knew that price fixing is illegal in Germany;
- a majority of respondents was of the view that "price fixing is as serious as fraud"; slightly over 50 % were of this view, and an additional slightly below 5 % thought price fixing was more serious than fraud, which is nearly identical to the percentage of US respondents;
- a clear majority of respondents was of the view that price fixing is as serious or more serious than insider trading; nearly 50 % thought that price fixing is as serious, and nearly 20 % thought it was more serious than insider trading;
- a clear majority of respondents was of the view that price fixing is more serious than illegally downloading music (Stephan 2015).

Fraud (§ 263 StGB), insider trading (§ 38 WpHG), and illegally downloading music (§ 106 UrhG) are criminal offences in Germany. With regard to the offence mentioned last, the legislature even rejected a de minimis exception that had been proposed. Considering price fixing as serious as or more serious than these offences therefore implies that a majority of respondents is for the criminalisation of price fixing.

It is true that when asked what sanctions the individual involved in price fixing should face, only 28 % of the German respondents included "imprisonment". This is similar to the proportion of respondents in the UK and Italian survey (27 % and 26 %, respectively), and somewhat lower than the percentage of respondents in the United States (36 %). It would seem, however, that the sanction of imprisonment was understood to mean the actual imposition of a custodial sentence in all cases, rather than providing for a sentencing range that also included a custodial sentence; otherwise, it would not make sense to consider price fixing as serious as or even more serious than the criminal offences fraud or insider trading, which both are criminal offences that include imprisonment in the sentencing range (Stephan 2016; Wagner-von Papp 2016: § 8).

Far from finding criminal sanctions for horizontal hardcore cartels abnormal, the public would arguably find it problematic that entering into an elaborate price-fixing cartel with a complex structure and refined subterfuges to conceal the scheme from the authorities, which results in losses of tens or hundreds of millions of euros, is an administrative offence, while the legal system has no compunction about imposing criminal penalties on the homeless person who steals a bread roll. Anatole France famously wrote: "*Ils y doivent travailler devant la majestueuse égalité des lois, qui interdit au riche comme au pauvre de coucher sous les ponts, de mendier dans les rues et de voler du pain.*" (France 1894, p. 118).[53] This was not meant as a policy prescription.

The argument here is not that horizontal hardcore cartels should be criminalised *because* the public considers price fixing at least as serious as fraud and insider trading. It is the opponents of criminalisation who claim, without empirical support, that the public would not agree with criminal sanctions for cartels. To the best of my knowledge, the YouGov survey summarised above is the best available evidence on this issue, and it provides evidence that the public understands the harmfulness of cartels and that they are comparably serious to, or more serious than, existing criminal offences.

While public sentiment is not irrelevant, there could be good reasons not to follow it. Just because the crowd demands that heads roll, and that individuals go to prison whenever a business decision has serious consequences for the economy, for example, this is not a reason to criminalise commercial decision-making as soon as it turns out to have been ill advised (in hindsight or even objectively). Nor would it be a good idea to let laypersons define the conduct that should be criminal in competition law. With regard to cartels, however, the vox populi also seems to be in accordance with a technical assessment. Hardly anyone denies that the overall social harm inflicted by cartels is considerable and exceeds the harm inflicted by many other forms of crime. While the case law currently finds the elements of the general fraud provision (§ 263 StGB) to be satisfied only in the special case of bid rigging, this is not the only possible interpretation of the elements in a legal assessment, and is not at all decisive for the moral assessment. What is more, given the criminalisation of the bid-rigging offence in Germany, it is difficult to argue that a minor bid-rigging agreement by local plumbers is more immoral than a large-scale price-fixing agreement (see already Möschel 1980, pp. 47–48, 57–58, but used there as an argument against the criminalisation of bid-rigging arrangements).

Of course, one can be of the view that the bar for criminalisation should *generally* be set higher. An outright abolitionist who believes that criminal law in its entirety is incapable or inappropriate to guide social conduct will inevitably consider the criminalisation of hardcore cartels inapposite. Even short of such an extreme position, one can advocate the decriminalisation of many non-violent crimes, and if such an overall revision were to take place, the comparators would shift. The argument above was made in the context of the existing criminal law, and

[53]"[The poor have] to work under the majestic equality of the law, which prohibits the rich and the poor to sleep under bridges, beg in the streets and steal bread".

tried to place horizontal hardcore cartels into the matrix of existing criminal offences. From this perspective, the moral culpability of those entering into horizontal hardcore cartels seems higher than for many existing criminal offences, so that from a moral perspective there is a good case for criminalisation.

8.4.5 Overall Assessment

From a moral perspective, cartel activity appears nearly indistinguishable from fraud, and often displays the special features of aggravated fraud, in particular organised conspiratorial conduct and the infliction of great harm. Even from a *de lege lata* perspective it can be argued that in Germany the elements of the offence are met not only in the case of bid rigging, but also in the case of other horizontal cartels such as price fixing—in today's market economy customers have a legitimate expectation that the prices have been arrived independently, and, empirically, the public indeed appears to have this expectation (Stephan 2015). Non-disclosure then constitutes implicit misrepresentation, induces a mistake which causes the value transfer; resulting harm can be established in the same way in which the German Federal Court of Justice has established it in the bid-rigging cases, namely by comparing the transaction price with the counterfactual price that would have resulted under independent price setting. The legal qualification of hardcore cartels (other than bid rigging) as fraud is, however, an extreme minority view.

Nevertheless, at a minimum hardcore cartels are on or near the borderline to criminal fraud. As the recent survey has shown, the public recognises this (above Sect. 8.4.4.3). Cartels inflict great social harm. They involve clandestine conspiracies, often perpetuated over a long period of time. The moral case for opprobrium by imposing criminal sanctions on cartels is clearer than for many existing criminal offences. From the perspective of coherence and consistency in the criminal justice system, the current qualification of cartels (other than bid rigging) as merely administrative offences is the outlier (Monopolkommission 2014: § 163). Criminalising horizontal hardcore cartels would restore coherence and consistency.

This leaves utilitarian and pragmatic arguments against criminalisation. It is true that criminalisation must take care not to impede the effectiveness of the competition authorities' cartel investigations. These administrative investigations and prosecutions are the bedrock of competition law enforcement, and they must not be endangered. These are the arguments that have traditionally been made by competition lawyers. At closer inspection, however, there are few reasons why criminalisation should interfere with the effectiveness of enforcement by the competition authorities, and all of them can be addressed and have to be addressed anyway, regardless of further criminalisation (*cf* Monopolkommission 2014: §§ 172–191). First, there is the necessity to provide for a criminal immunity provision for successful immunity recipients. Crucially, the introduction of such a criminal immunity provision is necessary anyway, even if one decided to criminalise further cartel conduct, because of the criminal sanctions for bid rigging in Germany (and the situation in France is similar). Secondly, public prosecutors may be less focused on competition offences and may lack the requisite specialist knowledge. This can be addressed by sufficient involvement of the competition authority in the criminal investigation and prosecution. Again, this is an issue that should be addressed anyway, because it creates problems even in the prosecution of cartels as administrative offences (Bundeskartellamt 2015b).

The cartel offence would have to be drafted narrowly in order to avoid type I errors and a chilling effect. An offence focused on horizontal hardcore cartels with a possibility of escaping criminal prosecution where the agreement was notified to the competition authority would not run these risks. The new UK cartel offence may serve as an already quite good model, even though some of the uncertainties of the new defences should be avoided. With regard to the chilling effect argument, one should see that the statutory law in the United States is much too broad, involving all conduct under sections 1 and 2 Sherman Act, and yet business goes on, based on the mere pronouncements of the Department of Justice that it will criminally prosecute only horizontal hardcore cartels.

A "cheap" criminalisation by creating mere "law in the books" that competition law infringements or cartel conduct constitutes a criminal offence without any complementing institutional reforms or active enforcement would indeed do more harm than good. This objection, however, cannot be made against the introduction of a criminal cartel offence that is narrowly tailored and accompanied by the introduction of a criminal immunity provision, the integration of the competition authority in the criminal investigation and prosecution, and the extension of the competence of the courts dealing with the administrative cartel offence to the new criminal cartel offence. Where this is the case, criminalisation can address the principal-agent problem effectively, effectively deter individuals from entering into cartels, and strengthen leniency programmes at the same time.

Criminalisation, if well done, is therefore desirable both from a moral and from a utilitarian perspective, provided the accompanying changes in the enforcement institutions are made at the same time.

8.5 International Aspects

8.5.1 Criminalisation and Extradition

The considerations above have looked at criminalisation from a purely national perspective. In reality, of course, many cartels have a cross-border element, an aspect that is often neglected in the criminalisation debate.

In particular where an international cartel has substantial and intended effects in the United States or, if import commerce is not affected, the cartel has direct, substantial and foreseeable effects in the US and gives rise to a claim in the US, US law applies (*United States v. Nippon Paper*), and the United States have made clear that they will aggressively enforce their laws against foreigners as well as against US nationals. Gone are the days when the Department of Justice granted foreigners "no-jail" plea agreements (O'Brien 2015, pp. 22–23). Nevertheless, enforcement jurisdiction is strictly territorial, and so criminal jurisdiction depended, until recently, on the voluntary submission of individuals to US American prosecution or their apprehension on US soil. Many individuals did submit voluntarily, in part because international travel would otherwise have become a great hassle because of red-flagging by Interpol.

Not all individuals did submit voluntarily to extradition. Over the last 2 decades, however, the United States has entered into numerous modernised extradition treaties (Girardet 2010). A condition of these modernised extradition treaties is "dual criminality". The numerous criminal offences in the EU (see the list in footnote 19), even to the extent that they are only "law in the books", may become relevant here.

The case of Mr Romano Pisciotti is instructive. Mr Pisciotti was allegedly a participant of the Marine Hose Cartel. The United States requested his arrest and extradition. When Mr Pisciotti wanted to connect flights at Frankfurt International Airport, he was detained. The Marine Hose Cartel was a bid-rigging cartel, so that it was criminal conduct under German law. The dual criminality requirement of the extradition treaty between United States and Germany was therefore fulfilled. Mr Pisciotti challenged the extradition before the German Federal Constitutional Court (BVerfG, 17 February 2014, 2 BvQ 4/14, WuW/E DE-R 4275; Röhrig 2015) and the European General Court (Case T-403/14, ECLI:EU:T:2014:692) and Court of Justice (Case C-411/14 P, ECLI:EU:C:2015:48), but to no avail. He was extradited to the United States. His experience has been summarised as follows:

> Romano Pisciotti spent 669 days in custody. This included two hours in a police station in Lugano, Switzerland; 10 months in a jail in Frankfurt, Germany, fighting extradition; and eight months in a US federal prison in Folkston, Georgia, in a room with around 40 mainly Mexican inmates and a single corner toilet. [...] 'I am totally ruined,' Pisciotti says wearily during an interview in his home north of Milan. 'They destroyed me, my bank account, my family, my career. Everything.' (Crofts 2015)

A German national would not be extradited from Germany due to Article 16 of the German Constitution, a provision which Mr Pisciotti argued should be applied to all EU nationals. Nor would a foreign price-fixer currently be extradited from Germany for lack of dual criminality. However, a price fixer of German (or for that matter, any other) nationality travelling to or connecting via London or possibly Paris could become the "next Pisciotti", regardless of the fact that German law does not consider cartels criminal offences, and regardless of the fact that criminal enforcement in the United Kingdom (so far) tends towards zero and in France is not very frequent either. Both the United Kingdom and France have "dual criminality" extradition treaties similar to Germany's with the United States.[54]

[54]For the United Kingdom, see already the earlier case of Ian Norris, who was eventually extradited to the United States from the United Kingdom. His extradition was not, however, based on the cartel offence, because s 188 EA 2002 had not been in force when he entered into a cartel; nor did the House of Lords consider cartel conduct to fall under the common law offence of conspiracy to defraud (*Norris v Government of the United States of America* [2008] UKHL 16, [2008] 2 WLR 673 (HL(E))). Instead, his extradition was based on obstruction of justice charges. Those participating in horizontal hardcore cartels after June 2003, however, would satisfy the dual criminality requirement.

In other words, to the extent a cartel has substantial and intended effects in the United States, horizontal hardcore cartels are de facto already "criminalised" worldwide. If there were significant chilling effects on legitimate conduct from cartel criminalisation, we should see them already at least in all markets that have a global dimension. Realistically, however, many actors in Germany and other European jurisdictions will not consider the criminal law in other jurisdictions, even where their conduct affects markets that are global in reach. Criminalising the conduct in their home jurisdictions may make them aware of the danger of going to prison for cartel conduct—a danger in which they already are, with or without criminalisation in their home jurisdiction.

8.5.2 The Need for a One-Stop Shop for Leniency with Criminal Immunity

The importance of complementing a criminal offence with a provision on criminal immunity for the immunity recipient under a leniency policy has been emphasised a number of times above.

And yet, more is required when one takes the international dimension into account. Assume that State A has a criminal offence and provides that the first successful leniency applicant will be immune from criminal prosecution. Taken by itself, this is a sensible way to approach the problem, and the leniency programme will remain effective. Indeed, the leniency programme will be especially effective, because the cartelists now fear criminal prosecution unless they are the first through the door, and because they know that the other cartelists also fear criminal prosecution. Mutual distrust is high. There is a "race to the competition authority" of State A.

Now assume that States B, C, D, E and F follow exactly the same scheme as State A. Again, in the case of purely domestic cartels, the scheme works well for each of them. However, in case there is an international cartel between members from A, B, C, D, E and F, a potential leniency applicant may not be the first applicant in all jurisdictions. Assume that a cartelist would indeed be the first in States A, B, C, D and E, but fails to be the first applicant in State F and therefore has to fear that State F prosecutes the responsible individuals criminally. Depending on the likelihood of prosecution, the severity of the sanction, and whether the decision-makers themselves would be criminally liable, this may deter the potential applicant from making use of the leniency policy.

The European Commission has highlighted the problematic impact which individual sanctions in Member States may have on the use of leniency programmes.[55]

[55]European Commission (2014a), § 41: "The majority of Member States provide for sanctions to be imposed on individuals for breaches of competition law, over and above fines on undertakings. If such systems do not provide for leniency for the employees of undertakings which are considering applying for corporate leniency, this may lead to disincentives to cooperate with authorities EU-wide. The threat of investigations and sanctions targeted at employees may deter

The Commission has indicated that a solution on the EU level may be necessary (European Commission 2014a: § 42; 2014b: § 102), possibly along the lines of the Swedish solution, which exempts from trading prohibitions individuals in undertakings that are granted immunity or a reduction in the fine under a leniency programme not only of the Swedish competition authority, but also of the Commission or another NCA. The advantage of a solution on the level of EU law would be that it would overcome any objections that may exist under national constitutional law against criminal immunity rules (Wagner-von Papp 2014). The CMA in its response to the consultation considered the Commission's intervention superfluous and recommended its own solution to other Member States, which grants criminal immunity to immunity recipients under the leniency programmes of the CMA and the European Commission (and discretionary criminal immunity to those who receive reductions under those leniency programmes). In contrast to the Swedish solution, this does not, however, capture the problem described above where immunity was granted not by the Commission, but the NCA of another state.

Preferable would be a third solution: a central clearing agency for leniency applications or at least markers on the global or—more realistically—European level (Wagner-von Papp 2016: § 41) with attendant automatic criminal immunity for the immunity recipient under the leniency programme.

8.6 Conclusions on Criminal Cartel Conduct and Compliance

Criminal sanctions for horizontal hardcore cartels are desirable from a moral perspective. Whether they are desirable from a utilitarian and pragmatic perspective depends on the institutional framework. In Germany, the conditions for a criminalisation of cartel conduct are good. All that is required is the introduction of a narrowly drafted cartel offence for horizontal hardcore cartels, a criminal immunity provision—which is long overdue anyway for the bid-rigging offence—, and provision for the Bundeskartellamt's involvement in the criminal prosecution of the cartel offence similar to the tax authorities' involvement in the prosecution of tax evasion. In other nations, the conditions for effective criminal enforcement may be better or worse than in Germany.

The European Commission could help Member States such as France and Germany to overcome their reluctance to create automatic criminal immunity, and it could help Member States such as the UK recognise that the interjurisdictional externalities are not fully resolved by national immunity provisions that cover only the national and the EU leniency programme.

potential corporate applicants from applying." Even more clearly European Commission (2014b), §§ 99–102, highlighting the interjurisdictional externalities of the threat of criminal sanctions.

The introduction of effective criminal enforcement of the cartel offence would make compliance training both more important and more effective. Criminalisation makes compliance training more important because training sessions help to spread knowledge about the criminal offence—and only a known threat can deter. The goal of criminalisation is, after all, not to send individuals to prison for their criminal conduct. It is to prevent them from engaging in cartel conduct. Criminalisation makes compliance training more effective because the participants of the compliance training realise that they have 'skin in the game': "the threat of prison sentences helps make compliance programs effective" (Werden et al. 2012).

The German "founding fathers" of the GWB, when opting for an administrative offence instead of a criminal one, indicated that this may be for a transition period only, and that a switch to genuine criminal sanctions may be appropriate once knowledge and familiarity with a competition regime are more widespread (Wagner-von Papp 2010a, p. 281; 2011, p. 164; Monopolkommission 2015 § 200). The time has come to make this switch: the fundamental notions of competition have permeated public knowledge (above Sect. 8.4.4.3), and thanks to compliance schemes the business community has a good understanding of the standards and ample opportunities to fill in any remaining gaps in their knowledge (*cf* Monopolkommission 2014: § 145).

References

Ablasser-Neuhuber, A., & Neumayr, F. (2015). Austria. In Campbell (2015), (p. 17).

Adams, C., & Boxell, J. (2006). UK drops BAE-Saudi bribery probe. *Financial Times*, 15 December 2006.

Allain, M.-L., Boyer, M., Kotchoni, R., & Ponssard, J.-P. (2013). Are cartel fines optimal? — Theory and evidence from the European Union. *CIRANO Scientific Series* 2013s-24 (July 2013), http://www.cirano.qc.ca/pdf/publication/2013s-24.pdf.

Almunia, J., & Lewandowski, J. (2010). Information note by Mr. Joaquín Almunia, Vice-President of the Commission, and by Mr. Janusz Lewandowski, Member of the Commission, Inability to Pay under paragraph 35 of the 2006 fining guidelines and payment conditions pre- and post-decision finding an infringement and imposing fines, SEC(2010) 737/2 (12 June 2010).

Andrews, P., & Collins, D. (2015). Ireland. In Campbell (2015), (p. 135).

Ashton, D., & Henry, D. (2013). *Competition damages actions in the EU: Law and practice*. Cheltenham: Edward Elgar.

Autorité de la Concurrences. (2015). Communiqué de procédure du 3 avril 2015 relatif au programme de clémence français. Available from http://www.autoritedelaconcurrence.fr/doc/cpro_autorite_clemence_revise.pdf.

Baumann, J., & Arzt, G. (1970). Kartellrecht und allgemeines Strafrecht. *Zeitschrift für das gesamte Handelsrecht und Wirtschaftsrecht, 134*, 24.

Beaton-Wells, C., & Ezrachi, A. (Eds.). (2011). *Criminalising cartels: Critical studies of an international regulatory movement*. Oxford: Hart Publishing.

Biermann, J. (2007). Neubestimmung des deutschen und europäischen Kartellsanktionenrechts: Reformüberlegungen, Determinanten und Perspektiven einer Kriminalisierung von Verstößen gegen das Kartellrecht. *Zeitschrift für Wettbewerbsrecht*, 1.

Blaise, J.-B. (2013). La Sanction Pénale. *Concurrence* No 1-2013, Colloque "Les Sanctions du Droit de la Concurrence", 23.
Blake, S. (2015). The UK steel tanks criminal cartel trial: Implications for criminalisation and leniency, 13 November 2015. Available from https://www.gov.uk/government/speeches/stephen-blake-on-the-uk-steel-tanks-criminal-cartel-case.
Bryant, P. G., & Eckard, E. W. (1991). Price fixing: The probability of getting caught. *The Review of Economics and Statistics, 73*(3), 531.
Bundeskartellamt. (2006). Notice no. 9/2006 of the Bundeskartellamt on the immunity from and reduction of fines in cartel cases – Leniency Programme (7 March 2006). Available from http://www.bundeskartellamt.de/EN/Banoncartels/Leniency_programme/leniencyprogramme_node
Bundeskartellamt. (2011). Erfolgreiche Kartellverfolgung — Nutzen für Wirtschaft und Verbraucher (August 2011). Available from http://www.bundeskartellamt.de/SharedDocs/Publikation/DE/Broschueren/Informationsbrosch%C3%BCre%20-%20Erfolgreiche%20Kartellverfolgung.pdf?__blob=publicationFile&v=9.
Bundeskartellamt. (2012). Fallbericht — Erste Bußgelder im Schienenkartell verhängt, Case B12 – 11/11 (14 December 2012). Available from http://www.bundeskartellamt.de/SharedDocs/Entscheidung/DE/Fallberichte/Kartellverbot/2012/B12-11-11.pdf?__blob=publicationFile&v=4.
Bundeskartellamt. (2015a). Tätigkeitsbericht des Bundeskartellamts 2013/14, *Bundestags-Drucksache* 18/5210.
Bundeskartellamt. (2015b). Zwischenbericht des Bundeskartellamts zum Expertenkreis Kartellsanktionenrecht — Reformimpulse für das Kartellbußgeldverfahren (12 January 2015). Available from http://www.bundeskartellamt.de/SharedDocs/Publikation/DE/Berichte/AG_Kartellsanktionenrecht_Zwischenbericht.pdf?__blob=publicationFile&v=2.
Caiazzo, R., & Costantini, F. (2015). Italy. In Campbell (2015), (p. 150).
Campbell, A. N. (2015). *Getting the deal through: cartel regulation 2015* (15th ed.). London: Law Business Research.
CMA. (2014). Cartel offence prosecution guidance. March 2014, CMA9. Available from https://www.gov.uk/government/uploads/system/uploads/attachment_data/file/288648/CMA9__Cartel_Offence_Prosecution_Guidance.pdf.
CMA, & COPFS. (2014). Memorandum of understanding between the Competition and Markets Authority and the Crown Office and Procurator Fiscal Service. July 2014. Available from https://www.gov.uk/government/uploads/system/uploads/attachment_data/file/328403/CMA_and_COPFS_MOU.pdf.
CMA. (2015a). CMA statement following completion of criminal cartel prosecution. *Press Release*, 24 June 2015. Available from https://www.gov.uk/government/news/cma-statement-following-completion-of-criminal-cartel-prosecution.
CMA. (2015b). Director sentenced to six months for criminal cartel. *Press Release*, 14 September 2015. Available from https://www.gov.uk/government/news/director-sentenced-to-6-months-for-criminal-cartel.
Coffee, J. (1980). Corporate crime and punishment. *American Criminal Law Review, 17*, 419.
Combe, E., & Monnier, C. (2011). Fines against hard-core cartels in Europe: The myth of overenforcement. *The Antitrust Bulletin, 56*(2), 235.
Coulon, J.-M. (2008). *La Dépénalisation de la Vie des Affaires, Rapport au garde des Sceaux, Ministre de la Justice* (Paris, January 2008). Available from http://www.ladocumentationfrancaise.fr/var/storage/rapports-publics/084000090.pdf.
Crofts, L. (2015). MLex interview with Romano Pisciotti (9 December 2015). Available from http://mlexmarketinsight.com/reports/mlex-interview-with-romano-pisciotti/, https://perma.cc/DT5U-JS26.
Cseres, K., Schinkel, M.-P., & Vogelaar, F. (2006). Law and economics of criminal antitrust enforcement: An introduction. In K. Cseres, M.-P. Schinkel, & F. Vogelaar (Eds.), *Criminalization of competition law enforcement* (p. 1). Cheltenham: Edward Elgar.

Department of Justice. (2012). HSBC Holdings plc and HSBC Bank USA N.A. Admit to Anti-Money Laundering and Sanctions Violations, Forfeit $1.256 Billion in Deferred Prosecution Agreement: Bank Agrees to Enhanced Compliance Obligations, Oversight by Monitor in Connection with Five-Year Agreement. *Press Release*, 11 December 2012.

Department of Justice. (2014a). Justice Department announces criminal charge against Toyota Motor Corporation and Deferred Prosecution Agreement with $1.2 Billion Financial Penalty. *Press Release*, 19 March 2014.

Department of Justice. (2014b). Antitrust Division, Workload Statistics FY 2005-2014. Available from https://www.justice.gov/atr/file/788426/download.

Department of Justice. (2016). United States files complaint against Volkswagen, Audi and Porsche for Alleged Clean Air Act Violations. *Press Release*, 4 January 2016.

de Pree, J. K., & Molin, S. (2015). Netherlands. In Campbell (2015), (p. 193).

Dreher, M. (2009). Die persönliche Verantwortlichkeit von Geschäftsleitern nach außen auf Schadensersatz bei Kartellrechtsverstößen. *Wirtschaft und Wettbewerb, 59*, 133.

Dreher, M. (2011). Wider die Kriminalisierung des Kartellrechts. *Wirtschaft und Wettbewerb, 61*, 232.

Eden, E. (2013). *Persönliche Schadensersatzhaftung von Managern gegenüber Kartellgeschädigten.* Baden-Baden: Nomos Verlag.

Eden, E. (2014). Haften Geschäftsführer persönlich gegenüber Kartellgeschädigten auf Schadensersatz? *Wirtschaft und Wettbewerb, 64*, 792, WUW0665591.

Emrich-Katzin, S. (2013). *Schwerpunktstaatsanwaltschaften im Wirtschaftsstrafrecht und die Stellung der Wirtschaftsreferenten.* Frankfurt: Peter Lang.

European Commission. (2014a). Communication from the Commission to the European Parliament and the Council: Ten Years of Antitrust Enforcement under Regulation 1/2003: Achievements and Future Perspectives (9 July 2014), COM(2014) 453 final.

European Commission (2014b). Commission Staff Working Document: enhancing competition enforcement by the Member States' competition authorities: institutional and procedural issues (9 July 2014), SWD(2014) 231 final

Federmann, B. (2006). *Kriminalstrafen im Kartellrecht: Eine rechtsvergleichende Untersuchung zur Frage der Kriminalisierung von Hardcore-Kartellen.* Baden-Baden: Nomos Verlag.

Fiala, T. (2015). Czech Republic. In Campbell (2015), (p. 63).

France, A. (1894). *Le Lys Rouge* (14th ed.). Paris: Calmann-Lévy.

Frese, M. J. (2014). *Sanctions in EU competition law: Principles and practice.* Oxford: Hart Publishing.

Gilbert, P. (2015). Changes to the UK cartel offence—Be careful what you wish for. *Journal of European Competition Law & Practice, 6*, 192.

Girardet, P. (2010). 'What if Uncle Sam wants you? Principles and recent practice concerning US extradition requests in cartel cases. *Journal of European Competition Law & Practice, 1*(4), 286.

Hammond, S. D. (2005). Caught in the act: Inside an international cartel, OECD Competition Committee Working Party No. 3, OECD, Paris, 18 October 2005. Available from https://www.justice.gov/atr/speech/caught-act-inside-international-cartel (permanent link: https://perma.cc/V2H2-FCRV).

Hansberry-Bieguńska, D., & Krasnodębska-Tomkiel, M. (2015). Poland. In Campbell (2015), (p. 212).

Harrington Jr, J. E., & Wei, Y. (2015). What can the duration of detected cartels tell us about the duration of all cartels? (4 December 2015). Available from http://assets.wharton.upenn.edu/~harrij/pdf/Cartel%20Duration_12.15.pdf.

Jenny, F. (2013). L'Articulation des Sanctions en Matière de Droit de la Concurrence du Point de Vue Économique. *Concurrence* No 1-2013, Colloque "Les Sanctions du Droit de la Concurrence", 1.

Jiménez-Laiglesia, J., Ois, A., Masía, J., Hervada, J., & Maldonado, R. (2015). Spain. In Campbell (2015), (p. 260).

Jones, K. R., & Harrison, F. (2014). Criminal sanctions: An overview of EU and national case law (25 March 2014). *e-competitions* No 64713.
Joshua, J. (2011). DOA: Can the UK cartel offence be resuscitated. In Beaton-Wells & Ezrachi (2011), (p. 129).
Kapp, T., & Hummel, K. (2011). Haftung von Managern und Mitarbeitern für Unternehmensbußgelder? *Zeitschrift für Wettbewerbsrecht,* 349.
Kartte, W., & von Portatius, A. (1975). Kriminalisierung des Kartellrechts? *Betriebs-Berater,* 1169.
Kolesnikovas, G. (2015). Lithuania. In Campbell (2015), (p. 172).
Kovacic, W. E. (2006). Competition policy and cartels: the design of remedies. In K. Cseres, M.-P. Schinkel, & F. Vogelaar (Eds.), *Criminalization of competition law enforcement* (p. 41). Cheltenham: Edward Elgar.
Kovacic, W. E. (2016). Criminal enforcement of competition law: implications of US experience. Concurrences No. 2–2016, 33. Available from http://ssrn.com/abstract=2782090
Lampert, T., & Götting, S. (2002). Startschuss für eine Kriminalisierung des Kartellrechts? *Wirtschaft und Wettbewerb, 52*, 1069.
Lebrun, B., & Bersou, L. (2015). Belgium. In Campbell (2015), (p. 23).
Levenstein, M. C., & Suslow, V. Y. (2011). Breaking up is hard to do: Determinants of cartel duration. *Journal of Law & Economics, 54*(2), 455.
LG Munich II. (2006). 3 May 2006, W5 KLs 567 Js 30966/04, partially reprinted in BeckRS 2008, 00736 "King of the Pipes".
Lianos, I., Jenny, F., Wagner-von Papp, F., Motchenkova, E., & David, E. (2014). An optimal and just financial penalties system for infringements of competition law: A comparative analysis. *CLES Research paper series* 3/2014, UCL Faculty of Laws: London (May 2014). Available from http://www.fne.gob.cl/wp-content/uploads/2014/11/Estudio.pdf.
Marques Mendes, M., & Vilarinho Pires, P. (2015). Portugal. In Campbell (2015), (p. 218).
Marvão, C., & Spagnolo, G. (2015). What do we know about the effectiveness of leniency policies? A survey of the empirical and experimental evidence. In C. Beaton-Wells & C. Tran (Eds.), *Anti-cartel enforcement in a contemporary age: Leniency religion* (p. 57). Oxford: Hart Publishing.
Massey, P., & Cooke, J. D. (2011). Competition offences in Ireland: The regime and its results. In Beaton-Wells & Ezrachi (2011), (p. 105).
Mayer Lux, L. (2013). *Die konkludente Täuschung beim Betrug.* V&R Unipress, Bonner rechtswissenschaftliche Abhandlungen N.F. 11.
Monopolkommission. (2014). *Eine Wettbewerbsordnung für die Finanzmärkte, XX. Hauptgutachten 2012/13.* Available from http://monopolkommission.de/images/PDF/HG/HG20/HG_XX_gesamt.pdf.
Monopolkommission. (2015). *Strafrechtliche Sanktionen bei Kartellverstößen, Sondergutachten 72.* Available from http://monopolkommission.de/images/PDF/SG/s72_volltext.pdf.
Möschel, W. (1980). *Zur Problematik einer Kriminalisierung von Submissionsabsprachen.* Cologne: Carl Heymanns Verlag.
Motyka-Mojkowski, M. (2015). Reform des polnischen Kartellrechts — Schwerpunkte der kartellrechtlichen Novelle 2014. *Wirtschaft und Wettbewerb, 65*, 1104.
National Audit Office. (2016). *The UK competition regime*, HC 737, Session 2015-16, 5 February 2016. Available from https://www.nao.org.uk/wp-content/uploads/2016/02/The-UK-Competition-regime.pdf.
Nikpay, A., & Taylor, D. (2014). The new UK competition regime: Radically different or more of the same? *Journal of European Competition Law & Practice, 5*, 278.
O'Brien, A. (2015). Leadership of leniency. In C. Beaton-Wells & C. Tran (Eds.), *Anti-cartel enforcement in a contemporary age* (p. 17). Oxford: Hart Publishing.
OFT. (2007). The deterrent effect of competition enforcement by the OFT — A REPORT prepared for the OFT by Deloitte. Office of Fair Trading, OFT962.

OFT. (2010). Office of Fair Trading, Project Condor Board Review. (December 2010). Available from https://assets.digital.cabinet-office.gov.uk/media/556876fce5274a1895000008/Project_Condor_Board_Review.pdf.

OFT. (2013). Applications for leniency and no-action in cartel cases. July 2013, Office of Fair Trading, OFT1495. Available from https://www.gov.uk/government/uploads/system/uploads/attachment_data/file/284417/OFT1495.pdf.

Ost, K. (2014). From regulation 1 to regulation 2: national enforcement of EU cartel prohibition and the need for further convergence. *Journal of European Competition Law & Practice, 5*, 125.

Papadopoulos, A., & Lovdahl Gormsen, L. (2015). Greece. In Campbell (2015), (p. 104).

Pettersson, T., Carle, J., & Lindeborg, S. P. (2015). Sweden. In Campbell (2015), (p. 266).

Pipan Nahtigal, N., & Lahovnik, T. (2015). Slovenia. In Campbell (2015), (p. 245).

Pound, R. (1910). Law in books and law in action. *American Law Review, 44*, 12.

Ransiek, A., & Hüls, S. (2009). Strafrecht zur Regulierung der Wirtschaft. *Zeitschrift für Unternehmens- und Gesellschaftsrecht, 38*, 157.

Rădulescu, M., & Iacob, V. (2015). Romania. In Campbell (2015), (p. 227).

Raum, R. (2014). § 81a. In E. Langen & H.-J. Bunte (Eds.), *Langen/Bunte Kartellrecht Kommentar* (Vol. 1, 12th ed.). Wolters Kluwer.

Rung-Hansen, A. (2015). Denmark. In Campbell (2015), (p. 69).

Sando, T., & Hageler, A. J. (2015). Norway. In Campbell (2015), (p. 206).

Shaffer, G., Nesbitt, N. H., & Weber Waller, S. (2015). Criminalizing cartels: a global trend? In J. Duns, A. Duke, & B. Sweeney (Eds.), *Comparative competition law* (p. 301). Cheltenham: Edward Elgar.

Sindhu, K. (2009). Anti-corruption compliance standards in the aftermath of the Siemens scandal. *German Law Journal, 10*, 1343.

Snyder, B. (2016). Individual accountability for antitrust crimes. Remarks at the Yale global antitrust enforcement conference, New Haven, 19 February 2016. Available from https://www.justice.gov/opa/speech/deputy-assistant-attorney-general-brent-snyder-delivers-remarks-yale-global-antitrust; permanent link: https://perma.cc/XW7J-XUMN.

Spagnolo, G. (2006). Criminalization of cartels and their internal organization. In K. J. Cseres, M. P. Schinkel, & F. O. W. Vogelaar (Eds.), *Criminalization of competition law enforcement: Economic and legal implications for the EU Member States*. Cheltenham: Edward Elgar.

Statistisches Bundesamt. (1999–2015). *Rechtspflege — Strafverfolgung*, Fachserie 10 Reihe 3, Wiesbaden (latest available: 2013, published 2015).

Stephan, A. (2008). The UK cartel offence: Lame duck or black mamba. *Centre for Competition Policy (CCP) Working Paper* No. 08-19. Available from http://ssrn.com/abstract=1310683.

Stephan, A. (2011). Disqualification orders for directors involved in cartels. *Journal of European Competition Law & Practice, 2*, 529.

Stephan, A. (2014). The UK cartel offence: A purposive interpretation. *Criminal Law Review, 12*, 879.

Stephan, A. (2014a). Is the Korean innovation of individual informant rewards a viable cartel detection tool? (January 15, 2014). CCP Working Paper 14–3. Available from http://ssrn.com/abstract=2405933.

Stephan, A. (2015). Survey of public attitudes to price fixing in the UK, Germany, Italy and the USA. *Centre for Competition Policy (CCP) Working Paper* 15-8. Available from http://competitionpolicy.ac.uk/documents/8158338/8368036/Working+Paper+15-8+CCP.pdf/0ae07f44-485e-4ff3-a0e5-2cdd8f0052e0.

Stephan, A. (2016). Is there public support for cartel criminalisation?. Concurrences No. 2–2016, 40. Available from http://ssrn.com/abstract=2782090.

Stucke, M. E. (2006). Morality and antitrust. *Columbia Business Law Review, 2006*(3), 443.

Szabó, L. (2015). Hungary. In Campbell (2015), (p. 117).

Tabuchi, H., & Ivory, D. (2016). 10th death is linked to airbag by Takata. *New York Times* (New York edn), 23 January 2016, B1.

Tiedemann, K. (1976). *Kartellrechtsverstöße und Strafrecht*. Cologne: Carl Heymanns Verlag.
Tiedemann, K. (2001). Wettbewerb als Rechtsgut des Strafrechts. In G. Britz, H. Jung, H. Koriath, & E. Müller (Eds.), *Grundfragen staatlichen Strafens: Festschrift für Heinz Müller-Dietz zum 70 Geburtstag* (p. 905). Munich: C.H. Beck.
Twele, M. (2013). *Die Haftung des Vorstands für Kartellrechtsverstöße*. Baden-Baden: Nomos.
van Bergeijk, P. A. C. (2008). On the allegedly invisible construction cartel. *Journal of Competition Law & Economics, 4*, 115.
van Duyne, P. C. (2007). All in the Dutch construction family: Cartel building and organised crime. In L. Holmes (Ed.), *Terrorism, organised crime and corruption: Networks and linkages*. Cheltenham: Edward Elgar.
Viros, D. (2016). Individual Criminal Sanctions in France. Concurrences No. 2–2016, 24. Available from http://ssrn.com/abstract=2782090.
Vlasic, B., & Stout, H. (2014). Auto industry galvanized after record recall year. New York Times (New York edn), 31 December 2014, A1.
Wagner-von Papp, F. (2010a). Privatrechtliche oder strafrechtliche Durchsetzung des Kartellrechts? In W. Möschel & F. Bien (Eds.), *Kartellrechtsdurchsetzung durch private Schadenersatzklagen?* (p. 267). Baden-Baden: Nomos Verlag.
Wagner-von Papp, F. (2010b). Kriminalisierung von Kartellen. *Wirtschaft und Wettbewerb, 60*, 268, WUW0347235.
Wagner-von Papp, F. (2011). What if all bid riggers went to prison and nobody noticed? Criminal antitrust law enforcement in Germany. In C. Beaton-Wells & A. Ezrachi (Eds.) (p. 157).
Wagner-von Papp, F. (2014). Kriminalisierung von Kartellabsprachen — tut sich da was? *Wirtschaft und Wettbewerb, 64*, 1155, WUW0666947.
Wagner-von Papp, F. (2016). Individual sanctions for competition law infringements: pros, cons, and challenges. Concurrences No. 2–2016, 14. Available from http://ssrn.com/abstract=2782090.
Wardaugh, B. (2014). *Cartels, markets and crime — A normative justification for the criminalisation of economic collusion*. Cambridge: Cambridge University Press.
Werden, G. J., Hammond, S. D., & Barnett, B. A. (2012). Deterrence and detection of cartels: Using all the tools and sanctions, 26th Annual Institute on White Collar Crime (1 March 2012). Available from https://www.justice.gov/atr/file/518936/download.
Werden, G. J., & Simon, M. J. (1987). Why price-fixers should go to prison. *The Antitrust Bulletin, XXXII*, 917.
Whelan, P. (2014). *The criminalization of European cartel enforcement: Theoretical, legal, and practical challenges*. Oxford: Oxford University Press.
Wils, W. P. J. (2003). Does the effective enforcement of Articles 81 and 82 EC require not only fines on undertakings, but also individual penalties, and in particular imprisonment? In C. D. Ehlermann & I. Atanasiu (Eds.), *European competition law annual 2001: Effective private enforcement of EC antitrust law* (p. 411). Oxford: Hart Publishing.
Wils, W. P. J. (2008). *Efficiency and justice in European antitrust enforcement*. Oxford: Hart Publishing.
Wils, W. P. J. (2013). Ten years of regulation 1/2003 — a retrospective. *Journal of Competition Law & Practice, 4*, 293.
Wils, W. P. J. (2016) The use of leniency in EU cartel enforcement: an assessment after twenty years. King's College London Law School Research Paper No. 2016–29; forthcoming in *World Competition: Law and Economics Review*, 39(3). Available from http://ssrn.com/abstract=2793717.
Wright, R. (2015). GM faces more than $1.5 bn over fatal ignition switch fault. *Financial Times*, 17 September 2015.
Zembla. (2001–2006). The Dutch construction cartel. Available from http://zembla.vara.nl/seizoenen/2006/afleveringen/12-11-2006/extras/the-duch-construction-cartel/.
Zimmer, D. (2016). Individual sanctions in German competition law: the case for a criminalisation of antitrust offences? Concurrences No. 2–2016, 28. Available from http://ssrn.com/abstract=2782090.

Part IV
Fine Reductions

Chapter 9
Can Compliance Programmes Contribute to Effective Antitrust Enforcement?

Florence Thépot

Abstract This chapter discusses the significance of corporate compliance programmes as a competition enforcement tool. Current enforcement challenges in the fight against collusive practices that are, a low probability of detection and under-deterrence of corporate fines, raise the need to move away from a strictly sanction-based type of enforcement. It is argued that competition authorities should steer companies' incentives towards implementing effective compliance programmes. Rewarding effective compliance programmes in the context of an investigation can improve the effectiveness of corporate sanctions in providing *ex ante* incentives to companies to deter and detect illegal behaviour internally. Outlining the key foundations of an effective compliance programme, this chapter also helps understanding how and when competition authorities should reward the compliance efforts of companies.

9.1 Introduction

The purpose of this chapter is to discuss whether and how competition authorities should encourage the compliance efforts of companies, with a view to achieving a better outcome in terms of the prevention and detection of anti-competitive collusive practices. The implementation of compliance programmes—schemes designed to educate employees about illegal activities, monitor their behaviour, and discipline them in cases of illegal conduct[1]—is highly valued by competition authorities as a necessary avenue for the creation of a culture of compliance. A number of

I would like to thank the participants in the ZiF Compliance Workshop in Bielefeld (November 2015) as well as J. Paha and an anonymous referee for their very helpful comments. The usual disclaimers apply.

[1]Angelucci and Han (2010), p. 2. Compliance programmes broadly refer to all of the management tools used to prevent and detect misconduct. Murphy (2011), pp. 14–15.

F. Thépot (✉)
School of Law, University of Glasgow, Glasgow, UK
e-mail: Florence.Thepot@glasgow.ac.uk

J. Paha (ed.), *Competition Law Compliance Programmes*,
DOI 10.1007/978-3-319-44633-2_9

guidelines describe the steps that companies should take to avoid the risk of competition law infringement in the first place, while acknowledging that a 'one-size-fits-all' approach is not adequate in the context of compliance programmes.[2]

In spite of acknowledging the value of corporate compliance programmes, competition authorities across jurisdictions are reluctant to provide concrete incentives (either positive or negative) for their implementation. After providing an overview of the existing regulatory approaches to compliance programmes (with a focus on the US, the EU and EU Member States), this chapter will analyse the contribution of corporate compliance to the enforcement objectives of prevention and detection of anti-competitive collusive practices. Among the different incentives that may be used by authorities, this chapter focuses on the possibility of giving credit to compliance programmes, in the form of a fine reduction in the context of an alleged infringement of the cartel prohibition.

9.2 Overview of Regulatory Approaches Towards Compliance

In a speech in 2011, Joaquin Almunia, Vice President of the Commission responsible for Competition Policy at that time, reaffirmed that compliance programmes implemented in companies that infringe EU competition law are 'failed' and therefore cannot constitute a mitigating factor in the assessment of the level of fine to be imposed: 'A successful compliance programme brings its own reward. The main reward for a successful compliance programme is not getting involved in unlawful behaviour. Instead, a company involved in a cartel should not expect a reward from us for setting up a compliance programme, because that would be a failed programme by definition.' (SPEECH/11/268, 14 April 2011) Consistent with that policy, compliance programmes have never been taken into account in the context of investigations of collusive practices in the EU.[3]

In the US, the Sentencing Guidelines foresee a possible reduction in the level of fine if a convicted corporation had in place at the time of the infringement an 'effective compliance and ethics programme'. There is, however, a rebuttable presumption that a compliance programme is not effective when the offence involves "igh-level" or "substantial authority" personnel.[4] Antitrust infringement

[2]The UK: Guidance provided by the CMA: OFT (2011); France: Autorité de la Concurrence (2012a); The EU: European Commission (DG COMP) (2012).

[3]Although in the 1980s and 1990s the Commission granted some fine reduction in export ban and abuse of dominance cases. E.g. *National Panasonic*, European Commission (1982), para 68; *Napier Brown - British Sugar*, European Commission (1988), para 86. However, British Sugar was later involved in a cartel, and its compliance programme was considered as an aggravating factor: European Commission (1998), para 208.

[4]US Sentencing Guidelines Manual (2012) §8C2.5 Culpability Score, (f) Effective Compliance and Ethics Program.

commonly involves individuals who are able to exercise substantial authority within the scope of their responsibility, such as setting prices, negotiating and approving commercial contracts etc.[5] Moreover, until recently, the Department of Justice ("DoJ") Antitrust Division had clearly excluded the consideration of compliance programmes in the context of antitrust, having 'established a firm policy, understood in the business community, that credit should not be given at the charging stage for a compliance program' (Murphy 2013). One of the reasons for this is that 'antitrust violations, by definition, go to the heart of the corporation's business' (United States Attorney's Manual 2008).

However, the wind seems to be changing, since top officials from the Antitrust Division, including Brent Snyder, have stated that the Division is actively considering ways in which it can credit companies that proactively implement or improve their compliance programmes after coming under investigation (see e.g. Snyder 2015). This change in direction materialised in the fact that in a couple of recent cases, compliance programmes implemented during the investigation have been considered as a mitigating factor in the amount of the fines imposed.[6] Only compliance programmes implemented or improved after the infringement may receive credit, and the Antitrust Division will retain full discretion so that companies cannot expect to receive credit for implementing 'cosmetic' or mere paper compliance programmes (Snyder 2015).

In the EU Member States, only a few authorities give credit to compliance programmes: in France, companies committing to set up or improve a compliance programme may benefit from a reduction of up to 10 % in the context of a settlement procedure, added to the 10 % reduction that is specific to the conclusion of a settlement agreement. The possibility of receiving credit only concerns programmes implemented or improved after the infringement (Autorité de la Concurrence 2012b). In the UK, the CMA may, under certain conditions, grant a discount of up to 10 % of the amount of the fine, for programmes existing prior to the infringement (OFT 2012, para 2.15) In 2014, Italy introduced fining guidelines confirming that compliance programmes (implemented after an infringement) may constitute a mitigating factor, with a possible reduction of up to 15 % of the amount of the fine (Global Compliance News 2014).

In some of these jurisdictions, anti-corruption laws in some of the same jurisdictions adopt a very different approach.[7] Although corruption and antitrust

[5]US Sentencing Guidelines Manual (2012) §8A1.2 Narrow circumstances under which the involvement of senior executives does not rule out the possibility of being credited for an effective compliance programme. Chapter 8, (f)(3)(C)(i) and §11.

[6]3 U.S. v. Barclays Plc, No. 3: 15-cr-00077-SRU, Plea agreement, available at http://www.justice.gov/file/440481/download; U.S. v. Kayaba Industry Co., Ltd, d/b/a KYB Corporation, Plea agreement available at http://www.justice.gov/atr/case-document/file/791911/download No information as to the actual content of the programme is given.

[7]Anti-corruption legislation is defined at EU level by a framework decision of the Council. Council of the European Union (2003), art 5-6. Member States are free to implement measures in order to achieve the required goals set out in the decision.

scandals may be quite similar in nature, the US anti-corruption policy foresees the possibility of not prosecuting the company at all, provided that it has an effective compliance programme In the case of prosecution, companies can receive a reduction in their fine for having an effective compliance programme, according to the Sentencing Guidelines provisions. The Morgan Stanley case, in which the company avoided charges despite corruption acts committed by a managing director, exemplifies such a contrasting approach:

> Morgan Stanley maintained a system of internal controls meant to ensure accountability for its assets and to prevent employees from offering, promising or paying anything of value to foreign government officials. Morgan Stanley's internal policies, which were updated regularly to reflect regulatory developments and specific risks, prohibited bribery and addressed corruption risks associated with the giving of gifts, business entertainment, travel, lodging, meals, charitable contributions and employment. [...] After considering all the available facts and circumstances, including that Morgan Stanley constructed and maintained a system of internal controls, which provided reasonable assurances that its employees were not bribing government officials, the Department of Justice declined to bring any enforcement action against Morgan Stanley related to Peterson's conduct.[8]

In the UK, Section 7 of the Bribery Act 2010 provides that companies can defend themselves from being liable for an employee's illegal conduct if "adequate procedures" are put in place by companies. Evidence brought by the company in their defence will be analysed on a case-by-case basis, in light of matters such as the level of control over the activities of the responsible employee and the level of corruption that requires prevention (Ministry of Justice, "Guidance about procedures which relevant commercial organizations can put into place to prevent persons associated with them from bribing" 2010). In Italy, a company can avoid liability by adopting an effective organisational, management and control model (Decreto Legge no. 231/2001). While corruption and antitrust infringements do not seem so different in nature, different liability regimes and different cultural perceptions towards the seriousness of the type of corporate crime may explain such divergent approaches towards companies' compliance efforts (Thépot 2015).

9.3 Rewarding Compliance Programmes in the Light of Current Enforcement Challenges[9]

There are currently two major enforcement challenges around antitrust infringements: a low probability of detection of anti-competitive agreements, as a result of which practices are typically well concealed—and the current level of corporate

[8]DoJ 'Former Morgan Stanley Managing Director Pleads Guilty for Role in Evading Internal Controls Required by FCPA' (April 2012) Press release available at http://www.justice.gov/opa/pr/2012/April/12-crm-534.html.'

[9]This section is an adapted version of a contribution to Lianos et al. (2014).

fines imposed is deemed to be under-deterrent.[10] A very important element of the effectiveness of sanctions is the perceived probability that an illegal act is detected. The threat of a jail sentence or a high pecuniary sanction deters the wrongdoing only if detection can be expected.

Firstly, the value of compliance programmes to the enforcement policy stems from the informational advantage of companies over agencies, which have better tools to prevent and detect illegal behaviour internally. Therefore, compliance programmes can improve the probability of detection, if strong incentives are provided to companies to undertake internal monitoring of antitrust infringements, according to the optimal sanction theory (Becker 1968). It has been argued that a company that detects the wrongdoing of an agent is likely to honestly report the wrongdoing to relevant authorities, because companies may face higher penalties for not reporting the illegal act of an agent since the wrongdoing of the agent may eventually be discovered or reported to the authority (Arlen 1994, p. 833). Moreover the internal discovery of a wrongdoing is likely to result in a leniency application.

In addition, giving credit to compliance programmes can improve the effectiveness of a corporate liability regime, especially in cases where companies have neither the incentives nor the means to detect or deter wrongdoing internally. Companies may be complex corporate structures, typically composed of a parent and different subsidiaries located in different jurisdictions. Corporate liability, in the absence of individual penalties, imposes a sanction on shareholders and not on the responsible individuals. A company can seek to mitigate the risk of individuals exposing the company to liability and, some argue, have a natural incentive to implement a compliance programme depending on the level of the fine and the probability of detection However, corporate liability does not automatically induce the adoption of internal compliance measures (Sokol 2012). Firstly, the incentive to adopt compliance programmes may be mitigated by the "perverse" effects of a strict corporate liability. A company may fear that implementing internal measures increases the probability of detection by the authority because companies would be likely to report any uncovered wrongdoing, which in turn increases the likelihood of receiving a fine (Arlen 1994). Weighing up the costs and benefits of implementing a compliance programme, a company may decide not to incur any of those costs if they expect that the costs of detection would be higher than the expected benefit of detecting the crime internally. This is likely to be the case if internal detection triggers an investigation by the authority leading to the imposition of a large fine on the company. In this case the company will incur costs in internally detecting a collusive practice, while bearing the cost of the cartel liability at the same time.

Second, companies may not have "effective methods of preventing individuals from committing acts that impose huge liabilities on them" (Posner 1976). First, companies can set up effective methods, but at a certain cost. The extent to which a

[10]Empirical studies estimated a probability of detection of between 13 and 17 % of cartels that were eventually detected. See: 1. Bryant and Eckard (1991); Combe et al. (2008), 2. Wils also concludes that based on such a probability of getting caught, the deterrent level of the fine would be about 150 % of the annual turnover in the products affected by the infringement (Wils 2002).

company is capable of monitoring its employees adequately depends on the quality of internal mechanisms such as corporate governance. Corporate governance schemes that fail to achieve the objectives for which they have been designed are not likely to be highly effective in preventing individuals from committing illegal acts either. Therefore, it is of utmost importance for competition authorities to take into account the agency nature of relations within the firms, together with the associated costs of monitoring employees. As such, in complex corporate structures, the mere imposition of large fines on companies does not automatically translate into compliance throughout the organisation.

In the presence of individual sanctions, compliance programmes potentially have a greater outreach on company's employees than when they are not personally liable. A senior executive may pay greater attention to compliance training if pecuniary or jail sanctions are part of the non-compliance risk. Therefore, compliance programmes may yield much greater value to the company. Competition authorities should leverage the potential of greater value that compliance programmes constitute to companies, in attributing more importance to internal prevention and detection. Competition authorities, facing the issue of cartel detection, would then benefit from the informational advantage that companies have with regard to their managers and employees.

Compliance programmes could also enhance the effectiveness of leniency if they enabled companies to better monitor and collect information relevant to a leniency application. A company that is better able to prevent and detect an infringement internally is also equipped with better tools to constitute a leniency application. In addition, this can help the company detect the infringement earlier than the other cartel members (Geradin 2013).

In considering the interaction with leniency, we should also consider whether leniency policy in itself gives the appropriate incentives for the internal detection of cartels, and whether or not leniency makes the reward of compliance programmes redundant.

First of all, while theoretically leniency programmes seem very powerful tools to uncover cartels, leniency policy is mostly used in the context of failing cartels (Stephan and Nikpay 2015). Therefore, one may question the actual deterrent impact that leniency has on cartels. In addition, in some jurisdictions such as the US, leniency policy is only available to the first company to self-report (Department of Justice 1993). There may be value for the investigation to give some credit to companies not benefiting from immunity. In addition, compliance programmes are not just about internal detection and play a different role to leniency—that of impacting the moral norms within companies towards greater prevention of collusive practices in the first place. According to game theory, leniency policy only prevents such practices to the extent that it makes collusion more costly, and is not intended to impact on employees' education and ethics.[11] In addition, leniency does not impose a requirement beyond cooperation with the authorities in the current

[11]Based on a game theoretical approach—and does not impact on ethics within companies.

investigation. The implementation or improvement of internal processes is a forward-looking means to prevent the occurrence of collusion in the future, while leniency can be used several times by companies who are repeat offenders and make strategic use of it.[12] Overall, compliance programmes complement leniency in the role of prevention and detection of cartels, with greater emphasis on internal prevention.

9.4 The Key Foundations of an Effective Compliance Programme

Studies on the drivers of compliance have identified corporate compliance as a very complex product of structure, culture and agency (see e.g. Parker and Gilad 2011). A compliance programme encompasses all types of compliance efforts and processes undertaken by a company, designed to impact the corporate culture—which means the values and behaviours that shape the environment of a company—translating into a strong moral commitment to comply at all levels. Corporate compliance is a matter of the degree and resources allocated to achieving compliance, and cannot be equated to a mere code of conduct or training sessions.

The first essential foundation of an effective corporate compliance programme lies in the culture from the top of the hierarchy. The CMA describes how clear and unambiguous commitment by senior management serves the purpose of setting a high compliance standard throughout the firm (OFT 2011, 2.1–2.3). Such a core commitment needs to be written down and strongly communicated within the company so as to reflect how compliance is rooted within the organisation. To ensure that the senior management's commitment is supported by a real awareness of the organisation of compliance, board members need to be part of the compliance effort.

Communication constitutes another key dimension of compliance programmes. Communicating a strong message of compliance throughout the organisation involves holding training sessions to teach employees and senior executives about compliance risks and procedures, especially those presenting exposure with competitors. In addition to delivering educational training about competition law, compliance programmes need to motivate the employees so as to increase their understanding of the need for ethical behaviour within the company. Therefore, compliance needs to work hand in hand with communication so as to 'impact emotionally' and avoid training fatigue.

Related to the communication dimension, the organisation of compliance needs to be structured around an 'ambassador' of competition law compliance. With a sufficient degree of responsibility, this person, either as part of the legal services or

[12]See empirical studies by C. Marvao showing how repeat offenders reap larger benefits from leniency (Marvão 2015).

compliance department, needs to have room to advocate compliance with competition law. The question of competition compliance cannot be diluted and given a lower level of priority compared to other areas of business, which may be the case if the compliance officer has no means of authority within the organisation. Although particularly true for large companies, the need for a 'compliance ambassador' also stands for smaller companies that can hand the compliance responsibility to someone particularly sensitive to such an issue. This assumes that the compliance officer is ethical and would not have any personal incentive to encourage price-fixing (and dissimulate), as opposed to sales manager who, for example, may benefit from price-fixing through compensation schemes incentivising them to sustain prices above competitive level.

Effective corporate compliance entails procedures of prevention, detection and response, which may involve sophisticated techniques such as screenings (Abrantes-Metz et al. 2010). To do so, procedures to monitor risky business activities or that provide legal advice need to be clearly established. In addition, the eventuality of an infringement needs to be addressed, for example by anonymous alert systems and credible sanctioning schemes.[13]

9.5 The Verifiability of Compliance Programmes

Most of the debate about compliance programmes crystallises around the verifiability of the quality of compliance programmes. Some argue that the inherent difficulty of evaluating a compliance effort may create perverse incentives: companies would then adopt 'cosmetic' compliance programmes to ensure a reduction in the level of fine (Wils 2013). As a result, infringing competition law would become less costly. This argument may be rejected on grounds similar to those advocating the use of leniency programmes. The fine eventually imposed no longer matches the gravity of the infringement, in order to stimulate the level of detection. Therefore, the competition authority operates a trade-off between reducing the potential deterrent effect of fines and the benefit of an increased level of detection. Rewarding compliance efforts entails a reduced level of fine, at the benefit for the purpose of an increased level of internal prevention and detection.

Based on the foundations of effective compliance programmes, tangible elements can be required by competition authorities to demonstrate that appropriate compliance efforts can be rewarded. To attest that there is a core commitment to competition compliance, competition authorities could require evidence that compliance is being discussed regularly at board meetings and that senior management

[13]The ICC provides a whole range of practical solutions to implement an effective compliance programme, relevant not only to large companies, but also to those of a much smaller size with constrained resources. Also, for example, J. Murphy proposes an organisation of compliance to small companies for "a Dollar a Day" that meets the principles set out in the US Sentencing Guidelines and OECD Good Practice Guidance (Murphy 2012).

have attended training. The authority may also want to verify that there is a board member responsible for compliance, and the frequency with which the compliance unit reports to the board. The communication dimension of effective compliance lies in internal communication and training material: the availability of a code of conduct, adopted internally and also in relation to business partners is part of compliance communication. In addition, evidence of compliance being mentioned in top executives' speeches or other internal communication, as well as the involvement of the communication department in compliance can attest to the effective communication of compliance. The actual implementation of compliance can be evidenced through training attendance records and the percentage of good results achieved. In particular, competition authorities can request proof that senior executives, sales managers or high-risk positions have attended training, and whether or not they can be disciplined if they do not attend. Companies can also demonstrate that clear procedures are in place, in hiring employees—human resources can indicate that their employees have no past history of antitrust infringement- and in monitoring risky business areas—such as trade association meetings. In addition, the availability of sanctioning procedures and a history of sanction cases are signs that compliance comprises a wider range of procedures than just training sessions. The availability of corporate compliance audit reports signals a willingness to continually adapt the compliance programme.

9.6 When Should the Authority Give Credit to a Compliance Programme?

Based on the elements outlined, the validity of compliance efforts seems verifiable. However such process, which needs to be undertaken by trained agency staff, involves gathering and checking a number of different types of evidence, which is not costless. In addition, such an inquiry may interfere with a company's internal affairs and may concern sensitive information. Therefore, competition authorities should give credit to compliance programmes, but only in the context of an investigation, during which authorities have access to a wide range of information about the company anyway. Carrying out a few interviews, and screening for evidence of the quality of the commitment to compliance in the company's email and documentation should provide hints of the existence (or not), of a strong commitment to compliance supported by clear internal processes. Because it holds informational advantage over the competition authorities, the burden of proof should lie with the company.

Upon cooperation and sufficient evidence of adequate compliance efforts, a company should benefit from a (possibly substantial) reduction in the level of fine, assessed on a case-by-case basis. The authority should of course retain full discretion in the decision to grant credit. The non-predictability of the fine reduction helps counteract the incentive to implement 'cosmetic' compliance programmes.

For the company, the value of such programmes not only stems from the possibility of getting a fine reduction in the case of a conviction, but also from the overall increased possibility of avoiding misconduct in the first place. In terms of timing, rewarded compliance programmes may have proven effectiveness at the time of the infringement. Commitment by a company to introduce or improve an existing compliance programme may be rewarded. However, in the light of optimal penalty policy, the reward should not just focus on post-infringement compliance programmes. The objective is to encourage the implementation of compliance effort *ex ante*. *Ex post* consideration of compliance may undermine the impact that such a reward is designed to have on the prevention of cartels in the first place. There are also factors that should preclude any credit given to compliance programmes—these include whether the company has repeatedly infringed antitrust laws, or when the top executives, while openly discussing compliance, have themselves initiated anti-competitive conduct.

Discretion given to authorities to decide whether or not to reward a compliance programme also needs to be balanced with the need for legal certainty for businesses (and transaction costs associated with large level of discretion). In addition to identifying conditions that preclude companies from receiving credit, guidelines on what constitutes effective compliance programmes may bring more certainty to businesses. Experience from the UK Bribery Act on how courts assess whether companies have taken 'adequate steps' to prevent the occurrence of the wrongdoing could also help competition authorities to establish standards that may be used in the assessment of the effectiveness of compliance programmes.

9.7 Conclusion

In spite of the increasing levels of fines and the introduction of individual sanctions, competition authorities face the difficulty of preventing and detecting cartels. Giving credit to compliance programmes could then leverage the potential deterrent effect of harsh sanctions, through increasing the possibility of internal detection. Concrete incentives should therefore be provided, in the context of an investigation, to companies who implement effective compliance measures capable of impacting effectively the commitment to the norm at all levels of the company's hierarchy, which were either in place prior to the infringement, or introduced during the investigation. The burden of proof should lie with the company—and some factors should also disqualify a company from receiving any credit.

References

Abrantes-Metz, R., Bajari, P., & Murphy, J. (2010). Enhancing compliance programs through antitrust screening. *The Antitrust Counselor, 4*(5).

Almunia, J. (2011). Speech/11/268 from 14 Apr 2011.
Angelucci, C., & Han, M. A. (2010). *Monitoring managers through corporate compliance programs*. Amsterdam Center for Law & Economics Working Paper No. 2010-14.
Arlen, J. (1994). The potentially perverse effects of corporate criminal liability. *The Journal of Legal Studies, 23*(2), 833–867.
Autorité de la Concurrence. (2012a). *Antitrust compliance and compliance programmes, Corporate tools for competing safely in the market place*. Paris.
Autorité de la Concurrence. (2012b). *Framework-Document of 10 February 2012 on Antitrust Compliance Programmes*. Available from http://www.autoritedelaconcurrence.fr/doc/framework_document_compliance_10february2012.pdf. Accessed 10 April 2016.
Becker, G. S. (1968). Crime and punishment: An economic approach. *Journal of Political Economy, 76*, 169–217.
Bryant, P. G., & Eckard, E. W. (1991). Price fixing: The probability of getting caught. *The Review of Economics and Statistics, 73*, 531.
Combe, E., Monnier, C., & Legal, R. (2008). *Cartels: The probability of getting caught in the European Union*. Bruges European Economic Research papers.
Council of the European Union. (2003). Council Framework Decision 2003/568/JHA of 22 July 2003 on combating corruption in the private sector. *Official Journal of the European Union* L192/54.
Department of Justice (DoJ). (1993). Corporate Leniency Policy.
European Commission. (1982). *National Panasonic* Case COMP IV/30.070, Decision no. 82/853/EEC. *Official Journal of the European Union* L284/41.
European Commission. (1988). *Napier Brown – British Sugar* Case COMP IV/30.178, Decision no. 88/518/EEC. *Official Journal of the European Union* L284/41.
European Commission. (1998). *British Sugar plc* Case COMP IV/F-3/33.708, *Tate & Lyle plc* Case COMP IV/F-3/33.709, *Napier Brown & Company Ltd* Case COMP IV/F-3/33.710, *James Budgett Sugars Ltd* Case COMP IV/F-3/33.711. Decision no. 1999/210/EC. *Official Journal of the European Union* L076/01.
European Commission (DG Competition). (2012). *Compliance matters, What companies can do better to respect EU competition rules*. Brussels.
Geradin, D. (2013). Antitrust compliance programmes & optimal antitrust enforcement: A reply to Wouter Wils. *Journal of Antitrust Enforcement, 1*(2), 18.
Global Compliance News. (2014). *Italy: Competition Compliance programs a mitigating factor for fines imposed by the Italian Antitrust Authority, 4 Nov 2016*. Available from http://globalcompliancenews.com/italy-competition-compliance-20141104/. Accessed 10 April 2016.
Lianos, I., Jenny, F., Wagner von Papp, F., Motchenkova, E., David, E., Thépot, F., Massman, J., and Strader, M.J. (2014). Just and Optimal Financial Penalties for Infringement of Competition Law: A Comparative Analysis. Project Report. UCL Faculty of Laws, London.
Marvão, C. (2015). The EU leniency programme and recidivism. *Review of Industrial Organization, 48*(1), 1–27.
Murphy, J. E. (2011). *In OECD, Policy Roundtable, Promoting Compliance with Competition Law, 14-15*. Report available from: http://www.oecd.org/daf/competition/Promotingcompliancewithcompetitionlaw2011.pdf. Accessed 10 April 2016.
Murphy, J. E. (2012). *A compliance & ethics program on a dollar a day: How small companies can have effective programs*. Available from: http://www.hcca-info.org/Portals/0/PDFs/Resources/ResourceOverview/CEProgramDollarADay-Murphy.pdf. Accessed 12 April 2016.
Murphy, J. E. (2013). *Making the sentencing guidelines message complete*. Available from: http://www.ussc.gov/Meetings_and_Rulemaking/Public_Comment/20130801/Public_Comment_Murphy_Proposed_Priorities.pdf. Accessed 10 April 2016.
OFT. (2011). *How your business can achieve compliance with competition law*. OFT1340, London.
OFT. (2012). *OFT's guidance as to the appropriate amount of a penalty*. OFT423, London.

Parker, C., & Gilad, S. (2011). Internal corporate compliance management systems: Structure, culture and agency. In C. Parker & V. Lehmann Nielsen (Eds.), *Explaining compliance: Business responses to regulation*. Edward Elgar.

Posner, R. A. (1976). *Antitrust law: An economic perspective* (p. 225). University of Chicago Press. In Wils (2002) *The optimal enforcement of EC antitrust law* (p. 200). Kluwer Law International.

Snyder, B. (2015). *Speech at the Sixth Annual Chicago Forum on International Antitrust, 08.06.2015*. Available from http://www.justice.gov/opa/speech/deputy-assistant-attorney-general-brent-snyder-delivers-remarks-sixth-annual-chicago. Accessed 10 April 2016.

Sokol, D. (2012). Cartels, corporate compliance, and what practitioners really think about enforcement. *Antitrust Law Journal, 78*, 202.

Stephan, A., & Nikpay, A. (2015). Leniency decision-making from a corporate perspective: Complex realities. In C. Beaton-Wells & C. Tran (Eds.), *Anti-Cartel enforcement in a contemporary age: Leniency religion*. London: Hart Publishing.

Thépot, F. (2015). Antitrust v. anti-corruption policy approaches to compliance: Why such a gap?. *Competition Policy International Antitrust Chronicle, 6*(2).

United States Attorney's Manual. (2008). *9-28.400, Special Policy Concerns*. Available from: http://www.justice.gov/usao/eousa/foia_reading_room/usam/title9/28mcrm.htm. Accessed 10 April 2016.

US Sentencing Guidelines Manual. (2012). United States Sentencing Commission, Washington, D.C.

Wils, W. P. J. (2002). *The optimal enforcement of EC antitrust law* (p. 200). Kluwer Law International.

Wils, W. P. J. (2013). Antitrust compliance programmes and optimal antitrust enforcement. *Journal of Antitrust Enforcement, 1*, 52–81.

Chapter 10
Legal Incentives for Compliance Programmes: Stick or Carrot?

Per Rummel

Abstract One way to improve antitrust compliance may be to incentivise compliance programmes. Compliance programmes can certainly help undertakings detecting and remedying illegal behaviour. Infringements might be avoided by providing undertakings with incentives to intensify their compliance efforts. On a basic level, legislators can use two different approaches to foster compliance programmes. Undertakings can be legally obliged to introduce compliance programmes. Without a legal obligation, undertakings can still introduce compliance programmes on a voluntary basis, and the legislator can use incentives to motivate undertakings to use compliance programmes. In this chapter, these two ways of promoting compliance programmes are discussed by taking a comparative approach, which takes into account different legal systems. Based on the analysis, reservations in respect of a compliance defence are formulated.

10.1 Introduction

Discussions during the ZIF workshop have shown once again that the opinions on the usefulness of a compliance defence differ. This also holds true on the legislative level. As an example, German legislation does not include a compliance defence. However, demands for introducing such a compliance defence are increasing. This chapter takes up the central points of this ongoing discussion. The key question to be dealt with is whether a legal obligation creates sufficient incentives for establishing compliance programmes making a compliance defence dispensable.

In the following, this question will be discussed based on the current legal framework in Germany. First, direct and indirect legal obligations for German undertakings to install compliance programmes will be outlined. Second, the question of whether a compliance defence should be introduced into German law

The author works as a senior analyst at the German Monopolies Commission. The views expressed in this article do not necessarily reflect the positions of the Monopolies Commission.

P. Rummel (✉)
German Monopolies Commission, Bonn, Germany
e-mail: per.rummel@monopolkommission.bund.de

J. Paha (ed.), *Competition Law Compliance Programmes*,
DOI 10.1007/978-3-319-44633-2_10

to promote the voluntary application of compliance programmes will be addressed. It will be shown that a compliance defence is not the best way to foster compliance programmes. Especially, negative side effects and legal obstacles count against introducing a compliance defence into German law.

10.2 Compliance Programmes as a Legal Obligation

10.2.1 Current Legal Framework in Germany

German company law contains provisions which limit the room for manoeuvre of directors and managers. In sec. 43 para. 1 of the Limited Liability Companies Act (GmbH-Gesetz) it is set that "[t]he directors shall conduct the company's affairs with the due diligence of a prudent businessman." A similar provision can be found in sec. 93 para. 1 of the German Stock Corporation Act (Aktiengesetz). Due diligence includes the obligation to ensure the lawfulness of a company's actions, which may require the installation of compliance programmes.

A more outright provision can be found in sec. 91 para. 2 of the German Stock Corporation Act. This provision states that "the management board shall take suitable measures, in particular surveillance measures, to ensure that developments threatening the continuation of the company are detected at an early stage". By using the term "surveillance measures", the German legislator refers mainly to measures for monitoring the current situation of an undertaking, like audit systems and managerial accounting. Nonetheless, the provision might also include the installation of compliance programmes, which rather concern the future behaviour of the company.

Sec. 130 para. 1 of the Act on Regulatory Offences (Ordnungswidrigkeitengesetz) and sec. 831 para. 1 of the German Civil Code can additionally trigger administrative liability of the management for not taking the required supervisory measures. Sector-specific provisions like sec. 25a of the German Banking Act (Gesetz über das Kreditwesen)[1] or sec. 29 para 1 of the Act on the Supervision of Insurance Undertakings (Versicherungsaufsichtsgesetz) contain the obligation to install an internal monitoring system with a compliance function.

The obligation to executive care does not necessarily mandate the installation of a compliance programme for every undertaking. Executives may refer to their discretionary power and argue that a compliance programme has to be installed only when there is a real danger of unlawful behaviour. Of course, the risks of an undertaking will often be hard to measure, even though economists have made efforts to evaluate such risks (cf. Scheld et al. 2015). German case law has,

[1]See also: Sec. 28 Code on financial investment (Kapitalanlagegesetzbuch), sec. 64a Insurance Supervision Act (Versicherungsaufsichtsgesetz).

however, already stated that due diligence comprises installing a compliance programme.[2] In that specific case, a company sued one of its managers for damages after having been fined for bribery. The Court held that the manager committed a breach of duty by not reviewing the company's compliance programme after being informed about suspicious actions hinting at bribery. Against this backdrop, executives would be negligent to refrain from installing a compliance programme. The required scope and features of such a compliance programme remain unclear. However, it can be reasonably assumed that the fact of just having a compliance programme installed is not sufficient to fulfil legal requirements. The compliance programme must, at least, be effective and adapted to the undertaking's compliance risks.

At first sight, it may seem unsatisfactory that the German legal framework does not impose unequivocal rules on how to implement a compliance programme. However, it should be kept in mind that a compliance programme remains a management tool to avoid unlawful behaviour and not an end in itself. Obviously, undertakings may not always have the intention to comply with the law. It could be in their best interest to optimise profits by breaching the law and taking the risk to be detected (c.f. Landes 1983). More generally speaking, an undertaking will only commit an antitrust infringement voluntarily if the expected benefit lies above the expected cost (see Tirole 1988, p. 239 et seq.). Consequently, a compliance programme could also be introduced to cover up an infringement.

It is clear, however, that management has to use appropriate and effective organisational measures to prevent unlawful behaviour. The realisation of the compliance programme must be individually adjusted based on the risks the company at hand is confronted with.

10.2.2 Avoiding Fines and Damages

Irrespective of potential legal obligations to install a compliance programme, operating a compliance programme may be in the best interest of an undertaking. By running such a programme, it can reduce financial risks and prevent reputation damages (cf. the conceptualisation in Paha and Götz 2015, p. 1206 et seq.). On the financial side, avoiding an infringement helps the undertaking to avoid fines and compensations for damages. Especially in the EU framework, fines can be very high, and thus become a significant economic risk to an undertaking. For example, the highest fine for an abuse of a dominant position ever imposed by the European Commission was 1.06 billion EUR.[3] This decision was recently upheld by the

[2]See LG Munich, Judgment of 10 December 2013, 5 HK O 1397/10, juris, para. 89.

[3]European Commission, Decision of 13 May 2009, COMP/C-3/37.990—Intel.

General Court.[4] Moreover, damage claims will become more and more important within the EU due to the new directive 2014/104/EU.[5]

When an infringement has already been committed, a compliance programme may still help to detect the infringement and to avoid some of the negative consequences for the undertaking. This is because fines can be avoided by a leniency application once an infringement has been detected. The first leniency applicant can even benefit from a complete remission of the fine, whereas later applicants often at least get their fines reduced. Even though leniency applicants may still face actions for damages, the new directive 2014/104/EU establishes some privileges for leniency applicants regarding their external and internal liability (Directive 2014/104/EU: art. 11, para. 4, and para. 5).

10.3 Compliance Programmes as a Mitigating Circumstance

Besides the legal obligations depicted in the preceding section, it has been discussed whether legislature could also foster compliance programmes by treating them as a (legally binding) mitigating circumstance. An undertaking convicted of an infringement could make use of a legal "compliance defence" to receive a reduction or even a remission of a fine.

10.3.1 The Possible Designs of a Compliance Defense

When introducing a legal compliance defence, important questions have to be answered. First, some thought must be dedicated to the question whether a compliance programme must have been installed before or during the infringement for the compliance defence to be applicable. In the former case, the compliance programme, obviously, was not able to prevent the infringement, which could serve as an argument for not rewarding the (mere) existence of the programme. As even the best programme will not prevent every offence, one could argue that a compliance programme should not be abandoned based on one single failure. Nonetheless, it seems unwarranted to grant compliance system benefits after it has been failed.

Second, it may be worth considering allowing compliance programmes installed after the infringements to lead to an alleviation of fines. On the one hand, this

[4]Judgment of 12 June 2014, T-286/09—Intel v Commission, ECLI:EU:T:2014:547.

[5]Directive 2014/104/EU of the European Parliament and of the Council of 26 November 2014 on certain rules governing actions for damages under national law for infringements of the competition law provisions of the Member States and of the European Union.

approach may help to prevent future infringements. One could conceptualise this type of compliance defence analogously to leniency programmes: Lawful behaviour after the infringement is incentivised by reducing or remitting fines. The analogy is, however, limited. Leniency programmes are mainly offered to raise the detection rate of cartels whereas fine reductions for compliance efforts aim to improve behaviour, even if it should be taken into consideration that raising the detection rate through leniency programmes can indirectly also lead to behavioural improvement (cf. Marvão and Spagnolo 2014). Moreover, a more dynamic approach may be needed to ensure compliance over time. A compliance defence based on compliance programmes installed after the infringement might incentivise infringers to hold back improvements of a running compliance programme in order to use possible ameliorations during negotiations with antitrust authorities. Contrary, only considering compliance programmes installed after the infringement might be considered unjust. Undertakings which have introduced a compliance programme before the infringement might have more difficulties to prove their efforts and to gain a fine reduction. The same holds true for small and medium enterprises, which are less likely to have the resources to install an elaborate compliance programme.

Third, the amount of the potential fine reduction must be determined. Several jurisdictions have opted for a fine reduction of up to 10 % (see below for some examples). This raises the question whether it really makes a sufficiently large difference for an undertaking if it has to pay 90 % of a fine instead of 100 %. In many jurisdictions, the amount of the fine for a certain infringement is not carved in stone either because the competition authorities have certain leeway in setting the fine. Therefore, a reduction of 10 % might not be a sufficiently high incentive to apply for leniency. Offering a higher reward could provide a stronger motivation to introduce a compliance programme. However, if the financial risks of getting caught were significantly reduced by a compliance defence, undertakings might take the obligation to comply with the law in the first place less serious.

10.3.2 The Comparative Perspective

Many jurisdictions, like Germany or the European Union, do not provide for a compliance defence. The former Vice President of the European Commission responsible for Competition Policy, Joaquín Almunia, put the EU approach very bluntly by asking: "[W]hy should I reward a compliance programme that has failed?" (Almunia 2010). That being said, you can find prominent examples for countries which included a compliance defence in their legal framework.

In 2012, the French Autorité de la concurrence (2012) issued a Framework Document on Antitrust Compliance Programmes offering a reduction of up to 10 % to settling undertakings. The Autorité only takes into account efforts for future behaviour. An undertaking that has not installed a compliance programme at the time of the settlement, will have to set up such a programme to receive a reduced fine. An undertaking that already has a compliance programme, will only receive a fine reduction if the company upgrades the existing programme.

Similarly, the guidelines from the Office of Fair Trading (OFT), which was abolished in 2014 and succeeded by the Competition and Markets Authority, mention that compliance efforts can lead to a penalty discount of up to 10 % (OFT 2012). In this case, both existing compliance programmes and steps to review compliance activities may lead to a fine reduction. In exceptional cases, however, the UK competition authority will treat the existence of compliance activities as an aggravating factor justifying an increase in monetary penalty. Such situations include that the compliance programme is used to conceal or facilitate an infringement, or to mislead the UK competition authority during its investigation.

In the US, the general rule is that compliance programmes should not be accounted for, when setting a fine. However, this rule seems to have been softened recently. In the Barclays Plea Agreement from 2015,[6] it is mentioned that Barclays' compliance efforts affected the calculation of the fine: "The parties further agree that the Recommended Sentence is sufficient [...] in considering, among other factors, the substantial improvements to the defendant's compliance and remediation program to prevent recurrence of the charged offense." (Ibid., para 13).

Shortly after the agreement, Brent Snyder, the Deputy Assistant Attorney General of the Antitrust Division of the Department of Justice, mentioned in a speech that the company's compliance efforts had led to "a modest reduction in its fine" and that the DOJ was "persuaded that there were demonstrable differences in the way that Barclays substantiated what it did to improve its compliance and corporate culture as compared to the other banks" (Snyder 2015). Most certainly, this will not be the last word in this development because companies are currently missing clear advice on when a compliance programme will be taken into account for the calculation of the fine. The approach taken in the Barclays Plea Agreement may remain an exception, though, as the behaviour of co-conspirators is usually not an adequate benchmark for evaluating compliance efforts.

The Canadian Competition Bureau published guidelines on Corporate Compliance Programmes in 2015 (Competition Bureau Canada 2015). According to this bulletin, "a credible and effective program" may be considered by the Bureau when determining how to proceed against companies or the magnitude of remedy to seek. As a consequence, the compliance defence does not only affect the amount of fines but also other legal aspects such as the choice between the civil and the criminal track. Even though the consequences go farther than in other jurisdictions, the decisions of the Bureau remain discretionary.

[6] U.S. v. Barclays PLC, 3:15-CR-77 (SRU), D.Conn.

10.3.3 Introducing a Compliance Defense in Germany?

On the international level, the compliance defence seems to be on the rise. Under these circumstances, the ongoing discussions on introducing a compliance defence into German law are not surprising. In 2014, the German Institute for Compliance and the Association of in-house counsels put forward even two separate legislative proposals (Deutsches Institut für Compliance 2014, Bundesverband der Unternehmensjuristen 2014) which aimed to set up a compliance defence. The content of the two proposals was quite similar: Section 30 and section 130 of the Administrative Offences Act should be amended allowing for a reduction or even a remission of the fine in reward of compliance efforts. The proposals covered compliance programmes installed both before and after the infringement. The main difference between the two proposals relates to the features a compliance programme must have in order to qualify as a mitigating circumstance. Whereas the association of in-house counsels provides clear orientation on how a compliance programme would have to be organised to alleviate the fine (inter-alia training for employees, whistleblowing system) the German Institute for Compliance refrains from precisely defining a sufficient compliance programme.

Both documents, unfortunately, do not discuss any further effects of the proposed changes aside from the fine reduction. Because of a specific aspect of German liability law, the liability of mother companies might be undermined by the proposed amendments to the Administrative Offences Act. In Germany, the legal entity which has committed an infringement is held liable. Therefore, other than in the EU, where the economic entity has to answer for an infringement, parent and sister companies will only be held responsible if they are actively involved in the infringement (sec. 14 of the Act on Regulatory Offences) or if they omit measures of supervision (sec. 130 para. 1 of the Act on Regulatory Offences). The proposed amendments to sec. 130 para. 1 of the Act on Regulatory Offences could further weaken the responsibility of parent companies by offering a reduction or remission of the fine.

The company liability question is subject to lively discussions and ongoing debates concerning the reform of the Act against Restraints of Competition in Germany. The legal opinion, however, tends to develop towards the idea of a broader scope of liability by adopting the EU concept of liability of the economic entity. Legal gaps, which may allow companies to avoid fines by restructuring their company and winding up the legal entity that had committed the infringement (cf. "German sausage cartel"), are likely to be closed soon. Creating new loopholes at the same time for parent companies thus does not seem appropriate. Moreover, a compliance defence would downplay the seriousness of the infringement and, thereby, work against the establishment of a compliance culture among decision makers.

10.4 Conclusions

Today, the German legislator rather uses the stick than the carrot to support undertakings' compliance efforts. Even though there is no clear legal obligation for an undertaking to install a compliance programme, diligent management of an undertaking probably includes operating a compliance programme. The interest of avoiding fines, compensation for damages, and harm to reputation provide additional incentives for undertakings to install compliance programmes. However, the legal framework leaves some freedom concerning the manifestation of programmes.

A compliance defence might serve as an additional tool to motivate management to voluntarily increase their engagement in compliance programmes beyond legal obligations. However, negative side effects (i.e. conflicts with EU law and the menace of trivializing infringements) must be considered. In the light of such trade-offs, the usefulness of introducing a compliance defence remains questionable.

There are other ways, however, to foster compliance via legal means. One of the main weaknesses of the current legal framework in many European countries follows from fines that are imposed on the undertaking only without having negative consequences for the causal agents. Whereas undertakings do have a clear interest in complying with the law and avoiding fines, management might have incentives to do the opposite. Notably, personal criminal liability might be an efficient instrument to solve this principal-agent-dilemma.

References

Almunia, J. (2010). Speech of 25.10.2010, Speech/10/586. Available from http://europa.eu/rapid/press-release_SPEECH-10-586_en.htm. Accessed 16 April 2016.

Autorité de la concurrence. (2012) Framework Document of 10 February 2012 on Antitrust Compliance Programmes.

Bundesverband der Unternehmensjuristen. (2014). Gesetzgebungsvorschlag für eine Änderung der §§ 30, 130 des Ordnungswidrigkeitengesetzes (OWiG). Available from http://www.buj.net/resources/Server/BUJ-Stellungnahmen/BUJ_Gesetzgebungsvorschlag_OWiG.pdf. Accessed 16 April 2016.

Competition Bureau Canada. (2015). Corporate Compliance Programs. Bulletin of 03.06.2015. Available from http://www.competitionbureau.gc.ca/eic/site/cb-bc.nsf/vwapj/cb-bulletin-corp-compliance-e.pdf/$FILE/cb-bulletin-corp-compliance-e.pdf. Accessed 16 April 2016.

Deutsches Institut für Compliance – DICO e.V. (2014). Compliance-Anreiz-Gesetz.

Landes, W. (1983). Optimal sanctions for antitrust violations. *University of Chicago Law Review, 50*, 652–678.

Marvão, C., & Spagnolo, G. (2014). What do we know about the effectiveness of leniency policies? A survey of the empirical and experimental evidence. Available from: http://ssrn.com/abstract=2511613. Accessed 8 March 2016.

Office of Fair Trading. (2012). OFT's guidance as to the appropriate amount of a penalty. Office of Fair Trading, Reference number OFT423, 1 Sept 2012.

Paha, J., & Götz, G. (2015). Screening und das Compliance-Risikomodell: Konzepte zur unternehmensinternen Aufdeckung von Verstößen gegen das Kartellverbot. *Wirtschaft und Wettbewerb, 12*, 1198–1206.

Scheld, D., Paha, J., & Fandrey, N. (2015). *A risk governance approach to managing antitrust risks in the banking industry*. Joint Discussion Paper Series in Economics by the Universities of Aachen, Gießen, Göttingen, Kassel, Marburg, Siegen No. 35-2015. Available from: http://www.uni-marburg.de/fb02/makro/forschung/magkspapers/paper_2015/35-2015_scheld.pdf. Accessed 16 April 2016.

Snyder, B. (2015). *Leniency in multi-jurisdictional investigations: Too much of a good thing?* Annual Chicago Forum on International Antitrust. 08.06.2015, Chicago, Illinois.

Tirole, J. (1988). *The theory of industrial organization*. Cambridge: MIT Press.

Part V
The Psychology of Compliance

Chapter 11
Psychological Contributions to Competition Law Compliance

Agnieszka Paruzel, Barbara Steinmann, Annika Nübold, Sonja K. Ötting, and Günter W. Maier

Abstract Price fixing and corruption cause immense economic damage. Measures of competition law compliance present a possibility to prevent price fixing and cartelisation. Taking a psychological perspective may help to understand which individual, group, and organisational factors may foster compliance. We explore factors driving compliance and propose the psychological onion model of competition law compliance. The model contains individual, group, and organisational factors determining competition law compliance. These factors are influenced by environmental factors. Within each layer of the onion model, we focus on particularly relevant examples by discussing implicit motives and core self-evaluations (individual), justice (group), and corporate social responsibility (organisation) in detail. Practical recommendations for the establishment of compliance structures in organisations are given, accompanied by theoretical considerations and future research directions.

11.1 Introduction

It started rather harmlessly: Daniel Peters and Peter Hannsen attended the trade fair three times, stayed at the same hotel, and wrapped up their exhausting day at the hotel bar. They started a nonbinding conversation and talked about their products. Quickly they realised that they share the same product range. Before they went to their rooms, Peter Hannsen invited Daniel Peters to dinner the next evening. Two weeks later, Peter Hannsen called Daniel Peters to talk about setting a target range for their prices, knowing that this would have several advantages for both of them. 'So what?', Daniel Peters thought, 'I'm doing it for the company.' One year later, Daniel Peters becomes aware of the fact that price fixing is illegal, but he does not want to, and even cannot, leave the cartel at this time. Too many companies have

A. Paruzel (✉) • B. Steinmann • S.K. Ötting • G.W. Maier
Work and Organizational Psychology, Bielefeld University, Bielefeld, Germany
e-mail: a.paruzel@uni-bielefeld.de

A. Nübold
Psychology and Neuroscience, Maastricht University, Maastricht, The Netherlands

J. Paha (ed.), *Competition Law Compliance Programmes*,
DOI 10.1007/978-3-319-44633-2_11

joined in, and business is flourishing. Instead of with him, Daniel Peters' employees began communicating with Peter Hannsen's company now. So far, he is not worried because no written material exists and all members have always communicated via prepaid phones.

As this fictitious example illustrates, price fixing can occur deliberately and non-deliberately, actively (as an initiator, such as Peter Hannsen's role) and passively (as an acceptor, such as Daniel Peters' role), with or without awareness of legal implications. Moreover, it can or cannot have a personal benefit incremental to the benefit for the company (e.g., the supervisor's appreciation, a bonus, or personal satisfaction). Whereas the underlying processes of the formation of a cartel have not been researched yet, the consequences are known, as illustrated by the following examples.

A prominent example of a cartel is the German sausage cartel, which involved 21 companies. Thirty-three company members fixed prices over decades. Owing to a clue given by an anonymous person, the cartel was detected. Due to the duration of the cartel and the multitude of companies, the sum of fines was €338 million. Eleven companies admitted price fixing and were granted reduced fines (Wood 2014). In the United Kingdom, another cartel, the Marine Hoses Cartel, was detected in 2009. It involved six producers who fixed prices over a period of at least 21 years. The cartel was detected because a producer applied for immunity to the EU Commission who had introduced a leniency programme in 2006. The fines for the six producers amounted to €131 million (Pino 2009). Cartelisation not only has negative consequences for the companies involved, but undoubtedly for the economy and society as a whole (e.g., for consumers who suffer from excessive pricing). The economic damage cartelisation causes is hard to calculate, but the fines imposed indicate the extent of devastation caused. In Germany in 2014, fines in an amount of €1 billion were imposed on companies of six large cartels (sausage, beer, and sugar, among others) with €338 million being the highest fine for a single company (Bundeskartellamt 2014). Cartel detection, though, does not solely result in financial penalties. The loss of reputation also entails declining business confidence in consumers, and furthermore, damages non-participating firms, shareholders, and society in general (Morgan 2009).

The European Commission defines cartels as groups of similar, independent companies aiming to fix prices, limit production, or share markets (http://ec.europa.eu/competition/cartels/overview/index_en.html). Although there are different views concerning the relationship between cartelisation and corruption, our understanding is that cartelisation and price fixing can be regarded as a specific form of corruption, following the opinion of Bannenberg (2002), Freund et al. (2008) and Stephan (2010). The crucial point of these constructs is the following: maximising your own benefit while simultaneously breaching the rules (Genkova and Schwarz 2011). The motivation to fix prices with competitors is primarily the company's economic benefit, but this benefit will also often have favourable personal consequences for the initiator (e.g., pride, satisfaction of contributing to profitability, income gain). Price fixing is different from other types of crimes, such as theft or fraud, which aim to maximise an employee's personal benefit and harm the organisation.

Price fixing and corruption are violations of competition laws. In the field of psychology, we can find three constructs that are related to cartelisation and price fixing: counterproductive work behaviour, workplace deviance, and unethical pro-organisational behaviour. Considering price fixing and corruption from a psychological viewpoint helps to understand about factors and processes relevant for the prevention of price fixing. **Counterproductive work behaviour** is defined as employee behaviour that is likely to do harm but no benefit to other employees or the organisation (Marcus et al. 2002), including absenteeism, substance use, aggression, or theft; whereas **workplace deviance** focuses on negative consequences for the organisation and refers to voluntary behaviour shown by employees that violates organisational norms and, as a consequence, threatens the goals and the prosperity of the organisation (Bennett and Robinson 2000). This may either show in employees' lack of willingness to conform to norms and regulations, or to actively violating expectations of the social context, for example, by discussing confidential company information with an unauthorised person. Counterproductive work behaviour can be both voluntary and non-voluntary, whereas workplace deviance is characterised by voluntariness. **Unethical pro-organisational behaviour** is unethical employee behaviour with the aim to benefit the organisation (Umphress et al. 2010). Although employees behaving in this way may intend to benefit the organisation, the final result of their actions will ultimately cause harm. Criminal forms of workplace deviance as well as counterproductive work and unethical pro-organisational behaviour can be considered among the broad term *white-collar crime*: "a crime committed by a person of respectability and high social status in the course of his occupation" (Sutherland and Holt 1949). These constructs are related to price fixing and have rule-breaching behaviour in common. For example, unethical pro-organisational behaviour relates to price fixing because it emphasises the intent to benefit the organisation, which also applies to price fixing. This illustrates the sometimes paradoxical nature of price fixing: Although it is illegal, people decide to engage in price fixing because they expect a benefit for the organisation. When confronted with the decision to engage in price fixing or not, people may predominantly perceive the benefit resulting from such actions, regard it as a promising reward, and therefore do not think about negative consequences because the expectation of rewards prevails. The benefit is immediately recognisable and is a strong short-term perception that suppresses other perceptions, such as risks. In the long term, people who engage in price fixing may become aware of the risks, damage, and illegality. However, obeying the law ensures compliance and is defined as follows: "Compliance means respecting the law. In the competition field, it means business proactively respecting competition rules" (European Commission 2013). We regard compliance as a possibility to prevent cartelisation and price fixing. Moreover, taking a psychological perspective on price fixing becomes necessary because there is disagreement concerning the effectiveness of punishment (e.g., Piquero et al. 2011), and it should be supplemented by other approaches which have motivational power (Tyler et al. 2015), which emphasises the importance of psychological factors.

In this chapter, we explore intraorganisational factors driving competition law compliance and propose the psychological onion model of competition law compliance. The model contains individual, group, organisational, and environmental factors determining competition law compliance, which constitute the layers of the model. In the following, we first discuss the layers and the constructs that determine competition law compliance, and then we focus on specific constructs of each layer to discuss them in detail.

11.2 Psychological Onion Model of Competition Law Compliance

We identify further scope for using the results of research on psychological factors of white-collar crime, corruption, and other related constructs to enhance competition law compliance. For example, Ayal et al. (2015) have proposed three principles to prevent unethical behaviour—reminding, visibility, and self-engagement—but they yet have to be proven effective in the specific context of competition law compliance. Competition law compliance is a behaviour characterised by respecting the law (European Commission 2013), which includes omitting unlawful acts or behaving proactively to respect competition laws (Frankel 1964). Organisational behaviour in general (behaviour that takes place in organisations), and compliant behaviour in specific, has several antecedents on the individual, group, organisational, and environmental level, determining whether behaviour is shown or avoided.

In our onion model (Fig. 11.1), the individual is at the core of the model. Compliant behaviour, same as other behaviours, depends strongly on an employee's personality features, such as traits, attitudes and emotions. Concerning stable personality traits, five prominent personality traits, the so-called Big Five (Goldberg 1993), predict behavioural tendencies: emotional stability (neuroticism), extraversion, openness to experience, agreeableness, and conscientiousness. Neuroticism is an individual's tendency to experience psychological distress, and extraversion includes sociability, activity, and the tendency to experience positive emotions. Individuals high in openness to experience are characterised by imagination, sensitivity to art, having a rich emotional life and being intellectually curious, and being behaviourally flexible and non-dogmatic in their values. People high in agreeableness are described as trusting, sympathetic, and cooperative. Conscientiousness is characterised by scrupulosity, organisation, and diligence (Costa and McCrae 1992). With regard to counterproductive work behaviour, conscientiousness was of specific interest to personality researchers. Occasionally, low conscientiousness was associated with white-collar crime (Ragatz and Fremouw 2010; Collins and Schmidt 1993). Collins and Schmidt's (1993) study,

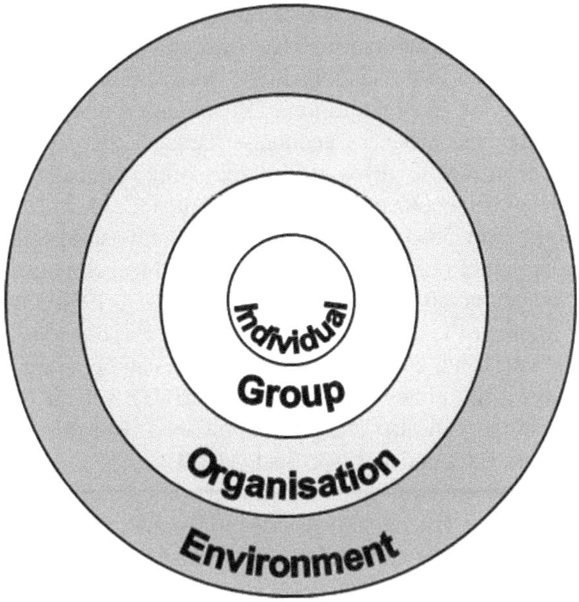

Fig. 11.1 Psychological onion model of competition law compliance

conducted in the United States, was later extended and conducted in Europe. The authors report opposite findings and discuss that criminals feel obliged to their company, which is why they engage in white-collar crime (Blickle et al. 2006). A study of the relation between personality and corruption on the international level (nation-level scores) showed that countries that score high on conscientiousness and neuroticism, and low on openness to experience, tend to be more corrupt (Connelly and Ones 2008).

The individual at the core is surrounded by layers of the group, organisation, and environment because these factors also determine why an individual acts compliant or noncompliant. Organisational members are organised into groups: divisions, workgroups, teams, and relationships of leaders and their followers. Groups are characterised by dynamic and interactional processes that shape behaviour (Hackman and Morris 1974). For example, *norms* are a factor determining compliance (Rabl 2011). Social norms are agreed-upon standards of behaviour (Pretty 2003). Determinants of whether an individual engages in corrupt behaviour include the social norms the group holds concerning corruption. They increase or decrease the probability of engaging in price fixing. Later, we will discuss ethical leadership and justice—conceptualised as a group-level justice climate—in detail (see Sect. 11.3.2). We assume that the justice climate in a group, depending on the type of justice as well as ethical leadership, relate to (non)compliant behaviour.

The third layer contains the organisation itself. A central concept concerning compliance in this layer is an ethical work climate. Employee perceptions of a certain ethical climate in their organisation are associated with ethical behaviour (e.g., Deshpande et al. 2000). Ethical climate consists of "prevailing perceptions of typical organisational practices and procedures that have ethical content" (Victor and Cullen 1988) and includes prescriptions and permissions regarding moral obligations in organisations (Victor and Cullen 1988). As it harms society in general and produces economic damage, the decision to fix prices or not is a decision that involves ethical reasoning. Ethical climate is associated with the ethical behaviour of employees (Deshpande et al. 2000; Fritzsche 2000; Peterson 2002; Treviño et al. 1998). Therefore, a favourable ethical climate should promote compliance (e.g., the emergence of an ethical climate can be promoted by a code of conduct or an ethics code; Treviño et al. 1998). Another factor that supports compliance is an organisations' policy (corporate social responsibility, CSR). On the one hand, compliance programmes can be an integrative part of an organisations' CSR policy (van Marrewijk 2003), yet on the other hand, specific CSR initiatives can also increase compliance (Houghton et al. 2009). Later, we will discuss CSR in detail (see Sect. 11.3.3).

As we are interested in intraorganisational psychological processes, we concentrate on the three inner layers: the individual, the group, and the organisation. Please note that environmental factors probably also play a role in competition law compliance. We think of culture or physical proximity of the competitors interacting with factors of the other layers.

In the following, we will discuss specific examples of each layer in detail: implicit motives and core self-evaluations (individual), organisational justice and ethical leadership (group), and corporate social responsibility (organisation).

11.3 Intraorganisational Key Aspects Derived from the Onion Model

We introduced the psychological onion model of competition law compliance by describing its layers and by giving a short overview. In the following, we discuss factors from each layer in detail: personality traits (implicit motives and core self-evaluations) as individual factors, justice and ethical leadership as a group factor, and corporate social responsibility as an organisational factor. These factors are especially relevant because personality traits in general, as well as justice are related to counterproductive work behaviour (e.g., Greenberg 1993; Kolz 1999), and compliance is regarded as a part of CSR (van Marrewijk 2003). Moreover, ethical leadership has the potential to facilitate compliance because employees prefer working for ethically responsible companies (Karpoff et al. 2008).

11.3.1 Personality Traits as Individual Factors Facilitating Compliance

We suggest that individual characteristics, such as implicit motives and personality traits, also drive the compliance of employees. Although people may differ with regard to their ability to self-reflect, research on both implicit motives (referring to motivational content that is not consciously accessible) and personality traits may prove extremely helpful for behavioural change and, thus, organisational interventions to improve individuals' compliance.

11.3.1.1 Implicit Motives

According to McClelland (1985), who decisively shaped the scientific field of human motivation, implicit motives are among the three major determinants of a person's behaviour. Implicit motives are conceived of as lasting affective preferences for certain classes of incentives for which an individual is striving (McClelland 1985; McClelland et al. 1989). Incentives that arouse implicit motives are of an affective nature and incorporate promising, rewarding emotions (Schüler et al. 2015). As these motives develop early during childhood, they are not consciously represented (Brunstein 2010). Yet, they orient, select, and energise a person's spontaneous conduct and long-term behavioural trends (McClelland 1985; McClelland et al. 1989). Implicit motives orient a person's attention toward cues that are of assistance in predicting opportunities to attain the incentives one is striving for. They foster the selection of behaviours instrumental in approaching the rewarding emotions, and energise these behaviours so that they are executed with greater persistence, vigour, and energy (Schultheiss and Brunstein 2010).

Research on implicit motives mainly concentrated on three important needs: the implicit need for achievement (*n*Ach), the implicit need for affiliation (*n*Aff), and the implicit need for power (*n*Pow). People with high levels of need for achievement strive for a standard of excellence, value performance, seek pleasure from successfully competing with others, and are concerned with reaching unique accomplishments through their own personal efforts (Winter 1994). People who are characterised by a high need for affiliation are concerned with establishing, maintaining, and restoring positive affective relationships with those around them (Heyns et al. 1992). They seek pleasure from companionate activities and express negative feelings in situations of separation (Winter 1994). People with a high need for power, by contrast, strive for strong and energetic actions that have an impact on others (Winter 1973). They are concerned with reputation or position and seek to impress the ones nearby or the world at large (Winter 1994). The way implicit motives find expression in a person's behaviour is not straightforward, though. For example, people may act out their concern for impacting others either through assertive and aggressive behaviours directed at regulating or controlling those around, or through giving unsolicited advice, help, or support, thus using their influence for the benefit of others (Magee and Langner 2008; Winter 1994, 2000). Whether the behavioural manifestation of motives tends to one side or the other depends on the degree of activity inhibition (AI) developed in a person. Activity inhibition is not an implicit motive itself, but a stable tendency that refines and modulates the behavioural expression of motives (Schultheiss et al. 2009). If people are high in AI, they are able to inhibit their implicit motivational and emotional impulses (McClelland 1979), and to act out their strivings in socially responsible ways. In various regards, the motivational Big Three *n*Ach, *n*Aff, and *n*Pow (Schultheiss and Brunstein 2001) may contribute to the corruptive or compliant behaviour of employees.

On theoretical grounds, it may be reasoned that high levels of need for achievement may preserve employees from engaging in price fixing, as cartelisation restrains or even prevents competition with potential competitors does not satisfy the achievement motivated person's need to attain accomplishments through personal efforts, and involves coming to agreements with competitors. Empirical evidence, however, suggests that employees high in achievement motivation are rather susceptible to unethical behaviours and may hence run a higher risk of engaging in cartelisation. As such, research acknowledges that if their motivational striving is not constrained by high levels of AI, people high in *n*Ach tend to ignore interpersonal or political aspects during task-completion in order to attain the standard of excellence they set for themselves and to reach the unique accomplishments they desire (Spangler et al. 2014). Similarly, a person's competitive orientation potentially influences ethics issues in various areas of life (Ryska 2002). In a sample of more than 260 senior-level undergraduate business students, hypercompetitiveness has been found to relate to poor ethics (Mudrack et al. 2012). People characterised by a hypercompetitive orientation strive for successfully competing with others and winning out over them, and are concerned with avoiding failures. Hypercompetitiveness is hence a personality trait closely associated with *n*Ach. Whereas the authors found those high in hypercompetitive orientation to show a tendency to favourably judge immoral actions beneficial in maximising their own gains at the expense of others, there also was a group of students concerned with self-improvement, task-enjoyment, and mastery when competing with others, who judged these immoral actions to be inappropriate. This finding lends evidence to the modulating function ascribed to activity inhibition. In an academic context, highly achievement motivated persons have likewise been found to be more prone to cheating compared to those with low levels of *n*Ach (Johnson 1981). On this basis, it has been questioned whether individuals high in achievement really strive for competing with a standard of excellence and seek pleasure from working on challenging tasks, or if they are solely motivated by achieving success (Johnson 1981). If ends really matter more than means (Johnson 1981), people high in need for achievement are at a higher risk of acting corruptly for the sake of obtaining their objectives compared to those with low levels. In any case, those high in *n*Ach are more concerned with attaining success than those low in *n*Ach (Atkinson 1964). Based on these findings, it may be reasoned that people high in *n*Ach tend to also consider unethical ways of achieving if their striving for unique accomplishments and their pleasure from competing with others is not channelled into socially responsible ways by high levels of activity inhibition. Along with their concern for exceptional performance, people with a highly developed need for achievement are inclined to take chances when decisions have to be made in uncertain situations (McClelland 1976). Such risk-taking behaviour—although only moderately developed in people high in *n*Ach (McClelland 1985)—may additionally facilitate an employee's involvement in corrupt conduct (i.e., illegal price fixing), especially if the way a person acts out a need for achievement is not inhibited (see Spangler et al. 2014).

High levels of need for affiliation may similarly drive employees to behave non-compliantly. In the organisational context, leaders especially have been said to practice favouritism and to place relationships above necessary organisational decisions if they are motivated by high levels of affiliated concern (House et al. 1991). In this way, they attempt to build positive relations with their followers and try to ensure their attachment. People high in need for affiliation are characterised by their striving for belongingness and for the preservation of relationships as well as their pronounced sense of community. On the contrary, however, they are also driven by their fear of being rejected or left alone (see Boyatzis 1973). Therefore, affiliation-motivated people try to please others and do what they can in order to maintain the affection of those around them (McClelland 1975). They shun conflicts and tend to avoid controversies (Exline 1962). In experimental research, it has been shown that affiliation-motivated people are prone to change their attitudes if they are unanimously opposed by a group (Hardy 1957). That way, they may escape potential conflicts and may preserve their affiliation to this group. Such a striving for conformity even holds if affiliation motivated people are confronted with obvious erroneous judgments (McGhee and Teevan 1967). Accordingly, if employees high in *n*Aff relate to competitors who are unanimously determined to arrange prices, they are likely to join the cartel and participate in the regulation of price fixing in order to not put this relationship at risk. Price fixing, however, may not only ensure an employee's belongingness to a group of competitors, but also to their own group of colleagues. Only recently, Thau et al. (2015) demonstrated in a two-wave study among employees in work groups as well as university students that under the condition of having a highly developed need for affiliation or need for inclusion, employees engaged in more unethical behaviour directed at the good of the group when they perceived a risk of being excluded from their team. Whereas affiliation motivated individuals showed more pro-group unethical behaviour facing this risk, pro-self-unethical behaviour did not increase in this situation. Accordingly, participants were not concerned with maximising profits as such, but with contributing to the group's welfare. Given that price fixing may result from good intentions directed at the economic vitality of the organisation, people high in need for affiliation may have a higher probability of joining a cartel if they perceive the risk of being excluded from their organisation or work group. Through these pro-organisational unethical behaviours, employees aim at benefitting their organisation so as to improve their own inclusionary status within the organisation or work group (Thau et al. 2015). Apart from ensuring and maintaining one's belongingness to a group, research has also shown that engaging jointly in ethical violations or "partnering-in-crime" constitutes one means of generating social bonding (Nikolova et al. 2015). In experimental studies (Nikolova et al. 2015), it has been demonstrated that students engaged in more dyadic as compared to individual unethical decision making if the two participants did not know each other. If these two persons, however, had already established some kind of a relationship to each other, they did not show more unethical decision making compared to single individuals. Moreover, the involvement in unethical decisions was higher if participants were high in need for social bonding, which clearly overlaps with the implicit need for affiliation. Findings of this study hence suggest that engaging jointly in unethical decision making may be one way of initiating interactions. Since individuals high in *n*Aff also long for the establishment of relationships within work settings, they may engage in price fixing in order to build and extend their networks. As such, joining a cartel may not only ensure affiliation motivated employees' belongingness to a group, but may also be a means of strategically intensifying and deepening contacts with competitors. Accordingly, participating in price fixing may serve the affiliation motivated employees' need in two regards at a time. Nonetheless, in the paragraph referring to the practical implications of the psychological contributions to competition law compliance, we point out how compliance officers may yet take advantage of highly developed levels of need for affiliation in fostering employees' compliance.

Additionally, high levels of implicit power may also contribute to employees' corruptive or compliant behaviour. Dependent on their ability to inhibit their motivational impulses, power motivated people do not necessarily pay attention to the welfare of those around them when satisfying their drive to influence others. In the context of leadership, for example, the concern for influencing other people and coming to fame may lead supervisors to use their power for self-serving purposes and to aggrandise themselves (McClelland and Wilsnack 1972). Accordingly, leaders characterised by high levels of uninhibited power—that is, leaders showing a personalised use of power—have commonly been described as leading unethically and at the detriment of organisations (Howell and Avolio 1992; House and Aditya 1997; Padilla et al. 2007). Instead of aligning efforts to long-term organisational success, they long for immediate personal gains. However, it is not only in leadership positions where individuals high in personalised power are concerned with maximising their own benefits. Also within a prisoner's dilemma, people high in an unconstrained display of *n*Pow showed more exploitative behaviour compared to those low in power or those high in *n*Ach (Terhune 1968). Being socially intelligent, power motivated individuals are sensitive toward their counterparts' behaviours to which they neatly adapt their own conduct in order to increase their personal gains (Terhune 1968). Besides, those high in power motivation seek pleasure for their own glory, and strive for prestige, fame, and reputation (Winter 1994). If cartelisation grants organisations a promising position within the competition or ensures employees recognition within their company and strengthens their status, price fixing may prove exceptionally gratifying for those high in uninhibited power motivation, who do not care about costs and long-term consequences for those around them. People characterised by high levels of need for power further are more likely to take risks. Barring the possibility of getting caught by authorities, price fixing is hazardous. Research by McClelland and Watson (1973), though, corroborated that power motivated persons are inclined to take more risks and to gamble more in public as opposed to private situations. Only if others are able to notice the risks they dare to take, then power motivated people may get the admiration and reputation for which they strive. Accordingly, covert arrangements on prices—although risky—may not directly serve as an incentive for power motivated people. Yet another way for a person's striving to exert an influence on others to become behaviourally manifest is to convince other people (Winter 1994), that way, affecting their behaviour (Winter 1973). Schultheiss and Brunstein (2002) found that persons who are high in *n*Pow, but act out their implicit power motive in socially intelligent ways, are perceived as particularly persuasive in controversial discussions. Strategically, they try to convince others to build alliances and define the situation in groups (Winter 1992). Within an organisational context, employees high in *n*Pow and high in AI are motivationally inclined to exert their influence so as to contribute to the attainment of organisational goals. As cartelisation may be driven by good intentions aligned to the welfare of one's organisation, initiating price fixing and convincing competitors to join a cartel may be especially satisfying for those people who are concerned with using their power for the benefit of others. As such, price fixing may likewise satisfy the employee's need for a socialised use of power in two different ways: they may convince competitors and may use their power in order to contribute to the organisation's economic vitality.

Although implicit motives have been related to various instances of unethical behaviour, evidence on how the needs for achievement, affiliation, and power relate to employees' involvement in price fixing, on their differential and interactive contribution to the initiation of cartelisation, as well as on possible ways of how to integrate implicit motives into compliance efforts within organisations still needs to be accumulated in research to come.

11.3.1.2 Core Self-Evaluations

When focusing on the inner layer of the onion model (i.e., the individual), it is crucial to evaluate the impact of individuals' personality as one of the most influential determinants of behaviour. One of the most popular and most researched personality characteristic in the field of work and organisational psychology are core self-evaluations. Core self-evaluations (CSE) represent the fundamental appraisals individuals make about their self-worth and capabilities (Judge et al. 1997). CSE is conceptualised as a higher order construct representing the core of the highly correlated traits of emotional stability, generalised self-efficacy, self-esteem, and locus of control. Individuals with high levels in CSE are confident and self-assured, and believe that they can affect what happens to them in life. By contrast, those with low levels in CSE are easily irritated and insecure, and do not trust themselves to be able to make an impact. A multitude of empirical studies have evidenced the value of high CSE for the individual and the organisation as a whole. Individuals with high levels of CSE show higher job and life satisfaction, better job performance, and greater career success, and report lower levels of stress and conflict while coping more effectively with setbacks (Chang et al. 2011).

Although research has not yet specifically focused on the relationship between CSE, corruption, and compliance with regard to price fixing, there is evidence that CSE is associated with broader, conceptually related concepts, such as workplace deviance and organisational commitment. Ferris and colleagues (Ferris et al. 2009a, b, 2011) have extensively investigated how CSE and its core components contribute to employees' deviant behaviours at work. The beneficial effect of high self-evaluations—preventing individuals from engaging in deviant behaviours toward the organisation (Ferris et al. 2009a, b, 2011)—is also in line with research showing that one of the core traits of CSE, emotional stability, is negatively related to corruption on a national level (Connelly and Ones 2008). This effect may be explained by individuals' approach and avoidance work orientations, and the self-regulatory processes involved. Whereas approach work orientations (i.e., striving to achieve positive work outcomes) only direct efforts toward a limited number of means to achieve a goal, avoidance work orientations (i.e., striving to avoid negative work outcomes) require much more resources in order to find and eliminate every possibility that may lead to a negative outcome. As an example, in order to do well in a meeting with a client, an approach-oriented person may simply prepare well by rehearsing the main facts and figures, whereas an avoidance-oriented person would need to detect all possible ways in which the meeting may go wrong. Thereby, one will probably not only rehearse the main information, but also anticipate different kinds of questions and critiques from the client, check the slides of the presentation again, look up the location again, and so on. Consequently, self-regulatory resources will be more easily depleted in avoidance-oriented individuals. As individuals with high CSE have high approach and low avoidance work orientations (Ferris et al. 2011), they possess more self-regulatory resources to abstain from unethical behaviours that may harm the organisation in the long run.

When focusing on the opposite behaviour—compliance to rules and regulations—we may refer to the literature on CSE and organisational commitment, specifically, affective commitment, which refers to an emotional attachment to an organisation (Allen and Meyer 1990). Assuming that employees are aware of both the short- and long-term consequences of their behaviour, it may be inferred that those employees are also more willing to adhere to official rules and regulations in order to not harm the organisation and its goals. In cases where employees only see the short-term benefit of their (non-compliant) behaviour for the organisation and ignore or are unaware of the potential detrimental long-term effects, commitment may potentially also lead to non-compliance. The positive relationship between CSE and affective commitment has been evidenced in a recent meta-analysis (Chang et al. 2011). This relationship can be explained by the way individuals with high CSE perceive their jobs. As individuals with high CSE are confident and strongly believe in their abilities, they tend to evaluate critical events at work as less threatening and view them rather as a challenge (Judge et al. 1997). Thus, individuals with high CSE tend to focus more on the positive aspects of their jobs, such as the significance of their tasks, and perceive their jobs as more intrinsically enriching (Judge et al. 2000; Stumpp et al. 2009). Therefore, they are also more committed to the organisation (Joo et al. 2012; Stumpp et al. 2009) and potentially also more motivated to behave in a compliant and collaborative way.

As a word of caution, it is important to also highlight the potential disadvantages of extreme levels of CSE, which may lead to corruption and may harm compliance behaviour in organisations. Individuals with extremely high levels of CSE may, due to their overconfidence and ambition, be prone to make decisions that serve their own best interests, for example, by price fixing and maximising the company's economic benefit, rather than to follow the official rules and regulations. Judge et al. (2009) stated in their work on the dark side (expressions that are viewed negatively by most individuals in society) of personality traits that *hyper-CSE* (Hiller and Hambrick 2005) indeed shows conceptual overlap with hubris (overconfidence) and narcissism (self-love), potentially leading to the same adverse effects. The adverse effects of narcissism have been recently evidenced by a meta-analysis (O'Boyle et al. 2012) on the dark triad, referring to narcissism, Machiavellianism, and psychopathy. The authors found that narcissism was associated with counterproductive behaviour at work, but that this detrimental effect could be buffered by a company culture that is high in in-group collectivism (i.e., emphasising duty and loyalty to the organisation and its members). Further, research on the downside of (extreme levels of) confidence in CEOs has suggested that it may be related to suboptimal decision making because individuals with extreme levels of self-esteem may ignore negative information and overestimate their abilities, thereby making bad choices and taking unwarranted risks (Hiller and Hambrick 2005; Hayward and Hambrick 1997; Simon and Houghton 2003).

Although CSE has been originally conceptualised as a stable dispositional trait, Judge (2009) explicitly acknowledged that "evaluations of our self-concept are intimately tied to our environment" (p. 61). Recent research has demonstrated that CSE is indeed malleable and shows short-term fluctuation and long-term change. This opens up the possibility for organisations to influence the personality of their employees in beneficial ways, for example, via self-reflection, coaching, and training. Research has shown, for example, that changes in trait CSE were predicted by changes in employees' job satisfaction (Wu and Griffin 2012)—a factor that may be enhanced through beneficial working conditions, such as autonomy, ethical leadership, and organisational justice. Further, research on the state level of CSE has evidenced that work pressure and task complexity may negatively affect individuals' CSE in a specific moment (Dóci and Hofmans 2015; Hofmans et al. 2015). These findings imply that the specific work environment, which can well be improved by the organisation, may also play a crucial role for employees' CSE and, thus, also their commitment and ethical conduct.

11.3.2 Justice and Ethical Leadership as Group Factors Facilitating Compliance

In addition to compliant and non-compliant behaviour being related to various personality features, such as implicit motives and CSE, research also in the fields of justice climate and ethical leadership allows one to conclude the circumstances under which group-level individuals tend to behave compliantly or not.

11.3.2.1 Justice

The concept of group-level justice climate emerged in the late 1990s from research on organisational justice, originally solely conceptualised as an individual-level construct (Li et al. 2015). Justice climate forms within workgroups from shared perceptions of justice, and is described as the "group-level cognition about how a work group as a whole is treated" (Naumann and Bennett 2000, p. 882). Research has shown that justice climate explains variance above and beyond the variance explained by its individual-level counterpart (Mossholder et al. 1998; Naumann and Bennett 2000). These results and recent research on the third-party justice effects demonstrate that individuals not only respond to the justice they experienced personally, but also take into account their co-workers' justice experiences when they respond to justice in the workplace (Rupp et al. 2007).

Justice climate, same as organisational justice, is composed of four dimensions, namely distributive, procedural, interpersonal, and informational justice (for an overview, see Greenberg 2011 and Rupp and Thornton 2014). *Distributive justice* focuses on the justice of decision outcomes. A decision outcome is perceived as fair if the ratio of one's contributions to one's outcomes is equivalent to that of a comparable other. *Procedural justice* describes the justice of the decision-making procedures. A decision process is perceived as fair if the recipients have voice during the process or influence over the outcome, and if justice criteria, such as consistency, lack of bias, accuracy, correctability, and ethicality, are included in the process design. Having voice or process control seems to be even more important than having control over the actual decision: individuals were willing to give up control over the decision outcome as long as they had control over the decision process (Thibaut and Walker 1975). The last two dimensions concern the justice of the decision communication: *Interpersonal justice* describes the justice of the decision authority's behaviour toward the recipient. The communication of a decision is perceived as interpersonally fair if it is respectful, polite, and dignified. *Informational justice* refers to the adequacy of the information used to explain how the decision process is formed. Informational justice is fostered where information is truthful, well-reasoned, specific, and timely.

Although justice research has not yet specifically focused on relationships between justice (neither on the individual nor on the group level) and competition law compliance, evidence on relationships with general law compliance, counterproductive work behaviours, and organisational commitment hints at such a relationship. Meta-analytic research has shown that organisational justice is, similar to CSE, negatively related to counterproductive work behaviours and positively related to affective commitment (Colquitt et al. 2013). We presume that employees are aware of both the short-term and long-term consequences of price fixing, especially that they are aware that price fixing is unethical and constitutes a risk for the organisation in the long term.

Being treated fairly and being witness of others being treated fairly has been shown to shape future law compliance in the context of taxation law and compliance with the police (e.g., Hough et al. 2013; Murphy 2003). Here, a growing number of studies has shown that procedural, interpersonal, and informational justice can be more effective in influencing compliance than fair outcomes or fear about punishment (e.g., Feld and Frey 2002; Hough et al. 2013; Magner et al. 1998; Murphy 2005; Wenzel 2002, Wenzel 2006). These studies mostly have built on the research of Tyler and colleagues, demonstrating that people who have been treated fairly by an authority, or who know people who have been treated fairly, are more likely to view this authority as entitled to be obeyed, and as more legitimate, regardless of the decision outcome (e.g., Magner et al. 1998; Tyler 1997; Tyler and Lind 1992). Tyler (1997) also has argued that if an organisation is perceived as being legitimate, people are more likely to comply with the decisions of those in authority. Hough and colleagues (2013) followed this argumentation and confirmed this model by showing that, through the perception of legitimacy, trust in procedural fair treatment shapes compliance with the police. We believe that this legitimisation refers not only to governmental authorities and organisations, but is especially important for group leaders.

11.3.2.2 Ethical Leadership

On the group layer, leader–follower interactions may be considered a determinant that essentially contributes to the emergence and maintenance of employee compliance. Current research has emphasised that in establishing a culture of ethics within teams and in fostering ethical conduct among followers, especially those leaders play an important role who employ ethical leadership behaviours (Mayer et al. 2009; Schaubroeck et al. 2012). Ethical leadership can be defined as "the demonstration of normatively appropriate conduct through personal actions and interpersonal relationships, and the promotion of such conduct to followers through two-way communication, reinforcement, and decision-making" (Brown et al. 2005). Apart from being moral, upright, and fair persons themselves, ethical leaders are uniquely characterised by the moral management they show (Treviño et al. 2000). On the one hand, ethical leaders align their words and actions and keep their promises, that way, becoming role models of ethically appropriate behaviour (Kalshoven et al. 2011). On the other hand, they explain and clarify integrity guidelines to followers, make sure employees follow codes of conduct, stimulate the discussion of integrity-related topics, and clearly articulate moral expectations

(Kalshoven et al. 2011). Through these means of ethical guidance, ethical leaders substantially shape their followers' conduct. They reward those who act in accordance with the established integrity guidelines, and punish those who violate the rules (Steinmann et al. 2016). Using these transactional leader behaviours, ethical leaders lessen deviance within the team and promote pro-social behaviour of team members (Mayer et al. 2009). Ethical leadership influences followers across hierarchical levels (Schaubroeck et al. 2012) and trickles down from top management to lower supervisory levels (Mayer et al. 2009). Mayer and colleagues (2009) have argued that ethical leadership cascades down by means of social learning (Bandura 1986) and social exchange theory (Blau 1964). Followers emulate the ethical conduct of their leaders and return their trust, honesty, and integrity. That way, compliance and ethical conduct of employees in organisations rise. Within their work groups, followers of ethical leaders perceive higher levels of group cohesiveness and psychological safety, and report higher levels of commitment to and trust in their organisation (Steinmann et al. 2016). As such, through their moral management, ethical leaders may also lessen the possibility of team members to engage in price fixing and keep them resistant to cartelisation.

11.3.3 Corporate Social Responsibility as an Organisational Factor Facilitating Compliance

Nowadays, the business community has to deal with several challenges: among global environmental problems, poor labour conditions, discrimination, and racism, hot topics are also corruption, bribery, and price fixing. In order to overcome these challenges, companies have to take responsibility for their actions. This commitment is called Corporate Social Responsibility (CSR) and is an organisational policy. Among others, one aim of CSR is to identify, prevent, and mitigate the organisations' possible adverse impacts (European Commission 2011), for example, the economic damage of price fixing. CSR includes both "doing good" and "avoiding bad" (Lin-Hi and Müller 2013).

CSR affects various stakeholder groups: the community in general, employees, suppliers, customers, shareholders, the natural environment, and the government (El Akremi et al. 2015; Türker 2009). Most CSR initiatives affect several stakeholder groups at the same time. As a prevention of price fixing, compliance in the competition field concerns the government, customers, employees, and the community in general. A hierarchical conceptualisation of CSR considers compliance as essential to CSR: the first level of CSR is compliance-driven CSR, which is about contributing to the welfare of society within the limits of governmental regulations (van Marrewijk 2003). In this context, CSR is regarded as correct behaviour or an obligation.

CSR affects employee-related outcomes by creating a feeling of belongingness to an organisation. Social identity theory suggests that CSR initiatives have the potential to increase organisational identification (Dutton and Dukerich 1991) if the initiatives are distinct and prestigious (Ashforth and Mael 1989). Organisational identification has an effect on several employee attitudes and behaviours (e.g., commitment and job satisfaction; Kim et al. 2010; Riketta 2005). Over-identification, which is regarded as pathological (Vadera and Pratt 2013), however, is likely to increase unethical pro-organisational behaviour (Umphress et al. 2010; Vadera and Pratt 2013), so that compliance issues should explicitly be integrated into CSR strategies. A meta-analysis quantified the relationship between CSR and identification and found a moderate relationship ($\rho = 0.47$) based on 14 studies with 3837 participants overall (Paruzel et al. in prep.), so it remains questionable if CSR is able to induce over-identification, or rather, is associated with a *non-pathological* type of identification.

Quasi-experimental research has indicated that participation in CSR initiatives possibly could enhance compliance in employees. It was investigated if a specific CSR initiative—a volunteer programme—increased compliance among employees in terms of adhering to regulations (Houghton et al. 2009). Companies having a volunteer programme release employees from work to give them the opportunity to volunteer while being paid full-time. This kind of CSR initiative targets two stakeholder groups: employees have the chance for self-fulfilment and the volunteerism serves a common good. The authors recorded how much time the employees spent volunteering during the last year and presented three vignettes to the study participants, varying in their subject (discrimination, accounting dilemma, and a strategic confidentiality breach). They had to choose between six different reactions to the three described situations, varying in the degree of compliance. For one of the three vignettes—the situation of the confidentiality breach—they found that extensive volunteerism is related to compliant behaviour.

The mere presence of CSR leads to an expectation or signal (Rynes 1989) that an organisation is compliant (Scheffer and Kaeb 2011). This is relevant in the recruitment process. Applicants who attach importance to compliance are attracted to socially responsible organisations. If they attach importance to compliance, it can be assumed that they are likely to be compliant themselves. The positive implications of this person–organisation fit can be fostered by CSR.

All in all, we have learned that the constructs of CSR and compliance have much in common. CSR helps to make corporate codes of conduct more credible and to absorb harm due to an allegation of corruption. Compliance will not directly be regarded as "doing good" because by "avoiding bad," it helps to prevent social irresponsibility, but this is a prerequisite for being perceived as socially responsible in the long term (Lin-Hi and Müller 2013).

11.4 Practical Recommendations

The psychological onion model of competition law compliance reveals several factors that can be taken into account when designing compliance programmes or establishing compliance in an organisation: implicit motives, CSE, justice, ethical leadership, and CSR. We will discuss how to improve compliance by integrating it into the personnel selection process and organisational interventions, and then discuss how to establish a favourable organisational climate for compliance, and finally give recommendations for compliance officers.

First, CSE, implicit motives, and other personality traits should be integrated into personnel selection. We propose including questions about compliance in a Behavioural Event Interview (BEI)—a standardised interview developed for personnel selection processes. The major underlying assumption of BEIs is that past behaviour is the best predictor for future behaviour. Talking about critical situations concerning price fixing or corruption will reveal how the applicant has behaved in the past. Moreover, the material of the personnel selection process (e.g., application documents) can be analysed with regard to implicit motives by means of coding schemes.

Second, the idea that CSE is subject to change opens up the possibility for systematic organisational interventions, such as compliance training, coaching, and codes of conduct. These interventions may either focus on the individual itself or on the organisation as a whole. In the first case, employees' core self-evaluations may be affected directly via training and coaching and by providing positive and appreciative feedback, such as by means of praising employees explicitly when behaviour toward a compliant organisation is shown; in the latter case, job design approaches and interventions aiming to benefit the organisational culture and climate and the interaction patterns of employees may benefit employees' CSE indirectly. For example, reducing the complexity of specific tasks and lowering work pressure may prevent employees from mental overload and from experiencing the depletion of too many resources and, as a consequence, lowered levels of CSE and deviant behaviours. Another possibility to prevent breach of rule is job rotation (Abbink 2004). In job rotation programmes, employees change their workplaces regularly and get to know other colleagues while working in another workplace, so they are assigned to new groups frequently. In order to make illegal pricing agreements, a stable network has to be established. Accordingly, experimental research findings have shown that job rotation decreases corrupt decisions significantly (Abbink 2004). The frequency of corrupt decisions decreased from 43.8 to 14.3 % under the condition of job rotation. If there are more than two employees of a company involved in the process of price fixing, job rotation could facilitate compliance because the networks become less stable.

Third, an organisation should strive for a beneficial climate fostering compliance. In order to achieve a climate for compliance on the group as well as on the organisational level, employees should be treated fairly in general and especially in situations of a (suspected) wrongdoing. Concentrating on procedural, interpersonal, and informational justice has proven to be most effective (Hough et al. 2013; Murphy 2005). Moreover, an ethical climate is assumed to foster compliance, too. To reach this goal, compliance should become a norm that is accepted and acted upon by all members of the organisation, for example, by means of a code of ethics or by leaders serving as good role models.

In addition, an organisation should attach importance to transparency (e.g., meetings with members of competitive organisations should take place in the presence of many people). Another possibility to enhance compliance is to foster the salience of respective peer groups by increasing the visibility of those who refuse price fixing or those who may suffer from these arrangements. This may contribute to heightened compliance, especially of people considered to have a strong *n*Aff who are characterised by their motivational drive to initiate and maintain relationships as well as their sympathy toward others (Koestner and McClelland 1992). Moreover, compliance programmes could be integrated into the CSR policy as a whole, and communicated to all members. They should focus on "avoiding bad," but the CSR policy should be complemented by initiatives that focus on "doing good." Initiatives that focus on financial support should be avoided. Communication of CSR to the outside is also relevant for attracting compliant staff. Clear codes of conduct help to establish a culture of ethics and guide the employee's behaviour. It is crucial that the code of conduct is not only communicated, but that it becomes a guideline for behaviour that is heeded by every member in the organisation (Sokol 2012). Compliance should also be integrated into employee appraisal systems, so it becomes an obligation to every single employee. In the annual appraisal interview, leaders should talk about compliance issues with their employees in order to increase awareness and imbed compliance in the agreement on objectives. Compliance training programmes should address this specific group of leaders in the first place.

11.4.1 Recommendations for Compliance Officers

According to our previous remarks, compliance officers should be integrated into various human resource practices. They should be involved in the personnel selection process as well as requirements analysis, and should develop questions for interviews. They can also analyse application documents with regard to implicit motives by using coding schemes. Moreover, compliance officers should include compliance issues into human resource development by taking part in planning training sessions (e.g., compliance training or leadership training). If employees are highly committed to and satisfied with their leader, the leader's ethical behaviour can spill over. Additionally, people high in *n*Aff tend to avoid conflicts, so the leader's disapproval of price fixing reduces the probability of the follower engaging in price fixing, as he would prefer to avoid a conflict. We recommend compliance officers as official justice representatives. In that capacity, they can use screenings to detect a high risk climate for justice. Besides, they should create awareness of the negative consequences of price fixing among all employees and emphasise that the organisation strictly refuses to engage in price fixing. The awareness that rule-breaking behaviour is sanctioned decreases corruption (Abbink 2002; Schulze and Frank 2003).

With regard to implicit motives, compliance officers should, on the one hand, and as already mentioned, participate in the personnel selection process, yet on the other hand, be sensitised to implicit motives and their consequences with regard to people already employed (e.g., to detect employees characterised by a high *n*Ach). Thau et al. (2015) have stated that leaders should particularly pay attention to employees who are at risk of exclusion because they tend to engage in unethical behaviour in order to improve their inclusion in their work group. Compliance officers should include these issues in leadership training.

With regard to CSE, organisations may not only focus on hiring individuals with high levels of trait CSE, but may also beneficially affect commitment via leadership or job design interventions. Compliance officers may advise supervisors to support and strengthen their employees' self-evaluations (e.g., through positive feedback and role-modelling) and try to create a more fulfilling work environment via job design. As an example, providing more autonomy to employees (e.g., via job enrichment interventions) may cause them to perceive their job in a more beneficial light, and may also strengthen their self-esteem.

11.5 Discussion

The psychological onion model of competition law compliance suggests several factors determining compliance that have to be taken into account when developing compliance programmes: implicit motives, CSE, justice, ethical leadership, and CSR. Concerning theory, the relationship between compliance and price fixing/ corruption is still not clear. Are price fixing and compliance opposites of the same construct, or different constructs? Is compliance rather a means of preventing price fixing? We took the more conservative position and assumed that compliance is a means of preventing corruption and price fixing, but future research should shed light on the relationship of these constructs.

Concerning future research, first, our theoretical assumptions concerning compliance, implicit motives, core-self-evaluations, justice, and corporate social responsibility have to be empirically tested in the context of price fixing. Second, the process of cartelisation has to be researched. Which psychological processes underlie an employee's decision to engage in price fixing? Future research should examine whether escalation of commitment (Staw 1981) also applies in the context of price fixing. Do price-fixing employees intensify their commitment to the cartel—an ineffective course of action which likely harms the organisation in the long run in the case of detection—in order to justify the allocation of previous resources, such as time and risk (see Brockner et al. 1986)? Third, a psychometric scale measuring noncompliance has to be developed. Such a scale could serve as an early warning system. It should take into account factors of the individual, group, and organisational level of the psychological onion model of competition law compliance. Research should also evaluate the implementation of systematic organisational interventions in order to learn about the effectiveness of different interventions. When researching price fixing and competition law compliance, our taxonomy is a useful tool for intra- and interdisciplinary communication, and for structuring and categorising research by declaring the focus of the research (deliberately or non-deliberately, actively or passively, with or without awareness of illegality, personal benefit and/or benefit for the company).

Whereas compliance has been researched mainly by legal and business scholars in the past, we have shown that it is worthwhile to consider compliance from a psychological point of view. By examining employees, we have identified individual, group, and organisational factors determining competition law compliance, and have derived practical recommendations for the establishment of compliance in organisations.

References

Abbink, K. (2002). An experimental bribery game. *Journal of Law, Economics, and Organization, 18*(2), 428–454. doi:10.1093/jleo/18.2.428.

Abbink, K. (2004). Staff rotation as an anti-corruption policy: An experimental study. *European Journal of Political Economy, 20*(4), 887–906. doi:10.1016/j.ejpoleco.2003.10.008.

Allen, N. J., & Meyer, J. P. (1990). The measurement and antecedents of affective, continuance and normative commitment to the organization. *Journal of Occupational and Organizational Psychology, 63*(1), 1–18. doi:10.1111/j.2044-8325.1990.tb00506.x.

Ashforth, B. E., & Mael, F. (1989). Social identity theory and the organization. *Academy of Management Review, 14*(1), 20–39. doi:10.5465/AMR.1989.4278999.

Atkinson, J. W. (1964). *An introduction to motivation*. Princeton, NJ: Van Nostrand.

Ayal, S., Gino, F., Barkan, R., & Ariely, D. (2015). Three principles to REVISE people's unethical behavior. *Perspectives on Psychological Science, 10*(6), 738–741. doi:10.1177/1745691615598512.

Bandura, A. (1986). *Social foundations of thought and action: A social cognitive theory*. Prentice-Hall, Inc.

Bannenberg, B. (2002). *Korruption in Deutschland und ihre strafrechtliche Kontrolle. Eine kriminologisch-strafrechtliche Analyse*. Neuwied: Luchterhand.

Bennett, R. J., & Robinson, S. L. (2000). Development of a measure of workplace deviance. *Journal of Applied Psychology, 85*(3), 349–360. doi:10.1037/0021-9010.85.3.349.

Blau, P. M. (1964). *Exchange and power in social life*. Transaction Publishers.

Blickle, G., Schlegel, A., Fassbender, P., & Klein, U. (2006). Some personality correlates of business white-collar crime. *Applied Psychology, 55*(2), 220–233. doi:10.1111/j.1464-0597.2006.00226.x.

Boyatzis, R. E. (1973). Affiliation motivation. In D. C. McClelland & R. S. Steele (Eds.), *Human motivation: a book of readings* (pp. 252–276). Morristown, NJ: General Learning Press.

Brockner, J., Houser, R., Birnbaum, G., Lloyd, K., Deitcher, J., Nathanson, S., et al. (1986). Escalation of commitment to an ineffective course of action: The effect of feedback having negative implications for self-identity. *Administrative Science Quarterly, 31*(1), 109. doi:10.2307/2392768.

Brown, M. E., Treviño, L. K., & Harrison, D. A. (2005). Ethical leadership: A social learning perspective for construct development and testing. *Organizational Behavior and Human Decision Processes, 97*(2), 117–134. doi:10.1016/j.obhdp.2005.03.002.

Brunstein, J. C. (2010). Implizite und explizite Motive. In: J. Heckhausen & A. Heckhausen (Eds.), *Motivation und Handeln* (pp. 237–255). Springer.

Bundeskartellamt. (2014). Das Bundeskartellamt - Jahresbericht.

Chang, C., Ferris, D. L., Johnson, R. E., Rosen, C. C., & Tan, J. A. (2011). Core self-evaluations: A review and evaluation of the literature. *Journal of Management, 38*(1), 81–128. doi:10.1177/0149206311419661.

Collins, J. M., & Schmidt, F. L. (1993). Personality, integrity, and white collar crime: A construct validity study". *Personnel Psychology, 46*(2), 295–311. doi:10.1111/j.1744-6570.1993.tb00875.x.

Colquitt, J. A., Scott, B. A., Rodell, J. B., Long, D. M., Zapata, C. P., Conlon, D. E., et al. (2013). Justice at the millennium, a decade later: A meta-analytic test of social exchange and affect-based perspectives. *Journal of Applied Psychology, 98*(2), 199–236. doi:10.1037/a0031757.

Connelly, B. S., & Ones, D. S. (2008). The personality of corruption: A national-level analysis. *Cross Cultural Research, 42*(4), 353–385. doi:10.1177/1069397108321904.

Costa, P. T., & McCrae, R. R. (1992). Normal personality assessment in clinical practice: The NEO personality inventory. *Psychological Assessment, 4*(1), 5–13. doi:10.1037/1040-3590.4.1.5.

Deshpande, S. P., George, E., & Joseph, J. (2000). Ethical climates and managerial success in Russian organizations. *Journal of Business Ethics, 23*(2), 211–217. doi:10.1023/A:1005943017693.

Dóci, E., & Hofmans, J. (2015). Task complexity and transformational leadership: The mediating role of leaders' state core self-evaluations. *The Leadership Quarterly, 26*(3), 436–447. doi:10.1016/j.leaqua.2015.02.008.

Dutton, J. E., & Dukerich, J. M. (1991). Keeping an eye on the mirror: Image and identity in organizational adaptation. *Academy of Management Journal, 34*(3), 517–554. doi:10.2307/256405.

El Akremi, A., Gond, J., Swaen, V., de Roeck, K., & Igalens, J. (2015). How do employees perceive corporate responsibility?: Development and validation of a multidimensional corporate stakeholder responsibility scale. *Journal of Management.* doi:10.1177/0149206315569311.

European Commission. (2011). Communication from the Commission to the European Parliament, the Council, the European Economic and Social Committee and the Committee of the Regions. A renewed EU strategy 2011-14 for Corporate Social Responsibility.

European Commission. (2013). *Compliance with competition rules: What's in it for business?*. Available from: http://ec.europa.eu/competition/antitrust/compliance/index_en.html.

European Commission Cartels. Available from: http://ec.europa.eu/competition/cartels/overview/index_en.html.

Exline, R. V. (1962). Need affiliation and initial communication behaviour in problem-solving groups characterized by low interpersonal visibility. *Psychological Reports, 10*(1), 79–89. doi:10.2466/pr0.1962.10.1.79.

Feld, L. P., & Frey, B. S. (2002). Trust breeds trust: How taxpayers are treated. *Economics of Governance, 3*(2), 87–99. doi:10.1007/s101010100032.

Ferris, D. L., Brown, D. J., & Heller, D. (2009a). Organizational supports and organizational deviance: The mediating role of organization-based self-esteem. *Organizational Behavior and Human Decision Processes, 108*(2), 279–286. doi:10.1016/j.obhdp.2008.09.001.

Ferris, D. L., Brown, D. J., Lian, H., & Keeping, L. M. (2009b). When does self-esteem relate to deviant behaviour?: The role of contingencies of self-worth. *Journal of Applied Psychology, 94*(5), 1345–1353. doi:10.1037/a0016115.

Ferris, D. L., Rosen, C. R., Johnson, R. E., Brown, D. J., Risavy, S. D., & Heller, D. (2011). Approach or avoidance (or both?): Integrating core self-evaluations within an approach/

avoidance framework. *Personnel Psychology, 64*(1), 137–161. doi:10.1111/j.1744-6570.2010.01204.x.

Frankel, L. H. (1964). Criminal omissions: A legal microcosm. *Wayne Law Review, 11*, 367.

Freund, M., Kallmayer, A., & Kraft, O. (2008). *Korruption und Kartelle bei Auftragsvergaben: Prävention-Sanktionen-Verteidigung*. Beck.

Fritzsche, D. J. (2000). Ethical climates and the ethical dimension of decision making. *Journal of Business Ethics, 24*(2), 125–140. doi:10.1023/A:1006262914562.

Genkova, P., & Schwarz, C. (2011). Motive fairen und nicht-solidarischen Verhaltens. In T. Kliche & S. Thiel (Eds.), *Korruption. Forschungsstand, Prävention, Probleme* (pp. 53–75). Lengerich, Westf: Pabst Science Publishers.

Goldberg, L. R. (1993). The structure of phenotypic personality traits. *American Psychologist, 48* (1), 26–34. doi:10.1037/0003-066X.48.1.26.

Greenberg, J. (1993). Stealing in the name of justice: Informational and interpersonal moderators of theft reactions to underpayment inequity. *Organizational Behavior and Human Decision Processes, 54*(1), 81–103. doi:10.1006/obhd.1993.1004.

Greenberg, J. (2011). Organizational justice: the dynamics of fairness in the workplace. In S. Zedeck (Ed.), *APA handbook of industrial and organizational psychology, maintaining, expanding, and contracting the organization* (Vol. 3, pp. 271–327). Washington, DC: American Psychological Association. doi:10.1037/12171-008.

Hackman, J. R., & Morris, C. G. (1974). *Group tasks, group interaction process, and group performance effectiveness: A review and proposed integration*. Citeseer.

Hardy, K. R. (1957). Determinants of conformity and attitude change. *Journal of Abnormal & Social Psychology, 54*(3), 289–294. doi:10.1037/h0048374.

Hayward, M. L. A., & Hambrick, D. C. (1997). Explaining the premiums paid for large acquisitions: Evidence of CEO hubris. *Administrative Science Quarterly, 42*(1), 103. doi:10.2307/2393810.

Heyns, R. W., Veroff, J., & Atkinson, J. W. (1992). A scoring manual for the affiliation motive. In C. P. Smith (Ed.), *Motivation and personality* (pp. 211–223). Cambridge: Cambridge University Press.

Hiller, N. J., & Hambrick, D. C. (2005). Conceptualizing executive hubris: The role of (hyper-) core self-evaluations in strategic decision-making. *Strategic Management Journal, 26*(4), 297–319. doi:10.1002/smj.455.

Hofmans, J., Debusscher, J., Dóci, E., Spanouli, A., & de Fruyt, F. (2015). The curvilinear relationship between work pressure and momentary task performance: The role of state and trait core self-evaluations. *Frontiers in Psychology, 6*, 16. doi:10.3389/fpsyg.2015.01680.

Hough, M., Jackson, J., & Bradford, B. (2013). Legitimacy, trust and compliance: an empirical test of procedural justice theory using the European Social Survey. In J. Tankebe & A. Liebling (Eds.), *Legitimacy and criminal justice: an international exploration*. Oxford: Oxford University Press.

Houghton, S. M., Gabel, J. T. A., & Williams, D. W. (2009). Connecting the two faces of CSR: Does employee volunteerism improve compliance? *Journal of Business Ethics, 87*(4), 477–494. doi:10.1007/s10551-008-9954-2.

House, R. J., & Aditya, R. N. (1997). The social scientific study of leadership: Quo Vadis? *Journal of Management, 23*(3), 409–473. doi:10.1177/014920639702300306.

House, R. J., Spangler, W. D., & Woycke, J. (1991). Personality and charisma in the U.S. presidency: A psychological theory of leader effectiveness. *Administrative Science Quarterly, 36*(3), 364. doi:10.2307/2393201.

Howell, J. M., & Avolio, B. J. (1992). The ethics of charismatic leadership: Submission or liberation? *The Executive, 6*(2), 43–54. doi:10.5465/AME.1992.4274395.

Johnson, P. B. (1981). Achievement motivation and success: Does the end justify the means? *Journal of Personality and Social Psychology, 40*(2), 374–375. doi:10.1037/0022-3514.40.2.374.

Joo, B., Jun Yoon, H., & Jeung, C. (2012). The effects of core self-evaluations and transformational leadership on organizational commitment. *Leadership & Organization Development Journal, 33*(6), 564–582. doi:10.1108/01437731211253028.

Judge, T. A. (2009). Core self-evaluations and work success. *Current Directions in Psychological Science, 18*(1), 58–62. doi:10.1111/j.1467-8721.2009.01606.x.
Judge, T. A., Bono, J. E., & Locke, E. A. (2000). Personality and job satisfaction: The mediating role of job characteristics. *Journal of Applied Psychology, 85*(2), 237–249. doi:10.1037/0021-9010.85.2.237.
Judge, T. A., Locke, E. A., & Durham, C. C. (1997). The dispositional causes of job satisfaction: A core evaluations approach. *Research in Organizational Behavior, 19*, 151–188.
Judge, T. A., Piccolo, R. F., & Kosalka, T. (2009). The bright and dark sides of leader traits: A review and theoretical extension of the leader trait paradigm. *Leadership Quarterly, 20*(6), 855–875. doi:10.1016/j.leaqua.2009.09.004.
Kalshoven, K., Den Hartog, D. N., & De Hoogh, A. H. (2011). Ethical leadership at work questionnaire (ELW): development and validation of a multidimensional measure. *The Leadership Quarterly, 22*(1), 51–69. doi:10.1016/j.leaqua.2010.12.007.
Karpoff, J. M., Lee, D. S., & Martin, G. S. (2008). The cost to firms of cooking the books. *Journal of Financial and Quantitative Analysis, 43*(03), 581. doi:10.1017/S0022109000004221.
Kim, H., Lee, M., Lee, H., & Kim, N. (2010). Corporate social responsibility and employee–company identification. *Journal of Business Ethics, 95*(4), 557–569. doi:10.1007/s10551-010-0440-2.
Koestner, R., & McClelland, D. C. (1992). The affiliation motive. In C. P. Smith & C. P. Smith (Eds.), *Motivation and personality* (pp. 205–210). Cambridge: Cambridge University Press.
Kolz, A. R. (1999). Personality predictors of retail employee theft and counterproductive behavior. *Journal of Professional Services Marketing, 19*(2), 107–114. doi:10.1300/J090v19n02_06.
Li, A., Cropanzano, R. S., & Molina, A. (2015). Fairness at the unit level: Justice climate, justice climate strength, and peer justice. *The Oxford Handbook of Justice in the Workplace* (p. 137).
Lin-Hi, N., & Müller, K. (2013). The CSR bottom line: Preventing corporate social irresponsibility. *Journal of Business Research, 66*(10), 1928–1936. doi:10.1016/j.jbusres.2013.02.015.
Magee, J. C., & Langner, C. A. (2008). How personalized and socialized power motivation facilitate antisocial and prosocial decision-making. *Journal of Research in Personality, 42*(6), 1547–1559. doi:10.1016/j.jrp.2008.07.009.
Magner, N., Sobery, J. S., & Welker, R. B. (1998). Tax decision making in municipal governments: Citizens' reactions to outcomes and procedures. *Journal of Public Budgeting, Accounting & Financial Management, 9*(4), 552.
Marcus, B., Schuler, H., Quell, P., & Humpfner, G. (2002). Measuring counter productivity: Development and initial validation of a German self-report questionnaire. *International Journal of Selection & Assessment, 10*(1&2), 18–35. doi:10.1111/1468-2389.00191.
Mayer, D. M., Kuenzi, M., Greenbaum, R., Bardes, M., & Salvador, R. (2009). How low does ethical leadership flow?: Test of a trickle-down model. *Organizational Behavior and Human Decision Processes, 108*(1), 1–13. doi:10.1016/j.obhdp.2008.04.002.
McClelland, D. C. (1975). *Power: The inner experience*. New York, NY: Irvington [u.a.].
McClelland, D. C. (1976). *The achieving society*. New York, NY: Irvington [u.a.].
McClelland, D. C. (1979). Inhibited power motivation and high blood pressure in men. *Journal of Abnormal Psychology, 88*(2), 182–190. doi:10.1037/0021-843X.88.2.182.
McClelland, D. C. (1985). *Human motivation*. Glenview, IL: Scott, Foresman and Co [u.a.].
McClelland, D. C., Koestner, R., & Weinberger, J. (1989). How do self-attributed and implicit motives differ? *Psychological Review, 96*(4), 690–702. doi:10.1037//0033-295X.96.4.690.
McClelland, D. C., & Watson, R. I. (1973). Power motivation and risk-taking behavior. *Journal of Personality, 41*(1), 121–139. doi:10.1111/j.1467-6494.1973.tb00664.x.
McClelland, D. C., & Wilsnack, S. C. (1972). The effects of drinking on thoughts about power and restraint. *The drinking man* (pp. 123–141).
McGhee, P. E., & Teevan, R. C. (1967). Conformity behavior and need for affiliation. *Journal of Social Psychology, 72*(1), 117–121. doi:10.1080/00224545.1967.9922305.
Morgan, E. J. (2009). Controlling cartels – Implications of the EU policy reforms. *European Management Journal, 27*(1), 1–12. doi:10.1016/j.emj.2008.04.006.

Mossholder, K. W., Bennett, N., & Martin, C. L. (1998). A multilevel analysis of procedural justice context. *Journal of Organizational Behavior, 19*(2), 131–141. doi:10.1002/(SICI)1099-1379(199803)19:2<131:AID-JOB878>3.0.CO;2-P.

Mudrack, P. E., Bloodgood, J. M., & Turnley, W. H. (2012). Some ethical implications of individual competitiveness. *Journal of Business Ethics, 108*(3), 347–359. doi:10.1007/s10551-011-1094-4.

Murphy, K. (2003). Procedural justice and tax compliance. *Australian Journal of Social Issues, 38* (3), 379–408.

Murphy, K. (2005). Regulating more effectively: The relationship between procedural justice, legitimacy, and tax non-compliance. *Journal of Law & Society, 32*(4), 562–589. doi:10.1111/j.1467-6478.2005.00338.x.

Naumann, S. E., & Bennett, N. (2000). A case for procedural justice climate: Development and test of a multilevel model. *Academy of Management Journal, 43*(5), 881–889. doi:10.2307/1556416.

Nikolova, H., Lamberton, C. P., & Coleman, N. V. (2015). When and why we partner in crime: Comparing the unethical decisions of dyads and individuals. *SSRN Journal*. doi:10.2139/ssrn.2574712.

O'Boyle, E. H., Forsyth, D. R., Banks, G. C., & McDaniel, M. A. (2012). A meta-analysis of the Dark Triad and work behaviour: A social exchange perspective. *Journal of Applied Psychology, 97*(3), 557–579. doi:10.1037/a0025679.

Padilla, A., Hogan, R., & Kaiser, K. B. (2007). The toxic triangle: Destructive leaders, susceptible followers, and conducive environments. *Leadership Quarterly, 18*(3), 176–194. doi:10.1016/j.leaqua.2007.03.001.

Peterson, D. K. (2002). Deviant workplace behaviour and the organization's ethical climate. *Journal of Business and Psychology, 17*(1), 47–61. doi:10.1023/A:1016296116093.

Pino, M. (2009). The Marine Hoses cartel.

Piquero, A. R., Paternoster, R., Pogarsky, G., & Loughran, T. (2011). Elaborating the individual difference component in deterrence theory. *Annual Review of Law and Social Science, 7*, 335–360. doi:10.1146/annurev-lawsocsci-102510-105404.

Pretty, J. (2003). Social capital and the collective management of resources. *Science, 302*(5652), 1912–1914. doi:10.1126/science.1090847.

Rabl, T. (2011). Wie Korruption entsteht - Eine Analyse der Entscheidungsprozesse korrupter Akteure.

Ragatz, L., & Fremouw, W. (2010). A critical examination of research on the psychological profiles of white-collar criminals. *Journal of Forensic Psychology Practice, 10*(5), 373–402. doi:10.1080/15228932.2010.489846.

Riketta, M. (2005). Organizational identification: A meta-analysis. *Journal of Vocational Behavior, 66*(2), 358–384. doi:10.1016/j.jvb.2004.05.005.

Rupp, D. E., Bashshur, M., & Liao, H. (2007). Justice climate past, present, and future: Models of structure and emergence. *Research in Multilevel Issues, 6*, 357–396.

Rupp, D. E., & Thornton, M. A. (2014). The role of employee justice perceptions in influencing climate and culture. *The Oxford handbook of organizational climate and culture* (p. 360).

Rynes, S. L. (1989). Recruitment, job choice, and post-hire consequences: A call for new research directions. CAHRS Working Paper Series, 398.

Ryska, T. A. (2002). Perceived purposes of sport among recreational participants: The role of competitive dispositions. *Journal of Sport Behavior, 25*(1), 91–112.

Schaubroeck, J. M., Hannah, S. T., Avolio, B. J., Kozlowski, S. W. J., Lord, R. G., Trevino, L. K., et al. (2012). Embedding ethical leadership within and across organization levels. *Academy of Management Journal, 55*(5), 1053–1078. doi:10.5465/amj.2011.0064.

Scheffer, D., & Kaeb, C. (2011). The five levels of CSR compliance: the resiliency of corporate liability under the Alien Tort Statute and the case for a counterattack strategy in compliance theory. *Berkeley Journal of International Law, 29*(1), 344–397. doi:10.15779/Z38T65N.

Schüler, J., Brandstätter, V., Wegner, M., & Baumann, N. (2015). Testing the convergent and discriminant validity of three implicit motive measures: PSE, OMT, and MMG. *Motivation and Emotion Journal, 39*(6), 839–857. doi:10.1007/s11031-015-9502-1.

Schultheiss, O., & Brunstein, J. (2010). *Implicit motives*. Oxford University Press.

Schultheiss, O. C., & Brunstein, J. C. (2001). Assessment of implicit motives with a research version of the TAT: Picture profiles, gender differences, and relations to other personality measures. *Journal of Personality Assessment, 77*(1), 71–86. doi:10.1207/S15327752JPA7701_05.

Schultheiss, O. C., & Brunstein, J. C. (2002). Inhibited power motivation and persuasive communication: a lens model analysis. *Journal of personality, 70*(4), 553–582. doi:10.1111/1467-6494.05014.

Schultheiss, O. C., Riebel, K., & Jones, N. M. (2009). Activity inhibition: A predictor of lateralized brain function during stress? *Neuropsychology, 23*(3), 392–404. doi:10.1037/a0014591.

Schulze, G. G., & Frank, B. (2003). Deterrence versus intrinsic motivation: Experimental evidence on the determinants of corruptibility. *Economics of Governance, 4*(2), 143–160.

Simon, M., & Houghton, S. M. (2003). The relationship between overconfidence and the introduction of risky products: Evidence from a field study. *Academy of Management Journal, 46*(2), 139–149. doi:10.2307/30040610.

Sokol, D. D. (2012). Cartels, corporate compliance, and what practitioners really think about enforcement. *Antitrust Law Journal, 78*(1), 201–240.

Spangler, W. D., Tikhomirov, A., Sotak, K. L., & Palrecha, R. (2014). Leader motive profiles in eight types of organizations. *Leadership Quarterly, 25*(6), 1080–1094. doi:10.1016/j.leaqua.2014.10.001.

Staw, B. M. (1981). The escalation of commitment to a course of action. *Academy of Management Review, 6*(4), 577–587. doi:10.5465/AMR.1981.4285694.

Steinmann, B., Nübold, A., & Maier, G. W. (2016). Validation of a German version of the Ethical Leadership at Work questionnaire by Kalshoven and colleagues (2011). *Frontiers in Psychology, 7*, 446. doi:10.3389/fpsyg.2016.00446.

Stephan, A. (2010). Cartel laws undermined: Corruption, social norms, and collectivist business cultures. *Journal of Law and Society, 37*(2), 345–367. doi:10.1111/j.1467-6478.2010.00507.x.

Stumpp, T., Hülsheger, U. R., Muck, P. M., & Maier, G. W. (2009). Expanding the link between core self-evaluations and affective job attitudes. *European Journal of Work and Organizational Psycology, 18*(2), 148–166. doi:10.1080/13594320802281110.

Sutherland, E. H., & Holt, R. (1949). *White collar crime*. New York: Dryden Press.

Terhune, K. W. (1968). Motives, situation, and interpersonal conflict within prisoner's dilemma. *Journal of Personality and Social Psychology, 8*(3, Pt. 2), 1–24. doi:10.1037/h0025594.

Thau, S., Derfler-Rozin, R., Pitesa, M., Mitchell, M. S., & Pillutla, M. M. (2015). Unethical for the sake of the group: Risk of social exclusion and pro-group unethical behaviour. *Journal of Applied Psychology, 100*(1), 98–113. doi:10.1037/a0036708.

Thibaut, J. W., & Walker, L. (1975). *Procedural justice: A psychological analysis*. L. Erlbaum Associates.

Treviño, L. K., Butterfield, K. D., & McCabe, D. L. (1998). The ethical context in organizations: Influences on employee attitudes and behaviors. *Business Ethics Quarterly, 8*(3), 447. doi:10.2307/3857431.

Treviño, L. K., Hartman, L. P., & Brown, M. (2000). Moral person and moral manager: How executives develop a reputation for ethical leadership. *California Management Review, 42*(4), 128–142. doi:10.2307/41166057.

Türker, D. (2009). Measuring corporate social responsibility: A scale development study. *Journal of Business Ethics, 85*(4), 411–427. doi:10.1007/s10551-008-9780-6.

Tyler, T. R. (1997). The psychology of legitimacy: A relational perspective on voluntary deference to authorities. *Personality and Social Psychology Review, 1*(4), 323–345. doi:10.1207/s15327957pspr0104_4.

Tyler, T. R., Goff, P. A., & MacCoun, R. J. (2015). The impact of psychological science on policing in the United States procedural justice, legitimacy, and effective law enforcement. *Psychological Science in the Public Interest, 16*(3), 75–109. doi:10.1177/1529100615617791.

Tyler, T. R., & Lind, E. A. (1992). A relational model of authority in groups. *Advances in Experimental Social Psychology, 25*, 115–191. doi:10.1016/S0065-2601(08)60283-X.

Umphress, E. E., Bingham, J. B., & Mitchell, M. S. (2010). Unethical behaviour in the name of the company: The moderating effect of organizational identification and positive reciprocity beliefs on unethical pro-organizational behaviour. *Journal of Applied Psychology, 95*(4), 769–780. doi:10.1037/a0019214.

Vadera, A. K., & Pratt, M. G. (2013). Love, hate, ambivalence, or indifference?: A conceptual examination of workplace crimes and organizational identification. *Organization Science, 24* (1), 172–188. doi:10.1287/orsc.1110.0714.

van Marrewijk, M. (2003). Concepts and definitions of CSR and corporate sustainability: Between agency and communion. *Journal of Business Ethics, 44*(2-3), 95–105.

Victor, B., & Cullen, J. B. (1988). The organizational bases of ethical work climates. *Administrative Science Quarterly, 33*(1), 101. doi:10.2307/2392857.

Wenzel, M. (2002). Principles of procedural fairness in reminder letters: A field experiment.

Wenzel, M. (2006). A letter from the tax office: Compliance effects of informational and interpersonal justice. *Social Justice Research, 19*(3), 345–364. doi:10.1007/s11211-006-0011-y.

Winter, D. G. (1973). The power motive.

Winter, D. G. (1992). Power motivation revisited: 301–310. doi:10.1017/CBO9780511527937.022.

Winter, D. G. (1994). *Manual for scoring motive imagery in running text* (version 4.2). Ann Arbor, MI: University of Michigan.

Winter, D. G. (2000). Power, sex, and violence: A psychological reconstruction of the 20th century and an intellectual agenda for political psychology. *Political Psychology, 21*(2), 383–404. doi:10.1111/0162-895X.00194.

Wood, Z. (2014). *German sausage cartel caught bangers to rights*. Available from: http://www.theguardian.com/world/2014/jul/15/german-sausage-cartel-caught-bangers-to-rights-wurst.

Wu, C., & Griffin, M. A. (2012). Longitudinal relationships between core self-evaluations and job satisfaction. *Journal of Applied Psychology, 97*(2), 331–342. doi:10.1037/a0025673.

FSC
www.fsc.org
MIX
Papier | Fördert
gute Waldnutzung
FSC® C083411

Kolibri 360 GmbH
Ferdinand-Jühlke-Straße 7
99095 Erfurt, Deutschland
produktsicherheit@kolibri360.de